D1087461

MUSIC
IN THE
GALANT STYLE

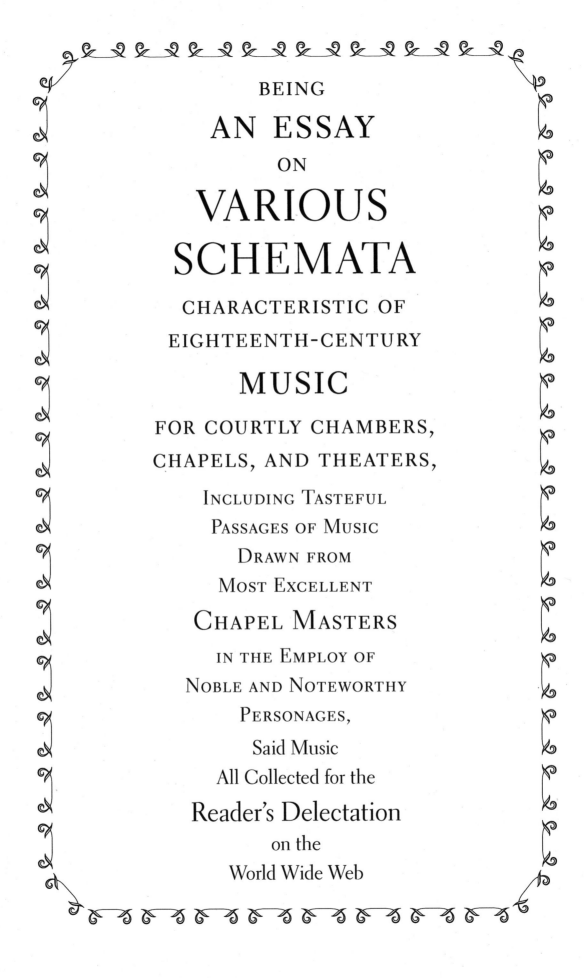

BEING

AN ESSAY

ON

VARIOUS
SCHEMATA

CHARACTERISTIC OF

EIGHTEENTH-CENTURY

MUSIC

FOR COURTLY CHAMBERS,

CHAPELS, AND THEATERS,

INCLUDING TASTEFUL

PASSAGES OF MUSIC

DRAWN FROM

MOST EXCELLENT

CHAPEL MASTERS

IN THE EMPLOY OF

NOBLE AND NOTEWORTHY

PERSONAGES,

Said Music

All Collected for the

Reader's Delectation

on the

World Wide Web

MUSIC
IN THE
GALANT STYLE

ROBERT O. GJERDINGEN

OXFORD
UNIVERSITY PRESS
2007

OXFORD
UNIVERSITY PRESS

Oxford University Press, Inc., publishes works that further
Oxford University's objective of excellence
in research, scholarship, and education.

Oxford   New York
Auckland   Cape Town   Dar es Salaam   Hong Kong   Karachi
Kuala Lumpur   Madrid   Melbourne   Mexico City   Nairobi
New Delhi   Shanghai   Taipei   Toronto

With offices in
Argentina   Austria   Brazil   Chile   Czech Republic   France   Greece
Guatemala   Hungary   Italy   Japan   Poland   Portugal   Singapore

Published by Oxford University Press, Inc.
198 Madison Avenue, New York, New York 10016
www.oup.com

Oxford is a registered trademark of Oxford University Press

Library of Congress Cataloging-in-Publication Data
Gjerdingen, Robert O.
Music in the galant style / Robert O. Gjerdingen
p. cm.
Includes index
ISBN 978-0-19-531371-0
1. Music—Europe—18th century—History and criticism.
2. Style, musical. 3. Musical analysis. I. Title.
ML240.3.G54 2007
780.9'033—dc22   2006050659

1 3 5 7 9 8 6 4 2

Printed in the United States of America
on acid-free paper

To all who,

like Mary in *Pride and Prejudice,*

have spent an afternoon

"deep in the study of

thoroughbass and human nature."

Acknowledgments

I HAVE ALWAYS RELIED ON THE KINDNESS OF LIBRARIANS. I send my heartfelt thanks to those who, during my visits and residencies, guided me through the North American university libraries of Berkeley, Chicago, Harvard, Michigan, Northwestern, Pennsylvania, Stanford, and Stony Brook, and the Italian conservatory libraries of Naples, Milan, and Bologna. Within these vast collections I have found not only the many manuscripts by eighteenth-century students and teachers that offer such an instructive glimpse into how this rich musical tradition was conceived and transmitted, but also the thousands of modern editions of eighteenth-century music that testify to the continuing engagement of succeeding generations with this distant courtly art. Those editions were prepared by talented scholars whose erudition and careful historical judgments form the vital foundation for any research in this area, and anyone who studies eighteenth-century music owes them a great debt.

This book began to take physical form while I was a fellow at the Center for Advanced Study in the Behavioral Sciences, Palo Alto, California. I want to thank Robert Scott (Associate Director), Lynn Gale (Statistician), and other staff members at the center for all their help and support. That year was one of three during my career funded by the Mellon Foundation, and I hope that this small contribution to the understanding of a great music may partially repay their generous investments. The University Research Grants Committee at Northwestern University underwrote my studies in Naples and Milan. They also provided follow-on grants to assemble what is now a microfilm collection of over eight thousand manuscript pages of *partimenti* (instructional basses) and galant *solfeggi* (elegant vocal lines paired with *partimento* basses). Online dissemination of this extensive corpus of eighteenth-century music-pedagogical material is being supported by the National Endowment for the Humanities (NEH) under the project title *Monuments of Partimenti* (http://faculty-web.at.northwestern.edu/music/gjerdingen/partimenti/index.htm). A subvention provided by the American Musicological Society through its Dragan Plamenac Publication Endowment Fund has been greatly appreciated, and I extend thanks to its awards committee for their support.

I want to acknowledge the important influence of both the wise teachers who inspired me and the bright students who participated in my seminars on galant music. I have been the beneficiary of the former's indulgence and the latter's forbearance. Many of the best musical examples in this book stem from pieces uncovered by students. And many of my ideas are but echoes of what I learned from the philological approach of Lewis Rowell, the psychological insight of Leonard B. Meyer, the theoretical rigor of Eugene Narmour, and the historical virtuosity of Eugene K. Wolf. Meyer's books and articles, models of humanistic scholarship informed by contemporary cognitive science, have been particularly influential, as have, perhaps less obviously, Robert Rosenblum's *Transformations in Late Eighteenth-Century Art*, Eric Auerbach's *Mimesis*, Albert Lord's *Singer of Tales*, Robert Darnton's *The Great Cat Massacre*, and E. H. Gombrich's *Art and Illusion*. The encouragement and advice of Christopher van Bayer, Gaston Dufresne, Robert Vernon, Leonard Stein, Ricardo Trimillos, Paul Lyddon, Alan Trubitt, David Slepian, Lewis Lockwood, David Lewin, William Caplin, Fred Lerdahl, Lawrence Bernstein, Thomas Bauman, Lee Rothfarb, Robert Hatten, Diana Deutsch, Carol Krumhansl, Thomas Christensen, Howard Mayer Brown, Carl Dahlhaus, and Albert Lord have been deeply appreciated. It was my great fortune to come into contact with these musicians and scholars, and I only regret, as Samuel Johnson lamented in the preface to his dictionary (1755), that "I have protracted my work till [some] of those whom I wished to please have sunk into the grave." I take consolation in returning to their books or recordings to hear echoes of the wisdom, imagination, and beauty of thought that first inspired me. With respect to the volume at hand, my notions of auditory pattern perception were strongly influenced by the adaptive-systems tradition of Stephen Grossberg and Gail Carpenter, and my interpretation of galant musical society owes a large debt to Pierre Bourdieu and Norbert Elias. Jesse Rosenberg, my colleague at Northwestern, kindly shared with me his extensive collection of printed Italian partimenti, and my research into the eighteenth-century Italian roots of the partimento manuscript tradition was generously assisted by Professors Giorgio Sanguinetti, Rosa Cafiero, and Elisabetta Pasquini. Stefan Eckert shared with me his convincing readings of Riepel's inimitable prose style and his research into the *ars combinatoria*.

The recent appearance of Daniel Heartz's magisterial, thousand-page *Music in European Capitals: The Galant Style, 1720–1780* (New York: Norton, 2003)—the finest conspectus of eighteenth-century music since the eighteenth century—provides a wealth of historical and biographical detail that complements my own, more modest volume. For example, while I have included complete arias by Leo and Jommelli for comparison, I was able to insert only a word or two about their lives. Heartz provides only brief excerpts from their operas but paints a rich portrait of their musical careers, complete with the telling observation by one of Jommelli's friends, Saverio Mattei, that, "according to those who know, Jommelli made a searching study of Leo's scores, and often reclothed the master's designs in better shades of color" (Heartz, p. 75). In the following chapters it will be possible for the modern reader to make "a searching study" not only of "the master's designs" but also of Jommelli's reclothing of them. Heartz's volume and mine, though produced from quite different points of departure, thus together form, as it were, a "history and theory" of the galant style.

In the course of this book I will describe hundreds of passages from the works of nearly eighty composers. These musical creations, collectively spanning 150 years, originated in the vast area bordered by Lisbon to the west, St. Petersburg to the east, Edinburgh to the north, and, most importantly, Naples to the south. I mention this not to boast but to apologize for the inevitable oversights and errors that accompany any scholarly landscape painted with so broad a brush. Every composer, performer, and patron, every chapel, chamber, and theater, every court, city, and cathedral had a unique location in the cultural web of eighteenth-century society. In focusing on the basic musical tradition shared by all, I risk effacing the details of unique individuals, situations, and locations. I look forward to thanking those experts willing to share with me their better grasp of the particulars so that I might emend any future edition.

This book benefited enormously from the typographical design of Rebecca Dixon, the editorial assistance of Catherine Gjerdingen, and the music-notation software of Keith Hamel (Noteability Pro™).

Lastly, I offer a listener's appreciation of the talented soloists and chamber ensembles whose wonderful performances have breathed new life into this musical world so full of charm, wit, sophistication, and joy. To hear Enrico Gatti play Pugnani, Elizabeth Wallfisch play Tartini, or Gérard Lesne sing Bononcini is like hearing a great actor bring to life one of the best roles of Sheridan, Goldsmith, or Marivaux. Though this book is more about scripts than individual performances, the surviving scripts of eighteenth-century music require interpretation through performance if they are to speak to us today.

CONTENTS

MUSIC
IN THE
GALANT STYLE

1

INTRODUCTION

COURTIERS IN THE TIME OF BACH OR MOZART artfully modulated all their social behaviors—their every gesture, word, glance, step, tone, inflection, posture—to optimize their success in the moment-to-moment interactions of society. The Earl of Chesterfield (1694–1773) gave the following advice to his son, who in the spring of 1749 had just arrived in that musical country Italy:

> I was very glad to hear, from one whom I think so good a judge, that you wanted [= lacked] nothing but *des manieres* [some manners], which I am convinced you will now soon acquire, in the company which henceforward you are likely to keep. But I must add, too, that if you should not acquire them, all the rest will be of little use to you. By *manieres*, I do not mean bare common civility; everybody must have that who would not be kicked out of company; but I mean engaging, insinuating, shining manners; distinguished polite-ness, an almost irresistible address; a superior gracefulness in all you say and do. It is this alone that can give all your other talents their full lustre and value; and, consequently, it is this which should now be the principal object of your attention. Observe minutely, wherever you go, the allowed and established models of good-breeding, and form yourself upon them.[1]

The modern sociologist Norbert Elias observed that "court etiquette which, by the values of bourgeois-industrial societies, may well seem something quite unimportant, something merely 'external' and perhaps even ridiculous, proves, if one respects the autonomy of the structure of court society, an extremely sensitive and reliable instrument for measuring the prestige value of an individual within the social network." He goes on to note that "court people develop an extraordinarily sensitive feeling for the status and importance that should be attributed to a person in society on the basis of his bearing,

3

speech, manner or appearance. . . . These people experience many things that we would be inclined to dismiss as trivial or superficial with an intensity that we have largely lost."[2]

Today, when motion picture directors attempt to re-create a realistic eighteenth-century milieu, the results often fail precisely in the small behaviors that once meant so much. Screenwriters can emulate phrases from eighteenth-century novels, those responsible for the mise-en-scène can copy period paintings or drawings, and costume designers can re-create preserved garments, but the important minutiae of human interactions are likely to be filled in with the habits of our own time. Strong habits in the present easily mask differences in the past. I can imagine few today who, viewing a motion picture set in the eighteenth century, would be shocked if a young nobleman said "hello" to his mother. But in the eighteenth century, *hello* was a very rare word, akin to *ahoy*. In the entire text of Jane Austen's *Pride and Prejudice* no one says hello, nor does anyone in *Emma* or in *Sense and Sensibility*.[3] If so basic a habit of speech was quite different in the eighteenth century, could it also be that basic habits of music were different? Could it be that eighteenth-century composers had a different musical vocabulary and applied it toward different aims? Could composers have had, as their "principal object of attention," the acquisition of musical manners—"engaging, insinuating, shining manners"—in order to give their works "full lustre"? Could recognizing the prestige value of a "superior gracefulness" in musical behavior have required that one "observe minutely" differences and "established models" to which, over the intervening centuries, we have become less sensitive?

I believe the answers are yes, and I will present evidence supporting my case in the course of this book. Yet I face a dilemma like that of the manufacturers who, in the 1960s, touted the benefits of color television in commercials received on black-and-white sets. Consumers could see those commercials over and over, and marketers could stress the analogy to color motion pictures, but until people actually experienced a functioning color television set, the message did not fully register. My ensuing exhortations to experience a more colorful picture of eighteenth-century music may likewise be received on "black-and-white sets": our modern habits of listening. In the world of classical music, habits of listening became transformed in the nineteenth century. If I might be permitted to caricature Romantic listening, which still dominates the reception of classical music, I would note that it favors music that affords sonic analogues to a thrill ride, a quest, the supernatural, or a melodrama. By contrast, eighteenth-century courtly listening habits seem to have favored music that provided opportunities for acts of judging, for the making of distinctions, and for the public exercise of discernment and taste. Because modes of listening change only through new experiences of listening, I beseech the reader to take the time to absorb the many musical examples that lie ahead. Savor them, listen to their basses, sing their melodies, evaluate their subordinate and superordinate patterns, compare them to preceding examples, judge them as small works of courtly art. Do not, please, just read about them. In 1765 the diplomat and writer Friedrich Melchior, Baron von Grimm (1723–1807) remarked that one could not really "hear" the higher forms of music "without a delicate sensibility, without a refined and trained ear."[4] Because interest in the music of Mozart, Haydn, and other galant composers extends well beyond the ranks of professional musicians, every musical example in this volume has been recorded and made available for listening on the World Wide Web.[5] This book describes galant music, of course. But equally important, it presents galant music as a performing art.

Galant was a word much used in the eighteenth century. It referred broadly to a collection of traits, attitudes, and manners associated with the cultured nobility. If we imagine an ideal galant man, he would be witty, attentive to the ladies, comfortable at a princely court, religious in a modest way, wealthy from ancestral land holdings, charming, brave in battle, and trained as an amateur in music and other arts. This perfect courtier, as Baldassare Castiglione described him in 1529, would have the natural grace "to use in every thing a certain *sprezzatura* [nonchalance] that conceals its art and demonstrates what he does and says to be done effortlessly, and, as it were, without concern."[6] His female counterpart[7] would have impeccable manners, clothes of real sophistication, great skill as a hostess, a deep knowledge of etiquette, and training in one or more of the "accomplishments"—music, art, modern languages, literature, and the natural sciences.[8] Courtiers sent to locate a suitable bride for George III echoed Castiglione's recipe for the perfect gentlewoman—a lady with some skill in "letters, music, painting, and who can dance and devise entertainments"[9]—when they described Charlotte Sophia of Mecklenburg-Strelitz as full of "Youth, Sprightlyness, good Nature, and good Sense, adorned with all the female accomplishments, (amongst which musick, of which the young King being fond, was not forgot)."[10] Female courtiers and courtesans often achieved a high degree of skill in music, and as connoisseurs they played a major role in shaping the kind of music and musicians that prospered in galant society. That same Charlotte, who later married George III and became his queen consort, was to choose no less a figure than J. C. Bach as her master of music. Galant music, then, was music commissioned by galant men and women to entertain themselves as listeners, to educate and amuse themselves as amateur performers, and to bring glory to themselves as patrons of the wittiest, most charming, most sophisticated and fashionable music that money could buy.

Today *Baroque* and *Classical* are the terms most frequently used to describe musical style in the eighteenth century. Yet these terms are hardly more representative of indigenous eighteenth-century concepts than an American real-estate agent's notion that all old houses must be either *Tudor* or *Colonial*. Categorizing San Souci, a palace of Frederick the Great, as Colonial or Tudor, for example, would make little sense. And neither would categorizing the music at his court as Baroque or Classical. "Baroque"—today meaning roughly the style of J. S. Bach—was a word Bach likely never heard in reference to music.[11] Similarly, "Classical"—meaning roughly the style of W. A. Mozart—was a word that Mozart never used in reference to music.[12] These terms were developed in the nineteenth and twentieth centuries for the purposes of those later times, but they obscure rather than illuminate eighteenth-century music. The terms *Rococo* and *pre-Classical* offer little improvement. "Rococo" describes aspects of the visual arts, and to call the music of the great galant musicians pre-Classical is no more enlightening than to call George Gershwin pre-Rock or Elvis Presley pre-Hip-Hop. By contrast, the term *galant* was actually used in a positive way by the men and women who made and supported eighteenth-century music. Leonard Ratner, author of the book *Classic Music*, wrote that "if we were to rename this period according to late eighteenth-century views, it would be called the *galant* style."[13] And Daniel Heartz subtitled his recent book on European music from 1720 to 1780 "The Galant Style."[14] I agree with those authors. Yet I also acknowledge that other careful scholars have their own, more narrow definitions of the galant style, and that these definitions find support in the divergent ways the term *galant* was used in the eighteenth century.[15] My position, as developed here and in earlier publications, is that a hallmark of the galant style was a particular repertory of stock musical phrases employed in conventional sequences. Local and personal preferences among patrons and musicians resulted in presentations of this repertory that favored different positions along various semantic axes— light/heavy, comic/serious, sensitive/bravura, and so on. But as long as the music is grounded in this repertory of stock musical phrases, I view all its manifestations as *galant*. Even J. S. Bach, whom the general public has long viewed as the paradigmatic Baroque composer, created galant music when it suited his and his patrons' purposes.[16]

I have resisted the temptation to make one type of galant music—say, Italian harpsichord movements intended for aristocratic amateurs—emblematic of the whole style. Such works are indeed characteristic, but they define just one location in a richly varied musical landscape. While many galant works do have a thin texture, a sprightly mood, a clearly defined melody and bass, frequent points of articulation and cadence, and simple schemes of repetition or contrast, many other equally galant works do not. There were tightly woven fugues, sacred masses with full chorus, complex orchestral works, grand scenes of serious opera, tedious pedagogical works, fantastic *bravura* works—everything, in short, to serve the diverse needs of the courts and wealthy homes of galant patrons. My focus is thus on "galant" as a code of conduct, as an eighteenth-century courtly ideal (adaptable to city life), and as a carefully taught set of musical behaviors.

The popular view of the composer—a Romantic view inherited from the nineteenth century—does not fit eighteenth-century reality. The composer of galant music, rather than being a struggling artist alone against the world, was more like a prosperous civil servant. He typically had the title chapel master (Ger., *Kapellmeister*; It., *maestro di capella*) and managed an aristocrat's sacred and secular musical enterprises. He worried less about the meaning of art and more about whether his second violin player would be sober enough to play for Sunday Mass. The galant composer necessarily worked in the here and now. He had to write something this week for an upcoming court ceremony, not tortured masterworks for posterity. Even a conservative musician like Johann Joseph Fux (1660–1741), imperial court chapel master in Vienna, had to admit that a court's "eagerness for novelty" resulted in music changing "every five years or so." Comparing music to clothing, he explained that "if a middle-aged man appeared today dressed in the clothes worn fifty or sixty years ago, he would certainly run the risk of ridicule." And so he advises a young composer that "music too must be accommodated to the times."[17] A court composer, rather than expressing his deep personal feelings for all to share, strove to touch his patron's sentiments. The patron, whether a king, an emperor, a countess, or a queen, had little or no interest in the common emotions of his or her musical lackey. The notion that a sad piece by the court composer was about the composer's sadness would have seemed just as strange as the idea that a tart sauce prepared by the court chef was about the chef's tartness. In short, the galant composer lived the life of a musical craftsman, of an artisan who produced a large quantity of music for immediate consumption, managed its performance and performers, and evaluated its reception with a view toward keeping up with fashion.

The art of galant music, like the art of figure skating, is replete with compulsory and free-style "figures." Whereas casual observers of ice-skating competitions may see only a variety of glides, spins, and jumps, a connoisseur sees salchows, axels, lutzes, and camels. Knowledge of the proper execution of each figure is a prerequisite for anyone officially assigned to judge a skater's abilities. Here are the figures used by the young Danish skater Mikkeline Kierkgaard in a recent performance:[18]

Triple salchow/double toe combination
Steps into triple toe loop
Flying camel spin
Double axel
Circular step sequence
Combination spin including:
    Camel spin
    Sit spin
    Layback spin catching her foot
(change of foot)
Sit spin
Upright spin
Spiral sequence including:
    Forward outside spiral
    Backward outside spiral
    Forward outside Chinese spiral
Layback spin

For comparison, here are the musical figures or schemata presented in the second half of a slow movement by the eighteenth-century Venetian composer Baldassare Galuppi (1706–1785; see chap. 15):

Quiescenza, diatonic, repeated
Fonte/Monte combination
Ponte, to Passo Indietro

Comma, followed by Cudworth cadence

Clausula Vera

Meyer

Ponte, tonic

Monte/Converging cadence combination

Fonte, repeated

Monte, diatonic

Clausula Vera

Ponte

Cudworth cadence . . . deceptive

Passo Indietro to Mi-Re-Do cadence

This book is for the person who wants to become more knowledgeable about galant music. The names of the musical schemata listed above may now sound as fanciful as the leaps of figure skating, but each schema will be explained in the following chapters. In learning to recognize the schemata of galant music, one becomes better able to appreciate the art of the galant composer. And in learning to judge the manner in which the schemata are presented in a particular composition, one becomes better able to understand the equally important art of the galant listener and patron. As the Earl of Chesterfield remarked, "every ear can and does judge . . . style."[19]

COMMEDIA DELL'ARTE

Should the art of modern figure skaters seem too remote an analogue to the art of eighteenth-century court musicians, then perhaps the art of eighteenth-century comedians can provide a closer comparison. Like musicians, troupes of comic actors were employed by courts to enliven a variety of festivals, weddings, and evening entertainments. Especially popular was the form of improvised comedy—*commedia all'improviso*—better known since the second half of the eighteenth century as *commedia dell'arte*.[20] Central to the training of an actor in this tradition was a *zibaldone*, a manuscript assemblage of stock speeches (*concetti*), slapstick (*lazzi*), jokes (*burle*), and plots (*scenarii* or *canovacci*) passed down from actor to actor, usually within the same family or troupe. A great deal of this material needed to be committed to memory before an actor could begin to function in one of the stock roles like Pulcinella (the male simpleton), Dottore (the elderly father), Coviello (the cunning suitor), or Fravoletta (the ingenue). Here is the *scenario* for act 1 of *Good Luck Not Recognized* [*La fortuna non conosciuta*], from a collection made in Naples around 1700:[21]

SCENE 1. DOTTORE AND PULCINELLA
   [They do] a stock speech, and Dottore exits. Pulcinella [speaks] of his love

for Fravoletta, and knocks at [her door].

SCENE 2. PULCINELLA AND FRAVOLETTA

They do a love scene and depart.

SCENE 3. COVIELLO, ALONE

[He speaks] about his love for Pimpinella, and knocks at [Pimpinella's].

SCENE 4. PIMPINELLA AND [COVIELLO]

[They do a] love scene, and they leave.

SCENE 5. GIANGURGOLO, ALONE

[He speaks] about his love for Pimpinella, and knocks at [Pimpinella's].

SCENE 6. PIMPINELLA AND [GIANGURGOLO]

She refuses him. At that,

SCENE 7. COVIELLO AND THE ABOVE

Coviello, out of jealousy, ties his [ankle], attaching the rope to the side of the
stage. Then he beats him and runs away. Giangurgolo tries to run after him
and falls down. At that,

SCENE 8. DOTTORE, PIMPINELLA, AND GIANGURGOLO

[Dottore] sees the man with his foot tied, near his house, and asks his
daughter why. She says he tried to violate her, and so she tied him up like
that. Dottore believes this and beats him. So ends the first act.

The scenario of all three acts would be pinned to the back of the stage curtain so that
actors could consult it before their entrances. As you can see, the scenario provided only a
bare skeleton of the play. In scene 1, for example, the actors playing the Dottore and
Pulcinella are reminded to do a "stock speech" (*scena di memoria*), just as at the beginning
of the next act the Dottore and Coviello do their "usual scene" (*scena solita*). The actors
would improvise a usual scene by weaving their learned repertories of banter, stunts, solil-
oquies, jokes, and other types of comic "business" (*lazzi*) into the framework of the scenario. The scenario provided a context, but the moment-to-moment dialogue and action
depended on actors knowing when and how to knit small set-pieces into an apparently
continuous mode of entertainment. As the great seventeenth-century comedian Niccolò
Barbieri noted (1634), improvising actors "study and fortify their memory with a wide variety of things such as sayings, phrases, love-speeches, reprimands, cries of despair, and
ravings, in order to have them ready for the proper occasion."[22]

Understanding the way in which the actors of commedia dell'arte fashioned scintillating and seemingly spontaneous theater from presentations of stock characters performing
stock "business" can serve as a model for understanding how galant composers made
music. The multi-act play becomes the multimovement sonata or multipart aria. The
stock characters become the stock moods or "affections." And the stock comic business —
the memorized speeches, dialogues, and well-practiced physical comedy — find analogues
in the repertory of stock musical phrases or passages: musical schemata. A galant musical
score was like a scenario in that it often provided only a bare notation of the sequence of

schemata, with the graces, ornaments, and elegant variation left to the skilled performer. Many musicians could improvise entire pieces as soloists, drawing upon their family's or teacher's musical *zibaldone* for standard phrases and cadences. In one case, the composer and violinist Carl Ditters von Dittersdorf (1739–1799) jointly improvised a sonata with his keyboard accompanist.[23] Like two actors of the commedia dell'arte performing their "usual scene," Dittersdorf and his accompanist must have ably connected a string of well-learned musical schemata to form a seemingly spontaneous and continuous musical performance.

   Zibaldone was also the word used to describe a music student's notebook of exercises and rules. Francesco Galeazzi (1758–1819; see chap. 29) recommended that the good maestro fill a student's *zibaldone* with custom-tailored lessons.[24] The collections of lessons that Mozart wrote for Thomas Attwood or Barbara Ployer would be of this type.[25] Because Galeazzi decried the practice of "some maestros" who, "with the aid of a *zibaldone* or notebook of stale lessons, pretend to give the appropriate lessons to any and all students," we can be fairly sure that certain standard *zibaldoni* were in wide use, at least in particular cities or conservatories. As the following chapters will demonstrate, a *zibaldone* of figured and unfigured basses (*partimenti*), along with examples of graceful melodies paired with unfigured basses (*solfeggi*), provided an important repository of stock musical business from which a young composer could later draw.

Defining Schemata

What does it mean to refer to a musical pattern as a schema? The term itself has a long history first in philosophy and then in psychology. "Schema" (Kant) refers to what is broadly called a mental representation or category, and thus shares meanings with terms like "idea" or "form" (Plato), "ideal type" (Weber), "family resemblance" (Wittgenstein), "archetype" (Frye), "prototype" (Posner), "essence" (Putnam), "natural type" (Rosch),[26] and so forth. There is no doubt that humans are very good at rapidly developing useful categorizations from the "blooming, buzzing confusion" of sensations and experiences,[27] but the richness and adaptability of human categorizations suggest that we may derive schemata in various ways. Three contemporary approaches to understanding the formation and employment of schemata focus on *prototypes*, *exemplars*, and *theories*. Many psychologists have noted that we naturally abstract the common features of similar experiences and create from those abstractions a generalized experience termed a *prototype*.[28] We can use a prototype as a point of comparison to evaluate whether a particular instance of something is a good example of its schema. A person who developed a schema for "final cadence" from listening to popular songs of the 1940s might perceive the picardy third at the end of a work by Bach as being highly atypical and unexpected, while another person who listened only to Bach and Handel might perceive the same cadence as a perfect instance of its type. Their very different prior experiences would lead to different schemata and hence to different judgments. Other psychologists note that we can also base such judgments on references to well-learned individual cases—*exemplars*.[29] A person who grew up loving Beethoven's Ninth Symphony might well use it as a reference point for the schema "symphony," even though the Ninth is historically atypical of the genre. Still other psychologists point to studies showing how children's perceptions change when they begin to form *theories* about their world.[30] A child's naive theory, for example, that the sound of a saxophone is part of the schema "jazz" could strongly affect his or her reception of Maurice Ravel's *Bolero*. The social and ethnic stereotypes held by many adults would be further evidence of theories that, however derived and however inaccurate in individual cases, nonetheless characterize many people's perceptions. *Schema* is thus a shorthand for a packet of knowledge, be it an abstracted prototype, a well-learned exemplar, a theory intuited about the nature of things and their meanings, or just the attunement of a cluster of cortical neurons to some regularity in the environment. Knowing relevant schemata allows one to make useful comparisons or, as the saying goes, to avoid "comparing apples with oranges." Experts in a particular subject may distinguish more relevant schemata than non-experts. Becoming acquainted with a repertory of galant musical schemata can thus lead to a greater awareness of subtle differences in galant music. The music may seem to develop more meaning.

Defining a schema can be difficult. There are both temptations to over-systematize—what Carl Dahlhaus termed *Systemzwang*[31]—and temptations to oversimplify. Our perceptions are far more fluid and richly nuanced than our ability to describe those perceptions in words. To explore more concretely some of the issues that arise in describing a schema, let us turn first to the well-studied repertory of German fairy tales. The brothers Grimm published the first important collection of these tales in 1812, using for their sources elderly informants who had learned the tales in the mid-eighteenth century.[32] These fairy tales contain a great deal of stereotyped material, as revealed by the following seven opening passages:[33]

> Just outside a great forest there lived a woodcutter with his wife; he had but an only child, a little girl of three. [Tale 3]

> Just outside a great forest there dwelled a poor woodcutter with his wife and two children; the little boy was called Hansel and the little girl Gretel. [Tale 15]

> Once upon a time there was a miller who was poor, but he had a beautiful daughter. [Tale 55]

> There once was a poor man and a poor woman who had nothing but a little cottage and fed themselves by catching fish, and they were living hand-to-mouth. [Tale 85]

Once upon a time there was a poor woodcutter who worked from morning till late at night. [Tale 99]

Once upon a time there was a man and a wife who had but an only child, and they lived all alone in an out-of-the-way valley. [Tale 166]

A poor woodcutter lived with his wife and three daughters in a little cottage at the edge of a lonely forest. [Tale 169]

Is there a single schema underlying all these sentences, a learned pattern useful for recognizing or initiating this type of tale? The answer depends very much on how one evaluates similarity. The openings of tales 3 and 15, for example, begin almost word for word, but then tale 15 diverges by introducing a male child, Hansel. The openings of tales 15 and 166, by contrast, use very different words and yet convey a very similar content. Similar story motifs are shared by tales 3, 15, and 169 (a forest), 3 and 166 (an only child), and 15, 55, 85, 99, and 169 (poverty). Indeed, as documented by the history of folktale research, the same repertory of utterances will support many different approaches to defining similarity and thus schemata.[34] Traditional folktale collectors, for example, focused on a protagonist—woodcutter, fisherman, miller—and categorized tales through this central agent: a woodcutter's tale, a fisherman's tale, and so on. The tale *Jack and the Beanstalk* is thus known as a "Jack tale." But what of tales 85 and 166? A "man-and-wife tale" was not a category recognized by folktale collectors. Nineteenth- and early twentieth-century researchers surmounted this obstacle by defining more abstract schemata. They distinguished quest tales from joke tales, tales of the supernatural from tales of cunning. And certain later twentieth-century researchers have extended those trends in the newer directions of psychoanalysis and political critique.[35] A continental literary theorist, for instance, might define the schema of the above sentences as the figurative expression of an urban petty bourgeoisie's fascination with a marginalized rural poor. The humble woodcutter (or miller or couple) does, after all, live "just outside" ("hand to mouth," "all alone," "out of the way," "at the edge," "at the foot of the mountain").

These approaches, however interesting they may be, all suffer from the defect of attempting to reduce complex phenomena to single essences. The opening sentence of tale 3 is neither essentially about woodcutters nor fundamentally about the marginalized rural poor. The sentence introduces a woodcutter, to be sure. But it goes on to place that woodcutter in a relationship with his wife, to place the two of them in a parental relationship with their three-year-old daughter, to color that parental relationship with the special phrase "only child," and to place the whole family unit in a setting near a large forest. Such a tabulation of relationships and constituent motifs played a large role in the taxonomic approach of the early twentieth-century Finnish school of folktale study.[36] The resulting mammoth compilations of tale schemata—"tale types," as they are called in folktale research—are based on analyses of constituent motifs and shared complexes of motifs. Our tale 15 turns out to be tale type 327A, *Hansel and Gretel*, which is a subtype of 327, *The Children and the Ogre.*[37]

The *Hansel and Gretel* schema, like a scenario from the commedia dell'arte, has three main episodes, each with subsidiary episodes in which are embedded various motifs (e.g., bread crumbs, gingerbread house, oven):

1. Arrival at the Witch's House
   (a) The children are abandoned by poor parents in a wood,
   (b) but they find their way back by cloth shreds or pebbles that they have dropped.
   (c) The third time birds eat their bread crumbs.
   (d) They wander until they come to a gingerbread house that belongs to a witch.
2. The Witch Deceived
   (a) The witch captures the children and begins to fatten Hansel.
   (b) Hansel sticks out a bone instead of his finger for the witch to measure.
   (c) The witch is burned in her own oven.
3. Escape
   (a) The children are carried across the water by ducks.

A tale type has many correspondences to what psychologists today term a "story schema."[38] Both assume different levels of analysis—subordinate narrative episodes each with its own subordinate motifs—and both eschew the single defining essence in favor of complexes of defining features, often hierarchically nested. Yet neither is the last word in defining a schema, especially a schema that unfolds in time. As past generations of philosophers and the present generation of cognitive psychologists have been at pains to point out, a complex mental category is something more than a fixed list of defining features. Take, for example, the case of the three woodcutter's tales (3, 15, and 169). All three omit "Once upon a time." Is the consistent omission of this stock opening phrase thus an integral part of a "woodcutter" schema? If this is true, then knowledge of a broader category, that of fairy tales in general, affects the definition. The point may seem trivial, but it does have significant ramifications. First, it suggests that individual exemplars of a schema may not contain all the features that define the schema. Second, it demonstrates that a schema may have defining features that are not overt, in the sense of articulated words or phrases. Third, it indicates that defining features may specify a temporal location or other relational attributes. And fourth, it leads to the conclusion that the notion of levels of structure is an oversimplification. In particular, "Once upon a time" is both subordinate and superordinate to the sentence in which it may appear—subordinate as part of a particular sentence, but superordinate as an important feature of the entire repertory.

Defining musical schemata is no less complex. Example 1.1 presents seven opening bass lines from the Opus 2 flute sonatas (1732) of Pietro Locatelli (1695–1764), all transposed to the key of C major for purposes of comparison. Though taken from movements in four different keys and five different tempos, these basses have obvious similarities. For example, on each bass I have marked a square on beat one, a circle on beat three, and a square again on beat seven to show that they all share, at analogous moments, an initial C, a move to A, and then a return to C. At a smaller scale, I have marked asterisks above the stepwise descent through the tones F–E–D–C. Note that in Sonata VIII, *Largo*, the asterisks are missing, suggesting that this stepwise descent was a very common but nonetheless optional continuation of the first half of this type of bass. Looking for still smaller motifs, one can see that Locatelli always writes ascending octave leaps on beat seven, usually adds ascending runs of three notes on the second half of beat seven, and usually includes descending runs on the second half of beat three.

EX. 1.1   Locatelli, Op. 2, various opening basses (Amsterdam, 1732)

Locatelli's basses exhibit numerous other similarities and differences. But more factors would need to be brought into the discussion before one could begin to clarify how these individual basses drew upon the "compulsory figures" known to Locatelli and other galant composers. For Locatelli and his musical colleagues, the frame of reference was the musical experience of their entire lives, not solely the sonatas of Opus 2. Beyond the further consideration of melody, harmony, rhythm, meter, and form, an understanding of how these passages were perceived requires examining the traditions of different genres, the predilections of national styles, and the particular repertories of music then known and performed. I have presented the details of that sort of inquiry in a previous book, *A Classic Turn of Phrase*, which explored the schema of one common musical phrase.[39] In the book at hand I summarize the results of several such inquiries so that the reader can develop a broad view of the repertory of important galant phrase schemata. Many of the following chapters are devoted to individual schemata. They present numerous musical examples — exemplars — that allow the reader to explore variants and stylistic changes typical of different decades and courts. Other chapters introduce whole movements by the great composers of the galant style so that the reader can experience the phrase schemata in their full context. Small, simple movements appear in the early chapters, longer, more complex movements later. The overriding theory behind my presentation of these schemata is that they formed one of the cores of a galant musician's *zibaldone*, his well-learned repertory of musical business, and that in the social setting of a galant court, these schemata formed an aural medium of exchange between aristocratic patrons and their musical artisans.

Chapter 2 will make it clear that Locatelli's basses each begin as variations on an opening schema known since the sixteenth century as the *Romanesca*. And chapter 3 will demonstrate that the asterisks mark the bass voice of a schema used as a standard riposte to an opening Romanesca. These relationships were not a "secret schematic art," to paraphrase Edward Lowinsky.[40] Rather, these schemata were designed to be noticed by anyone who listened to enough of this music. For modern devotees of classical music, every schema in this volume may sound quite familiar.

Around 1709, the North German musician Johann David Heinichen (1683–1729) wrote a treatise in which, among other things, he discussed how to harmonize certain pairs of tones in a bass. He then showed how several such pairs could be combined into a larger pattern that he termed a "schema."[41] His schemata for scalar passages of the major and minor modes were similar to what Italian musicians termed the *regola dell'ottava* ("Rule of the Octave"), yet different enough to seem out of fashion.[42] Heinichen himself recognized his imperfect grasp of the Italian style and so set off for Venice in 1711. There he perfected his knowledge and eventually made a triumphant return as chapel master to the lavish German court at Dresden. Like Heinichen, we will examine various pairings of tones in the following chapters, and we will see how they were combined into the most common schemata. Like Heinichen, we will travel to Italy to perfect our knowledge, studying exemplars by the great maestros. And like Heinichen, we will close by returning to German-speaking lands, in our case to view the lavish work of Mozart through the lens of the Italian galant style.

An Archaeology of Galant Musical Behaviors

Though this book is primarily about the musical patterns taught to and used by galant composers, the discussions inevitably raise questions about past modes of listening. If, for instance, a galant composer studied a particular repertory of patterns from an early age and employed them in his compositions for decades, would those patterns not resonate for him when he heard them in compositions by others? Would these acts of recognition not affect his experience of the music? If he and his fellow composers shared nearly the same repertory of schemata, would the repeated presentation of those patterns not affect their patrons' experiences too? If these schemata constituted a musical medium of exchange between court artisans and their patrons, did this aesthetic commerce not in some way depend on at least a general recognition of these patterns by many of the courtiers? Did familiarity with the normal presentation of these schemata not determine standards for judging musical propriety, invention, and taste?

Eighteenth-century documents cannot answer those questions directly. Then, as now, most people assumed that other people heard music in much the same way as they did themselves. Music affects listeners so directly, so viscerally, that they can easily mistake it for a natural phenomenon whose meanings should be patent and self-explanatory to any sentient being. Baron von Grimm stated without reservation that music was "a universal language that strikes our sense and our imagination immediately. . . . Its expressions . . . [go] straight to the heart without passing, so to speak, through the mind.[43] Music's meanings do seem to be shared within social groups of similar age, education, ethnicity, and class. But as the social distance between people increases, so can the distance between their modes of listening. A distant musical "language" may then require translation.

For much of the twentieth century it was common to view the automobile, airplane, motion picture, and radio as signs of a "brave new world," to use the Shakespearean phrase that became the title of Aldous Huxley's 1932 novel of modernism run amok.[44] Many composers played up this perceived break with the past, and a by-product of their musical modernism was the retrospective formation of a preceding "common-practice period." In particular, eighteenth- and nineteenth-century musics became lumped together as a pre-Modern style that came in three standard flavors—Romantic, Classical, and Baroque. The appeal and convenience of this construction, with its master narrative of musical growth and progress aided by the invisible hand of tonality and developments in the "science" of harmony, no doubt led to its wide acceptance. Yet as a prime example of Whig history,[45] this construction conceals the very discontinuities and ruptures that, if widely known, would undermine its legitimacy. In practical terms, the broad sweep of this dominant music-historical discourse has placed significant obstacles in the path of an accurate "archaeology" of the craft of musical composition.[46]

The twentieth century did not invent the sense of disquiet and alienation in response to rapid social and technological change. The people who lived through the shift from a courtly to a commercial musical culture were more likely to notice disjunctions than a continuing "common practice." The writer and art historian Henry Adams (1838–1918) described in the third person how the world into which he was born was assaulted by new technologies:

> [Henry Adams] and his eighteenth-century, trogloditic Boston were suddenly cut apart,— separated forever,—in act if not in sentiment, by the opening of the Boston and Albany Railroad; the appearance of the first Cunard steamers in the bay; and the telegraphic messages which carried from Baltimore to Washington the news that Henry Clay and James K. Polk were nominated for the Presidency. This was in May, 1844; he was six years old; his new world was ready for use, and only fragments of the old met his eyes.[47]

Adams, privileged grandson and great-grandson of early American presidents, felt all his life that he was culturally an eighteenth-century man lost in a nineteenth-century world of raw power. "One found one's self in a singular frame of mind,—more eighteenth-century than ever,—almost rococo,—and unable to catch anywhere the cog-wheels of evolution."[48] Beethoven and the dynamic world of nineteenth-century music were as foreign to young Adams as the steam locomotive. Only after this "eighteenth-century American boy fresh from Boston"[49] arrived at a nineteenth-century German university did he begin to understand Beethoven, and when that happened "he could not have been more astonished had he suddenly read a new language."[50] Adams would likely have concurred with the thrust of Michel Foucault's contention that,

> on the archeological level, we see that the whole system of positivities was transformed in a wholesale fashion at the end of the eighteenth and beginning of the nineteenth century. Not that reason made any progress: it was simply that the mode of being of things, and of the order that divided them up before presenting them to the understanding, was profoundly altered.[51]

Some nineteenth-century musicians in the post-Beethoven era did have an interest in the musical past and explored the surviving manuscripts and prints. Yet many Romantics, rather like conquistadors who discarded the Incas' finest treasures—cloaks of intricate feather work—in their search for gold, colonized their eighteenth-century musical heritage, looting a few extraordinary items—late Mozart, some works of J. S. Bach—but discarding the works that had been the most highly regarded by the patrons of the ancien régime. Almost like an Old Testament strongly reinterpreted by a New Testament, eighteenth-century music came to be heard through the filter of nineteenth-century music. Meanings changed, and to paraphrase Adams, "only fragments of the old" would be heard by the new ears. Galant works would become judged by the degree to which they were amenable to Romantic reception. In the words of the French novelist André Gide, "The classical work of art will not be strong and beautiful save by virtue of its subjugated romantisicm [*romantisme dompté*]."[52] Though Gide's dictum can be profitably applied to the neoclassicism of the 1920s and to the early twentieth-century reception of eighteenth-century art, it stands as a very poor guide to the tastes and values of galant society.

In a study of village life in Ireland, the folklorist Henry Glassie described the type of commitment needed to explore the past of a culture different from one's own:

> Serious study of a community's history does not begin with a raid to snatch scraps to add color or flesh or nobility to the history of another community. It begins when the observer adopts the local prospect, then brings the local landmarks into visibility, giving the creations of the community's people—the artifacts in which their past is entombed, the texts in which their past lives—complete presence.[53]

This post-Modern attitude toward recovering the "complete presence" of the cultural past, with its presumption of difference, is not shared by every classical musician. Many performers can recite a lineage that extends from their own principal teacher back through a chain of teachers to the time of Beethoven or beyond. The great Chilean pianist Claudio Arrau (1903–1991), for example, was a proud student of Martin Krause (1853–1918), who was a student of Franz Liszt (1811–1886), who was a student of Carl Czerny (1791–1857), who was a student of Ludwig van Beethoven (1770–1826), who was a student of Joseph Haydn (1732–1809), who was a student of Nicola Porpora (1686–1768), who was a student of Gaetano Greco (ca. 1657–1728). Greco taught the first generation of galant composers in Naples, so one might leap to the conclusion that Arrau's performances of eighteenth-century music benefited from this apparently unbroken connection to the roots of the galant musical past. One might even assume that Arrau played Haydn "as it really was."[54]

Wax cylinder recordings from the end of the nineteenth century have made it clear that traditions of performance changed dramatically during the twentieth century. Historical studies of still earlier traditions chronicle the equally dramatic changes that also occurred during the eighteenth and nineteenth centuries. Today numerous soloists and ensembles offer "historically informed" performances of eighteenth-century music. They feature a reversion to eighteenth-century technology (wooden flutes, strings made of catgut, horns without valves, timpani covered in calfskin, etc.), a lowering of the pitch, and changes in bowing, tonguing, phrasing, and ornamentation. The attendant claim to authenticity, which has commercial repercussions, has not escaped challenge.[55] Arguments have raged over whether a carefully researched yet still speculative "period" re-creation of the musical past is truer than a living yet mutated tradition passed down from teacher to teacher.

As mentioned earlier, I suspect that traditions of listening have also been slowly transformed. To recover something of the older, galant tradition, I attempt an archaeology of utterances from that distant musical civilization, one whose courtiers share with us relatively few social structures or modes of thought. As the potsherds from my excavations I present musical phrases—simple musical behaviors from a different time, now given voice in a different social setting. Can we hear them as Voltaire, Jefferson, or Mozart heard them? Perhaps that is an unrealistic question. The scholars of classical archeology have taught us that the temples of ancient Greece and Rome were gaudily painted.[56] Yet we do not rush out to paint the Parthenon.[57] The all-white classical building has become fully integrated into the modern worldview as a symbol of various staid institutions. My studies and those of other scholars show that the late works of Mozart were difficult for galant listeners to understand. Yet I do not expect Mozart to be suddenly dethroned from his current position as child-god of purity, clarity, and rationalism, no matter how mannered and extravagant were his manipulations of the galant style. What *can* be done is to provide an option for the modern listener, a method for developing a historically informed mode of listening to galant music. This other mode, to be sure, is conjectural and not necessarily superior. Like "authentic" performance, it is a modern reconstruction of an imagined past. But this conjectured galant mode of listening is nonetheless intriguing and well supported by the writings and practices of eighteenth-century musicians. It may help to put some of the color back into the experience of galant music.

Arnold Dolmetsch, a pioneer of the early-music revival, titled his 1915 magnum opus *The Interpretation of the Music of the XVII and XVIII Centuries Revealed by Contemporary Evidence.*[58] His interpretation was directed at the tangible—at the rebuilding of instruments and the performance of melodic ornaments. My interpretation of eighteenth-century music will focus on the intangible—on the mental constructs used by court musicians to create and perform their art. My "contemporary evidence" will be gleaned not only from the artifacts of musical phrases but also from the traces of how professional musicians learned their craft. Though today Haydn and Mozart are as distant in time as Purcell and Corelli were to Dolmetsch, I believe it is still possible to recover something of a galant musical *mentalité* through a close analysis and comparison of galant musical behaviors. The following chapters document those behaviors in detail.

Notes for the Reader

INTENDED AUDIENCE. While at times the discussion may become quite technical, I avoid hiding behind technical terms. Anyone with a love of classical music and the ability to read musical notation should find most of this tome accessible.

LIMITATIONS. There have been, of course, more than two centuries of critical and scholarly discourse between Mozart's time and our own. During that long period the music of the galant era has meant many different things to many different types of people. Indeed, the Romantic/Modern reinterpretation of galant music has itself become a great

musical tradition with its own authenticity. I cannot attempt to survey or review that important literature in this single volume. Rather, to the extent possible, I seek to engage
eighteenth-century writers and musicians through their own terms, concepts, and behaviors. Of course the writings of that time can be difficult to interpret unambiguously. As Dr.
Johnson noted (1773), "all works which describe manners require [explanatory] notes in
sixty or seventy years or less."[59] Today, at a far greater historical distance, eighteenth-
century accounts of galant musical manners may require quite a few "explanatory notes,"
which I derive in part from my studies of regularities in galant musical behaviors.

The names of all but a few eighteenth-century musicians have, alas, already slipped
into obscurity, so I attempt to provide for each a sentence or two that outlines the musician's location in galant society. These outlines are jejune substitutes for real biography,
attempting only to highlight for the non-specialist reader the web of personal and professional connections that linked musicians in different courts, chapels, and cities.

NAMES OF SCHEMATA. I follow in the footsteps of Joseph Riepel, the eighteenth-
century writer and chapel master at Regensburg who gave names to several important
musical schemata. I use Riepel's names and other names known in the eighteenth century
where possible, but I do not hesitate to add new names to the canon. For some schemata
I will choose a word, often an Italian word, that captures an aspect of their function. That
was Riepel's practice in the 1750s. And for other schemata I will choose a name that hon-
ors a significant scholar or teacher. It is, of course, possible to have musical knowledge that
does not correspond to a name. The musical knowledge of ordinary listeners is of that type.
But just as one can hardly imagine a serious inquiry into the characteristics and habits of
different species of birds without using the names of birds, so it would be difficult to compare and contrast the species of galant musical phrases without the ability to name them.
Naming, of course, has a style of its own. I have avoided the scientistic overtones of music-
theoretic discourse, favoring instead the direct, insouciant approach of galant composers
themselves. A review of each schema can be found in Appendix A.

NAMES OF PITCHES. When I mention specific tones, I use the forms standardized by
the Acoustical Society of America. Middle "C" on the piano is thus C4, the orchestral
tuning standard of 440 cycles per second is A4, the "A" an octave higher is A5, an octave
lower A3, and so on.

NAMES OF SCALE STEPS. When I refer to the steps of a scale or key from an eighteenth-
century perspective, I often use the names favored at that time. In place of the nineteenth-
century English syllables doh, ray, me, fah, soh, and lah, the earlier musicians used the
Latin forms *ut* (or *do*), *re*, *mi*, *fa*, *sol*, and *la*. In referring to the steps of a scale or key as
features of a schema, I use numbers within circles. For features of the melody, the circles
are black, as in ❶–❷–❸. For features of the bass, the circles are white, as in ①–⑦–①. In
passages that modulate between keys, such fixed scale-degree designations poorly repre-

sent the mobile cognition of pitch. I will argue that older forms of note naming may have been superior for those contexts.

NAMES OF CHORDS. In describing the chords chosen by galant composers, I generally avoid the roman numeral system of the nineteenth and twentieth centuries (I, IV, V, etc.), favoring instead the normal eighteenth-century shorthand of thoroughbass (6, 6/5, 7, etc.). In those places where I do use roman numerals, they indicate degrees of the scale treated as chordal reference points (Ger., *Stufen*) or local key centers, and I follow the older practice of using only uppercase roman numerals.

LOCAL KEY VERSUS GLOBAL TONALITY. The relationship between local and global meanings of chords and keys was fluid in galant music. Many of the methods of musical analysis in vogue today often overstate the degree to which one can clearly distinguish between local and global significance. Indeed, the craft of the galant composer depends heavily on the ability to modulate between perceived certainty and uncertainty, between, on the one hand, giving the courtly audience a sense of security and groundedness and, on the other hand, taking listeners down dark alleys of strange chords and keys where they may feel utterly lost. The lodestar of galant music was not a tonic chord but rather a listener's experience, which the masters of this art modulated with consummate skill. The nineteenth-century term *tonality*, which was never used by galant composers, was foreign to their more localized preoccupations. I too avoid its use, losing nothing, I would argue, in the process.

FORM. Some musical patterns could be described as having a clearly defined form but a loosely specified content (e.g., a "four-bar theme"). Other patterns could be described as having a loosely specified form but a clearly defined content (e.g., a "dominant pedal point"). Still others fall at some midpoint between those poles. For the midsize schemata that are the subject of much of this book, aspects of this form/content interrelationship are captured by the terms *event* and *stage*. Take, for example, an imaginary music schema with three events occurring in a predictable order, say A–B–C (see fig. 1.1). In a simple presentation each event may constitute its own stage, as when, for example, A, B, and C

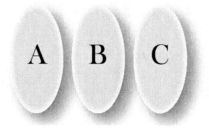

FIGURE 1.1   A schema of three musical events

are each a single chord. But in a more involved presentation, the core events may function as points of reference or as signs of punctuation. In that case, *stage* refers to the longer utterance into which the *event* is embedded. In figure 1.2, these three core events are now presented with three associated stages, where the first two stages are similar and the third is something different. Stages one and two might involve lengthy arpeggios that end with events *A* and *B*. Stage three might feature multiple echoes of event *C*.

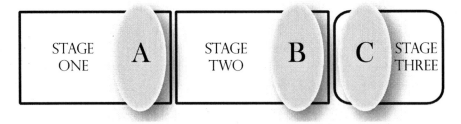

FIGURE 1.2   A schema of three core events embedded in three stages

The schemata presented in this book will be defined with reference to their events, and the important parallels or contrasts of the associated stages should be evident in the many musical examples provided for each schema. These issues and other questions of form will be revisited and given a fuller treatment in chapter 29. There we will see that another term rarely used by galant composers, *sonata form*, is more a hindrance than a help in understanding how galant compositions were made and understood in their own time. To judge by a considerable body of twentieth-century writing on eighteenth-century musical style, one might infer that tonality and sonata form were almost the only topics of any significance. If I declare those topics anachronistic before even beginning to discuss this music, and if I refuse to locate each piece on a Baroque/Classical axis, will there be anything left to say? I hope the reader will allow, at least provisionally, that something of worth might remain for discussion even if one forswears these pillars of a Romantic/Modernist approach to an unromantic art.

REPERTORY. This volume examines music written for the world of eighteenth-century courts. Court culture, of course, extended beyond the ranks of the hereditary nobility to the court-emulating world of the haute bourgeoisie in the growing cities. According to Nolivos de Saint-Cyr (1759), "the town, as they say, apes the court,"[60] and many wealthy financiers and traders established *maisons* complete with smaller versions of courtly entertainments. High churchmen also had courts with musical establishments (the phrase "princes of the church" was more than just a figure of speech, and the patronage of wealthy churchmen was vital for many galant composers). Excluded from this volume are those musics exclusively intended for middle-class home performance, for the congregations of Protestant churches, for "common" commercial concerts, and for popular theatricals, even though such music formed part of the web of eighteenth-century life. Mozart, for example, began his career almost exclusively devoted to court music. Yet as an adult he ventured into popular theater (*The Magic Flute*), commercial subscription concerts (many of his piano concertos), and music for the Masons (secular hymns), a group that most European courts considered seditious. His gradual shift toward more commercial and urban traditions was paralleled by many musicians in the second half of the eighteenth century. So for some music written after about 1760, my reference to court music may be best understood as indicative of a stylistic orientation and heritage rather than a literal provenance.

Within the courtly, galant style proper, I present hundreds of musical examples from nearly eighty composers. Thus the schemata are, as Samuel Johnson (1709–1784) said of the words in his dictionary (1755), "deduced from their originals, and illustrated in their various significations, by examples from the best writers."[61] Even so, many areas of galant music will be unavoidably underrepresented. The centrality of opera in galant culture cannot be overstated. I nevertheless have selected a large number of examples from small instrumental works. This will be especially apparent in the earlier chapters, where simplicity and comprehensibility are paramount. Later in the book, after a sufficient number of schemata have been introduced, I include whole arias by some of the best Italian masters. The raucous and somewhat different style of opera overtures has been slighted in my treatment. I do not examine recitative or melodrama, nor was it possible to include adequate coverage of schemata favored in the extraordinarily rich tradition of galant sacred music. In particular, I bypass the doleful inventory of chromatic depictions of woe, damnation, and the torments of hell. The schemata presented were chosen on the basis of their importance and prevalence in the central repertories of music for courtly chambers, for court opera theaters, and for the more progressive chapels. Because music in the major mode came to dominate this repertory, especially in the second half of the eighteenth century, the examples presented here are overwhelmingly in the major mode. To make musical illustrations of the schemata easier to comprehend aurally, I will often present movements of a slow or moderate tempo.

LABELING OF MUSICAL EXAMPLES. In the main text, musical examples are labeled by chapter, place in the series of examples, composer's name, movement, tempo, and measure number. Thus "EX. 7.14 Locatelli, Opus 4, no. 2, mvt. 3, Allegro, m. 1" indicates that the fourteenth musical example in chapter 7 is an *allegro* excerpt from the start of the third movement of the second sonata of Locatelli's Opus 4. Information about the further provenance of specific musical examples, or references to modern editions, can be found in the index of musical works. Copyists rarely added dates to galant musical manuscripts, and music printers often collected and published works that had been written some years earlier. Where an approximate time frame is all that can be ventured, the reader will find datings like "ca. 1780s," meaning "probably written sometime during the 1780s." In the case of the pedagogical manuscripts known as *partimenti*, which were copied by students for generations, the dates provided here often represent only vague suppositions based on the lifespans of the relevant maestros.

SHORTCUTS. Some of the following chapters introduce new schemata. Others feature whole movements that contain examples of the previously introduced schemata. Readers who might chafe at the leisurely eighteenth-century pace of this presentation, and who desire a quick overview of the schemata, may wish to refer first to appendix A. There they will find a pictorial representation of each schema prototype, a list of each schema's central features, and short paragraphs concerning each schema's typical functions and historical prevalence. They might then return to one of the "featured works" chapters to hear the schemata in context. Other readers, desiring to encounter this repertory more directly, without any interpretive gloss or theorizing on my part, may wish to bypass the text and listen first to the recorded exemplars. Many other paths through this material are possible, including starting with a featured work and then exploring its constituent schemata in the relevant chapters.

PARTIMENTI. The text makes frequent reference to the large repertory of pedagogical works known as *partimenti*. These works, which progressed from the very simple to the fiendishly difficult, were predominantly bass lines to which the student was expected to add upper voices or chords in order to create a complete keyboard work. The text focuses on partimenti as a means for young composers to, in Barbieri's words, "study and fortify their memory with a wide variety of things" such as galant schemata. Should the reader have an interest in the performative aspects of partimenti, or in learning to realize a partimento, appendix B provides a brief introduction.

2

THE ROMANESCA

FOR THE PATRONS OF GALANT MUSIC, making informed judgments about compositions and their performances required familiarity with the important schemata of the style. For the composers, making works worthy of praise required being able to produce exemplars of every schema correct in every detail. The more passive knowledge of patrons could be gleaned from frequent listening to the typical phrases of galant music. The active, operationalized knowledge of composers was carefully taught to them by music masters—maestros. The greatest maestros of the age worked in Italy, and they developed a unique method of instruction centered on the partimento—the instructional bass. A partimento resembled the bass part given to eighteenth-century accompanists, with the difference being the lack of any other players or their parts. The partimento was the bass to a virtual ensemble that played in the mind of the student and became sound through realization at the keyboard. In behavioral terms, the partimento, which often changed clefs temporarily to become any voice in the virtual ensemble, provided a series of stimuli to a series of schemata, and the learned responses of the student resulted in the multivoice fabric of a series of phrases and cadences. From seeing only one feature of a particular schema—any one of its characteristic parts—the student learned to complete the entire pattern, and in doing so committed every aspect of the schema to memory. The result was fluency in the style and the ability to "speak" this courtly language.

Like commedia dell'arte actors memorizing all the scenes and "business" in their troupe's *zibaldone*, so young composers memorized all the schemata in the partimenti of their maestros. As apprentices in the guildlike system of court musicians, students did not learn about the schemata through verbal descriptions or speculative theories, but rather learned them by rote, realizing them in every possible key, meter, tempo, and style. This calculated and concentrated regimen, guided by what Giovanni Maria Bononcini (1642–

1678) called the "living voice of a well-established maestro,"[1] allowed students to build up a robust knowledge of which variations and exceptions were permissible and which were not. Three such "well-established" maestros were Giacomo Tritto (1733–1824) and Giovanni Paisiello (1740–1816), both of Naples, and Stanislao Mattei (1750–1825) of Bologna. Paisiello, of course, was among the most famous opera composers of the eighteenth century, and the students of Tritto and Mattei included giants like Spontini, Donizetti, Bellini, and Rossini, who dominated early nineteenth-century opera. Below I have excerpted a passage from one partimento by each master. From Tritto comes a bass of simple whole notes intended as a beginner's exercise. Above the bass, in smaller notes, I show a likely realization with two additional parts. Below his bass, in measures 4–5, I show the figure "6" in brackets to indicate where the student would have been expected to play a 6/3 chord instead of the default 5/3:[2]

EX. 2.1   Tritto, from a partimento in F major, m. 1 (ca. 1810–20)

From Mattei comes a similar bass. Mattei's own numeric figures—hence a "figured bass"—indicated a chain of dissonances and their resolutions:[3]

EX. 2.2   Mattei, from a partimento in C major, m. 1 (ca. 1780s)

Notice that, on the last beat of measure 1 (ex. 2.2), Mattei adds the figure "5" to overrule the student's tendency to play a "6" there (C5 instead of B4), as was implied in Tritto's example.

From Paisiello comes another similar bass, also with indicated dissonances. But while Mattei sets the imagined upper voices against each other, Paisiello moves them in concert to make dissonances against the bass:[4]

EX. 2.3   Paisiello, an E♭-major passage from a partimento in C minor, Andante, m. 10 (1782)

Each of these partimenti is unique, and yet the three excerpts share many features. Their first five bass tones are identical in relation to their local keynotes. Their first three sonorities are the same, again in relation to the keynote. The imagined upper parts begin by descending in parallel thirds, whether by implication (Tritto), complete specification (Paisiello), or abstraction (Mattei, whose dissonances can be viewed as arising from the delay or "suspension" of an alto part that would normally be a third below the soprano). And each example represents, in its larger context, the entry of an important new musical theme or subject. They all, in fact, are common variants of a schema known as the Romanesca.

As its name implies, the Romanesca has an Italian provenance (as do most galant schemata).[5] It was first widely noticed and named by musicians in the sixteenth century, and during the seventeenth century it reigned as one of the most common ground basses. In more recent times, the Romanesca has been described as a common solution to a practical problem in composition: how to add a third voice, without introducing parallel fifths or octaves, to a pair of voices that move in parallel descending thirds.[6] If the added voice is a bass, the solution will closely resemble the music that made a forgotten seventeenth-century composition a household name among late twentieth-century devotees of classical music—Pachelbel's Canon (ca. 1680; see ex. 2.4). Its first three-voice combination, in measure 5, presents an obvious Romanesca where simple quarter notes mark each stage of the schema.

The horizontal braces in example 2.4 serve to highlight the general location of the schema. Again, the black-circled numbers indicate the scale degrees of the melody, and white-circled numbers indicate the scale degrees of the bass. Partimento manuscripts

EX. 2.4   Pachelbel, from his Canon in D Major, Andante, m. 5 (ca. 1680s)

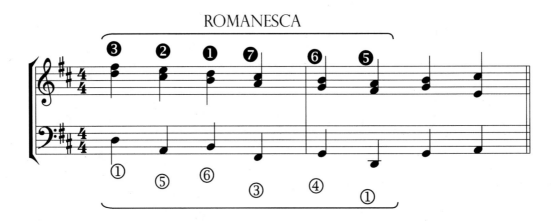

in Naples may have been the first texts to treat scale degrees as an organizing principle and point of departure. In the brief rulebooks or *regole* sometimes attached to collections of partimenti, the ①–⑤–⑥ . . . bass of the Romanesca was described as *prima di tono, quinta di tono, sesta di tono,* and so on. Thus my scale-degree markings are less a modern gloss than a graphic depiction of indigenous galant concepts.

In eighteenth-century terms, the above basses represent *partimenti semplici* or basic patterns shorn of ornament. Florid basses, with the underlying longer notes "diminished" into shorter notes, were far more common. Georg Frideric Handel (1685–1759) served as music tutor and hence maestro to Anne, daughter of George II, from 1724 until her marriage in 1734. As a carryover, perhaps, from his previous years in Italy, Handel used partimenti in his teaching. He gave the Princess Royal florid partimenti as assignments, and some of these exercises have been preserved. Handel likely intended the excerpt below to be realized as a Romanesca:

EX. 2.5   Handel, from his exercises for Princess Anne, Allegro, m. 4 (ca. 1724–34)

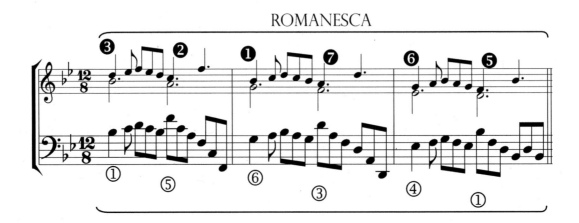

Because the princess's completed exercise has been lost, I have provided a realization in smaller notes above the partimento. In this florid bass, each stage of the schema lasts for six eighth-notes, with the core events occurring on the first eighth-note of each stage.

All these differing exemplars of the Romanesca imply a more abstract concept of the underlying schema, perhaps something with (a) six stages, (b) a descending stepwise melody, (c) a bass that alternates descending leaps of a fourth with ascending steps of a second, (d) an alternation of metrically strong and weak events, and (e) a series of 5/3 sonorities, as shown in figure 2.1.

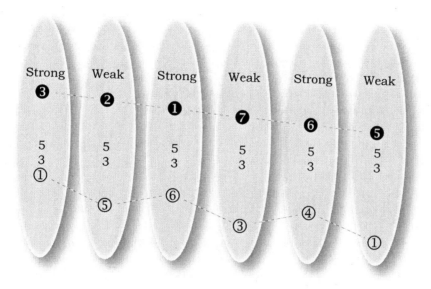

FIGURE 2.1   A schema of the Romanesca with a leaping bass

Even this brief introduction to the Romanesca should enable one to recognize, with some confidence, the same schema in the excerpt below:

EX. 2.6   Cimarosa, from his student notebook (*zibaldone*) of partimenti, m. 1 (Naples, 1762)

The only thing remarkable about its straightforward presentation of the Romanesca is its provenance. The example comes from a notebook of partimenti used at the Conservatorio di Santa Maria di Loreto, Naples, by the thirteen-year-old Domenico Cimarosa (1749–1801), later to become one of the most famous chapel masters in Europe.[7] The conservatory had taken the boy in following the death of his father. The next year, 1762, he dated and signed his name on a *zibaldone* of partimenti, most of which can be attributed to the great Neapolitan maestro Francesco Durante (1684–1755). This is a rare case where detailed biographical information about an indigent boy taken in by one of the great conservatories can be linked to a dated partimento manuscript.

The treble staff of example 2.6, added by me, shows a likely realization of two upper parts. The choice of those tones was highly constrained by the series of "5s" shown above Cimarosa's bass. The "5s" were a shorthand for "every bass tone should carry a 5/3 sonority." The original manscript, probably done by a professional copyist, only used figures at the cadence. A student, possibly Cimirosa himself, added the 5s to specify what was already self-evident to an adult musician.

During this same period Cimarosa was also studying the schema known as the Folia, which shares with the Romanesca a series of 5/3 sonorities and implied upper voices in parallel thirds. Example 2.7 presents the Folia partimento from Cimarosa's notebook, along with added, typical upper voices:

EX. 2.7   Cimarosa, from his student notebook of partimenti, m. 1 (Naples, 1762)

These forms of the Romanesca and Folia, part of the patrimony of late seventeenth- and early eighteenth-century musicians, were frequently modified as time passed. For the

Romanesca, the compositional problem posed earlier, "how to add a third voice, without introducing parallel fifths or octaves, to a pair of voices that move in parallel descending thirds," also has a solution in which the added voice is a treble. The "treble solution" may resemble this passage sung by the Three Ladies in Mozart's *Magic Flute* (KV620), where the parallel thirds are sung by the lower two voices:

EX. 2.8   Mozart, from *The Magic Flute* (KV620), act 1, no. 5, Andante (1791)

Johann Schobert (ca. 1735–1767), a celebrated keyboard player working in Paris and someone whose music the young Mozart studied assiduously, provided a more florid example of this Romanesca variant in the opening of his F-major trio:

EX. 2.9   Schobert, Opus 6, no. 1, mvt. 1, Andante, m. 1 (Paris, ca. 1761–63)

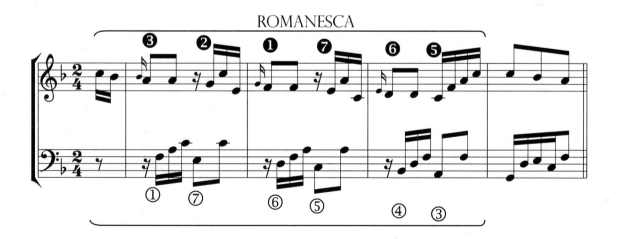

As an abstraction, this variant of the Romanesca features a stepwise descending bass in place of the previous leaping bass, and an alternation of 5/3 and 6/3 chords:

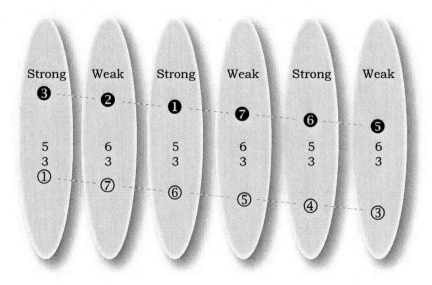

FIGURE 2.2   A schema of the Romanesca with a stepwise bass

While both types of solutions result in the same sequence of sonorities, the leaping variant (Pachelbel and Handel) is more characteristic of the seventeenth and very early eighteenth centuries, while the stepwise variant (Mozart and Schobert) is more characteristic of the later eighteenth century. Neither, however, was the preferred type for most galant musicians.

The Czech musician Wenceslaus Wodiczka (ca. 1715/20–1774) dedicated his Opus 1 violin sonatas (Paris, 1739) to the Duke of Bavaria, in whose orchestra he served as *primo violino*. In the dedication, Wodiczka effusively thanked the duke for having chosen him as a member of the duke's musicians, the *Filarmonici*, and for having arranged for his instruction in Italy under the guidance of "a most wise maestro." In Italy a young musician from the north could apprentice himself to one of the great masters of the galant style, and the diligent student could commit to memory the entire repertory of currently fashionable schemata. An examination of Wodiczka's compositions suggests that he was that sort of student, and I view his Opus 1 as a public presentation of the fruits of his Italian studies. Each page shows, with unusual clarity, the "compulsory figures" of the Italian galant.

The opening slow movement from the third of Wodiczka's sonatas begins with a good example of the preferred galant Romanesca (see ex. 2.10). The dashed lines at the right of the horizontal braces indicate that this type of Romanesca almost always blended into a following schema, often a cadence. Wodiczka's melody features the tonic and fifth of the key, with the descending stepwise melody of the older Romanescas now consigned to an inner voice. The particular contour of the melody—whether, indeed, ❶ preceded ❺ or vice versa—was not an important factor in the galant Romanesca. Wodiczka's first four sonorities alternate between 5/3 and 6/3 chords, somewhat like the stepwise variant (the figures shown between the staves are original). The 6/3 chord at the fourth stage over ③ in the bass, a feature not found in "pure" forms of the leaping or stepwise variants, was

EX. 2.10   Wodiczka, Opus 1, no. 3, mvt. 1, Adagio, m. 1 (1739)

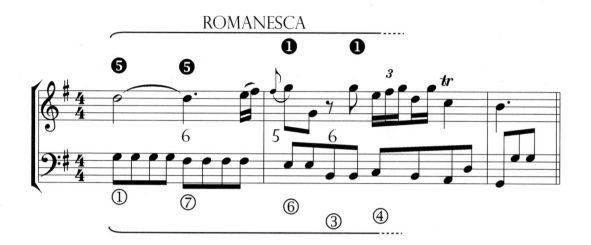

nonetheless very common, and it was implied in the partimento of Tritto shown earlier (ex. 2.1). Thus Wodiczka's bass—one used by countless other court musicians—resembles an abbreviated hybrid of the two main variants:

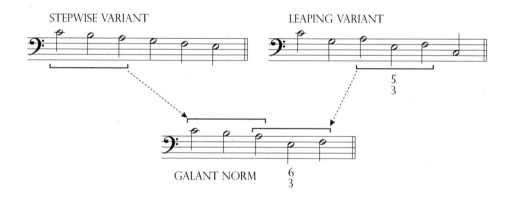

FIGURE 2.3   The galant Romanesca bass as a hybrid

The first three tones of the galant bass match the stepwise variant, while its third through fifth tones match the leaping variant, though with a slightly different sonority. In place of the 5/3 sonority for the fourth event, the galant Romanesca usually has a 6/3 sonority. That is, for the bass shown above (in the key of C major), the galant version would sound a C-major chord at the point where the leaping or stepwise variants sound an E-minor chord. Why?

When I have posed this question to students and colleagues, they generally answer in ways that would have puzzled the musicians who conceived this music. My beginning students' training in "chord grammar" does not help them explain why, in the key of G major, Wodiczka would follow an E-minor chord with a G-major chord in first inversion. Even the advanced student who invokes the post–World War I "theories and fantasies" of Heinrich Schenker (1868–1935), with that heavy-handed discourse of "the Will of Tones" and "the Spirit of Voice-Leading," is typically unsure whether training rusty artillery on a galant butterfly does justice to either the butterfly or the artillery.[8] The particular musical choice described above was not based on "chord grammar," the "rise of tonality," the "spirit of voice leading," or other grand abstractions. The proximate cause of that 6/3 sonority was a low-level nexus between the once common, concrete skills of solfège and the realization of unfigured basses (the more advanced type of partimenti), skills that were themselves merely codifications of a living musical praxis.

Creating a proper harmonic accompaniment from a plain bass part required the performer to make educated guesses about the musical context. The more obvious of those educated guesses became codified as rules or "laws." One of many such codifications was published in 1707 by Monsieur de Saint Lambert (fl. Paris, ca. 1700). As his very first law for realizing an unfigured bass, he declared: "A Si, a Mi, & a Sharp are always presumed to be figured with a 6 . . . , provided that the following note ascends by a semitone."[9] That is precisely the circumstance that obtains at the fourth bass tone of the galant Romanesca. Readers with a low tolerance for this sort of technical minutia might now wish to skip ahead to the following chapter, taking it for granted that eighteenth-century musicians played by eighteenth-century rules. For others who would like to understand how "a Si, a Mi, & a Sharp" could each trigger the "mi-rule," I provide the following excursus on eighteenth-century solmization.

Doh, a Deer . . . ?

The seven-syllable solfège in use at the Paris Conservatory for generations provides a unique verbal tag for every step of the diatonic scale:

EX. 2.11   A seven-syllable solfège

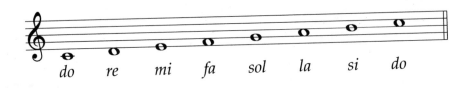

Whether one treats these syllables as note-names that persist regardless of the key or mode (fixed-*do*, the later Parisian practice) or as position-labels that move as the key center moves (movable-*do*), they can provide a one-to-one mapping between a syllable and a musical location.

The earlier six-syllable solfège introduced in the eleventh century by Guido of Arezzo also associated syllables with tones:[10]

EX. 2.12   A six-syllable solfège

But this hexachordal solfège only defined a local context. The syllable *mi*, for example, could refer to a tone in at least three different hexachords. So to identify an exact global position, the Renaissance musician would resort to a many-to-one mapping, where the intersection of two or three local contexts would fix a global position. The modern A3 would become "A *la-mi-re*" by virtue of its separate locations in three cardinal hexachords (see ex. 2.13). Italian musicians maintained these triangulated names for specific pitches until well into the nineteenth century.

EX. 2.13   Three hexachords used to define one location

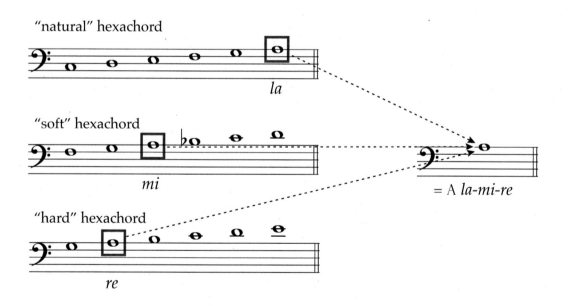

Somewhere between these two systems—between the global generality of the seven-syllable solfège and the local particularity of the hexachords—lies the common practice of the eighteenth century. What Giuseppe Tartini (1692–1770), the violin maestro of Padua, termed the "usual Italian solfeggio" is neither fully local nor fully global:[11]

EX. 2.14   The "usual Italian solfeggio"

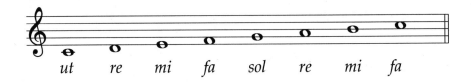

Important intervals like semitones are treated locally, so that both E4–F4 and B4–C5 become *mi–fa*, as though they inhabit separate hexachords. Yet as we shall see, when the scale is extended beyond the range of a single octave, the patterns that emerge repeat after *seven* syllables.

Eighteenth-century practice was far from uniform. In some German texts one finds only the alphabetical note-names—A, B, C, D, E, F, and G. The violin treatise (1756) of Leopold Mozart (1719–1787) falls into that category.[12] Many French musicians were among the first to adopt a seventh syllable. The harmony treatise (1722) of Jean-Philippe Rameau (1683–1764), for example, uses *si* for the seventh degree, as Saint Lambert did earlier.[13] The Italian writer Fausto Fritelli noted (1744) how chromatic and widely leaping melodies could confound the old system of hexachordal solfège.[14] Indeed, by midcentury some younger writers like Joseph Riepel and Johann Friedrich Daube had begun to ridicule all solfège systems as the imposition of needless complexity.[15] Nevertheless, the "usual Italian solfeggio" was widely known wherever the Italian style of music was cultivated. And in the eighteenth century, that was nearly everywhere.

A more detailed exposition of Italian practice as it was received abroad in the latter part of the seventeenth century can be found in the *Musicalischer Schlissl* [The Key to Music] (1677) by Johann Jacob Prinner (1624–1694).[16] Prinner begins with the hexachord, ascending and descending:

EX. 2.15   Prinner, *Musicalischer Schlissl*, a two-location hexachord

His use of two clefs indicates that the pattern of syllables is the same whether one sings the natural hexachord beginning on C4 (with the soprano clef) or the hard hexachord beginning on G2 (the bass clef). More generally, the point is that such hexachords share the same syllables and hence the same pattern of intervals. Thus the subject and "real" answer of a fugue, or the themes in sonatas that become transposed up or down a fifth, are the "same" by virtue of requiring the same syllables.

Prinner then shows how to extend the solfège beyond a single hexachord. The ascending pattern of syllables initially matches Tartini's scale, with subsequent alternating three- and four-tone groups that begin on *re*:

EX. 2.16   Prinner, *Musicalischer Schlissl*, the pattern of syllables when ascending

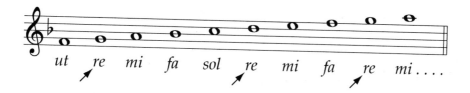

The descending pattern of syllables also alternates three- and four-tone groups that begin with *la*. The descending dyad *fa–la* may seem unusual, but it does conform to the then well-known precept that "a note above *la* should always be sung as *fa*" (*una nota super la / semper est canendum fa*):

EX. 2.17   Prinner, *Musicalischer Schlissl*, the pattern of syllables when descending

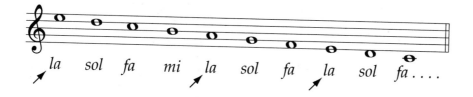

Adding a flat sign to the signature, which signals a change to the "soft" or *molle* system, transposes the syllables:

EX. 2.18   Prinner, *Musicalischer Schlissl*, the pattern of syllables in the "soft" system

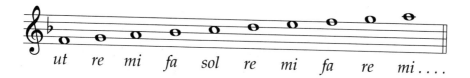

Thus the "usual Italian solfeggio" was, at least in some respects, "movable-*do*," although as we will see, different modes required different patterns of syllables. For Prinner, one might want to say "movable-*ut*," but for many Italians the syllable *do* was already replacing *ut*. Giovanni Maria Bononcini, in *Musico Prattico* [The Practical Musician] (1673), attributed the change to difficulties in singing the older syllable.[17] Tartini was probably adopting a scholastic stance by using *ut* almost a century later.

In reading Prinner or Bononcini today, a common confusion involves equating a solfège syllable with a scale degree. They are not the same. *Mi*, for example, defined a tone with a half step above it and a whole step below it, regardless of the location in a scale. Prinner, closely following Bononcini's treatise, displays an ascending scale for each mode with the semitones *mi-fa* highlighted as black noteheads. Here is his mode on D:

EX. 2.19   Prinner, *Musicalischer Schlissl*, the D-mode with *mi–fa* highlighted in black noteheads

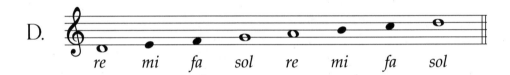

Some central precepts of the "usual solfeggio" should now be clearer:

One should consider all semitones as *mi–fa* when ascending and as *fa–mi* or *fa–la* when descending, regardless of the mode.

One should change hexachords on a new *re* if ascending and a new *la* if descending, when a passage moves beyond the range of a single hexachord.

One should treat an accidental as a change of syllable. Thus ♭ means "treat as *fa*," and ♯ means "treat as *mi*."

One can fit a short solfeggio fragment—*re, mi, fa*, for example—into multiple tonal contexts even with a single diatonic system: as (1) ❶–❷–❸ of the D or A modes, (2) ❷–❸–❹ of the C or G modes, (3) ❸–❹–❺ of the F mode, (4) ❹–❺–❻ of the E or A modes, (5) ❺–❻–❼ of the D or G modes, (6) ❻–❼–❶ of the F or C modes, and (7) ❼–❶–❷ of the E mode—twelve possibilities in all.

For a "practical musician" like Prinner, Saint Lambert's law about "a Si, a Mi, & a Sharp" would have been a rule about "a Mi, a Mi, & a Mi," since *si* was just another name for a *mi*-degree, and a sharp was an instruction to treat a tone as *mi*. These *mi*-degrees, when in the bass and followed by a *fa*, corresponded with musical contexts in which a locally unstable event preceded a locally stable event. Since the more stable events tended to have 5/3 chords, the *mi*-degrees, to avoid parallel fifths, should not have 5/3 chords (6/3 worked best, or 6/5/3). Hence the *mi*-rule, and hence an important reason why, when the fourth tone of the Romanesca bass preceded a tone one half-step higher (as *mi* preceding *fa*), galant musicians responded with a 6/3 chord on *mi* and a 5/3 chord on *fa*. To do otherwise would have been a faux pas.

Saint Lambert's observations were fully in line with the doctrine of the Neapolitan conservatories. Francesco Durante, a major figure in Naples who numbered Pergolesi among his many talented students, summed up the rule in his collection of partimenti: "When the partimento ascends a semitone, it takes the 6th".[18]

EX. 2.20 Durante, *Regole*, for an ascending semitone in the partimento (ca. 1740s)

So a musical schema can be a patchwork, the result of interactions between numerous small practices and the larger forces of both historical precedent and contemporary fashion. The musicians who developed the galant Romanesca preserved a number of venerable traits from its sixteenth- and seventeenth-century antecedents. But they also added the melodic focus on ❶ and ❺, shortened its length from six events to four, blended the stepwise bass with the leaping bass, and chose to make the fourth event a 6/3 sonority that would seamlessly connect to a following cadence or other schema:

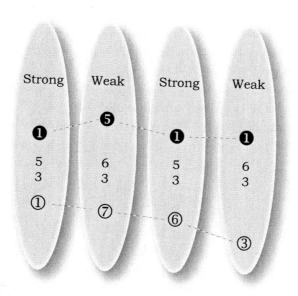

FIGURE 2.4   A schema of the preferred galant Romanesca

This galant Romanesca proved so popular that during the first half of the eighteenth century it became something of a cliché, especially in slow movements like that of the

Wodiczka Adagio shown earlier. It was one of the first patterns one might think of to begin any number of works. When Naples-trained Johann Adolf Hasse (1699–1783), the famous composer of court operas in Dresden, married the prima donna Faustina Bordoni (1697–1781) and wrote for her a dozen vocal exercises or *solfeggi*, he chose to begin the second one with a Romanesca:

EX. 2.21   Hasse, *12 Solfeggi*, no. 2, Allegro, m. 1 (ca. 1730s)

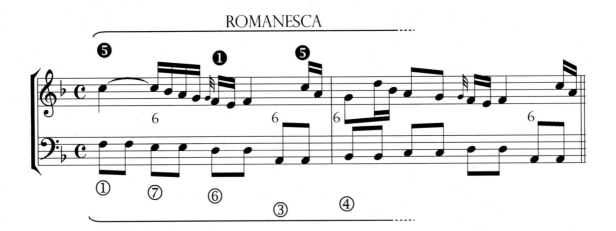

Note that Hasse's solfeggio includes a lightly figured bass, for which Neapolitan musicians also used the term *partimento*. The melody thus was schematically contextualized by its companion partimento, and the partimento was partially realized by its companion melody. Rather than being a single melodic line intended to teach some aspect of vocal gymnastics, as in the nineteenth century, an eighteenth-century Neapolitan solfeggio was a *two*-voice composition intended to teach melodic elegance and refinement in the context of the particular schemata codified by its companion partimento. Students who worked through these solfeggios would have an advantage when called upon to create keyboard realizations of free-standing partimento basses. That is, they could use solfeggios to "fortify their memory" with appropriate melodies, which could then be recalled when prompted by particular contexts or "occasions" in the partimento bass.

In the manner of a "usual scene" from the commedia dell'arte, the galant Romanesca depended for its effect on the quality of its presentation, not its originality. Yet it was never a completely fixed pattern. Further variation was possible if the overall schema remained recognizable. As a final variant, here is a Romanesca from a motet by the Milanese composer Giovanni Battista Sammartini (1700/01–1775), who was the maestro of Gluck. It conforms in most respects to the schema of figure 2.4, but holds the harmony of the first stage through the second stage, creating a lovely dissonance as the bass descends from ① through ⑦ to ⑥:

EX. 2.22   Sammartini, *Psalm* (J-C105), mvt. 6, *Gloria Patri*, Andante, m. 9 (ca. 1750s)

In many respects Sammartini's phrase is a performance of the same "scene" as Hasse's, with each composer making slightly different choices from among a set of known alternatives. The schema that they shared was "essentially" neither chord grammar nor voice leading, "fundamentally" neither harmony nor melody. Rather, each transcribed performance was a successful negotiation among a number of well-learned musical schemata within the constraints both of the practical requirements of particular musical situations and of each composer's background and training.

Sammartini was the premier church musician in Milan during the period when a young J. C. Bach (1735–1782) served as organist at the Milan cathedral. One can hear echoes of Sammartini's special treatment of the Romanesca in one of Bach's keyboard sonatas from 1766, written after the "Milan" Bach had acquired a reputation as an opera composer and been recruited to England where he became the "London" Bach:

EX. 2.23   J. C. Bach, Opus 5, no. 3, mvt. 1, Allegro, m. 63 (London, 1766)

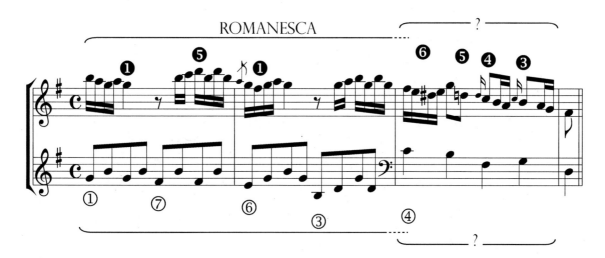

Bach's follow-on riposte to the Romanesca, labeled with question marks in example 2.23, was itself one of the most common galant schemata, and it forms the subject of the following chapter.

After listening to these many examples of the galant Romanesca, you may have now acquired a "refined ear" and the ability to judge whether a particular presentation of it possesses a "superior gracefulness." Imagine yourself at the Vatican in 1750, in conversation with a devotee of galant sacred music. As musicians enter the chamber of Cardinal Albani, you sit and await the Naples-trained *maestro di capella*, Niccolò Jommelli (1714–1774). The portly maestro finally arrives and signals for a performance of his motet *Domus mea* to commence. It opens with a *largo* Romanesca. The two high male voices are supported by an organist softly playing the bass in his left hand and harmonies in his right:

EX. 2.24   Jommelli, *Domus mea*, m. 1 (Rome, 1750)

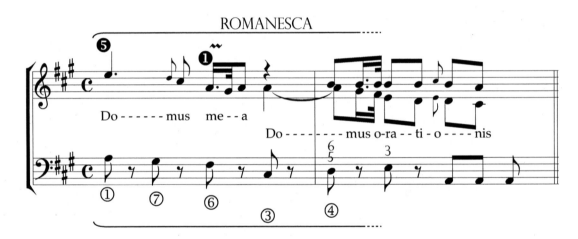

There were several possible choices for the second chord (above ⑦), three of which are shown in example 2.25. The organist played version (a), to which your noble friend later objects. She speaks of its "harshness," and after the musicians have left you recommend either the normal model of Hasse (cf. ex. 2.21, adapted as ex. 2.25b) or the more piquant model of Sammartini (cf. ex. 2.22, adapted as ex. 2.25c). Your friend is impressed by your display of discernment, and compliments you on your taste.

As fanciful as that scenario might seem, it does put the focus squarely on informed, educated taste, and especially on taste as a topic of conversation and good-natured disputation. To speak artfully of art was a social grace and distinction worth cultivating. The tiny differences in the organist's options may once have mattered a great deal. Quoting Norbert Elias from chapter 1 above, "These people experience many things that we would be inclined to dismiss as trivial or superficial with an intensity that we have largely lost." Though perhaps only musicians could have verbalized the options for harmonizing Jommelli's bass, the opinions of highly placed musicians mattered a great deal at any prestige-conscious court.

EX. 2.25   Three harmonizations of ex. 2.24: (a) "harsh"; (b) "normal"; (c) "piquant"

"Harsh"

à la **Hasse:**

the most common
type, with "6" above ⑦

à la **Sammartini:**

tonic harmony extends
through stage two,
with "4/2" above ⑦

Ironically, and perhaps reinforcing my remark about distinctions to which, "over the intervening centuries, we have become less sensitive," the "harsh" option, the one least appropriate, was the one chosen for the otherwise exemplary modern edition of this work.[19] The general sequence of schemata was not, fortunately, subject to revision. Jommelli gave his Romanesca the same type of riposte and continuation chosen by J. C. Bach (ex. 2.23). The nature of this preferred galant riposte is, as mentioned, discussed at length in the following chapter.

3

THE PRINNER

GALANT SOCIETY VALUED POLITE YET PLAYFUL CONVERSATION. In the skillful turn-taking that animated courtly banter, the ability to come up with an elegant riposte was at least as important as the ability to lead off. The slyest, most teasingly ambiguous opening gambit could fall flat if no one found a riposte to counter it. The chosen riposte could be effective even if it were conventional—perhaps an old saying or proverb—as long as it was employed with a certain flair at just the right moment. An ill-chosen riposte could be a social disaster. Isabelle de Charrière (1740–1805) was a brilliant, highly educated woman in courtly society at The Hague. She had real gifts as a writer, and many critics feel that her letters are among the finest of her time. In 1764 she wrote to her secret male correspondent about a young man who had the notion of marrying her. Her letter mentions that she had asked the suitor, alluding to Corneille's French tragedy about an ancient Roman general, "Do you know *Cinna?*" The poor man, guessing she must be referring to something in antiquity, responded, "Oh yes, I read it in Latin."[1] His riposte doomed him.

In courtly musical society, an opening gambit like the Romanesca invited an elegant musical riposte, and one of the favorite choices was a pattern I call "the Prinner," in honor of the humble seventeenth-century pedagogue introduced in the previous chapter. Prinner's treatise, important more for its typicality than its originality, covered a range of topics deemed necessary for the aspiring provincial musician. Under the heading "Instruction for the Organ," he treats what an accompanist should know of figured and unfigured basses. His discussion follows the time-honored practice of describing counterpointing voices as proper responses to a motion in a reference voice. In earlier centuries the reference voice would have been a tenor. In Prinner's seventeenth century, it had become the bass. He dutifully shows how the counterpointing voices should behave if the bass ascends or descends one step, two steps, three steps, and so on. When he comes to a bass that descends four steps, he notates the proper responses as follows (I have added the indications of scale degrees for comparison with later examples):[2]

EX. 3.1   Prinner, *Musicalischer Schlissl* [The Key to Music], fol. 58 (1677)

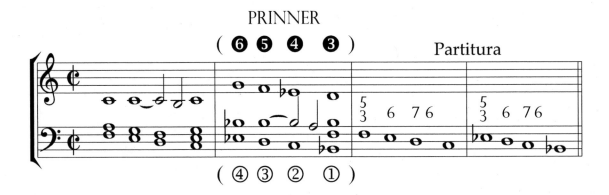

His intent may have been to show that two different voicings (mm. 1, 2) in two different keys (C and B♭) share the same figured-bass pattern given under his rubric *Partitura* (mm. 3, 4). Yet his two voicings also represent the old and the new. The voicing in his first measure had long functioned as a form of the ancient *clausula vera* (see chap. 11), while the voicing in his second measure—what I term the Prinner—would become a preferred riposte in the nascent galant style.

The Romanesca of Wodiczka shown in chapter 2 was the type of opening gambit that demanded a suitable riposte:

EX. 3.2   Wodiczka, Opus 1, no. 3, mvt. 1, Adagio, m. 1 (1739)

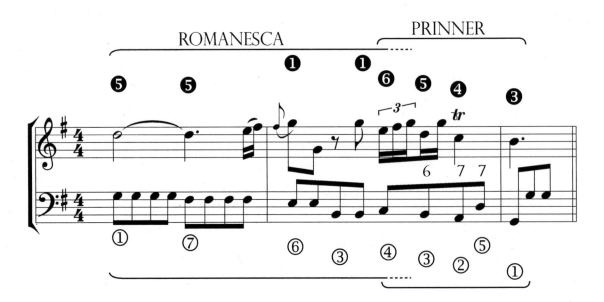

Wodiczka chose a popular variant of the Prinner that featured a lengthened third stage. That is, while each of the first two stages of Wodiczka's Prinner lasts for only an eighth note, the third stage, with its melodic trill on ❹, lasts for a quarter note and allows for the interpolation of ⑤ between ② and ① in the bass. This adjustment places the Prinner's fourth event squarely on the downbeat of measure 3, a stable place at which Wodiczka gives both the listener and the soloist time to pause before the music sets forth with a new phrase.

Extending the third stage was but one of many common options available to galant musicians who wished to vary the Prinner riposte. When Wodiczka repeated his Romanesca-Prinner combination later in the same movement (immediately following the double bar), he took advantage of this latitude to introduce a number of minor alterations:

EX. 3.3   Wodiczka, Opus 1, no. 3, mvt. 1, Adagio, m. 6 (1739)

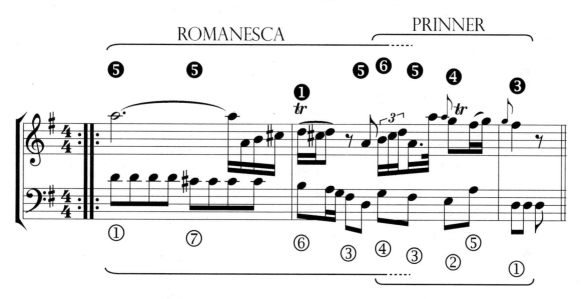

For instance, in its opening appearance, his Romanesca's melodic ❺ moved *up* to ❶, whereas after the double bar the ❺ moves *down* to ❶. Similarly, the Prinner's ❻–❺ was initially *higher* than its ❹–❸, but the reverse is true when the Prinner reappears after the double bar. Yet this second passage, even with these and other changes, would still have been perceived as a restatement of the opening theme (in the key of the dominant) because Wodiczka respected the range of variation allowed for both the Romanesca and its Prinner riposte.

Wodiczka, who will serve as galant Everyman in this text, could have studied with any of several "most wise maestros" of the Italian galant. His treatment of the Romanesca-Prinner pairing finds echoes in many works of the period. An excerpt from the Opus 1 sonatas of Benedetto Marcello (1686–1739;), for instance, is easy to imagine as Wodiczka's point of departure and compositional model, though as a nobleman Marcello would not have taken students (see ex. 3.4).[3]

EX. 3.4   Marcello, Opus 1, no. 1, mvt. 1, Largo, m. 1 (Amsterdam, 1732)

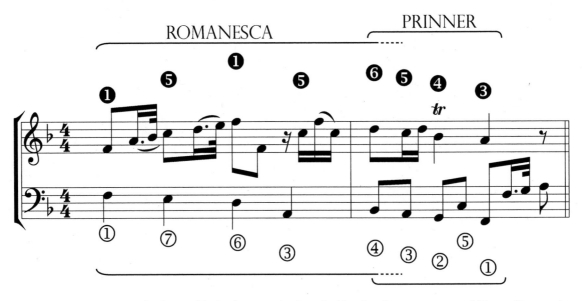

Wodiczka could also have studied works like the Opus 2 sonatas of Pietro Castrucci (1679–1752). Castrucci, a violin pupil of Corelli in Rome, was—like many in a long line of Italian and Italian-trained musicians—recruited to work in the north.[4] In Castrucci's case that meant England, where he met with considerable success as the leader of Handel's opera orchestras in London. Although Castrucci left Italy in 1715 and thus could not have been Wodiczka's direct teacher, their styles are nonetheless similar. Note how, in the fourth of these sonatas for violin and thoroughbass, Castrucci presents a Prinner riposte that adopts a cadential bass in place of the usual ④–③–②–①:

EX. 3.5   Castrucci, Opus 2, no. 4, mvt. 1, Andante, m. 1 (London, 1734)

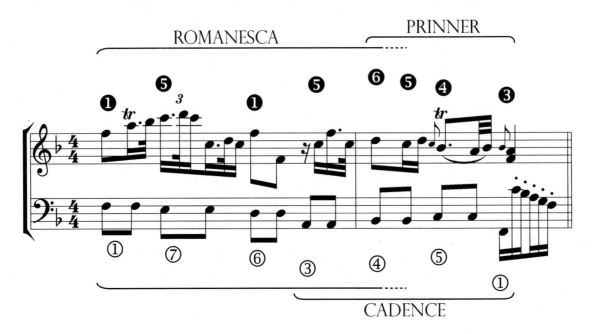

Wodiczka might also have learned and mimicked the Opus 6 sonatas of Pietro
Locatelli (1695–1764). Again, a personal connection is unlikely, since this great violinist
from the Corelli orbit seems not to have taken students. He had already left Italy in the
late 1720s for work in the north, centering on Amsterdam:

first composer to write cappricio (violin cadenzas so elaborate that they become independent pieces in concerto)

EX. 3.6   Locatelli, Opus 6, no. 11, mvt. 1, Adagio, m. 16 (Amsterdam, 1737)

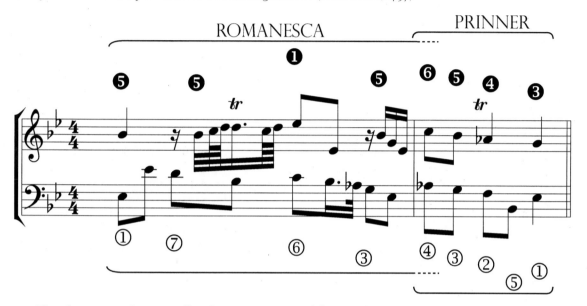

The above example is actually a later restatement of the initial, more playful theme
(see ex. 3.7). Locatelli begins his Prinner, then halts, and then begins it again. Though
only hinted at here, in later decades it became common to separate ❻–❺ from ❹–❸:

EX. 3.7   Locatelli, Opus 6, no. 11, mvt. 1, Adagio, m. 1 (Amsterdam, 1737)

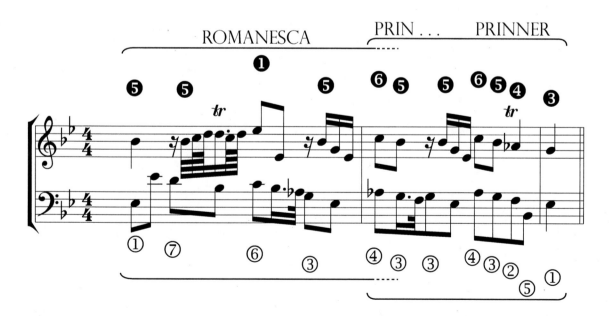

Many of the elite young musicians from this era studied in Naples with the famous maestros of its four conservatories. Leonardo Leo (1694–1744) taught a whole generation of galant composers. The following passage from the slow movement of his flute concerto in G major could have served Wodiczka as a model for a slow, stately presentation:

EX. 3.8   Leo, Concerto in G Major for Flute, mvt. 2, Largo (Naples, ca. 1730s)

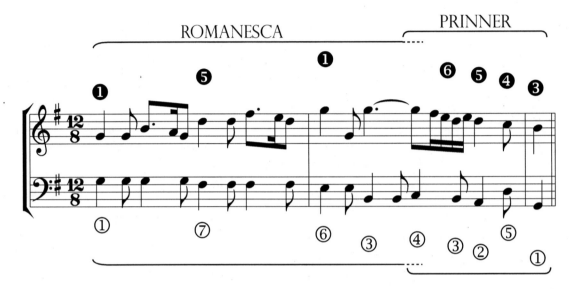

Whatever the specific pieces that Wodiczka learned, and whoever served as his "most wise maestro," he obviously absorbed what was happening in Italian music of the 1730s. If these examples sound vaguely familiar, it is probably because many modern listeners have heard the work of Wodiczka's contemporary Domenico Gallo (fl. 1750s) in the famous retouching by Stravinsky for the Ballets Russes (*Pulcinella*, overture, mm. 1–2):

EX. 3.9   Gallo, Trio in G Major, mvt. 1, Allegro, m. 1 (ca. 1750s)

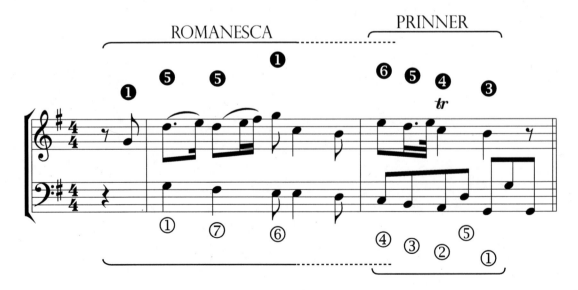

Gallo's movement, still frequently attributed to Pergolesi, begins with a Romanesca whose bass avoids the usual leap from ⑥ down to ③. The Prinner riposte, however, could hardly be more conventional.

The examples by Wodiczka, Marcello, Castrucci, Locatelli, Leo, and Gallo all embody an important tradition of how to present a Romanesca-Prinner pairing. To borrow the terminology used in eighteenth-century fugal partimenti, this conventional linkage of Romanesca *proposta* with Prinner *riposta* was important for any student to learn. Paisiello included an obvious example of this pairing in one of his partimenti, and one can set either version of Wodiczka's melody above Paisiello's bass without any modifications save the lengthening of note values required by the change of meter. Below is Paisiello's bass with Wodiczka's second melody. Though written more than four decades apart, the two fragments fit perfectly because both musicians knew the same "compulsory figures":

EX. 3.10   A Paisiello partimento bass (1782) with a Wodiczka violin melody (1739)

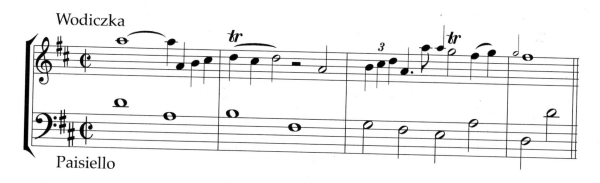

The speed and confidence with which many of the best eighteenth-century composers wrote multivoice works has long been a subject of marvel for modern musicians. Though the skill and invention of those composers remains impressive however one might try to explain their abilities, there are obvious advantages that a stockpile of "interchangeable parts" would give to the rapid, secure crafting of complex compositions. Anyone who knew the above tradition of a Romanesca leading to a Prinner could draw upon a number of stock melodies, basses, and harmonizations—everything would fit together. Today we tend to equate "compose" with "invent," yet the older, more literal meaning of "put together" (*com* + *posare*) may provide a better image of galant practice.

There were also other traditions for connecting a Romanesca with a Prinner. Among the earliest exponents of the galant style was Giovanni Bononcini (1670–1747, son of Giovanni Maria Bononcini). In example 3.11 from his opera *Il trionfo di Camilla* (1696), Bononcini incorporated the Romanesca into another opening gambit that I term, for obvious reasons, "the Do-Re-Mi" (see chap. 6). His Prinner riposte matches the length of his opening gambit, and he repeats the Prinner in perhaps an echo effect (the use of repeat signs below is a space-saving expedient and not a feature of the original manuscript).

EX. 3.11   Bononcini, *Il trionfo di Camilla*, Sinfonia, mvt. 3, Allegro, m. 1 (Naples, 1696)

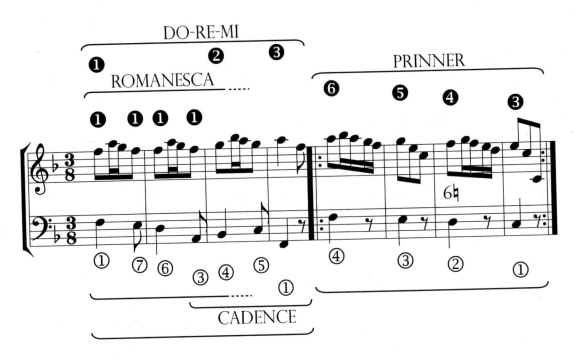

Bononcini's Prinner is in the key of the dominant, C major (note the B♮ indicated by the "6♮" in m. 7). In early eighteenth-century terms, this requires the Prinner's initial melodic tone, A5, to change its orientation from *mi* in the hexachord on F to *la* in the hexachord on C. A two-clef solfège example, like those from Prinner's own treatise (cf. ex. 2.15), can make the point in a manner consistent with Bononcini's era:

EX. 3.12   The core Prinner melody in two different hexachords

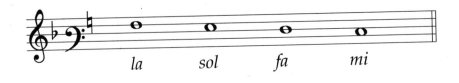

That is, *la–sol–fa–mi* in the "soft" system (shown by the treble clef with one flat) is "the same" as *la–sol–fa–mi* in the "natural" system (shown by the baritone clef with no sharps or flats).

A Prinner heard to end in the key of the dominant, which I call a "modulating Prinner," was very common in galant music. It provided an excellent means of moving rapidly to the dominant while at the same time fulfilling the expectation for a riposte.

Among the maestros of the Neapolitan conservatories its use was considered standard
practice. Saverio Valente, a maestro from 1767 until the early nineteenth century, recommended the following *esempio* (It., "example"), an almost exact copy of the partitura from
Prinner's treatise, "for a departure to the fifth of a key in the major mode":[5]

EX. 3.13   Valente, an example of how to move to the key of the dominant (ca. 1790s)

The modulating Prinner of Valente's example begins in the key of F major and then
shifts toward C major. Had the same passage followed a C-major context, it would represent an ordinary, non-modulating Prinner. Below is a Prinner, also by Valente, from a
florid partimento (for its opening Sol-Fa-Mi, see chap. 18). Its bass (mm. 14–17) corresponds closely to the four notes shown above, but the context is entirely that of C major:[6]

EX. 3.14   Valente, from a partimento in C Major, m. 11 (1790s)

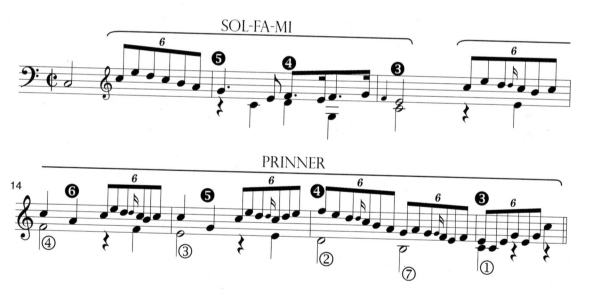

The choice of which type of Prinner to use depended on a number of factors, including the size of the intended movement (small movements needed to move more quickly
to a second key). Bononcini's younger rival Handel also knew how to incorporate an opening Romanesca into a larger Do-Re-Mi opening gambit. But in example 3.15 the German
musician leaves his Prinner in the main key and expands it with a circle-of-fifths bass and
a corresponding harmonic sequence, all in keeping with the greater breadth of his movement as compared to Bononcini's.

EX. 3.15   Handel, Suite in G Major, Courante, m. 1 (before 1720)

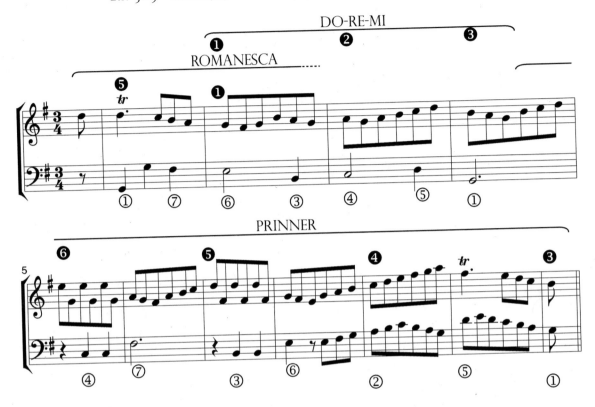

"Well-established maestros" taught these same combinations of schemata. The Naples-trained castrato Giuseppe Aprile (1732–1813) gave his students the following solfeggio. It opens with a Romanesca and Do-Re-Mi that lead into a canonic, non-modulating Prinner. The downward scalar motion of the canonic Prinner extends to a half cadence:

EX. 3.16   Aprile, *Solfeggi per voce di soprano*, fol. 4v, m. 1 (Paris, 1763)

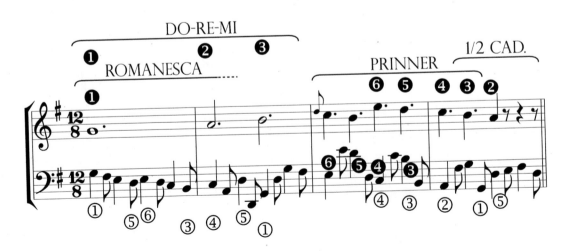

A charming passage by L'Abbé le Fils (1727–1803) can serve as a summary example of a large and complex Prinner from the 1760s (ex. 3.17). Taken from his Opus 8 violin sonatas (1763), this passage embodies a further extension of the Bononcini/Handel/Aprile template. Where Handel's Do-Re-Mi had a full cadence (m. 4), L'Abbé inserts a deceptive cadence, which he must then repeat with a full cadence. He also presents a large, non-modulating Prinner *twice*. On repetition, the Prinner gains additional melodic decoration and a circle-of-fifths accompaniment. The all-root-position, leaping-fifths-and-fourths bass of Handel had lost favor by midcentury, so L'Abbé was keeping up with fashion when, for his circle of fifths (mm. 11–14), he wrote the more modern bass with alternating 5/3 and 6/3 chords:

EX. 3.17   L'Abbé, Opus 8, no. 1, mvt. 1, Allegro, m. 1 (Paris, 1763)

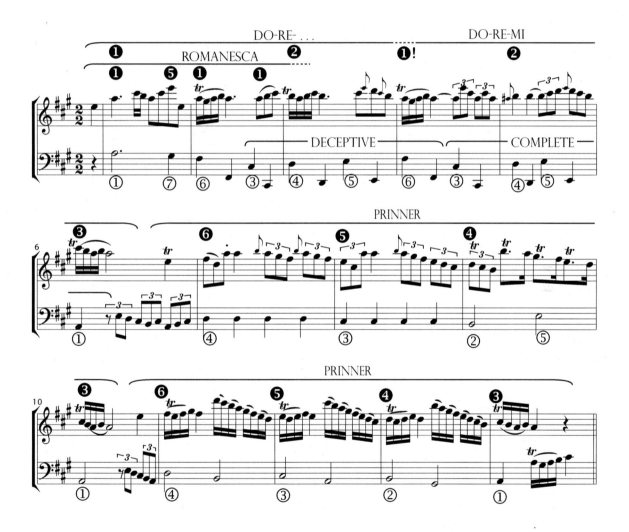

I expect that a listener even modestly familiar with Romanescas and Prinners will find this passage perceptually clear in spite of its ornate melody. Eighteenth-century courtiers with a taste for music must have heard thousands of instances of the Romanesca-Prinner pairing, and I presume that the aural recognition of these and other schemata would have been a matter of course. The musical paths at court were very well worn, and as soon as one perceived which path had been chosen, attention could shift toward appreciating the nuances of presentation. A Prinner in response to a Romanesca was no more surprising than a curtsy in response to a bow. It was the *manner* or style of presentation that mattered as the real object of aesthetic attention.

Isabelle de Charrière, as we read earlier, was a courtier who knew how to judge a riposte. As an amateur composer of keyboard sonatas, she wrote an opening gambit for which she provided an emphatic riposte of two Prinners :[7]

EX. 3.18   De Charrière, Sonata in D Major, mvt. 1, Allegro, m. 1 (The Hague, ca. 1790s)

Is this inspired music? No. Does it show proper behavior at court, executed with zest and confidence? Yes. It is securely in the galant style, though it may lack the "superior gracefulness" we might expect from a professional.

A title by Hugo Riemann (1849–1919), *Verloren gegangene Selbstverständlichkeiten . . .* [Things Once Self-evident but Now Lost to the Past . . .][8] might well describe the Prinner. Few patterns in galant music were more common, but the concept, regardless of what name one might apply to it, has all but disappeared. In the eighteenth century, even amateurs like de Charrière knew that a Prinner was a typical response to almost any opening gambit. What de Charrière knew about Prinners and other schemata came to her partly through osmosis, as an avid member of galant musical society, and partly through instruction from gifted teachers. For some time she employed the Neapolitan maestro Niccolò Zingarelli (1752–1837) as her private tutor (he was later to teach Bellini). Zingarelli had his own repertory of partimenti and solfeggi, and I imagine that de Charrière worked her way through them as part of her training.

Below I provide the opening phrases of three of Zingarelli's partimenti (exx. 3.19, 20, 22), with plausible realizations added in smaller notes. The thoroughbass figures are Zingarelli's. The annotations of schemata and scale degrees are mine. The first bass demonstrates a textbook example of the stepwise Romanesca, one that merges with a *clausula vera* (see chap. 11) or Prinner:[9]

EX. 3.19   Zingarelli, from a partimento in C Major, m. 1 (ca. 1790s)

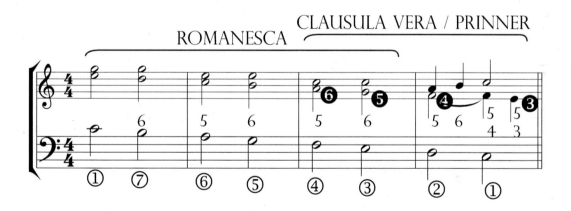

De Charrière was studying with Zingarelli at roughly the same time that another talented woman, Barbara Ployer (1765–1811), was studying with Mozart in Vienna. Mozart and Zingarelli were contemporaries, and though they had few if any personal contacts (Mozart visited Naples only briefly in the summer of 1770, when Zingarelli was still a senior student at one of the conservatories), the similarity in their approaches as teachers can be heard in the lessons they wrote. First Zingarelli. His second bass (ex. 3.20) begins with a brief Do-Re-Mi as opening gambit (the Do-Re-Mi "melody" is in the bass, and the normal bass is in the melody; see chap. 6 for details). The riposte is obviously a Prinner, with its third stage lengthened (m. 3):[10]

EX. 3.20   Zingarelli, from another partimento in C Major, m. 1 (ca. 1790s)

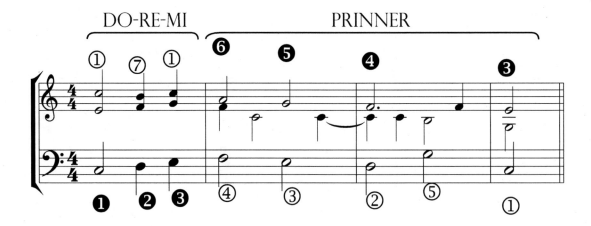

Compare Zingarelli's lesson with one that Mozart wrote for Ployer to complete and continue. The bass, melody, and figures are Mozart's, the annotations and alto voice are mine:

EX. 3.21   Mozart, from his exercises for Barbara Ployer (KV453b, mid 1780s)

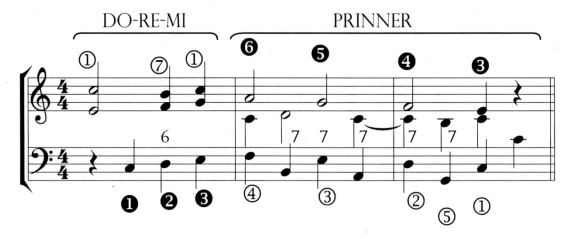

Finally, in a third example by Zingarelli (ex. 3.22),[11] we see him call for a modulating Prinner between an opening theme in C major and its restatement in the dominant key of G major. He added figures only for the first cadence, and wrote "sec: pos:" (*seconda posizione*) at the beginning of the modulating Prinner to alert the student that the third of the chord (E5) should be in the melody. Everything else was presumed to be self-evident.

EX. 3.22   Zingarelli, from another partimento in C Major, Andante, m. 1 (ca. 1790s)

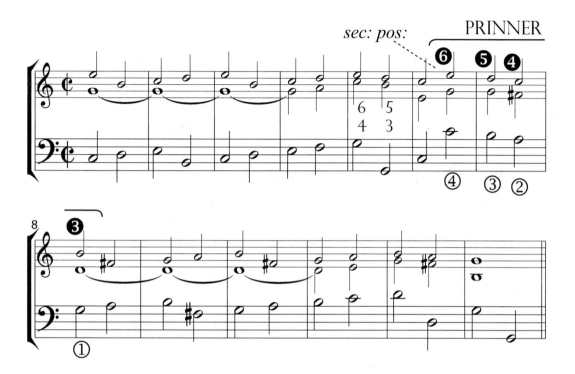

As we will see in chapter 16, this theme, with its canon between melody and bass, was a favorite galant schema. I name it "the Fenaroli," after the composer whose partimenti came to be the most famous of all in the nineteenth century, and who, more than coincidentally, was Zingarelli's own maestro. Like the Romanesca and Prinner, it was replicated time and time again within the close-knit world of teachers and students.

How did we become deaf to the Prinner? Answering that question would take us beyond the scope of this volume and into the history of nineteenth-century music theory, especially the rise of "harmony" as an imagined force of nature. Yet cognizance of the Prinner and other similar patterns need not be irretrievably lost. We can, through an archaeology of musical utterances, dust off the galant schemata and listen to what they have to tell us about this courtly mode of musical thought.

In archaeology, one can infer centers of influence and style based on the distribution and dissemination of potsherds and other fragments of material culture. When, as in this chapter, one encounters example after example of similar Romanesca-Prinner pairings, and when those "potsherds" are distributed among the works of violinists like Castrucci in London, Locatelli in Amsterdam, and L'Abbé le Fils in Paris, whose lineages of maestros are known to converge on Arcangelo Corelli (1653–1713) in Rome, one would expect to find the same or similar pattern in the works of this seminal figure. That is indeed the case. Castrucci's phrase shown earlier as example 3.5, for instance, is an almost note-for-note recasting of one of the several Romanesca-Prinner pairings found in Corelli's famous set of violin sonatas.

EX. 3.23   Corelli, Opus 5, no. 10, mvt. 2, Allemanda, m. 1 (1700)

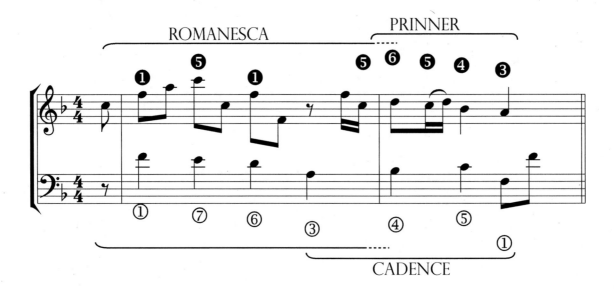

Almost every type of Romanesca and Prinner discussed so far can be found in Corelli's Opus 5. Castrucci was able to learn them from the maestro himself. But thousands of other violinists became familiar with Corelli's repertory of galant schemata through the independent study and frequent performance of this much lauded collection. Though Corelli's absence from the field of operatic composition limited his influence on the premier genre of galant music, and though Corelli did not invent the galant style, he played an important role in its dissemination.

4

THE FONTE

JOSEPH RIEPEL (1709–1782), surely one of the most colorful, prolix, and revealing eighteenth-century writers on music, was chapel master to the wealthy Prince of Thurn and Taxis at Regensburg.[1] For Riepel, certain galant schemata had so palpable a presence as to have their own names. In his fictional student-teacher dialogues (1752–65), Riepel has the teacher introduce three schemata—the Fonte, the Monte, and the Ponte—that are so important he implores the student to "keep this threefold example in mind as long as you live and stay healthy!"[2] In this chapter I will explain what he meant by the Italian word *fonte*, leaving the *monte* for chapter 7 and the more perplexing *ponte* for chapter 14.

The fictional teacher shows the student several versions of the Fonte (It., "a well"), each time writing down only the melody. Here is the version most frequently cited today:[3]

EX. 4.1   Riepel, a Fonte melody (1755)

Riepel's many treatises provide few basses because for knowledgeable devotees of galant music—his expected audience—the basses could be imagined from the melodic context. The laconic and occasionally completely nonverbal Italian collections of difficult partimenti basses were written by and for professionals. Riepel's readership was heavily populated with amateurs who would appreciate genial commentary and simple musical examples playable on the flute or violin.

Instead of defining the Fonte feature by feature, Riepel, as mentioned, provided multiple exemplars of its melody and allowed his fictional student or teacher to comment on each in the manner of a wine tasting. From just the example above, one can already infer that a Fonte has two main sections. Its first half (mm. 1–2) appears in the minor mode (D minor) while its second half (mm. 3–4), one step lower, appears in the major mode (C major). If one were to scan Italian partimenti for similar patterns, hundreds of examples would come to light. Here is a typical partimento fragment from Tritto, transposed for comparison with Riepel's Fonte:[4]

EX. 4.2   Tritto, a Fonte bass (ca. 1790s)

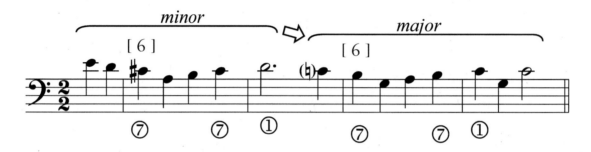

In Tritto's bass, the leading tone of each half, ⑦, first appears on a downbeat and then moves to the tonic, ①, in a direct stepwise connection that crosses a notated bar line. In a later treatise (ex. 4.3), Riepel provides his Fonte with a bass, and that bass, though simpler, has many features in common with Tritto's.[5] The ⑦–① ascent in the bass is matched by a ❹–❸ descent in the melody, often terminating a larger ❻–❺–❹–❸ descent that the Fonte shares with the Prinner. This coordinated movement of melody and bass across a metrical

EX. 4.3   Riepel, a Fonte with both melody and bass (1765)

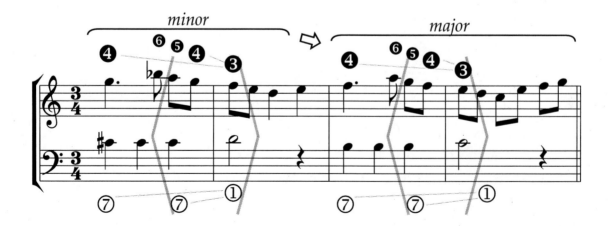

boundary is highlighted in the example by canted brackets superimposed on the score. The horizontal dashed lines indicate how the ⑦–① and ❹–❸ are doubly connected. One connection is indirect—from downbeat to adjacent downbeat—while the other is based on direct note-to-note succession. Galant melodies and basses are full of such subtleties, and I will not attempt to display them all. Because the bass's leading tones are *mi* degrees, they will have 6/3 or 6/5/3 sonorities, and the ensuing tonic basses will have 5/3 sonorities. All these features together suggest a Fonte prototype of four events arranged into two pairs:

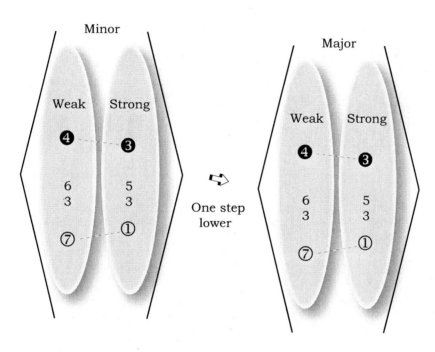

FIGURE 4.1   A schema of the Fonte as two pairs of events

I know of no direct evidence explaining how Riepel learned the term *fonte*. He never traveled to Italy, yet his matter-of-fact referencing of presumed Italian terminology suggests how strongly Italian music and musicians influenced German-speaking Catholic courts. Jan Zelenka (1679–1745), Riepel's own maestro at Dresden, may have studied in Venice at a time when Antonio Lotti (1666–1740) and Francesco Gasparini (1661–1727) were actively teaching there. Lotti and Gasparini served as maestros to many future musicians of note, including Domenico Scarlatti, Galuppi, Marcello, and Quantz. Since Zelenka later taught Quantz as well, the possibility exists that Riepel's terminology and his descriptions of compositional norms have their roots in Venetian practices from the first quarter of the eighteenth century. If so, one ought to find Fontes in the works of Gasparini.

Fontes, in fact, abound in his works. A characteristic use of this schema immediately following a double bar can be found in Gasparini's comic opera *Il Bajazet* (Venice, 1719). Gasparini uses a ⑤–① bass, setting the Fonte's leading tones, normally found in the bass, in the violins (the top staff of ex. 4.4). The vocal part (the middle staff) concludes each half of the Fonte with the typical **➏–➎–➍–➌** descent highlighted in Riepel's melodic prototypes (cf. exx. 4.1, 4.3):

EX. 4.4   Gasparini, *Il Bajazet*, act 2, scene 4, aria of Tamerlano (Venice, 1719)

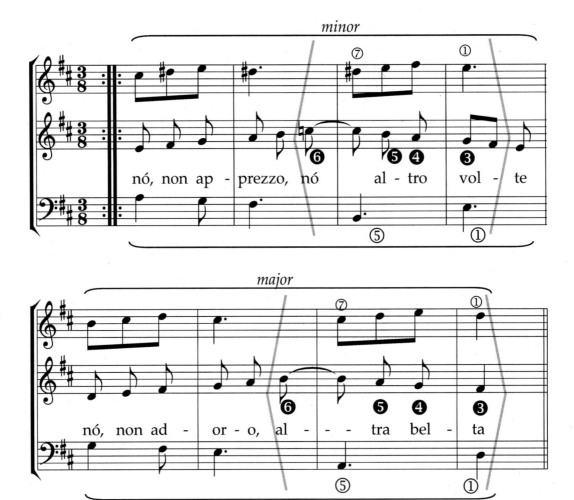

A later influence on Riepel may have been the great pedagogue Nicola Porpora (1686–1768), one of the premier Neapolitan teachers of singing, and chapel master to the Elector of Saxony at Dresden (1748–52) during the period when Riepel began writing his first treatise. Porpora had trained the leading castrati of Europe, Caffarelli and Farinelli among them, and in the 1750s he agreed to serve as maestro to Haydn, imparting the precepts of the Neapolitan conservatories to this talented young student. A hallmark of the castrato's art had always been ornate melodic passagework and florid runs. The Dresden court seems to have especially favored a luxuriantly complex melodic style. At times, the visual swarm of notes on the page can easily conceal the basic schemata being employed. In a Fonte from Porpora's 1754 set of violin sonatas (ex. 4.5), I have indicated how the composer anchors each half of the Fonte with a ⑤ in the deep bass until, at the conclusion of each phrase, the Fonte's standard dyads appear almost like closing punctuation:

EX. 4.5   Porpora, *Sonate XII*, no. 7, mvt. 4, Allegro, m. 26 (Vienna, 1754)

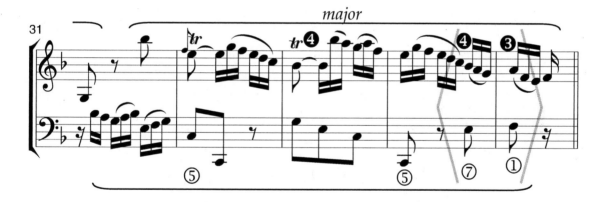

Notice in the above Fonte how Porpora's bass leads off with a flurry of sixteen-note triplets, which are then taken up by his melody. Many galant schemata could be described as a pas de deux with the part of the *danseuse* usually given to the melody and that of the *danseur* to the bass. In the Fonte, the bass's normal role was supportive: to ascend in clear fashion from the local leading tones to their tonics. The melody's normal role was more decorative: to trace a line that would close by descending through the local scale degrees ❹–❸. Yet these roles could at times be reversed. Niccolo Pasquali (ca. 1718–1757), an Italian violinist who became prominent playing in the theaters of London and Edinburgh, penned the following minuet in which the bass presents the prototype of the Fonte "melody," and the melody, after initial flourishes, presents the prototype of the Fonte "bass" (ex. 4.6).

EX. 4.6   Pasquali, Opus 1, no. 2, mvt. 3, Menuet, m. 9 (London, 1744)

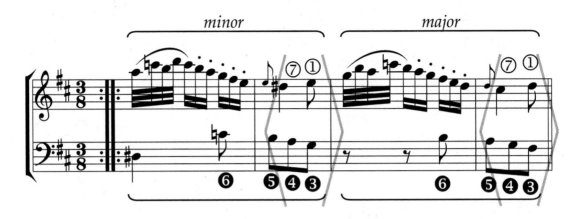

The same *la–sol–fa–mi* pattern, now in the normal upper voice, underlies the following more complex example by Pasquali's contemporary Johann Stamitz (1717–1757), director of instrumental music for the Elector Palatine in Mannheim. Stamitz embeds a Prinner in each half of his Fonte and employs the Prinner-like technique of isolating the melodic ❻–❺ and repeating it before finally introducing the expected ❹–❸:

EX. 4.7   J. Stamitz, Opus 6, no. 2, mvt. 3, Minuetto, m. 9 (ca. 1759)

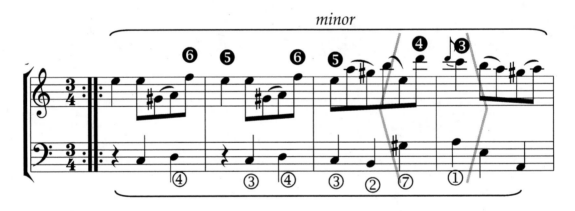

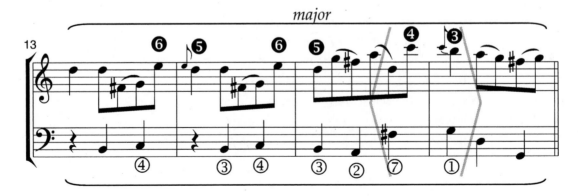

Today, *"la–sol–fa–mi"* and "**❻**–**❺**–**❹**–**❸**" are generally taken as equivalent expressions. Eighteenth-century musicians, however, tended to be far less glib about equating syllables with numerical scale steps. In the two halves of a typical Fonte, a difference in the position of the melodic semitones would have required a difference in syllables. The second half could remain *la–sol–fa–mi*. But if the first half began with a **❻**–**❺** semitone, the "usual Italian solfeggio" would require the syllables to be *fa–mi* (or *fa–la*). One thus could imagine the Fonte's first half as *fa–la–sol–fa*, which brings out the considerable scalar overlap between the two halves. Indeed, it might be historically more accurate, early in the century, to define the Fonte's first half as Dorian and its second half as Ionian:

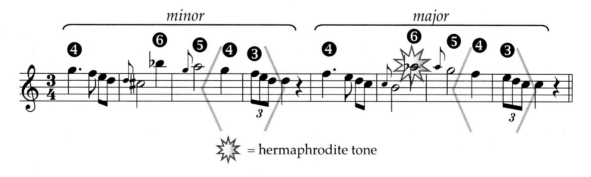

Dorian   *Ionian*

❻--*fa*
  ❺--*la* -------------------- *la*-- **❻**
    ❹--*sol* ------------------ *sol*-- **❺**
      ❸--*fa* ------------------- *fa*-- **❹**
                                        mi-- **❸**

FIGURE 4.2 The Fonte melody viewed as segments of adjacent modal scales

By midcentury, Riepel's own description (1755) seems to favor viewing the Fonte as being in two distinct keys with analogous scale steps: "The . . . Fonte makes . . . a half-phrase in D (with minor third) so as then to complete, one step lower, a full phrase in C."[6] In my student days, before finding a reference to Riepel's Fonte in an article by Leonard Ratner, I had routinely marked examples of this schema with the phrase "one step lower." When the Riepel scholar Stefan Eckert showed me the above quote twenty years later, you can imagine my surprise and delight at hearing Riepel utter the same words ("eine Stuffe tieffer").

However one chooses to interpret the tonal system of the Fonte, Riepel himself was highly sensitive about the position of semitones. He seems to have considered the first half, with its initial melodic semitone and minor cast, to be feminine,[7] and the second half, with its initial whole-tone and major cast, masculine. This gendered treatment may have encouraged him to label as "hermaphrodite" those instances where the second half is also given a prominent semitone between **❻** and **❺**:[8]

EX. 4.8   Riepel, the hermaphrodite Fonte (1755)

Riepel admits that the hermaphrodite Fonte has "a hundred fanciers,"[9] but he is resolutely not one of them. Although he might allow a Fonte's second half to be entirely in the minor mode, he disapproves of the way the hermaphrodite version implies the minor mode (with the melodic A♭) but then continues on in major "contrary to expectation." A passage from a minuet by the young Christoph Willibald Gluck (1714–1787), perhaps one of those hundred fanciers, shows a hermaphrodite Fonte in a context where the melody presents the normal Fonte bass, and vice versa:

EX. 4.9   Gluck, Trio Sonatas, no. 5, mvt. 1, Andante, m. 9 (London, 1746)

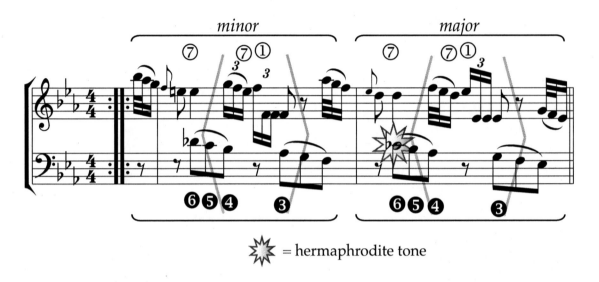

✴ = hermaphrodite tone

"Hermaphrodite" is certainly a colorful, strong term, and it demonstrates both Riepel's verbal flair and the extent to which the details of schemata mattered to a court composer. The proper execution of these details was part of court etiquette, and deviations from them could imply incompetence or impertinence. In the case of Gluck's Andante, the effect seems merely sly or piquant (Mozart often favored the hermaphrodite variant). The underlying Fonte remains clear and unchallenged.

A schema's objective features can be recognized and catalogued through careful observation and simple statistics. After all, both Riepel and I independently abstracted what he termed the Fonte, and we both made note of its second half being "one step lower" than its first half. But it can be much more difficult to divine how eighteenth-century listeners interpreted the musical meaning of individual schemata. Meaning is not easy to observe objectively. One might hope that vocal music could provide clues, since poetic texts clearly have meaning. Yet eighteenth-century composers tended to connect the meaning of a poetic text with, on the one hand, tiny melodic or rhythmic motifs or, on the other hand, the mood of an entire musical section or movement. Thus it can be difficult to link the Fonte with a particular poetic device or topic.

An interesting clue to how the Fonte was received in galant society comes from a pantomime ballet by the French ballet master Auguste Joseph Frederick Ferrère (fl. 1782). This ballet, *Le peintre amoureux de son modèle* [The Painter in Love with His Model], includes a Largo in which the artist stands by his easel, hard at work on a painting of a beautiful young woman. At a double bar in the score, a Fonte begins and the stage directions (shown below in quotes) provide a hint that the Fonte may have connoted a digression from, and then a return to, a previous state. The digression is in response to a problem, which achieves resolution with the return to the status quo. The meaning of this schema may thus have been connected less with an affect or mood and more with a detour in a narrative path:

EX. 4.10   Ferrère, *Le peintre amoureux de son modèle*, mvt. 5, Largo (Paris, 1782)

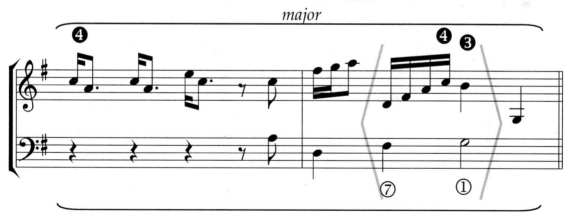

Just how common was the Fonte? The German scholar Wolfgang Budday listed about thirty Fontes in his book *Grundlagen musikalischer Formen der Wiener Klassik* (1983).[10] Yet Haydn alone wrote hundreds, and a list of ten thousand would still account for only a small fraction of its presentations during the eighteenth century. Within Wodiczka's Opus 1, for example, there are five minuets. If one looks only at the phrases immediately following the double bars, the results will tally one Monte, one modulation by fifth, and *three* Fontes. While I would hesitate to assign a numerical value to the probability of hearing a Fonte in a randomly selected galant work, the reader can be assured that the Fonte was a *very* common schema.

As a final example, let me present the Fonte from the first of Wodiczka's minuets. This minuet includes a theme and three variations of the melody to be played over the same bass, so the notation (see ex. 4.11) shows all the melodies above that bass (please note: the melodies play sequentially, not simultaneously, in the order Theme, Var. 1, Var. 2, Var. 3). A dotted line indicates the metrical boundary that separates the Fonte's dyads. In most previous instances in this chapter, that boundary coincided with a bar line. But in this case, and in many other minuets, the boundary separates beats 2 and 3:

EX. 4.11   Wodiczka, Opus 1, no. 2, mvt. 3, Menuetto (1739)

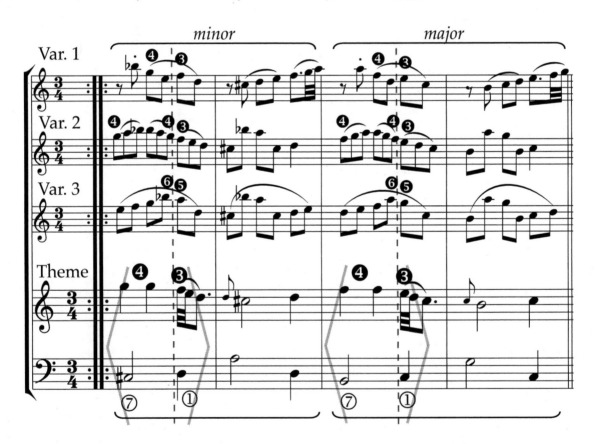

Variation 3 illustrates that, given the right context, no single feature is absolutely necessary for a particular schema. The melodic ❹–❸, for instance, is a central feature of a Fonte. But after listening to the theme and the first two variations, the substitution of ❻–❺ for

❹–❸ in Variation 3 does not suddenly force one to put the phrase in a different category. It remains a Fonte, though a less typical one. In all of Riepel's many examples of different types of Fontes, this "❻–❺" version occurs only once.[11] So a statistically accurate Fonte prototype should retain a ❹–❸ dyad, even if that dyad is not the sine qua non of the schema in every possible context.

As mentioned above, Fontes in minuets often had a scansion that was no doubt influenced by the steps of that courtly dance. There were, of course, many variants of the dance, but the common type required a six-beat pattern with a close on the sixth beat. As the dancing master to the Queen of Spain expressed it in the 1720s, at the sixth beat the dancer must ensure "that the Heel be set down to be able to make a Sink to begin another Step."[12] The first beat of each six-beat pattern (the first quarter note of each two-measure unit) was an initiation of movement, and Wodiczka's Fonte respects that dynamic as well.

In a short story by Guy de Maupassant (1850–1893), a young man meets a very old man who had been a dancing master during the reign of Louis XV. The nineteenth-century youth inquired of his eighteenth-century elder, "Tell me, what was the minuet?" The old man, startled, responded, "The minuet, monsieur, is the queen of dances, and the dance of queens, do you understand? Since there is no longer any royalty, there is no longer any minuet."[13] Minuets did fade away with the aristocrats who danced them. But the Fonte, so useful as a gentle move away from and then back to the main key, survived in various nineteenth-century social dances and songs. As late as the 1930s, popular composers in New York's Tin Pan Alley employed the Fonte in the bridge sections of songs that became "standards" still heard today.

5

A MINUET

BY

GIOVANNI BATTISTA SOMIS

Opus 6, no. 4, mvt. 3, Paris, 1734

RIEPEL ARGUED THAT LARGE WORKS IN THE GALANT STYLE—movements from sonatas, symphonies, concertos—were nothing more than expanded minuets.[1] While there was some rhetorical exaggeration in his claim, there is also a large measure of truth. Many of the skills needed to write a good minuet could be adapted to the requirements of larger pieces. The same general sequence of schemata used in a minuet could be used in a large movement, though with other schemata added and interpolated. And if one could not write a good minuet, there was little point in attempting a larger format. Riepel's point is further borne out by our records of eighteenth-century German instruction in composition. Thomas Attwood's lessons with Mozart, for example, show that systematic training neared its end with assignments to write minuets.[2] After students had successfully dealt with the minuet, they could be expected to work on their own to emulate the larger compositions of master musicians.

Only a few schemata are necessary to form a minuet, since its small size precludes more than a handful of musical phrases. A minuet by Giovanni Battista Somis (1686–1763), a master violinist whose family long served the court of Savoy at Turin, employs little beyond the Romanesca, the Prinner, and the Fonte, and so serves as a useful introduction to these schemata in their native habitat. An outline on the following page details how Somis organized his minuet. Its three columns list, respectively, the minuet's two sections (the terms "first half" and "second half" are used approximately), the various schemata and cadences in the order deployed, and the series of local keys with their modulations. The abbreviation "C ⇨ G" means "a move from the key of C major to G major." Because each half of a minuet is repeated in performance, the term "double-reprise form" is perhaps the best modern label for the minuet's overall design.

Section	Schema	Key
1st Half	Romanesca	C
	Prinner riposte	C
	Prinner, modulating	C ⇨ G
:‖:		
2nd Half	Fonte	Dm ⇨ C
	(modulation)	C ⇨ F
	Prinner, modulating	F ⇨ C
	Cadence, hemiola	C
:‖		

The following musical example—one of the most prevalent melodic clichés in the galant style—can be heard in measures 7–8 of Somis's minuet:

EX. 5.1   The High ❷ Drop

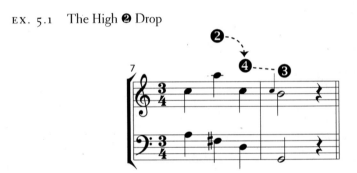

This figure, which I term "the High ❷ Drop" on account of its distinctive contour, served as a conventional sign of impending closure. It was featured in several of the Prinners already presented in chapter 3 and will be found in numerous examples in the chapters ahead.

Among the minuet's other commonplaces are (1) the matching of a two-bar Romanesca with a two-bar Prinner riposte, and (2) the appearance of a Fonte immediately following the double bar. Less common are the use of the modulating Prinner to end the first half (a Prinner rarely furnishes a strong cadence by itself) and the use of rising figures in the Fonte melody (which I assume to be in imitation of the minuet's opening melody). Because danceable minuets needed to maintain an even number of measures overall (as mentioned in chapter 4, the basic step required six beats to complete), the "odd," single measure used to set up the temporary move to F major (m. 13) is "evened" out by the final, three-measure hemiola cadence (mm. 18–20). It is sometimes argued that because no one danced to a minuet embedded within nondance movements, it makes no difference whether there is an odd or even number of measures. Riepel, however, maintained that producing a minuet with an odd number of measures was a mistake. He noted that while an even number of measures was more pleasing in most cases, it was "especially required for a minuet."[3] The reader may notice that the "odd" measure 13 is not shown as part of a larger schema. The goal here is not to force every note into a rigid framework of phrase schemata. Measure 13 clearly leads into measure 14, but that connection is based on different, localized factors.

Somis, like Wodiczka, provided a set of melodic variations on his minuet. In the rendering provided on the World Wide Web,[4] inspired by a recorded performance by Enrico Gatti, one can hear all the variations. No score of the variations is provided. Yet because the same bass and the same schemata recur in each variation, it should be possible to follow the course of the variations aurally with the same confidence and satisfaction that was so important to the experience of a galant patron. As in many galant sets of variations, the bass plays the supporting role while the melody adds new "diminutions" to each variation. The quarter notes of the theme are first "diminished" into eighths, then into triplet eighths, and finally into sixteenth notes. At the end, the theme returns "undiminished" to be lightly ornamented as the performer sees fit. This overall plan of increasingly bravura performance followed by return and relaxation was easily understood and remained remarkably stable for the entire century. Not only did it provide a stage for the performer to display his or her powers in a series of different tableaus, but it also took the listener on a journey from a simple tune through incrementally more abstracted schemata to the tune again, now heard as the central tendency of a range of decorative potentialities.

Like Wodiczka, Somis began his career as a violinist in a ducal orchestra, and he too was sent by his patron to an Italian maestro to perfect his art. For Somis, that maestro was Corelli in Rome. Returning from Rome late in 1706, Somis embarked on a career that not only brought him to musical supremacy at the Savoy court in Turin but also took him to Paris for important concerts. His first opus appeared there in 1717, dedicated to the Duchess of Savoy, Maria. Of necessity courtiers had to write fawning dedications to their patrons, and Somis was no exception. I will omit the most obsequious passages addressed to "that august name acclaimed in all the courts." But Somis's list of praiseworthy attributes is worth quoting, given the assertion that through musical notation he could "present to all the world a symbolic portrait" of his patron's "glorious qualities."

> In these my high and low notes, these acute and grave tones artfully reduced from contrariety and opposition to harmony and consonance, anyone will find certain virtues which by their nature seem opposed, yet in your person they unite in miraculous temperament and perfect concord; he will see highest majesty conjoined with highest sweetness, an affable reserve, a joyful and serene gravity, in sum a consort [*concerto*] of grandeur and intimacy, of moderation and splendor, of authority and gracious deference.[5]

Whether or not any patron could live up to these ideals, the mention of galant traits like sweetness, intimacy, moderation, and deference hint at the changing fashions in Paris associated with the passing of Louis XIV and the accession of the boy Louis XV (1715). In learning to fashion "musical portraits" for this new type of affable regency patron, Somis assured himself of continued courtly favor for decades to come.

EX. 5.2   Somis, Opus 6, no. 4, mvt. 3, Minuet (Paris, 1734)

6

THE DO-RE-MI

THE "RISING FIGURES" described in the discussion of Somis's minuet (chap. 5) were each part of a Do-Re-Mi schema.[1] The French violinist Jean-Marie Leclair (1697–1764), a famous pupil of Somis, knew all forms of the Do-Re-Mi common in the early 1720s and presented them in his first set of sonatas. Here is his version of the basic type, with *do–re–mi* (**❶**–**❷**–**❸**) in the melody and *do–si–do* (①–⑦–①) in the bass:

EX. 6.1   Leclair, Opus 1, no. 3, mvt. 2, Allegro, m. 1 (1723)

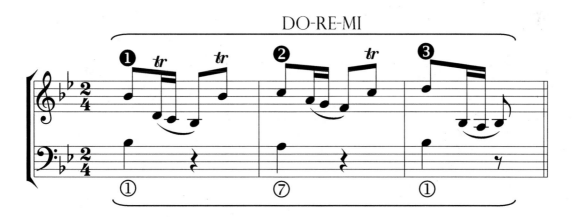

As the example implies, the schema's first and last stages feature stable tonic chords while the middle stage, with a *mi*-degree (see chap. 2) of ⑦ in the bass, sounds a less stable 6/3 or 6/5/3. In abstract form, the schema could be represented as shown in figure 6.1.

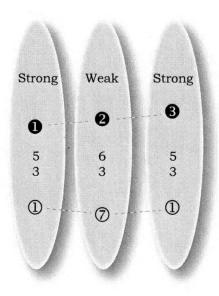

FIGURE 6.1   A schema of the Do-Re-Mi

Like the Romanesca, the Do-Re-Mi was a favored opening gambit in the galant style. In fact, both patterns could be presented simultaneously if the melody's ❶ were held or implied through the beginning of the Romanesca. We heard examples of this combination by Bononcini, Handel, Aprile, and L'Abbé le Fils in chapter 3. Leclair was in fact maestro to L'Abbé. One could imagine a young L'Abbé learning how to combine the Do-Re-Mi with the Romanesca by studying some of Leclair's simpler works, like this example in gavotte rhythm:

EX. 6.2   Leclair, Opus 1, no. 3, mvt. 4, Allegro ma non troppo, m. 1 (1723)

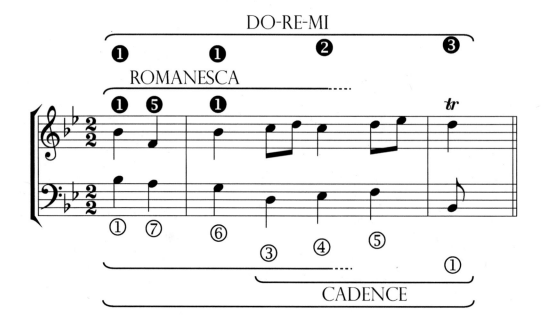

Leclair's normal style, however, was rarely that simple or direct. To aid the reader in unpacking his sometimes densely written scores, let me first explain his use of the "2–3" suspension in a Do-Re-Mi. In the standard Do-Re-Mi, the melody's ❷–❸ ascends in parallel thirds (or tenths) with the bass's ⑦–①. If, however, the bass holds on to its initial ① when the melody rises to ❷, the result is a dissonance highly prized by the school of Corelli and marked in the thoroughbass with a "2" to indicate the second between the simultaneous ❷ and ①. When the bass then resumes its "suspended" descent to ⑦, the dissonant second expands to a consonant third, hence "2–3." The explanation is more complex than the effect, which should be evident in example 6.3:

EX. 6.3   Leclair, Opus 1, no. 11, mvt. 3, Allegro, m. 1 (1723)

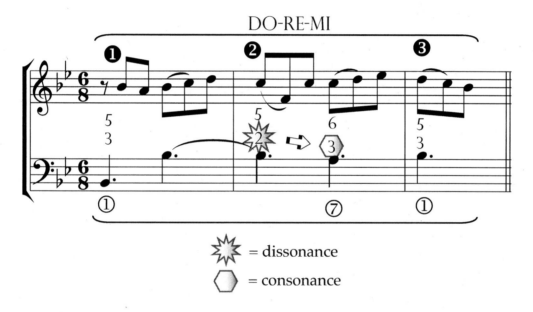

✦ = dissonance

⬡ = consonance

In his study of oral traditions in the epic poetry of the Balkans, Albert Lord pointed to "enjambment" as one mark of a literary, learned style.[2] Enjambment means that an individual poetic line is not an autonomous and self-contained unit; its syntax or sense overlaps the next line or lines. In contrast to literary poetic traditions, oral traditions often avoid enjambment because an improvising bard has greater freedom to mix and match good lines if they are self-contained and interchangeable. Suspensions obviously create small forms of musical enjambment, since they force one event to overlap another. But Leclair also favored larger forms of enjambment where one schema either overlaps another or morphs into another. The following two musical examples are thus literary in the ways in which each (1) embeds elements of the Romanesca in an opening Do-Re-Mi, (2) overlaps the close of the Do-Re-Mi with the beginning of what we might call a "false" Prinner, leading to a cadence, and then (3) presents the "real" Prinner with great clarity. We thus see Leclair giving two quite different "readings" of the same galant script, the first more assertive and showy (ex. 6.4), the second more pensive and restrained (ex. 6.5):

EX. 6.4   Leclair, Opus 1, no. 8, mvt. 2, Vivace, m. 1 (1723)

EX. 6.5   Leclair, Opus 1, no. 4, mvt. 1, Adagio, m. 1 (1723)

A contemporary of Leclair referred to his Opus 1 as "a kind of algebra capable of rebuffing the most courageous musicians."[3] The general taste for complexities of the type favored by Leclair's own generation (J. S. Bach, Handel, Domenico Scarlatti, Rameau, Marcello, Porpora, and Somis) waned rapidly after the 1720s. By the late 1730s, younger composers like Wodiczka were crafting streamlined versions of the earlier, richer combinations. Examples 6.6 and 6.7 from Wodiczka's Opus 1 bear comparison with the previous two examples by Leclair. Gone are the embedded Romanescas, the false Prinners, and the chains of suspensions. What remains is a simpler script of Do-Re-Mi, cadence, and modulating Prinner.

EX. 6.6   Wodiczka, Opus 1, no. 1, mvt. 1, Largo, m. 1 (Paris, 1739)

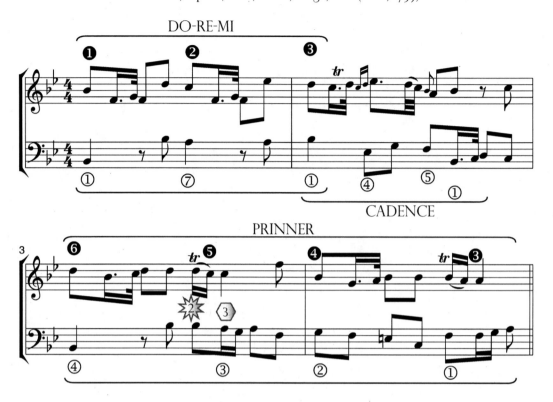

EX. 6.7   Wodiczka, Opus 1, no. 1, mvt. 2, Allegro ma non troppo, m. 1 (Paris, 1739)

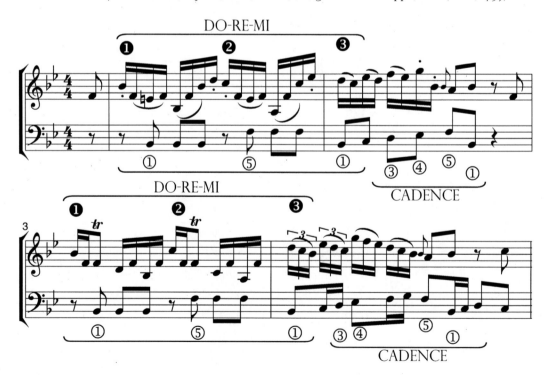

EX. 6.7   (continued)

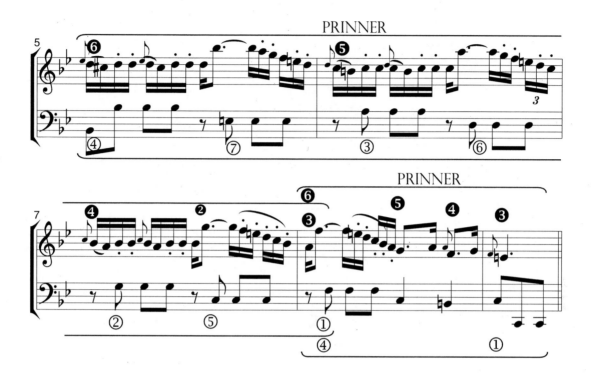

The Do-Re-Mi remained a staple throughout the eighteenth century. If we turn to keyboard sonatas by Domenico Cimarosa (1749–1801), one of the premier opera composers of the second half of the century and a chapel master sought after by imperial courts, we can find a number of cases where stock Do-Re-Mi opening gambits lead to clear Prinner ripostes. A pair of C-major examples features Cimarosa's tendency to add a melodic third above the main melodic tones, as in *Do–(mi)–Re–(fa)–Mi–(sol)*. The first is in a very light style, with an inverted Do-Re-Mi added after the Prinner riposte:

EX. 6.8   Cimarosa, Sonata C48, Allegro, m. 1 (ca. 1780s)

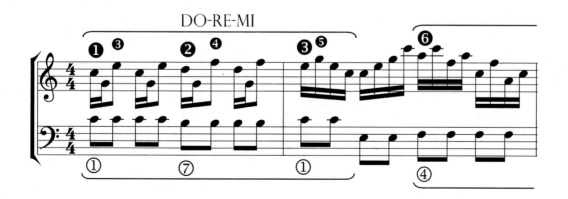

EX. 6.8   (continued)

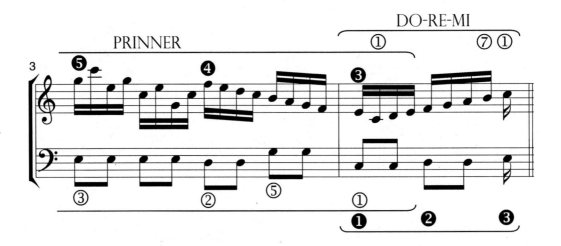

In the second example from the same set of keyboard works, Cimarosa lengthens his Do-Re-Mi to five measures and follows it with a four-measure Prinner riposte, again maintaining a rough parity between them.

EX. 6.9   Cimarosa, Sonata C56, Allegro, m. 1 (ca. 1780s)

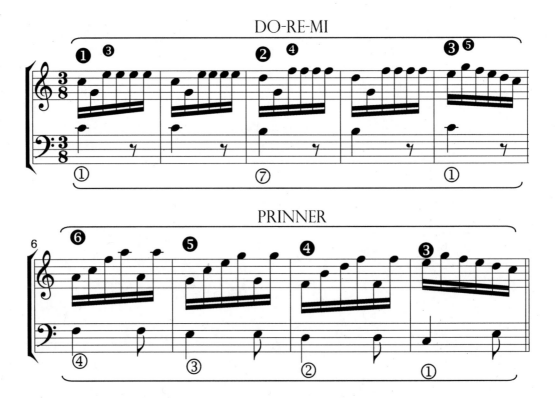

In the 1970s, Leonard B. Meyer noticed that many eighteenth-century phrases resembled the opening of the hymn tune "Adeste Fidelis."[4] Its melody, believed to date from the early eighteenth century, opens with a variant of the Do-Re-Mi that features melodic leaps down to, and up from, ❺:

EX. 6.10 "Adeste Fidelis"

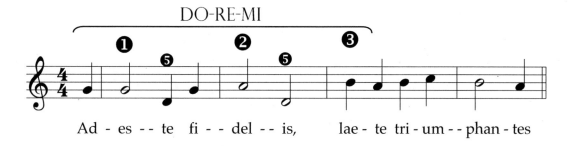

Meyer's observation certainly applies to Cimarosa. Both of the preceding examples use the Adeste Fidelis variant, with its leaps to and from ❺. The consistency with which Cimarosa presents the combination of Do-Re-Mi with both added upper thirds and lower Adeste Fidelis leaps suggests that he considered this a unitary package—a Gestalt. And because Cimarosa was a product of the conservatory system in Naples, it also suggests that this nexus of patterns was something taught there. For example, a partimento by Zingarelli, Cimarosa's classmate in Naples, calls for *prima posizione* and hence a starting ❶ in the melody over a bass that clearly invites this type of Do-Re-Mi (treble-staff realization mine):[5]

EX. 6.11 Zingarelli, from a partimento in D Major, Allegro molto, m. 1 (ca. 1790s)

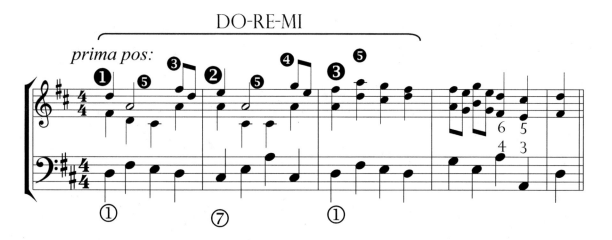

The trend toward using a pair of musical events that could function as a call and response, or question and answer, may have encouraged a replaying of the *re* in the

Do-Re-Mi. Instead of three events, one could have four—*do–re . . . re–mi* (❶–❷ . . . ❷–❸). As might be expected, Wodiczka furnishes a clear example that has affinities to the Adeste Fidelis variant:

EX. 6.12   Wodiczka, Opus 1, no. 2, mvt. 3, Menuetto, m. 1 (1739)

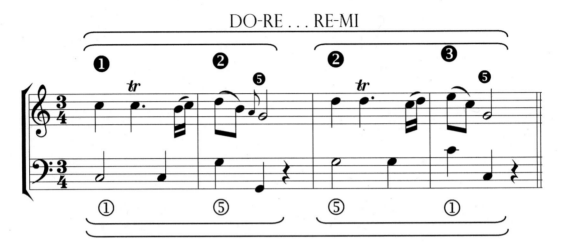

More than fifty years later, this paired Do-Re-Mi was still popular enough for Mozart to use it in his D-major horn concerto. Note how closely Mozart preserves the schematic norm represented by Wodiczka, even though Mozart adds a lovely one-beat delay of the final ❸ and bridges his two subsections with a thematically significant bass:

EX. 6.13   Mozart, Horn Concerto (KV386b), mvt. 1, Allegro, m. 1 (1791)

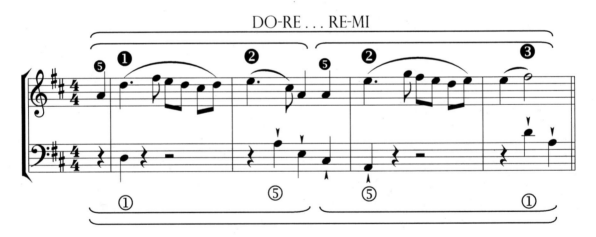

Mozart and Cimarosa were masters of adding delicate touches to the melodies of the standard schemata. In their approach to the paired Do-Re-Mi in the major mode, it appears that they both recognized the two ascending melodic whole steps as opportunities for inserting matching chromatic embellishments. In example 6.14, a short fragment from another keyboard work by Cimarosa, one sees how chromatic passing tones can be added to the paired Do-Re-Mi. Adding the same chromaticism to both halves of the schema enhances the musical rhyme.

EX. 6.14   Cimarosa, Sonata C86, Andante grazioso, m. 12 (ca. 1780s)

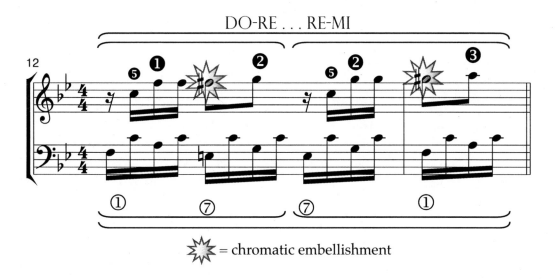

The resulting network of patterns—a paired Do-Re-Mi schema with Adeste Fidelis leaps and matching chromatic passing tones—became very popular. Mozart used it in another of his horn concertos:

EX. 6.15   Mozart, Horn Concerto (KV447), mvt. 3, Allegro, m. 1 (ca. 1787)

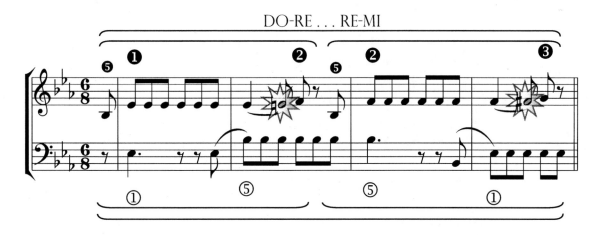

Note how the chromatic passing tones participate in the delay first of ❷ and then of ❸— what François-Joseph Fétis called *prolongations* (1844)[6]—just as they did in the previous example by Cimarosa.

The type of paired Do-Re-Mi promoted by Mozart and Cimarosa in the 1780s was still viable three decades later. Gioachino Rossini (1792–1868), who had studied with the partimento maestro Stanislao Mattei in Bologna, conceived a grand, eight-measure version of this schema for his overture to *The Barber of Seville*:

EX. 6.16   Rossini, *Il barbiere di Siviglia*, Overture, Allegro, m. 68 (Rome, 1816)

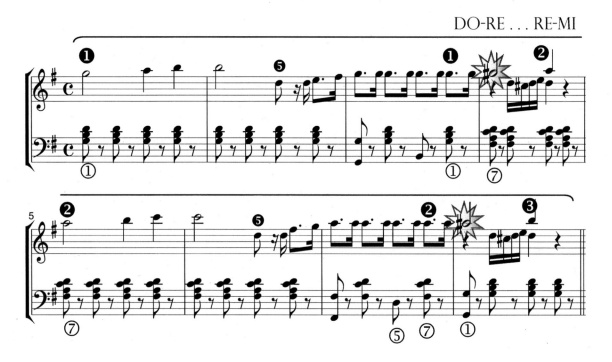

The excellent fit between the melody of the paired Do-Re-Mi and the tones of the natural horn might have explained the pattern's prevalence in Mozart's horn concertos, but in truth the Do-Re-Mi was ubiquitous across music for all instruments throughout the eighteenth and well into the nineteenth century. Composers were clearly fond of beginning a movement by figuratively climbing the first three rungs of the melodic ladder, *do–re–mi*. If we were to include the thousands of movements that begin with *do–mi–sol* (the first three rungs of the triadic ladder) under the same rubric of initial three-stage ascents, we would account for a significant fraction of all galant movements, and an even larger fraction of opening movements.[7]

In the mid-twentieth century the American lyricist Oscar Hammerstein II penned the phrase "When you sing you begin with *do–re–mi*."[8] His observation would have seemed like reasonable advice to any galant composer. When Hammerstein's collaborator Richard Rodgers set the chorus that begins "Doe, a deer . . ." and used scale degree ❶ for *doe*, ❸ for *deer*, ❷ for *ray*, ❹ for *drop*, and so forth, he was probably unaware of how closely he was following in the footsteps of Cimarosa. What both composers shared was a recognition of the abiding utility of this schema.

7

THE MONTE

WHEREAS THE SECOND SECTION OF A FONTE IS "ONE STEP LOWER," that of a
Monte (It., "a mountain") is one step higher. Like the Fonte, the Monte involves a sequential transposition of its first material. Unlike the Fonte, however, it may continue the
sequence through more steps. In Riepel's dialogues, the teacher instructs his student that
the Monte can be employed immediately after the double bar in a minuet. That was a
common usage, though the Monte was not limited to that position and was not as common there as was the Fonte. For a model Monte, Riepel gave only a melody, following his
custom:[1]

EX. 7.1   Riepel, a Monte melody (1757)

As mentioned in chapter 4, Riepel's readers could have associated the melody with
the typical complete context, mentally supplying an appropriate bass. In this C-major
context the implied bass would normally include the leading tone and tonic first of F
major and then of G major. In example 7.2, an excerpt from a partimento by Zingarelli
gives the important thoroughbass cue of "6/♭5" to begin the ascending chromatic line created by this rising sequence.[2]

EX. 7.2   Zingarelli, a Monte bass from a partimento, Allegro, m. 53 (ca. 1790s)

ignore key labels
probably not how 18C
musicians thought of keys

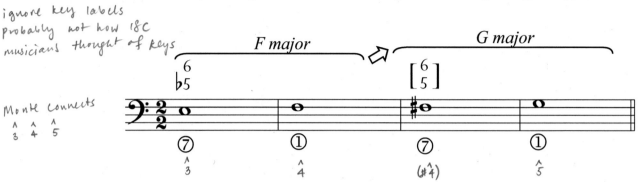

Monte connects
^ ^ ^
3 4 5

Viewed in the larger context of an entire minuet, Riepel's Monte focuses first on the subdominant (IV) and then rises to the dominant (V). Like the Fonte, the Monte coordinates each ⑦–① ascent in the bass with a ❹–❸ descent in the melody, with these dyads straddling a metrical boundary, usually a bar line. And again like the Fonte, the bass's *mi*-degrees on ⑦ will have 6/3 or 6/5/3 sonorities, and the ensuing tonic basses will have 5/3 sonorities. The Monte prototype of four events arranged into two pairs of events is thus very similar to that of the Fonte, with the main differences being the relative transposition of the second dyad and less specificity in the mode of each half (the Fonte is always major-then-minor):

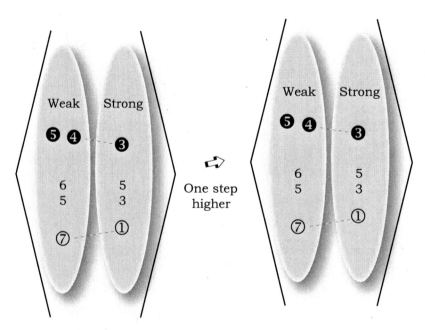

FIGURE 7.1   A schema of the Monte as two pairs of events

In an earlier treatise, Riepel had combined a melody very similar to the one shown above (ex. 7.1) with a bass very similar to Zingarelli's (ex. 7.2). The result was a Monte prototype (see ex. 7.3).[3]

EX. 7.3   Riepel, a Monte with both melody and bass (1752)

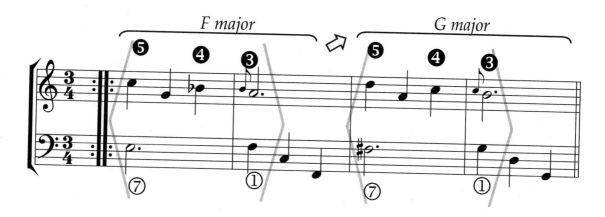

An E♭-major episode from a rondo by the celebrated keyboard player Muzio Clementi (1752–1832) presents a more elaborate and much later exemplar:

EX. 7.4   Clementi, Opus 4, no. 5, mvt. 2, Allegretto, m. 97 (London, 1780)

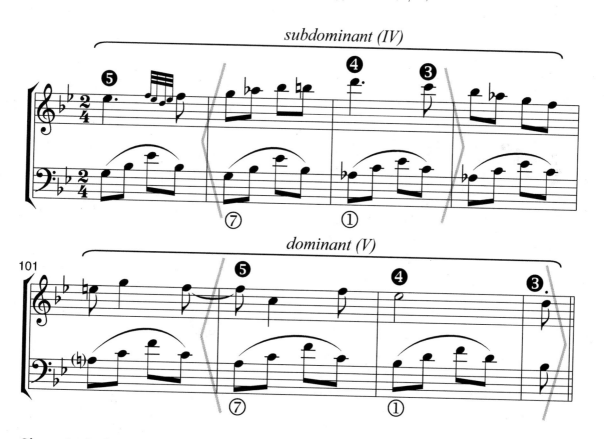

Clementi, who learned the galant traditions in Rome from his Naples-trained maestro Antonio Boroni (1738–1792), makes the required harmonic moves, the first being toward the subdominant (A♭) and the second being the move up a step to the dominant (B♭). Clementi's melody, however, is ornate and approaches C6, the ❸ of the subdominant (A♭), both from below (B♮5) and from above (D♮6), thus keeping the schema's main melodic tones within the diatonic scale of E♭ major. For ease of comparison with the Monte prototype, I have marked ❺–❹–❸ above both halves of Clementi's melody. That is, however, an oversimplification. Rather than adapt the key of his melody to each local tonic, he maintained a more global melodic adherence to the scale of E♭ major. Thus ❶–❼–❻ for the first half and ❷–❶–❼ for the second half would better reflect the diatonic nature of his melody. Further differences between chromatic and diatonic variants of the Monte will be discussed later in the chapter.

In his extensive writings, Riepel described a broad range of possibilities open to the musician who wished to use a Monte. One could, for example, write a three-part Monte. Because the norm is a two-part Monte with a one-step rise, Riepel noted that a listener, upon hearing the Monte rise yet a second time, might feel "deceived," though that was not necessarily a bad thing.[4] In fact Riepel's fourth "chapter" or treatise focuses specifically on the denial of expectation for artistic effect. His example of this technique moves from a local F major to G major, as before, and then continues on to A minor:[5]

EX. 7.5   Riepel, a three-part Monte (1765)

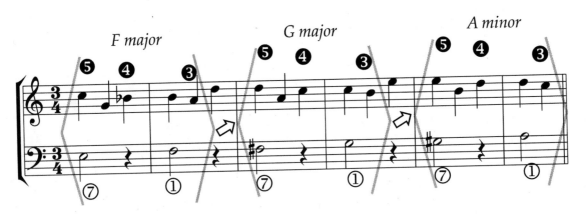

The three-part Monte could also appear in both chromatic and diatonic guises. Two additional examples by Clementi may help to clarify the differences between them. In a chromatic example (ex. 7.6), which occurs in the typical location immediately following the double bar, Clementi guides his Monte first toward the key of the subdominant (IV), then toward the key of the dominant (V), and finally on to the key of the submediant (VI), emphatically marking the tonal closure of each part with a High ❷ Drop. Note that each new part is a transposition of the previous one into a new key, with the accidentals adjusted for an implicit II–V–I chord progression in each new tonal context.

EX. 7.6   Clementi, Opus 4, no. 2, mvt. 2, Presto, m. 105 (London, 1780)

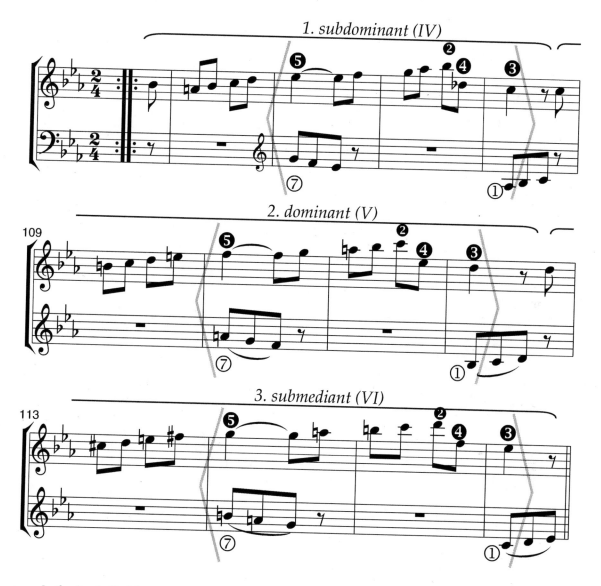

In the first half of the same movement (ex. 7.7) Clementi penned a three-part diatonic Monte. Unlike the chromatic example 7.6, with its shifting key centers, the Monte of example 7.7 stays within the tonal orbit of a single key, B♭ major, with its third part morphing into a *clausula vera* cadence (see chap. 11) on F major, the dominant of B♭ major. Save for chromatic neighbor tones (e.g., the B♮s in m. 4), the tones are all taken from the scale of B♭ major until the slight shift toward F major at the cadence. There are changes of harmonic color, to be sure, as when the second part ends on a G-minor chord. But that is technically different from a shift of key center, with a possible shift of mode.

EX. 7.7   Clementi, Opus 4, no. 2, mvt. 2, Presto, m. 24 (London, 1780)

Apart from the difference in detail, both types of Monte still go "up a mountain," and they both share an underlying "5–6" interval pattern, a centuries-old means of skirting prohibitions against parallel fifths. To make the 5–6 pattern clearer, example 7.8 shows a simplification of the bass in Clementi's diatonic three-part Monte (ex. 7.7), with thorough-bass figures added:

EX. 7.8   A simplification of the accompaniment of ex. 7.7

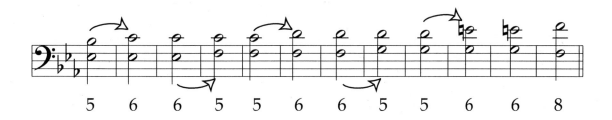

As with the Fonte, the different sections of a Monte mediate local and global meanings that seem incompatible when expressed in any single system of symbols. One could
try to define the Monte as pure counterpoint, but that would obscure the quite specific
scale degrees and tonal functions usually employed. There is, after all, an audible difference when one section of a Monte concludes with a minor, as opposed to a major, chord,
or when the underlying scale changes slightly for each new part. Conversely, expressing
the Monte as merely a pattern of scale degrees and key centers obscures the close relationship between its chromatic and diatonic variants. This dilemma was evident in the eighteenth century. At one point in Riepel's fictional dialogue between teacher and student,
the student notes that an ascending diatonic 5–6 sequence "really seems like a Monte."
The teacher agrees, but describes the plain, diatonic 5–6 as an archaism that "has yet to be
fully obliterated."[6]

Part of the difficulty resides in the word "key." By the second half the century—
Clementi's time—the meaning of "key" was approaching its modern sense, as in "the key
of B♮ major." In the first half of the century, "key" could also imply a note in a scale that
received some temporary focus, as in "G—the sixth key in the hexachord on B♭." If we
examine a repertory from the first half of the century, we ought to find more of the practices that were not yet "obliterated."

Domenico Scarlatti (1685–1757) was raised in a musical family. Much of this precocious musician's training was already completed in the late seventeenth century. He was
thus familiar with many of the older schemata that would eventually fall out of favor during the course of the eighteenth century. His early experiences included training in
Naples, in Rome (where Clementi would study years later), and, as mentioned, in Venice,
where his work with Gasparini made him a distant musical relative of Riepel. Scarlatti
went on to become a chapel master in both Rome and Lisbon, harpsichordist to the Queen
of Spain,[7] and one of the most flamboyant keyboard artists of the age. He seems to have
been quite comfortable in taking a Monte through almost any three adjacent "keys." At
times, as in his sonata K. 220 (ex. 7.9), the three keys may fit within a single modern key.
That is, the ascending sequence of keynotes C, D, and E could be construed as anchoring,
in the modern key of A minor, (1) the mediant or relative major, (2) the subdominant, and
(3) the dominant.

EX. 7.9   D. Scarlatti, Sonata K. 220, Allegro, m. 22 (ca. 1740s)

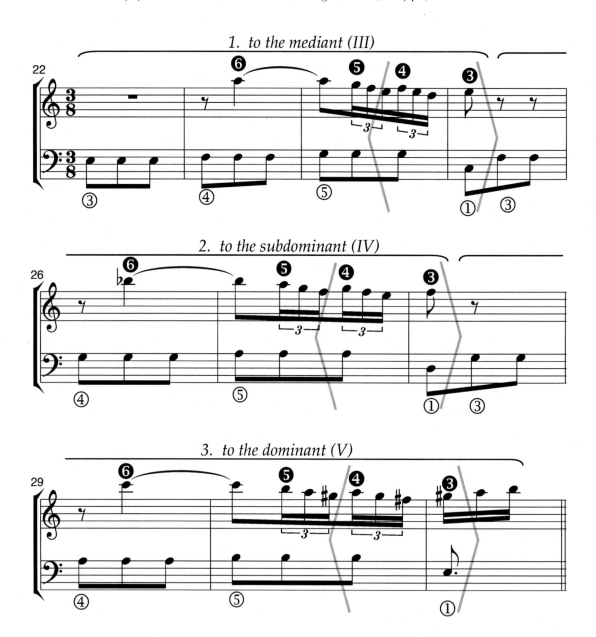

Note that each stage of the above Monte is tonally self-contained, with a clear caden-tial bass and a descending melodic **❻**–**❺**–**❹**–**❸**. In a modern notion of key, the passage could be described as leading smoothly from the relative major back toward the global key of A minor, the same type of move one might encounter in Viennese sonatas by Haydn or Mozart.

At other times, however, one senses that the modern notion of key would be misap-plied. A three-part Monte in a different A-major sonata, K. 219 (see ex. 7.10), also presents

EX. 7.10   D. Scarlatti, Sonata K. 219, m. 45 (ca. 1740s)

descending ❻–❺–❹–❸ melodies and a three-stage ascent. But its keynote sequence of B, C♯, and D♯, with all three in the minor mode, is impossible to ascribe to any single modern key. As "keys" in the older meaning, however, B, C♯, and D♯ fit comfortably in the hexachords on B or F♯, which though still relatively distant are not impossibly so, especially given an A-major context as the point of departure. Scarlatti is justly famous for this type of extravagant tonal excursion, although modern critics are more likely to ascribe such moves to his personality than to the traditions in which he was trained.

His Neapolitan contemporary Francesco Durante (1684–1755), who went on to become one of the most influential and revered of all the maestros, favored two additional, older types of Monte. Durante's great authority, and the success of so many of his students, ensured that these archaic seventeenth-century Montes continued to form part of the pedagogical curriculum long after they had left common usage in fashionable court music. The first type is described by one of his students, Fedele Fenaroli (1730–1818), as having a bass that "rises a fourth and falls a third." Fenaroli provided a realization of this bass in a famous set of partimenti that eventually became, in printed form, a staple of nineteenth-century conservatories:

EX. 7.11   Fenaroli, *Partimenti*, book 3, no. 10, m. 1 (ca. 1770s)

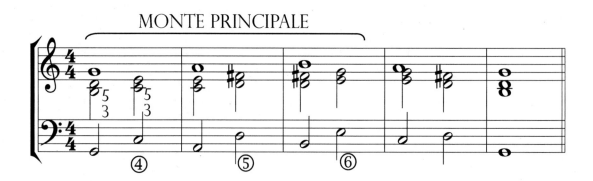

The result is a diatonic Monte in which all chords are in 5/3 position. Or put another way, the G-major diatonic Monte heard in the upper three voices is accompanied by its chordal roots in the bass, in what the Neapolitans called *movimento principale* ("root-position motion")—hence my term "Monte Principale."

Fenaroli describes another pattern as having a bass that "rises a fifth and falls a fourth," and he again presents a series of chords in root position. Here is his realization in melodic "second position" (the chordal third begins the melody):

EX. 7.12   Fenaroli, *Partimenti*, book 3, no. 12, m. 1 (ca. 1770s)

Because this pattern begins like a Romanesca but then rises where the Romanesca would fall, I term it a "Monte Romanesca." It could equally well be treated as a separate schema, given its different series of sonorities, or even as a variant of the Romanesca. The affinity with the Romanesca seems to have been noticed by C. P. E. Bach (1714–1788), who used a standard Romanesca in the first half of one of his more advanced keyboard movements and then replaced it with a Monte Romanesca at the analogous location in the second half. The two passages are shown one above the other for ease of comparison:

EX. 7.13   C. P. E. Bach, Sonata in A Major (H. 186), mvt. 1, Allegro assai, mm. 5, 47 (ca. 1765–66)

"Mannerist galant" might be a useful description of C. P. E. Bach's flamboyant and willful manipulations of galant conventions.[8] In many cases, his manipulations would be difficult to explain if one did not assume a prior and quite sophisticated knowledge of the basic galant schemata. Riepel ascribed the interchangeability of musical patterns to what philosophers then termed the *ars combinatoria*.[9] In the same movement, Bach further explored this "art of combinations" by substituting a "textbook" Fonte for the reprise of what had been a Monte (ex.7.14).

EX. 7.14   C. P. E. Bach, Sonata in A Major (H. 186), mvt. 1, Allegro assai, mm. 13, 95 (ca. 1765–66)

Durante filled his compositions with all the types of Montes that would be passed down through his students' partimenti. In his set of six keyboard sonatas of the late 1740s, each of which pairs a *studio* (It., "study") with a *divertimento*, one can find all three "genres" of Montes discussed above—the galant Monte with the 5–6 pattern, either chromatic or diatonic, the Monte Principale, and the Monte Romanesca. The standard galant Monte with chromatic bass occurs in the Adagio opening of the sixth "study." Because of Durante's central position in the Neapolitan tradition, it may be worth quoting the entire first section (see ex. 7.15). Durante's Romanesca invites comparison with those of Sammartini, J. C. Bach, and Jommelli given at the conclusion of chapter 2 (exx. 2.22–24). Durante's Prinner, although thoroughly ornate, "hits its mark" for each stage of the modulating version. The modulation to F major seems provisional, since the passage in measures 4–5 (what Riepel will term a Ponte) appears to expand on F as the dominant of B♭ major, the original tonic key. That B♭ focus is reinforced by the following Monte, which highlights IV and then V in B♭:

EX. 7.15 Durante, *Studio* no. 6, Adagio, m. 1 (Naples, 1747)

The Monte Principale is obvious in the theme of Durante's second study (see ex. 7.16). Allowing for transposition, Durante's bass sounds the very notes of the partimento by his student Fenaroli shown earlier in this chapter (ex. 7.11). Indeed, almost every collection of partimenti features at least one such bass as an opening gambit. Closer inspection of Durante's Monte Principale reveals a canon between melody (leading by one eighth-note) and bass. This particular setting of two parts in canon, each with a *movimento* up a fourth and down a third, was much prized and replicated in Naples.

EX. 7.16   Durante, *Studio* no. 2, Allegro, m. 6 (Naples, 1747)

MONTE PRINCIPALE

Finally, the Monte Romanesca provides a scaffolding for the playful triads in Durante's sixth and final divertimento:

EX. 7.17   Durante, *Divertimento* no. 6, Allegro, m. 1 (Naples, 1747)

MONTE ROMANESCA

The odd-numbered chords of the Monte Romanesca will likely have the mode appropriate to their place in the current hexachord, while the even-numbered chords will be either diatonic as well, or applied dominants of the preceding chord (as in ex. 7.17 above). As its bass passes through ②, ⑥, and ③ of the local key, a Monte Romanesca will take on a minor-mode cast (an observation made by the partimento maestro Giovanni Furno [1748–1837]) and, though not seen in Durante's *Divertimento*, a series of 4–3 suspensions.[10] In a description of how two soloists could perform an improvised cadenza, Gasparini's student Johann Joachim Quantz (1697–1773) presented the "intervals" shown in example 7.18 (the upper parts are his; the bass is mine). He was providing the upper parts, with 4–3 suspensions, to a Monte Romanesca which leads, by way of a small Fonte, to a *cadenza doppia* ("double cadence"; see chap. 11) with a double trill on the penultimate tones:[11]

EX. 7.18   Quantz, *Essay on the Art of Playing the Flute*, his Fig. 4, Table 21 (1752)

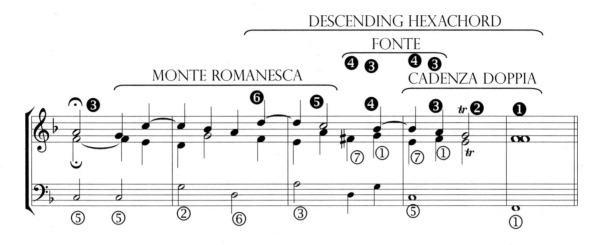

The Monte Romanesca was an important part of the "strict" or sacred style taught in many partimenti. As in Quantz's example, there was often a series of 4–3 suspensions, a trait made explicit in a partimento given by Mozart to his student Thomas Attwood (the bass and figures are Mozart's, the realization is mine):

EX. 7.19   Mozart, *Attwood Studies* (1785–86)

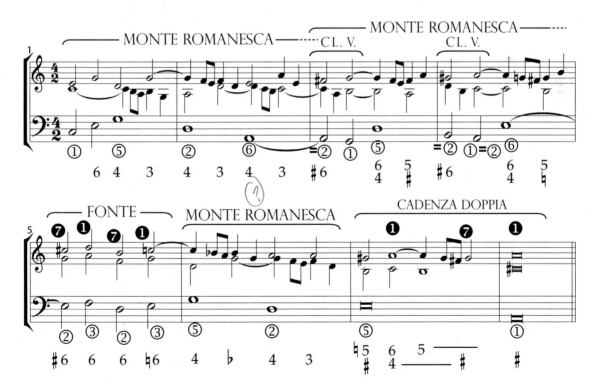

Attwood had come to Mozart after completing two years of study with conservative teachers in Naples. Perhaps that is why Mozart gave him an assignment that ends with the
signature cadence of the Italian partimento, the *cadenza doppia*. This cadence, a vestige
of seventeenth-century practice, had become rare in Mozart's time outside of partimenti.
Mozart's notation of explicit figures for all the 4–3 suspensions was unusual by Italian
standards. For the Neapolitans, the 4–3 suspensions were implicit parts of the schema.
The following unfigured partimento by the Neapolitan maestro Giacomo Tritto presents
a slightly less severe review of many of the same schemata that Mozart assigned to Attwood
(the bass is Tritto's, the realization is mine).[12]

EX. 7.20　　Tritto, *Partimenti* (ca. 1790s)

Tritto's combination of a small Do-Re-Mi with a larger Prinner (mm. 7–10) is very similar to the previously presented partimento of Zingarelli (ex. 3.20) probably used by Isabelle de Charrière, and to the exercise by Mozart (ex. 3.21) written for Barbara Ployer. That combination of schemata seems to have been a "usual scene" that any student of galant music needed to know.

In spite of the wide range of Montes available to them, younger generations of galant composers hewed to the line described by Riepel at midcentury. They probably shared the view of Riepel's fictional teacher who, when the student played for him first a Romanesca and then a Monte Romanesca, described them as sounding "old."[13]

The very first page of Wodiczka's Opus 1 contains a Monte of the standard type advocated by Riepel:

EX. 7.21   Wodiczka, Opus 1, no. 1, mvt. 1, Largo, m. 18 (1739)

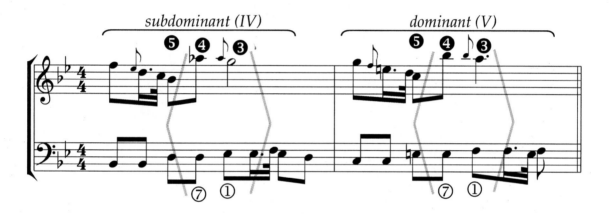

One of Riepel's many model Montes, if transposed to the key of B♭ major for comparison with Wodiczka's Monte, shows how closely his summary of the galant style matched the actual practice of his generation and its younger followers:[14]

EX. 7.22   Riepel, a model Monte (1755)

But note how Riepel goes slightly beyond Wodiczka by adding a small variation to the second half of this Monte (m. 4 compared to m. 2). When his fictional student wrote two halves of a Monte that, like Wodiczka's, were identical, the teacher rebuked him with a pronouncement that, in a world governed by ideas of good taste, the student could hardly gainsay: "two identical statements one after the other sound bad."[15] Since there are many, many Montes with identically notated halves, it remains unclear whether Riepel's voice of authority was articulating an idiosyncratic view, whether performers always added variations during performance, whether there were regional preferences for or against "elegant variation," and so forth. In any case, to understand the issue is to have already become something of a connoisseur. Riepel's treatises were addressed to the educated amateur, and questions such as this were tailor-made to stimulate discussions of taste, style, and the standards of elegant musical behavior.

8

A THEME AND VARIATIONS

BY

CARL DITTERS VON DITTERSDORF

Quartet No. 2 in B♭ Major (K. 192), mvt. 2, 1789

THE STRING QUARTETS OF CARL DITTERS VON DITTERSDORF (1739–1799), though contemporaneous with the onset of the French Revolution, nonetheless suggest the continuity of tradition, the stability of the ancien régime, and the careful refinement of decades of galant musical craftsmanship. Dittersdorf was fully conversant with the rapidly developing styles of quartet writing in Vienna. He had, after all, played in a string quartet whose members included Haydn, Mozart, and Johann Baptist Wanhal (1739–1813), with Dittersdorf likely taking the first violin part. Yet he had a conservative temperament. Over fifty years had passed since the publication of the minuet by Somis discussed in chapter 5, but the organization of the theme from the variations movement of Dittersdorf's second string quartet is fully comparable with the model set down by that earlier Italian master.

As shown in the list below, Dittersdorf, like Somis, lays out his movement in two repeated halves—the double reprise form. In both works, the first half features an opening gambit followed by a Prinner riposte, while the second half features a Fonte leading to a final cadence. Somis matched a two-bar Romanesca with a two-bar Prinner riposte; Dittersdorf matched a four-bar Do-Re-Mi with a combination of a two-bar Prinner and two-bar cadence.

Section	Schema	Key
1st Half	Do-Re-Mi, paired	B♭
	Prinner, modulating	B♭ ⇨ F
	Cadence	F

:||:

2nd Half	Fonte, chromatic	Cm ⇨ B♭
	Monte, diatonic	IV ⇨ V
	Prinner, modulating	F ⇨ C
	Cadence, evaded	B♭
	Cadence	B♭

This is in line with the clear tendency for composers to write longer versions of the stock schemata as the century progressed.[1] Both Somis and Dittersdorf wrote just eight measures of music for the first half of their respective minuets, but Dittersdorf's opening phrase seems distinctly broader. The paired Do-Re-Mi that begins the first half of the movement uses the Adeste Fidelis leaps and chromatic passing tones seen previously in works by Cimarosa and Mozart (exx. 6.14–15). The Fonte that begins the second half, however, is something new to our discussions.

In his book on "deceptive" compositional methods, Riepel allows the imaginary student to introduce the following phrase, mentioning to the teacher that it "seems like a workaday Fonte":[2]

EX. 8.1   Riepel, from the "student" (Regensburg, 1765)

The teacher neither agrees nor disagrees, but notes that "some composers ornament it as follows":[3]

EX. 8.2   Riepel, from the "teacher" (Regensburg, 1765)

Riepel seems to be exploring the many overlapping features of the Fonte, the Sol-Fa-Mi (see chap. 18), and the circle of fifths. Like Riepel, for the moment I will pass over the details of how these schemata interconnect. But his introduction of the F♯ in measure 2, followed by the F♮ in measure 3 (the cautionary accidental is mine), does suggest that he was aware of what I term the "chromatic" Fonte. For this schema, the chromatic descent through scale degrees ❺–♯❹–♮❹–❸ is more a melodic phenomenon than a harmonic one, an "ornament" or decoration in Riepel's words. While the chromatic Fonte appears in every variation in this particular movement, it was just one of several possible variants of the normal Fonte. That is the case in a theme-and-variations movement by Haydn presented in chapter 10, and in the galant repertory generally. Thus I still place the word "minor" above the first half of Dittersdorf's Fonte (ex. 8.3, mm. 9–10), even though his melody sounds E♮ rather than the E♭ expected of the minor mode.

Halfway through measure 5, the introduction of an F♯ in an inner voice (at the "♯6" shown between the staves) hints at an embedded Fonte within the larger Prinner. That is, the inner F♯ points toward G minor and the bass's ② at the start of measure 6. The bass's own F♮ then points to F major and the local ① at the start of measure 7. This small Fonte slightly darkens the mood before the sunny release of the cadence that begins, in measure 7, just as the embedded Fonte returns to the major mode.

The Monte that Dittersdorf presents in the second half of his theme is diatonic, quickly moving, and closely integrated into the final cadence, which is first evaded and then completed more emphatically. I present the notation of the theme alone. The theme with all its variations can be heard on the World Wide Web (see chap. 1 , n. 5). Dittersdorf slightly changes the bass, inner parts, or melody for each variation, but the sequence of schemata remains fixed until a playful rush to the cadence at the very end of the movement.

EX. 8.3   Dittersdorf, String Quartet (K. 192), no. 2, mvt. 2, Andante (1789)

9

THE MEYER

ALONG WITH NOTES ON

THE JUPITER, PASTORELLA, AND APRILE

GIACOMO TRITTO BEGAN HIS *Scuola di contrappunto* [The School of Counterpoint] by citing his pedigree.[1] He had studied "under the direction of the renowned maestro Signore Pasquale Cafaro, who was a student of the celebrated Signore Leonardo Leo." This pedigree, which was impeccable by eighteenth-century standards, meant that he had received a pure form of the largely oral tradition of instruction. Indeed, Tritto's own book contains more pages of partimenti than pages of verbal explanation. When Tritto began one of his *partimenti semplici* as follows, he was making a clear reference to part of that tradition:[2]

EX. 9.1   Tritto, from his *Scuola di contrappunto* (Naples, ca. 1816)

Other insiders would have recognized the reference as pointing toward the type of opening phrase shown in example 9.2 (the bass is Tritto's, the upper parts are mine). I surveyed the history of that small but highly characteristic tradition in *A Classic Turn of Phrase*,[3] a study inspired by one of my own renowned maestros, Leonard B. Meyer (1918–). He had identified a musical "archetype" that featured a melodic contour resembling the musical turn sign, ∞, which he termed the "changing-note archetype."[4] The Tritto partimento

EX. 9.2   Tritto, from his *Scuola di contrappunto* (Naples, ca. 1816)

has this shape in the bass and, in an abstract form, the reverse contour in the melodic dyads that close each half of my realization (C5–B♮4 and F4–E♭4 descend following the ascents C3–D3 and B♮2–C3 in the bass).

In terms of the schemata discussed in previous chapters, the coordinated moves by the dyads in the melody and bass associate Tritto's pattern with the schemata for the Fonte and Monte. But whereas those schemata are tonally mobile, this schema is tonally stable, which may explain why it was a preferred choice for important themes. I now call this schema "the Meyer," after the scholar who first drew attention to its importance.[5] In the diagram below, the words *open* and *closed* refer to the ancient terms still common in the eighteenth century for musical phrase endings that, respectively, lack and possess a sense of finality or closure:

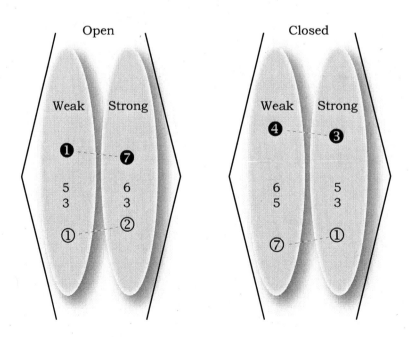

FIGURE 9.1   A schema of the Meyer as open and closed pairs of events

Examples of this schema become very common by the 1750s and 1760s. Here is one from a symphony that Haydn wrote in 1767:

EX. 9.3   Haydn, Symphony in B♭ (Hob. I:35), mvt. 1, Allegro di molto, m. 17 (1767)

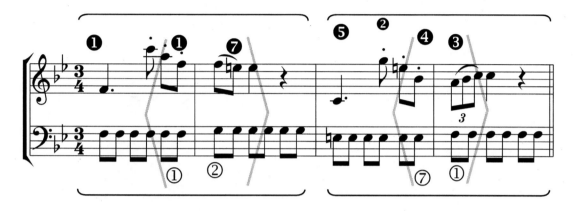

Haydn, recently promoted from assistant chapel master to chapel master by the Prince of Esterházy, provided a sprightly if nonetheless conventional theme whose drumlike bass was very much in vogue. Dittersdorf, who not long before had succeeded Haydn's brother Michael as chapel master to the bishop of Grosswardein, had penned a very similar theme the previous year:

EX. 9.4   Dittersdorf, Symphony in C (K. 1), mvt. 1, Allegro moderato, m. 1 (1766)

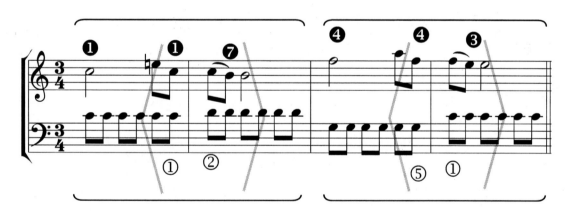

In Haydn's theme the melodic ❹–❸ of measures 19–20 sounds a fifth lower than the initial ❶–❼ of measures 17–18, whereas in Dittersdorf's theme it is played above. An indifference toward the register of the ❹–❸ is a common characteristic of this schema. Its second half "answers" its first half, but the exact register of the melody is of small significance.

This simple, sturdy scaffold could support a number of subsidiary patterns. For instance, Carl Heinrich Graun (1703/4–1759), chapel master at the court of Frederick the

Great in Berlin, embedded a two-measure Prinner within a four-measure Meyer in such a way that both schemata come together to close on the same *fa–mi* in the melody (❹–❸, heralded by a High ❷ Drop):

EX. 9.5   C. Graun, Trio Sonata, mvt. 2, Adagio, m. 1 (ca. 1750)

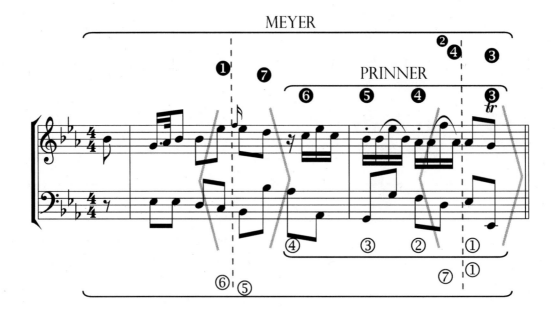

If a Prinner can be embedded within a Meyer, so can a Meyer be embedded within a Prinner. The "*la*-to-*sol* flourish" marked on example 9.6 was an ornamental motif closely associated with Prinners. We will encounter it again in the works of Mozart:

EX. 9.6   Haydn, Symphony in D (Hob. I:73, "La chasse"), mvt. 1, Allegro, m. 27 (ca. 1781)

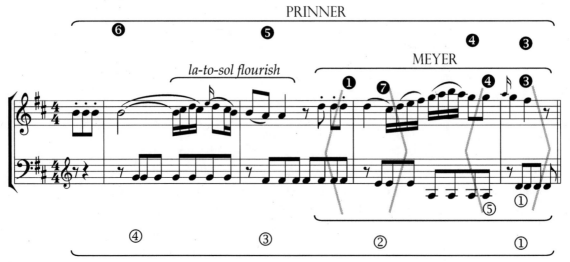

As a final instance of a Meyer in combination with another schema, example 9.7 shows a large Fonte by Wodiczka. Each of the Fonte's two sections presents a Meyer, and the second half of each Meyer features the Prinner melody above a cadential bass (cf. Castrucci, ex. 3.5). Because both parts of the Fonte modulate—from the preceding G major to D minor, and then from D minor to C major—the first stage of each Meyer involves subdominant rather than tonic harmonies. This passage is unusually complex for Wodiczka. Such pilings up of schemata became rare after the 1740s, returning only in the 1780s with any frequency.

EX. 9.7   Wodiczka, Opus 1, no. 1, mvt. 2, m. 18 (1739)

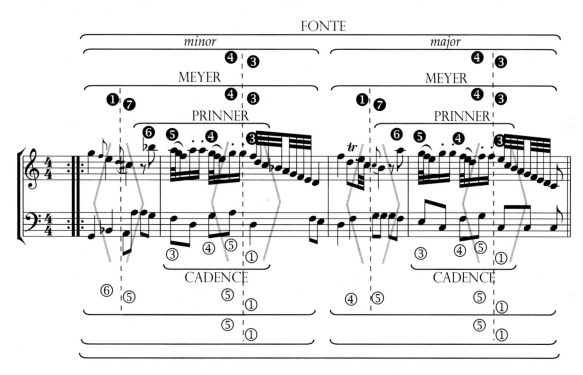

The fluid mixing and matching of schemata would seem to exemplify perfectly the *ars combinatoria*. As mentioned earlier, this was a philosophical tradition cited by Riepel and other eighteenth-century musicians.[6] Yet paradoxically these same writers seem loath to ascribe more than one pattern to each moment of music. In describing eighteenth-century scientific and philosophical writers—those in his "classical episteme"—Michel Foucault observed that they believed "words . . . are a constitution and evident manifestation of the order of things."[7] For Riepel, terms like Fonte, Monte, and Ponte seem to have signified unities that could no more be blended than could the words themselves. Riepel's position is not unusual. Even today most people do not think of the word "arm" as existing within the word "harm," or "harm" within "harmony." The meanings are too divergent. People do, of course, recognize that "harm" is a constituent of words like "unharmed" or "harmless," and eighteenth-century writers on music could certainly describe patterns as having musical prefixes, suffixes, or other modifications. But the inability of Riepel and others to separate a schema's imagined essence from its composite construction or its overlapping deployment meant that a Monte would always be a unitary schema and never something contained in or containing something else. So the rich *ars combinatoria* of professional compositional practice found its only verbal explanation in the description of simple sequences of independent figures. In place of describing an *ars combinatoria* that includes nesting, blending, reference, and allusion, eighteenth-century writers described parlor games in which a fixed set of musical fragments could be placed in a simple series governed by the laws of chance.[8] It was left to the nonverbal traditions of partimenti, solfeggi, and actual composition to demonstrate the richer possibilities of the art.

THE JUPITER

Mozart begins the final movement of his last symphony, known to later generations as the "Jupiter," with a melodic motto of four whole notes, C5–D5–F5–E5. He then pairs this opening gambit with a standard Prinner riposte:

EX. 9.8   Mozart, Symphony in C (KV551, "Jupiter"), mvt. 4, Molto allegro, m. 1 (1788)

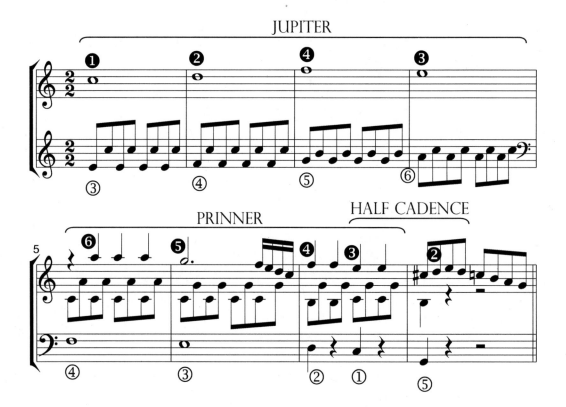

What I and many others call the "Jupiter" motto, which itself had an extensive history prior to Mozart's use of it,[9] fits very well into a number of contrapuntal combinations. In the example above, Mozart matched it with the bass of a deceptive cadence. In example 9.9, which is the continuation of example 9.8, he changed the bass to ①–⑤–⑤–① and added an upper voice to create a pair of 7–6 suspensions (in relation to the Jupiter motto):

EX. 9.9   Mozart, Symphony in C (KV551, "Jupiter"), mvt. 4, Molto allegro, m. 9 (1788)

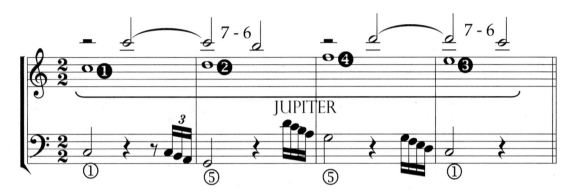

Extensive training in fugal partimenti and imitative solfeggi helped an aspiring composer to master a repertory of these stock contrapuntal combinations. The fruits of this training were most clearly evident in sacred music, especially in Amen fugues and the like. It is a characteristic of Mozart's late style that he took these techniques of counterpoint favored in sacred genres and developed them in genres associated with the court chamber or theater.

THE PASTORELLA

Lerner and Loewe's 1960 musical *Camelot* featured actor Richard Burton, in the role of King Arthur, singing the question "What do the simple folk do?" Among the real kings and courtiers of Europe the question seems to have been of perennial interest. Eighteenth-century answers, as represented by paintings, ballets, and operas, appear every bit as contrived as that scene in *Camelot*. The shepherds and shepherdesses of ordinary rural life became conflated with mythical Arcadian figures like Pan or Orpheus to represent an eternal type of "natural" person untouched by the stresses and temptations of court or urban life. Perhaps the ultimate case of the imagined pastoral was the construction for Marie Antoinette of a *ferme ornée* ("ornamental farm") known as the *Hameau de la Reine* (1783), a complete faux village where the queen could pose as a milkmaid. A contemporary treatise on gardens (1776) commented that an ornamental farm should "announce itself by its country air, careless and without pretension; like a naive shepherdess without guile whose simplicity would be her only ornament."[10]

The musical depiction of the pastoral was itself a rich tradition not limited to the literally rustic. Among the many ways to depict in sound a world where "simplicity would be [the] only ornament" was to use a schema that featured a melody, often accompanied in parallel thirds, that gently oscillated around the tones of the tonic triad. Near the close of the *Missa pro defunctis* by François-Joseph Gossec (1734–1829), where one leaves behind the terror of its famous *Tuba mirum* to contemplate "rising again" to a guileless paradise, two sopranos present an instance of what I term "the Pastorella," the "shepherdess":

EX. 9.10   Gossec, *Missa pro defunctis* [Requiem], mvt. 15, [Andante], m. 26 (1760)

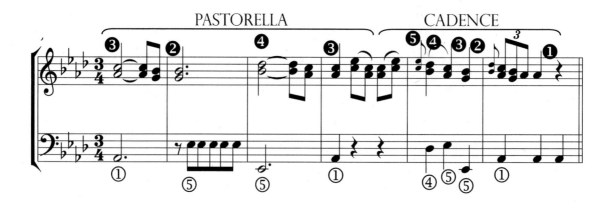

The Pastorella schema shares with the Meyer and Jupiter a ❹–❸ melodic termination, a similar harmonic pattern, and its function as opening gambit or important theme. In the larger context of Gossec's mass, the above phrase is part of the "Lacrimosa." That movement begins in a doleful F minor, which eventually leads to a half cadence followed by a grand pause. When the Pastorella begins in A♭ major, it is clearly the opening theme of a new section. The prized effect of "noble simplicity and quiet grandeur" ("edle Einfalt und stille Grösse"), an influential phrase from Johann Joachim Winkelmann's description (1755) of ancient Greek art,[11] is here musically abetted both by the dearth of melodic diminutions and by the way in which the opening ❸ in measure 26 leads broadly through the ❹ in measure 28 all the way to the high point of the ❺ in measure 30. The avoidance of vocal display is likewise evident in the mere five-note range of the melody.

Vocal display was the stock-in-trade of the great castrato Farinelli (1705–1782), a Neapolitan who studied with Porpora. Yet Farinelli was also renowned for his affecting performance of a simple, direct melody. One of his signature arias was Hasse's "Per questo dolce amplesso" ("For this sweet embrace"). The aria debuted in Hasse's first Metastasian opera, *Artaserse* (Venice, 1730). Farinelli took the aria with him to London (the version shown in ex. 9.11) and later used it to assuage the melancholia of Phillip V of Spain. Hasse's radiant yet restrained aria presents the "noble simplicity" of a young man wrongly accused

yet willing to die to save his father. The example gives the beginning of the opening ritornello. Farinelli's entrance with this same theme (not shown) is even simpler, with the
dotted rhythms replaced by two sixteenth-notes or plain eighth notes.

EX. 9.11   Hasse, *Artaserse*, "Per questo dolce amplesso," m. 1 (London, 1734)

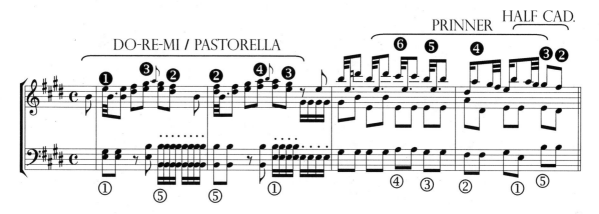

The first two measures present the Pastorella's parallel thirds in the treble and its ①–
⑤–⑤–① pattern in the bass. A Prinner riposte then leads to a half cadence. Note that
Hasse's melody also presents the Adeste Fidelis variant of the paired Do-Re-Mi, that is,
Do-Re (m. 1) ... Re-Mi (m. 2). The downbeats of measures 1–2 emphasize the Do-Re-Mi,
while the middle beats of the same measures emphasize the Pastorella. Had the second
measure begun with a prominent A5, one might hear the Jupiter. These schemata were
each subtly distinguished in the galant style. Only much later, when the distinctions no
longer had any force, were they all assimilated into the category "antecedent-consequent
phrase" or worse, "I–V–V–I."

One of the many concertos of the great Venetian musician Antonio Vivaldi (1678–
1741) was actually titled "La pastorella":

EX. 9.12   Vivaldi, Concerto in D, "La pastorella" (RV95), mvt. 2, Largo, m. 1 (Venice,
ca. 1710)

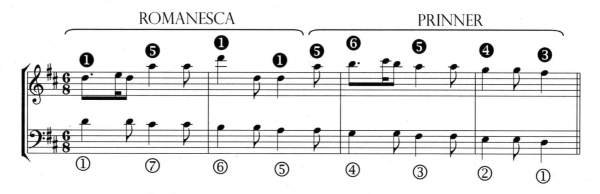

Its slow movement carries many of the external markers of the pastoral—simple texture, gently oscillating neighbor tones in triple rhythm, calm bass, the pipes of Pan (a recorder plays the melody)—and yet it presents the generic schemata of the Romanesca with Prinner riposte. Hence I do not want to suggest too strong a link between an abstract schema and the pastoral theme or "topic," to use Leonard Ratner's term.[12] Most of the galant schemata were adaptable to any topic, just as a particular dress pattern could be realized in any number of fabrics.

Nevertheless, the Pastorella schema did seem to have a certain affinity with the pastoral topic. In a similarly bucolic slow movement for the same instrumentation (ex. 9.13) Vivaldi chose to present the Pastorella along with the Jupiter. Note the Pastorella's characteristic ①–⑤–⑤–① bass, its mid-measure resolution of the melodic dyads, and its very simple melody. The Jupiter's characteristic ❹ falls squarely on the downbeat of the second measure:

EX. 9.13   Vivaldi, Concerto in G Minor (RV105), mvt. 2, Largo, m. 1 (Venice, ca. 1710)

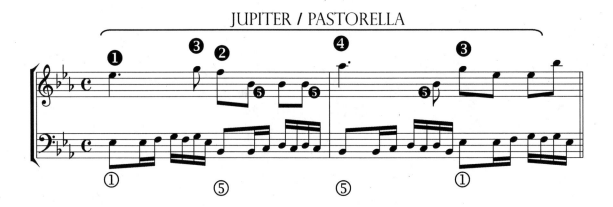

The Adeste-Fidelis–like melodic leaps down to and up from ❺ are a further indication that the Jupiter and Pastorella have close relationships with the Do-Re-Mi. Leonard Meyer grouped the Pastorella together with the Meyer (my terms) under the category of the "changing-note archetype."[13] While those schemata do share a turnlike or sigmoid melodic contour of the core tones, ∾, the Pastorella has more in common with the Jupiter and the paired Do-Re-Mi. For instance, whereas the Meyer's second event features a prominent melodic ❼, these other schemata all require a ❷ at that point: paired Do-Re-Mi (❶–❷ . . .), Jupiter (❶–❷ . . .), Pastorella (❸–❷ . . .). From the point of view of the galant composer, the psychological question of schema similarity or affiliation was less important than the pragmatic one of which schemata could be superimposed if one desired to achieve, in Leonard Meyer's apt phrase, both "grammatical simplicity and relational richness."[14]

Three opening themes from the solfeggi of Giacomo Insanguine (1728–1795) can demonstrate how, for instance, a young musician could learn to distinguish the Pastorella from the Meyer. A Neapolitan collection of maestro Insanguine's solfeggi for bass voice and partimento is preserved in the Noseda Collection of the Milan Conservatory Library. The first example below, no. 10 of that collection, presents the Meyer with its standard ①–②–⑦–① (or ③–②–⑦–①) bass. The melody descends a step for the first dyad **❶**–**❼**, and then continues to descend through a Prinner melody:

Ex. 9.14   Insanguine, solfeggi nos. 10–12, all beginning with m. 1 (Naples, ca. 1770s)

The second example, no. 11, presents the Pastorella. The ①–⑤–⑦–① bass is a variant of the ①–⑤–⑤–① basses seen earlier. The melody, after sounding the **❸**–**❷** dyad, restates the **❷**

as part of a scalar High ❷ Drop. The third example, no. 12, presents another Pastorella, this time forming another Prinner melody by transposing measures 1–2 up one step in measures 3–4. Solfeggi for bass can be instructive for the analysis of schemata because they generally present the basic forms, avoiding complex types of ornamentation. Solfeggi for soprano, as we shall see below, were written for more agile voices.

The Aprile

Giuseppe Aprile (1732–1813) had a brilliant career as a singer. Trained in Naples, where he later became a maestro, he premiered many of the choice operatic roles, including that of Timante in the Stuttgart premiere of Jommelli's *Demofoonte* (1764; see chap. 24). The solfeggi, or vocal exercises, that he, Durante, Leo, David Perez (1711–1778), Porpora, Insanguine, Nicola Sala (1713–1801), Pasquale Cafaro (1715/16–1787), and others wrote for students in Naples were not the arid scales and arpeggios that the term calls to mind today. Instead, they were often beautifully crafted melodies paired with partimento-like unfigured basses. Students thus practiced and absorbed a complete melody-bass framework. The lovely vocal gestures in Cimarosa's operas may owe a great deal to the time he spent as a student of Aprile. Castrati, among whom Aprile was one of the most prominent, have not been given much credit for composition, whether through prudery in Victorian times or through ignorance of the rich tradition of eighteenth-century solfeggi. Yet they were crucial carriers of galant traditions, and their knowledge of how to craft a moving melody, shaped as it was by their years on stage, could be matched by few others.

The Aprile schema, which I name in his honor, is closely associated with the Meyer. Both share the same pair of initial events. But whereas the Meyer closes with a ❹–❸ dyad, the Aprile closes a third lower with ❷–❶. Example 9.15, taken from one of Aprile's Neapolitan solfeggi for soprano (meaning a boy or a castrato in the male-only world of the conservatories) begins with the "open" half of a typical Meyer (mm. 1–2). Its "closed" half (mm. 3–4), with its ❷–❶ dyad, is what distinguishes it from the Meyer. This four-bar Aprile opening gambit leads to a four-bar Prinner riposte, with the *la-to-sol* ornament (mm. 5–6) applied twice. The Prinner's normal tenor voice is in the bass. Though the solfeggio looks very spare with its barely moving bass, the accompanist would have been expected to add, where appropriate, parallel thirds or sixths beneath the melody, thereby considerably enriching the texture and sonority. Such textures are quite common in the arias of Cimarosa, Paisiello, Piccinni, and Mozart. The rising scale in measure 8 "flees" the closure of the Prinner, ascending to begin in measure 9 a second descent toward a special type of galant half-cadence. A discussion of these and many other varieties of galant "closes" or *clausulae* will be the focus of chapter 11.

As shown earlier in example 9.9 from Mozart's Jupiter symphony, the Jupiter motive can form an alternate bass for an Aprile melody. Mozart fully exploited this *ars combinatoria* in the slow movement of his famous G-minor symphony, written the same summer as

EX. 9.15   Aprile, solfeggio, MS fol. 40v, Larghetto, m. 1 (ca. 1780s?)

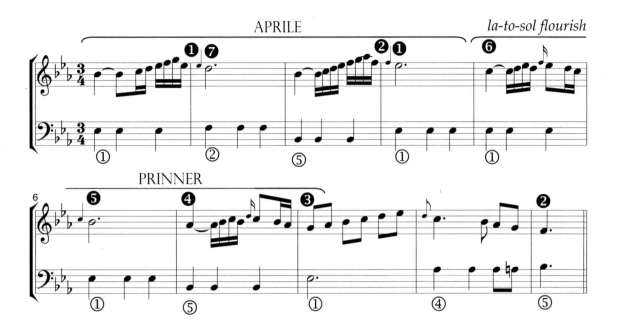

the Jupiter symphony. Examples 9.16–20 sketch the melody and bass of some of the combinations and transformations that abound in this movement, focusing on those that relate to the schemata previously introduced. Articulating Mozart's series of schemata are a variety of *clausulae* with differing strengths and functions.

Mozart selected a four-measure presentation of the Jupiter schema (see ex. 9.16) for the opening of his Andante. Its "melody"—that is, what a listener attends to as the theme unfolds—emerges from the composite effect of three successive entries by the violas, second violins, and first violins. The violas and second violins leap up from ❺ in a manner characteristic of the Adeste Fidelis Do-Re-Mi (see chap. 6). They perform a variant of the Corelli "leapfrog" (cf. ex. B.7 in appendix B). The violas leap first to E♭4. As they repeat that tone in a series of equal eighth notes, the second violins leap to F4 a second above it. The ensuing iterated clash of E♭4 and F4, the "2" of a 2–3 suspension, continues for a whole measure, resolving only in measure 3 when E♭4 descends to D4. The bass supporting the Jupiter is a variant of the standard bass clausula (③–④–⑤–①; see chap. 11). In measure 2 (at the asterisk), beneath the "2" of the 2–3 suspension, Mozart chromatically ornaments ④ and its movement toward ⑤. His Jupiter is followed by the traditional Prinner riposte. For its first half, Mozart prefaces each core tone in the melody with a lower chromatic appoggiatura (highlighted with starbursts in ex. 9.16). For the Prinner's second half, Mozart accelerates the pace, fitting two statements of the ❹–❸ dyad (with High ❷ Drops) in measure 7. The general descent of the Prinner melody thus pushes on to the ❷ in measure 8, ending in a chromatic slide to a half cadence.

EX. 9.16   Mozart, Symphony in G Minor (KV550), Andante, m. 1 (Vienna, 1788)

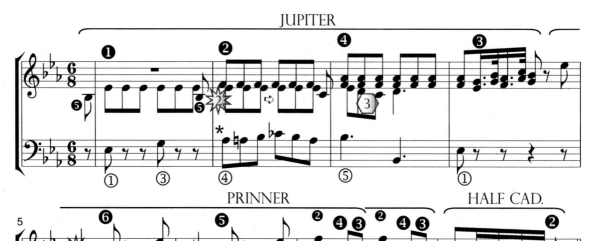

In his first transformation (ex. 9.17), he placed the "melody" in the lowest string parts and the bass in the first violins, thus exchanging the registers of melody and bass. In a further transformation, he simplified and extended the chromatic ornament (see the double asterisk, mm. 10–11), which first appeared in the bass of measure 2. As for the Prinner, with its "melody" in the bass, the ❹–❸ close functions as a conventional preface to a strong cadence, first evaded and then completed.

EX. 9.17   Mozart, Symphony in G Minor (KV550), Andante, m. 9 (Vienna, 1788)

EX. 9.17   (continued)

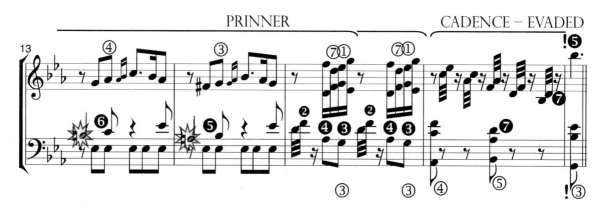

After a complete cadence in the main key (not shown), Mozart introduced a new theme in B♭ major. It features the Jupiter melody in the bass and an Aprile melody in the first violins (cf. ex. 9.9 from the Jupiter symphony). In place of the 2–3 suspensions of the opening theme (m. 2), this new theme features 7–6 suspensions (mm. 21, 23). A small Fonte ensues, followed by a *clausula vera* (see chap. 11) that closes with Fs in both bass and treble. That is, the music emerges from the digression of the Fonte to focus on Fs as both ① and ❶ of a local but relatively stable F-major context:

EX. 9.18   Mozart, Symphony in G Minor (KV550), Andante, m. 20 (Vienna, 1788)

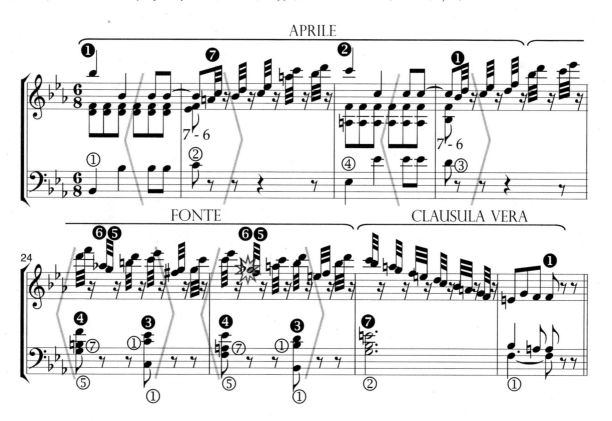

The next transformation takes as its point of departure the 2–3 suspension that occurs in measure 2 when the second violins leap to a tone a step above the tone being reiterated by the first violins. At the end of the previous example, rescored below as the beginning of example 9.19, all the principal parts play or ornament an F as ① or ❶. In measure 28, an analogue of measure 2, the upper parts introduce a dissonant G♭ one step above the F. The resolution of this unexpected 2–3 suspension leads quickly to the remote key of D♭ major (m. 29). There Mozart repeats the bass and composite melody of measure 1, with the addition of the decorative descending scale first heard in measure 27 (itself a transformation of the descending thirds of measure 16). What follows in measure 30 transforms the expected 2–3 suspension into the closely related 4–3 suspensions of a "textbook" Monte Romanesca (see chap. 7). In the late 1780s the Monte Romanesca was an archaism, and the overlay of the descending scales (not shown) gives this remarkable passage a Handelian grandeur:

EX. 9.19   Mozart, Symphony in G Minor (KV550), Andante, m. 28 (Vienna, 1788)

The opening theme returns unaltered in measure 74 (not shown). After the Prinner riposte, the second Jupiter and its expected exchange of parts follows, with the "melody" moving to the bass, and the prior bass moving to the first violins. This second Jupiter (ex. 9.20), now with both forms of the chromatic ornament in the first violins (marked with single and double asterisks), dissolves in a modulation to F minor before its Prinner riposte can appear.

EX. 9.19 · Mozart, Symphony in G Minor (KV550), Andante, m. 82 (Vienna, 1788)

In between the dissolving Jupiter and its interrupted Prinner, Mozart inserted a huge Fonte. Heinrich Christoph Koch (1749–1816; see chap. 29, exx. 29.1–2) described this technique as a musical "parenthesis" in the "connecting of melodic parts." Mozart's Fonte is so complex that it can only be described piecemeal, although it has a close analog in the large Fonte by Wodiczka shown earlier (ex. 9.7). As in the Wodiczka Fonte, each half of Mozart's Fonte is a Meyer. The second half of each Meyer presents the Prinner melody. The first half of each Meyer employs the motivic material of the Aprile (ex. 9 17), an association facilitated by the Meyer and the Aprile sharing the same opening dyad (①–② with ❶–❼). Within this large Fonte measure 89 warrants special mention. In a hypothetical simpler version, Mozart might merely have ended the first Meyer there, and then, in measure 90, begun the second one. In the actual version, Mozart takes the eighth-note melodic motive of measure 88 and echoes it, one step lower (shifted up an octave to the flute part) in measure 89. The flute's high C♭6 (♭❻) makes this a hermaphrodite Fonte within a larger, normal Fonte. The result is that measure 90 differs from its analog in measure 86. Whereas measure 86 merely begins a Meyer, measure 90 both begins a Meyer and ends an embedded Fonte-within-a-Fonte (note the small ❹–❸ in measure 90). After this grand "parenthesis" Mozart returns to the Prinner riposte as if nothing had happened. He then proceeds directly to the *clausula vera*, skipping the already employed Fonte. The Handelian Monte Romanesca follows as before (not shown). All the component parts from earlier in the movement are reused, but in amazing new combinations—a true *ars combinatoria*.

10

A THEME AND VARIATIONS

BY

JOSEPH HAYDN

Hoboken XVI, No. 27, mvt. 3, 1774–76

AS CHAPEL MASTER TO THE PRINCE OF ESTERHÁZY in western Hungary, Haydn served a provincial court where the galant style of music was clearly preferred. Some of his instrumental music was intended to be performed by the amateur musicians among the local aristocrats, the most important of whom was Haydn's patron, the prince. The necessity of keeping this music within the technical grasp of amateurs sometimes prevented Haydn from exploiting the full potential of each instrument. He did not, for example, match Locatelli's amazing passagework for the violin, or Scarlatti's for the harpsichord. But Haydn still managed to impress and delight with a combination of impeccable craftsmanship (which he credited to his Neapolitan teacher Porpora) and the seemingly inexhaustible ability to arrange conventional schemata in novel configurations.

Like Somis and Dittersdorf (see chaps. 5 and 8), Haydn presented his movement's theme in two repeated halves—the ubiquitous double-reprise form. The first half lasts eight measures (as it did in the movements by Somis and Dittersdorf), but the second half lasts eighteen, due not only to Haydn's addition of a Monte but also to his restatement of all the material from the first half (indicated below by the boxes enclosing the Meyer, Prinner, and Cadence).

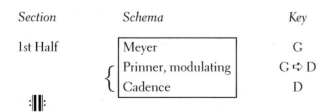

Section	Schema	Key
1st Half	Meyer	G
	Prinner, modulating	G ⇨ D
	Cadence	D

129

2nd Half	Fonte	Am ⇨ G
	Monte	C ⇨ D ⇨ Em
	Half cadence	G
	Meyer	G
	Prinner	G
	Cadence	G

In the list above, the braces linking the Prinner with the ensuing cadence are meant to show that Haydn melded these two schemata together. Somis, Dittersdorf, and Haydn all initiated a modulating Prinner in the fifth measures of their respective movements and cadenced in the key of the dominant in the eighth measures. As shown in example 10.1 (where each phrase has been transposed to G major for comparison), Somis simply presented a four-bar Prinner and used the High ❷ Drop to give closure to the first half of his movement. Dittersdorf began a two-bar Prinner (with a hint of a Fonte—here E minor then D major), extended its third stage, and then overlapped the end of the Prinner with the beginning of a two-bar cadence. Haydn began a four-bar Prinner but abandoned it as he switched onto the path of a two-bar cadence.

EX. 10.1   A comparison of mm. 5–8 in three movements

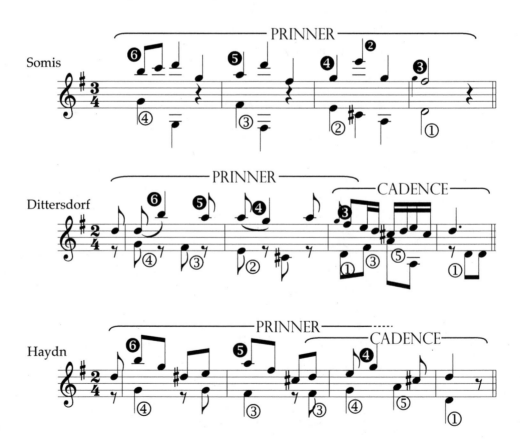

Haydn's procedure was not uncommon. As we will see in chapter 11, on clausulae, the first two tones of the Prinner bass—*fa–mi* or ④–③—were often a cue to begin a cadence, and many galant composers responded to that cue. The schemata of galant phrases were not immutable objects of the real world that could be bolted together in only a certain way. They coalesced, evanesced, and mutated in response to a variety of cues that could easily lead down divergent paths. A successful chapel master needed to understand and exploit those cues, but he had great latitude in choosing the particular paths down which he would lead his listeners.

Haydn was a master at recognizing the possibilities for alternate paths, and each new variation on the theme provided him with new opportunities to demonstrate that mastery.[1] For example, the bravura last variation (Var. IV) gave Haydn a chance to transform the final descending steps of a "regular" modulating Prinner (that is, ❺–❹–❸) into a descending, cadential run of sixteenth notes in which each new core tone is an octave lower than the previous one:

EX. 10.2   Haydn, Variation IV, m. 5

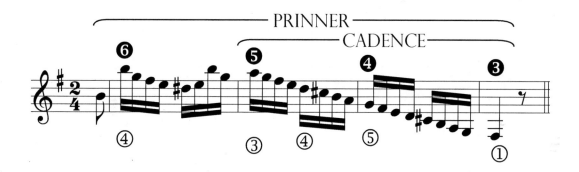

He had already transformed the melodic steps of the Meyer into descending scales in Variation II, where he also drew attention to the affinities between the first two stages of his theme's Prinner and the Fonte. He did so first by altering his modulating Prinner to resemble an uncommon type of Fonte and then by giving the following Fonte the same figuration as the Prinner-Fonte, as if to reinforce the association (see ex. 10.3).

Practical constraints motivated some of Haydn's alterations. In Variation III, which moves to the minor mode, he was forced to replace the main Fonte with a Monte because a Fonte's "minor-then-major" modal change is not easily adapted to a minor key.[2] But most of Haydn's many alterations represent his great capacity for "invention," an eighteenth-century approbation that signified the sanctioned exploitation of artful combinations—the *ars combinatoria*.[3] Each page of this technically easy but musically rich movement (ex. 10.4) is a small textbook of that art.

EX. 10.3   Haydn's gradual association of a Prinner with a Fonte

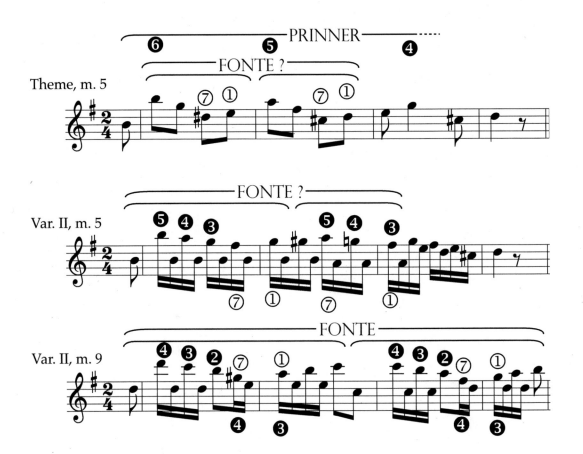

EX. 10.4   Haydn, Sonata (Hob. XVI, no. 27), mvt. 3, Presto (1774–76)

11

CLAUSULAE

THE LATIN TERM CHOSEN BY MEDIEVAL WRITERS to describe the perceived sense of closure and finality brought about by certain melodic figures was *clausula* (pl. *clausulae*; a close, conclusion, or end).[1] In time, this sense was transferred to formulae involving two contrapuntal voices, and then much later to formulaic successions of multivoice chords. The example below shows a four-voice formula that Johann Gottfried Walther (1684–1748), organist at Weimar, maestro to the young Prince Johann Ernst, and friend of J. S. Bach, described in 1708 as a *clausula formalis perfectissima*[2]—what is commonly described today as a "perfect authentic cadence." *Perfectissima* invites translation as "most perfect," but the intended meaning was nearer to "most complete," referring to the degree of closure. Hence the title of the example could be rendered as "a close in the most complete form."

EX. 11.1   Walther, *Praecepta der musicalischen Composition* (Erfurt, 1708)

Clausula formalis perfectissima

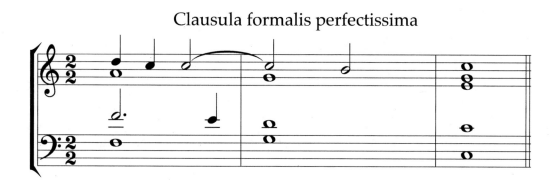

Generations of nineteenth- and twentieth-century music students have learned about musical phrase endings—cadences—from textbooks on harmony. This chord-centered view of musical articulation was fully appropriate to the aims of general musical education in the Romantic age, but it is too coarse-grained for an esoteric, courtly art like galant music. Or put another way, it highlights only what Locatelli has in common with Rimsky-Korsakov. Walther, following the lead of Andreas Werckmeister (1645–1706),[3] looked at clausulae more melodically, as was then the norm. For him, each of the four voices performed its own clausula, participating as an integral part in the "perfection" of the whole. The soprano performed the discant clausula, the alto performed the alto clausula, the tenor performed the tenor clausula, and the bass performed the bass clausula:[4]

EX. 11.2   A version of Walther's four melodic clausulae

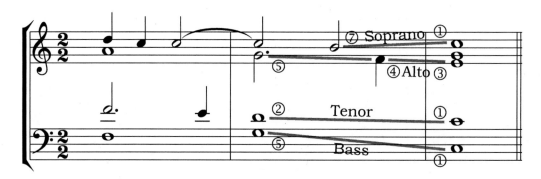

Any of these melodic clausulae could appear in the bass voice or part. Walther reserved the term *clausula perfectissima* for cadences where the normal bass performed the bass clausula (⑤–①). If the discant clausula (⑦–①) was performed by the lowest voice, he named the resulting cadence a *clausula cantizans* ("a cantus- or soprano-like clausula"); if the tenor clausula (②–①) appeared in the lowest voice, he named the resulting cadence a *clausula tenorizans* ("a tenor-like clausula"); and if the alto clausula (⑤–③) was played by the lowest voice, he named the resulting cadence a *clausula altizans* ("an alto-like clausula"). Walther's treatise was, after all, written in the era of figured bass and partimenti. It drew attention to specific patterns in the bass that could help a young accompanist recognize the intended type of clausula.

The conceit that four voices had four roles defining four categories of clausulae—a taxonomy neatly aligned with the then prevalent notions of four elements or four humors—conforms to eighteenth-century practice quite well except in the case of the alto. Walther's alto clausula (⑤–③) was not common as a bass and was not even the most common alto part in a "complete cadence." Much more frequent was, as shown above in my adaptation of Walther's example (ex. 11.2), the descending second *fa–mi* (④–③). Walther and the seventeenth-century sources that he drew upon in writing his treatise may have been reluctant to initiate a clausula from a dissonant tone. Galant composers did not share their scruples, at least not to the same degree.

In this chapter I present the galant versions of Walther's clausulae, going beyond the simple bass formulae to specify the several subspecies that had significance to eighteenth-century musicians and their audiences.[5] As with the other galant schemata, each type of clausula could be described as a *pas de deux* of bass and melody. The chapter is organized according to the different movements of the bass. I begin with *clausulae perfectissimae* (⑤–① in the bass), and then proceed with *clausula cantizans* of a rising half step in the bass (⑦–①), *clausulae tenorizans* of a falling whole-step in the bass (②–①), and *clausulae altizans* of a falling half step in the bass (④–③, a whole step in the minor mode). Within each section, the finer distinctions involve different movements of the melody. Some specific combinations or co-articulations of bass and melody had commonly used names in the eighteenth century or earlier, while others were named by later scholars and musicians. I have named additional types that, perhaps because they were ubiquitous in galant music, were not considered noteworthy at the time but are nonetheless essential for understanding galant musical discourse. Though I do not exhaust the possibilities of this *ars combinatoria*, the resulting bestiary of subtly differentiated clausulae may nevertheless tax some readers' patience. The remaining chapters will be intelligible without a knowledge of these fine distinctions, but the importance of recognizing the many shades of articulation in galant music cannot be overestimated.

THE ⑤–① CLAUSULAE: *Clausulae perfectissimae*
(THE MOST COMPLETE TYPES OF CLOSES)

The prototypical, standard clausula in galant music had a bass that rose from ③ to ④ to ⑤ before falling to ①. In Naples they called this direct ⑤–① close a *cadenza semplice*, a "simple ending" or "basic fall"—the Italian root of *cadenza* means both to fall and to terminate. If ⑤ was repeated an octave lower before continuing to ①, the clausula was called *cadenza composta*, a "compound ending" involving the addition of a "cadential" 6/4 or 5/4 chord. Here are two instantiations in two different meters:

EX. 11.3   The standard galant clausula in its "simple" and "compound" forms

In describing difficulties that arise when we seek to study improvised arts in the past, the theater historian Domenico Pietropaolo points out that while "our descriptive language

is similar to that of earlier periods of history, . . . our artistic forms and our cultural contexts are different, and so we risk being prevented from understanding earlier instances of the phenomenon by the words that apparently best equip us to grasp its essence."[6] Such a word is "cadence." Since the mid-nineteenth century, each ostensibly fixed type of cadence has been taught as a "chord progression" with a descriptive title intended to "grasp its essence" (e.g., "perfect," "imperfect," "deceptive," "plagal," "Phyrgian," and so forth). The delicate interactions of galant basses and melodies, however, were not fixed and go well beyond simple ascriptions of an essence. In the following discussions, a "cadence" is thus more properly understood as an instance of bass-melody co-articulation. And if, as suggested, one views such a co-articulation as a musical pas de deux, it is worth noting that the danseur of the bass and the danseuse of the melody might also work equally well with other partners. That is, their combination is not essential, and each part alone is still meaningful. In place of more accurate but cumbersome and tedious circumlocutions I will still employ the word "cadence," but understood with the caveats just mentioned.

In galant music, the standard bass clausulae were used countless times in every conceivable meter, tempo, style, and genre. They were paired, as mentioned, with melodies that, although quite diverse in structure and complexity, were generally expected to close on the keynote, **❶**. One prominent class of cadential melodies featured a **❸–❷–❶** or *mi–re–do* descent. A typical example occurs in a small keyboard work by Cimarosa:

EX. 11.4   Cimarosa, Sonata C30, Allegretto, m. 1 (ca. 1780s)

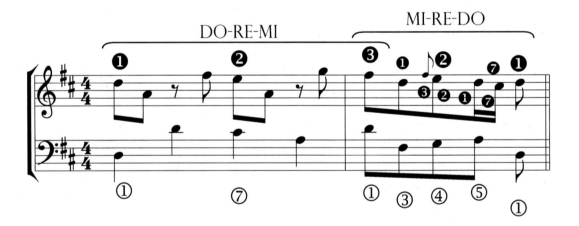

He presents a Do-Re-Mi theme with a pacing of two beats per stage, and then closes, at a faster pace, with a Mi-Re-Do melody fitted above the *semplice* bass. At the quarter-note pacing, the **❸–❷–❶** ending is obvious. Among the subsidiary patterns at an eighth-note pacing are descending thirds, **❸–❶** and **❷–❼**, as well as ascending seconds, **❶–❷** and **❼–❶**, all of which are significant melodic gestures. Even at a sixteenth-note pacing, the initiation of a rapid descending scale from a dissonant tone (the grace note F♯5, which is performed as a sixteenth note) above the bass's ④ is worth noting for later reference.

For comparison, example 11.5 shows the very first cadence written by a five-year-old Mozart (as transcribed by his father Leopold; see ex. 25.1 for the full context). If we think of Cimarosa's sixteenth notes ❸–❷–❶–❼ as a decoration, or to use the galant term, a "diminution," of the eighth notes ❷–❼, then we see that Mozart applied the same diminution to the previous two eighth notes, ❸–❶. For his bass, in place of Cimarosa's *cadenza semplice*, Mozart chose to employ what the Neapolitan maestro Nicola Sala termed a *cadenza lunga* ("long cadence"; see ex. 11.50 for a fuller discussion). The point of this comparison is to demonstrate that in galant practice the composer and performer retained a degree of freedom to "mix and match" stock basses, melodies, and diminutions, even in the case of highly stereotyped clausulae.

EX. 11.5   Mozart, KV1a, m. 5 (1761; age 5)

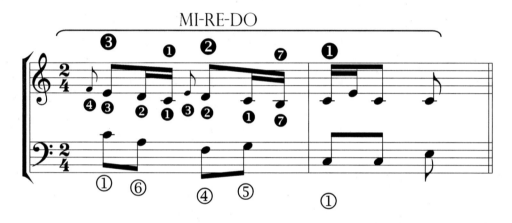

If a composer opted for the *cadenza composta*—two ⑤s, with the second one an octave lower—it was still possible to employ the ❸–❷–❶ melody, though ❸ would often be shifted to align with the bass's first ⑤ as in this minuet by violinist Pierre Gaviniés (1728–1800):

EX. 11.6   Gaviniés, Opus 3, no. 5, mvt. 2, Tempo di Minuetto, m. 29 (1764)

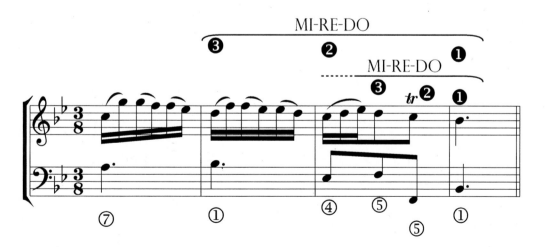

In this example we see the Mi-Re-Do descending at two different pacings. A direct ❸–❷–❶ descent with ❸ placed over the first ⑤, and ❷ over the second ⑤, begins in measure 31 on consecutive eighth notes. A broader, indirect ❸–❷–❶ descent occurs on the downbeats of the last three measures (mm. 30–32).

The prevalence of cadences with theses prototypical bass clausulae and stepwise descending melodies made them easily recognizable and highly predictable, which in turn allowed composers to subject them to extensive elaboration and variation with little loss of comprehensibility. In a Parisian trio by Johann Schobert, for instance, we see a flurry of thirty-second-note figurations, a trilled ❷ over both ⑤s, and the substitution of ① for the normal ❸, but the underlying cadence is still quite similar to that of Gaviniés:

EX. 11.7   Schobert, Opus 6, no. 1, mvt. 1, Andante, m. 6 (ca. 1761–63)

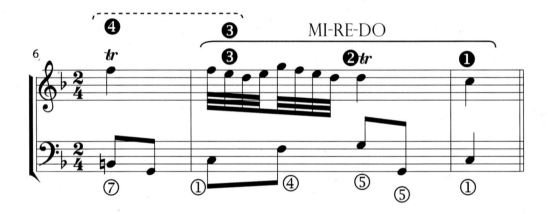

Notice that Schobert, like Gaviniés, began his cadential passage with a weaker articulation (shown under a dotted brace). These ⑦-to-① "soprano" clausulae will be discussed later in the chapter. In particular, a connection will be suggested between the older *cadenza doppia* and this newer combination of a soprano clausula with a following bass clausula.

Melodic descents were clearly the norm above the standard bass, and the ❸–❷–❶ close was often only the termination of a longer descent. A justly popular aria by Antonio Salieri (1750–1825; see ex. 11.8), later chosen by Mozart as the theme for a set of keyboard variations (1773), closes with a Prinner that Salieri incorporates into a final cadence. The melodic descent stretches from ❻ down to ❶. That broad descent was not, however, in a fixed relationship with the bass. In Mozart's last variation on Salieri's theme (see ex. 11.9), he retains the broad ❻–❺ dyad of the Prinner but accelerates the remaining descent so that the variation reaches ❶ and sounds ❶–❼–❶ where Salieri's theme sounded ❸–❷–❶. At the close, a Prinner-like alto part and a ③–②–① tenor part join in presenting all four of Walther's clausulae, though the upper voices artfully delay arriving at their destinations for half a beat.

EX. 11.8   Salieri, *La fiera di Venezia*, "Mio caro Adone," Andante, m. 13 (1772)

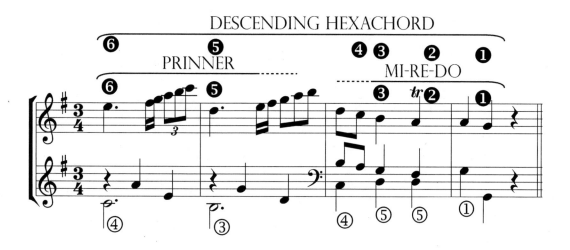

EX. 11.9   Mozart, Var. on a theme by Salieri (KV300e), Var. 6, Allegretto, m. 13 (1773)

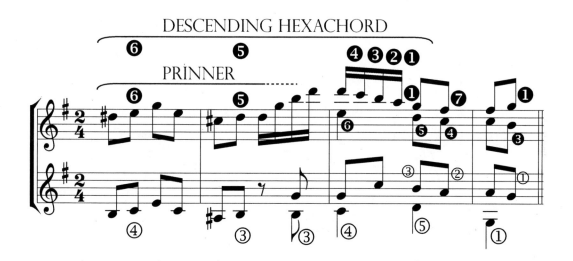

This combination of a soprano's ❶–❼–❶ with a tenor's ③–②–① was heir to a long contrapuntal tradition. The same pairing is clearly evident in an Adagio movement from a string quartet by Luigi Boccherini (1743–1805; see ex. 11.10), where a tenor-like ⑤–④–③–②–① in the second violin is paired with ❸–❷–❶–❼–❶ in the first violin). In Walther's terms, the first violin plays a *clausula cantizans*, the second violin a *clausula tenorizans*, and the violoncello a *clausula perfectissima*. Boccherini avoids the usual dissonance over ④ (cf. Salieri's aria, ex. 11.8) and instead arpeggiates tones of the local harmony (m. 23, beat 1). Descending thirds over ④ were almost as common as descending scales.

EX. 11.10   Boccherini, String Quintet, Opus 11, no. 1, mvt. 2, Adagio non tanto, m. 22, (1771)

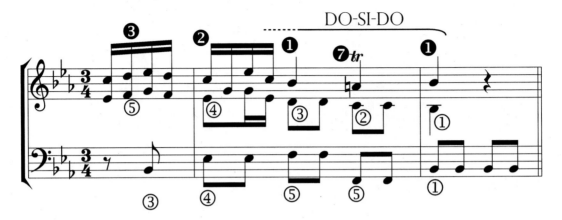

Versions of this type of Do-Si-Do cadence (to use a modern solfège), a favorite for slow movements, could also be presented with only hints of the descending inner voice, as in a cadence from an Andante for keyboard by J. C. Bach (1735–1782). In common with other cadences, it has a dissonance above ④ (the grace note G4 at the start of measure 6 in relation to the implied bass Ab2):

EX. 11.11   J. C. Bach, Opus 12, no. 6, mvt. 2, Andante, m. 5 (Paris, 1773–74)

The most famous of galant cadences was identified by the English musicologist Charles Cudworth (1908–1977). It uses the standard bass in conjunction with a melodic descent through the full octave from a high ❶ to the final ❶. In Cudworth's words, it was "so typical of the age that one can refer to it simply as 'the galant cadence.'" In the book at hand, which includes so many other varieties of thoroughly galant cadences, Cudworth's designation would be confusing. So in honor of his contributions to, and many wise words about, the study of galant music, I will call it the Cudworth cadence. Here is the model cadence as presented in his article for *The Monthly Musical Record*:[7]

EX. 11.12   Cudworth's *cadence galante* (1949)

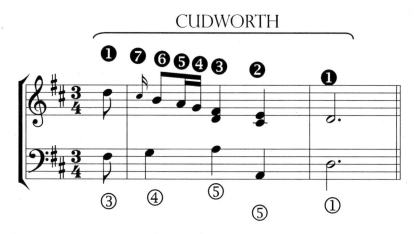

Many features of the Cudworth cadence have already been discussed, such as its initiation of a rapid scalar descent from a dissonance (❼) over ④ in the bass, its coordination of the melodic ❸–❷ over the two ⑤s in the compound bass (the "cadential 6/4"), and (though not in Cudworth's own example) the frequent use of a trill on ❷. So it is closely related to the other types of standard cadences. But the salience of the melody rising to the high ❶ before hurtling down to the final ❶ was such that a Cudworth cadence tended to serve as a main cadence placed at the end of an entire movement or at least a large section.

Because numerous instances of the Cudworth cadence will be found throughout this book, it is unnecessary to provide more examples here. But it may be useful to highlight some special cases. Like other cadences, the Cudworth cadence can be nested within a larger progression, as in the example below by Tartini (ex. 11.13). A descending scale ❺–❹– ❸–❷–❶ is both interrupted and then completed by the Cudworth cadence. The dotted brace indicates the weaker initial articulation that Tartini's passage shares with those of Gaviniés and Schobert presented earlier.

EX. 11.13   Tartini, Opus 6, no. 4, mvt. 1, Adagio, m. 17 (Paris, ca. 1748)

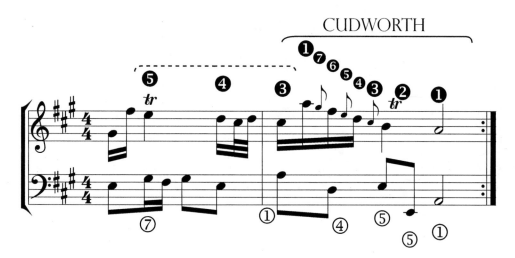

When used in the minor mode, the Cudworth cadence will sound the lowered seventh scale degree in the melodic descent over ④ in the bass, followed by the raised seventh degree in an inner voice over the last ⑤ in the bass, as in this passage by Baldassare Galuppi (1706–1785) (m. 42, 1st violin F♮, 2nd violin F♯):

EX. 11.14   Galuppi, *Concerto a quattro* in B♭ Major, mvt. 1, Grave sostenuto, m. 41 (ca. 1750s)

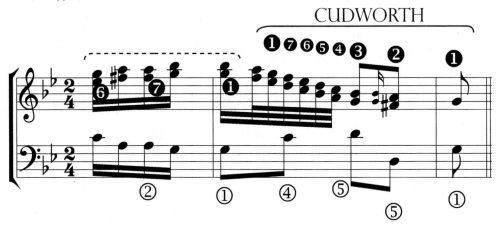

Here the initial, weaker articulation shown under the dotted brace is a *clausula tenorizans* or tenor clausula (to be discussed later in the chapter).

Two further variants of the Cudworth cadence depend on performance practice and are thus difficult to specify with confidence in any individual passage. The first of these usually occurs in a major-mode movement after a modulation to the dominant key. As shown in example 11.15 by Cimarosa, a Cudworth cadence in the local key of B♭ uses the lowered seventh degree (A♭5) in place of the expected A♮5:

EX. 11.15   Cimarosa, Sonata C37, Andantino, m. 11 (ca. 1780s)

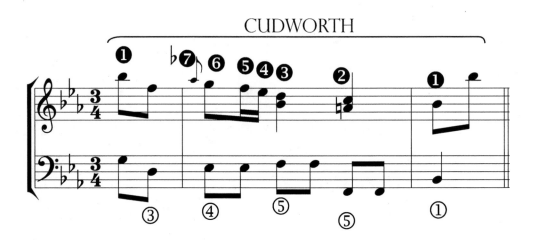

Eighteenth-century manuscripts were dashed off at great speed and consequently abound in errors of every kind. So it is possible that performers would play the raised seventh degree out of habit. Yet many clean, careful manuscripts and prints do seem to indicate the lowered seventh degree, which could be described as a Mixolydian variant, as an effect of the global key (E♭ major in ex. 11.14) on the local context, or as a tonicization of the subdominant ④. Another explanation would be that since many of these Mixolydian Cudworth cadences approach the seventh degree from below (F5 to A♭5 in the example), musicians invoked the rule that "a note above *la*" should be *fa*, which would result in the lowered seventh.

Similar questions could be raised about the following cadence, again by Cimarosa:

EX. 11.16   Cimarosa, Sonata C5, Allegretto, m. 21 (ca. 1780s?)

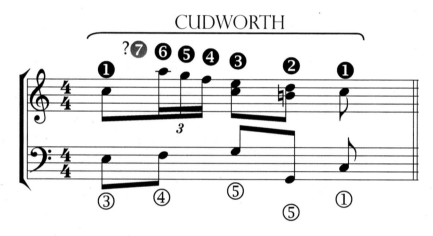

Only the descent from ❻ to ❶ is notated, but it is possible that performers conditioned by other similar cadences would add a ❼ (either raised or lowered) as an improvised appoggiatura to ❻. The ❼ in the normal Cudworth cadence is, after all, most commonly notated as a grace note.

On hearing a standard bass, listeners could project specific expectations about its outcome, and those expectations were a resource upon which composers could draw. As early as 1605, the philosopher Francis Bacon had remarked, "Is not the trope of music, to avoid or slide from the close or cadence, common with the trope of rhetoric of deceiving expectation?"[8] The rhetorical use of misdirection or digression is important in galant musical discourse. A variety of eighteenth-century terms referred to these unexpected outcomes— "evaded cadence," "avoided cadence," "feigned cadence," "deceptive cadence," "the deceit," and so on. Perhaps the best known today is the deceptive cadence, which features a standard bass that, rather than falling from ⑤ to ①, continues to rise to ⑥. The "deceit," or "trick" as it was sometimes called in Italian (*inganno*), was particularly well chosen since it balanced, against the learned expectation for the bass to fall from ⑤ to ①, the equally strongly learned expectation for stepwise movement to continue. The deceptive cadence was taught through partimenti, and the two examples below by the renowned Neapolitan maestros Carlo Cotumacci (ca. 1709–1785)[9] and Nicola Sala,[10] show that essentially the same bass and figures were used in both the major and the minor modes:

EX. 11.17   Cotumacci, from a partimento in C minor, m. 27 (Naples)

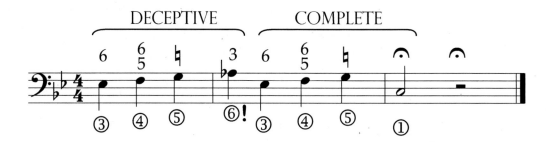

EX. 11.18   Sala, from a partimento in D major, m. 39 (Naples)

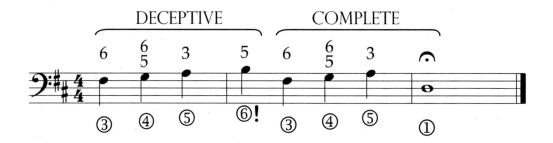

Other departures from expectation fell under the rubrics of "avoided" or "evaded" cadences, terms that were used interchangeably. A second partimento by Cotumacci shows how a cadence ending on ③ in the bass, rather than ①, evaded full closure and, like the deceptive cadence, required a second, successful attempt at cadencing (my exclamation point marks the point of evasion):[11]

EX. 11.19   Cotumacci, from a partimento in E minor, m. 27 (Naples)

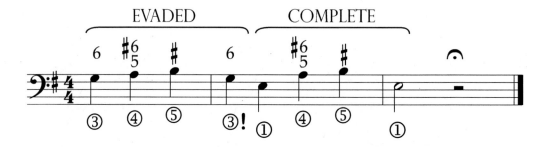

Evasions were especially common in the melody. The cadence by J. C. Bach presented earlier (ex. 11.11) was actually his second attempt to complete the melodic **❶–❼–❶**.

His first attempt (ex. 11.20) veered away from the final **❶** at the last moment, coming within a sixteenth note of sounding the goal before leaping up to **❺**.

EX. 11.20   J. C. Bach, Opus 12, no. 6, mvt. 2, Andante, m. 3 (Paris, 1773–74)

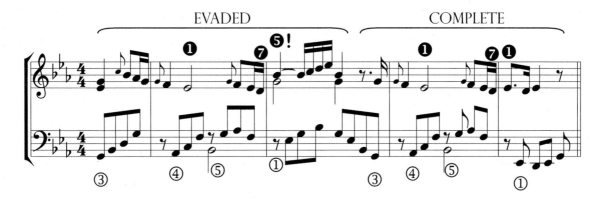

In an Andantino by Cimarosa (ex. 11.21), the same technique is used, but with the effect of forcing a premature restarting of the phrase. His Romanesca bass concludes as expected, but his melody reaches full closure only on the second attempt. Properly speaking, an entire passage like Cimarosa's first Romanesca (mm. 1–3) is not "evaded." Rather, a crucial moment of evasion affects our memory of the whole passage, which we then often characterize metonymically as "evaded."

EX. 11.21   Cimarosa, Sonata C37, Andantino, m. 1 (ca. 1780s)

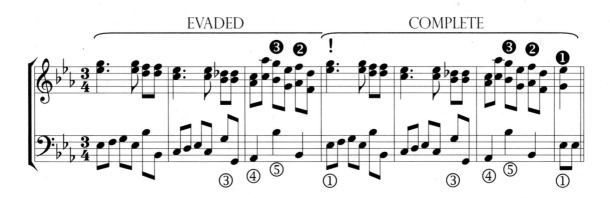

Similarly, deceptive cadences are only deceptive at a given moment. Up to that moment they are usually perceived as normal cadences. In some cases the sense of evasion can be almost entirely retrospective. For instance, the first Mi-Re-Do cadence shown at the beginning of this chapter (ex. 11.4) seems far less closed when one hears its larger context (see ex. 11.22). In measure 2, the failure to dwell long enough on the first cadential **❶**, performed staccato, seems in retrospect to launch a digression and then a restatement,[12] with the properly dilatory and satisfying close coming finally in measure 5.

EX. 11.22   Cimarosa, Sonata C30, Allegretto, m. 1 (ca. 1780s)

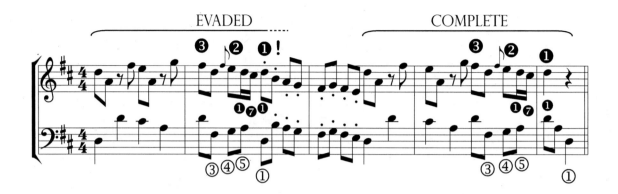

In the course of the century, as movements became ever longer, so did cadences. While the Cudworth cadence remained a staple of smaller movements, it was not easily enlarged. Its characteristic descending rush of notes would have lost much of its impact had the cadence been stretched out and hence slowed down. What took its place in longer movements—what I call "the Grand cadence"—borrows from the Cudworth cadence its point of initiation on high ❶ and the general descent toward the final ❶, but is in other respects a separate type. Over the ③–④–⑤ of the standard bass (whether "simple" or "compound"), the Grand cadence places a ❶–❻–❺ descent in the melody, as can be heard in the following example by Clementi, which closes an episode in E♭ major:

EX. 11.23   Clementi, Opus 4, no. 5, mvt. 2, Allegretto, m. 109 (1780)

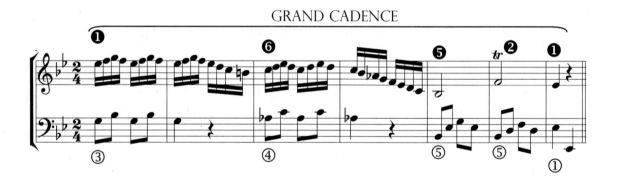

The grandest of Grand cadences involved repetitions engendered by the techniques of deception or evasion just discussed. An excerpt from a string quintet by Dittersdorf presents a first statement of a Grand cadence that ends with the deceptive bass and a melodic descent only as far as ❸. Upon repetition, of course, Dittersdorf provides the expected complete closure:

EX. 11.24   Dittersdorf, String Quintet (K. 190), no. 6, mvt. 1, m. 14 (1789)

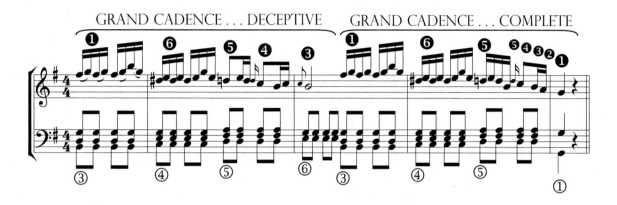

Perhaps the limit in avoidance or evasion would simply be to stop a cadence short of its goal—to leave it "half" finished. Half cadences would then be described as those that stop on the penultimate bass tone, ⑤, commonly with an appoggiatura in the melody ending on either ❷ or ❼. Yet half cadences seem not to have been perceived as deceptions or tricks. They had their own features and created their own expectations. In a minuet by Pasquali, for example, a half cadence ends the first half of the movement:

EX. 11.25   Pasquali, Opus 1, no. 2, mvt. 2, Menuet, m. 7 (London, 1744)

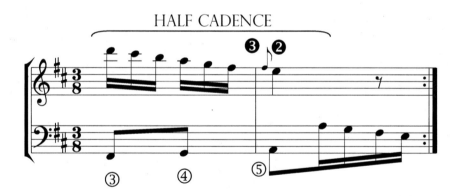

Notice that, in relation to the standard cadence, the half cadence is shifted metrically forward so that ⑤, rather than ①, falls on a downbeat (the sixteenth notes in the bass of measure 8 lead back to D major the first time and to E minor the second time). That is, although the half cadence has long been described as deriving its effect from an incomplete harmonic pattern, the difference in metrical scansion may be equally important.

Later in the century it became fashionable for a half cadence to have a trill on ❸. As shown in example 11.26 by Pietro Nardini (1722–1793), some forms of the half cadence no longer relied on the standard bass but leaped directly from ① to ⑤.

EX. 11.26   Nardini, Opus 5, no. 4, mvt. 3, Allegro, m. 15 (ca. 1769)

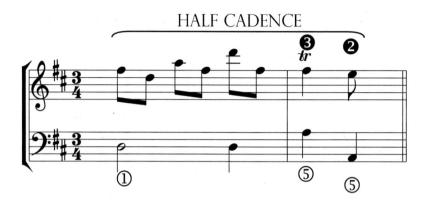

The last of the *clausulae perfectissimae* to discuss, and the most Italian of them all, featured the standard bass under an obstinate and unchanging ❶ and ❸ in the melody or the inner parts. This cadence was most often played twice, with a deceptive ending the first time and the expected ending the second. The example below by the Neapolitan composer Emanuele Barbella (1718–1777) appeared in a London print (1765) of six violin sonatas, five of whose final movements carry subtitles—"All'Italiana," "Alla Venetiana," "Alla Napolitana," "All'Inglese," and "Alla Francese"—that suggest a musical tour of European styles. The movement containing the cadence in question was the one depicting his home city of Naples, and Barbella gave it the further description "Sul fare di Pulcinella," which I take to mean "in the manner of Pulcinella." Though "Pulcinella" did not refer exclusively to the cadence, the connection with this stock comic character of the commedia dell'arte seems apt. The Pulcinella cadence ignores the strictures of conventional counterpoint and instead revels in the free interplay between the moving bass and the static upper parts:

EX. 11.27   Barbella, Six Solos, no. 4, mvt. 3, Presto, m. 63 (London, 1765)

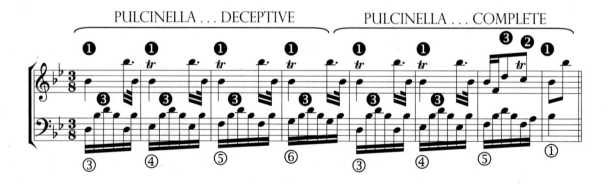

Nardini was musically related to Barbella through connections with the violin school of maestro Tartini at Padua. To show that the Pulcinella cadence was used beyond Naples,

I present example 11.28, from Nardini's Opus 5 violin sonatas, believed written in northern Italy or Austria. Nardini sets a deceptive Pulcinella twice with scintillating harmonic clashes, executes a cadenza-like solo that touches the high A5 and begins the descent of the hexachord (m. 40) before initiating a Cudworth cadence. He gives that Cudworth cadence a deceptive bass and an evaded melody (m. 43), which leads to a varied repeat of the small cadenza. Nardini finally closes with a complete and emphatic Cudworth cadence in the lower register.

EX. 11.28   Nardini, Opus 5, no. 4, mvt. 3, Allegro, m. 32 (1769)

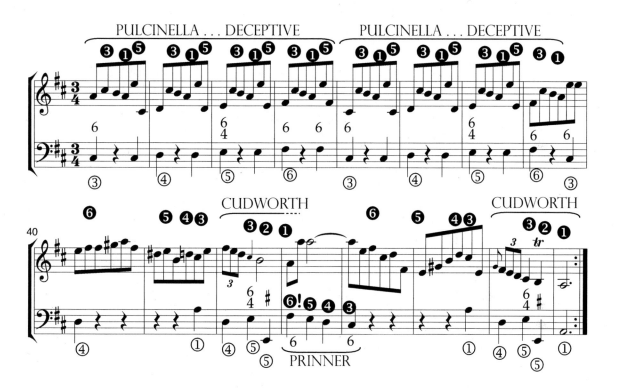

THE ⑦–① CLAUSULAE: *Clausulae cantizans*
(CLOSES CHARACTERISTIC OF A SOPRANO)

In 1797 Vincenzo Manfredini (1737–1799) wrote that "*cadence* signifies a close or state of repose . . . [that can] serve not only to end an entire composition but also to close off a musical phrase or period, it being the case that music, like verbal discourse, has its phrases, its periods, its punctuation marks of every sort, its digressions, etc."[13] Manfredini was expressing a widespread notion. Alexander Malcolm (1687–1763) had made the same points early in the century when he declared that "by a close or cadence is meant a terminating or bringing a Melody to a Period or Rest, after which it begins and sets out anew, which is like the finishing of some distinct Purpose in an Oration."[14] In the spirit of these similes one might liken the complete cadence to a period at the end of a sentence, and the half cadence to a colon or question mark. For the weaker articulation afforded by a comma I suggest the mild close in this brief example by Mozart (see chap. 16 for the entire movement):

EX. 11.29   Mozart, Sonata in C Major (KV545), mvt. 1, Allegro, m. 4 (1788)

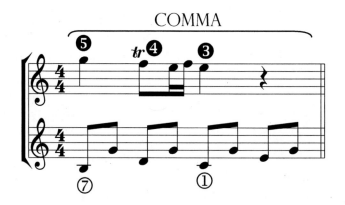

The ⑦–① ascent in the bass and the coordinated descent of ❺–❹–❸ (or just ❹–❸) in the melody create a small inflection that, like a comma, sets off a syntactical unit from what will come next. It its larger context, Mozart's Comma formed the end of a Prinner. It could equally well have formed any unit in a Monte, the second, major-mode unit of a Fonte, or the close of a Meyer, Jupiter, or Pastorella. But the Comma was not limited to forming a component of larger schemata. It could also stand on its own.

I first read Manfredini's simile that "music, like verbal discourse, has . . . its punctuation marks" during a visit to the Milan Conservatory Library in 2003. It prompted my selection of "comma," "colon," and "period" as reasonable analogues for the cadence-types discussed above (colon = half cadence, period = complete cadence). Two years later, in reading a discussion of cadences by Manfredini's contemporary Francesco Galeazzi (see chap. 29), I was both surprised and heartened to see nearly the same words applied to the same cadences. Galeazzi, who himself had read Manfredini, proposed a graded series of four cadence-types ranging from the very weak to the very strong, each related (where possible) to a mark of punctuation:

> The first [type A, a melodic evasion] has no analogue in [verbal] discourse; the second [type B, a Comma] has the effect of commas [*virgole*] and serves to distinguish the clauses [*clausole*]; the third [type C, a half cadence] has the effect of a semicolon or colon, distinguishing the phrases; the last [type D, a complete cadence] distinguishes the sentences and has the effect of a period.[15]

Galeazzi provided a melodic example, in the style of Riepel, and marked the four grades of cadences with the letters A, B, C, and D. As shown in example 11.30, type B—the

Comma—obviously has the ❺–❹–❸ melody. One can infer the ⑦–① Comma bass (or ⑥–⑦–① Long Comma bass, see below) from Galeazzi's comment that his type B has the cadential "fundamental bass" (presumably V–I or II–V–I) but does not have it in the "basso continuo," meaning the actual bass:

EX. 11.30   Galeazzi, *Elementi teorico-pratici di musica . . .* , vol. 2, ex. 19 (Rome, 1796)

A Comma would often precede stronger cadences. In the Adagio movement that begins the fifth of Nardini's Opus 5 violin sonatas, a Comma (with the High ❷ Drop) occurs just before the final cadence:

EX. 11.31   Nardini, Opus 5, no. 5, mvt. 1, Adagio, m. 15 (ca. 1769)

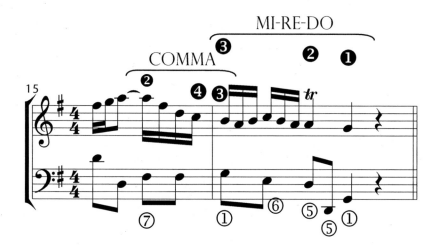

This was a very common practice, and several examples of Commas preceding stronger cadences have already appeared earlier in this chapter (e.g., exx. 6, 7, 13, and 14; for exx. 7, 13, and 14 the Comma is marked with a horizontal dotted brace). A feature worth noting in Nardini's treatment of the Mi-Re-Do cadence is the placing of ⑥ before ⑤. Nardini was a devoted student of Tartini, and that somewhat unusual bass was a cliché in the works of Tartini and his school at Padua.

In the opening movement of his fourth sonata from this set, Nardini placed a variant of the Comma twice before his final cadence. I term this variant "the Long Comma," and it features a ⑥–⑦–① rise in the bass matching the ❺–❹–❸ fall in the melody:

EX. 11.32   Nardini, Opus 5, no. 4, mvt. 1, Adagio, m. 21 (ca. 1769)

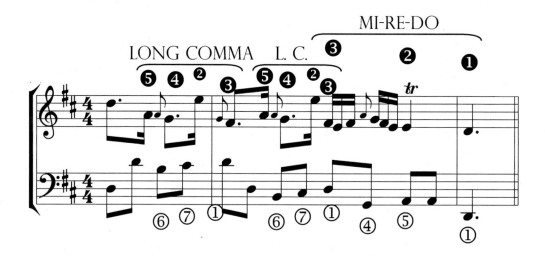

The Long Comma sometimes served as an intensification of the normal Comma. In an Andante movement by Castrucci, the second half of the movement begins with a Romanesca that dissolves into two Commas. Then a Long Comma, with a dissonance between ⑥ in the bass and ❺ in the melody, leads back to the overall key of F major:

EX. 11.33   Castrucci, Opus 2, no. 4, mvt. 1, Andante, m. 4 (London, 1734)

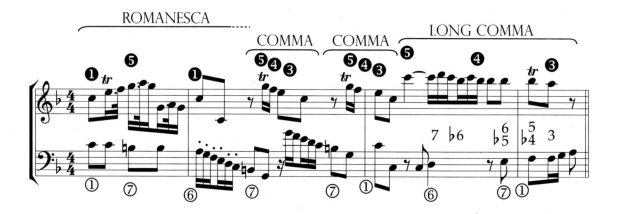

Johann Friedrich Daube (ca. 1730–1797), an eighteenth-century musician and writer who worked in Stuttgart and Vienna, took note of a pairing of chords that, although some-

what frowned upon in the past, had become "utterly essential."[16] Daube was referring to a
⑦–① *clausula cantizans* common in the repertory at Stuttgart, where he served as second
flute under senior chapel master Niccolò Jommelli (1714–1774), who was among the most
brilliant products of the Neapolitan conservatories. The following passage from Jommelli's
opera *Demofoonte* shows his fondness for this relative of the Comma, which I call "the
Jommelli" in his honor:

EX. 11.34   Jommelli, *Demofoonte*, act 2, scene 10, m. 31 (Stuttgart, 1764)

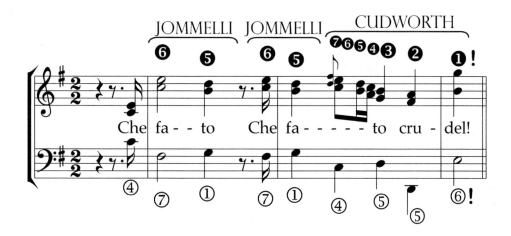

The two statements of the Jommelli precede a Cudworth cadence that is doubly *sfuggite*
(It., "fled" or "evaded"), to use Daube's term, by the deceptive ending in the bass and the
evasive leap up to G5 in the soprano. There is, of course, much more that follows this
excerpt, and I present the complete aria in chapter 24.

    Two final species of *clausulae cantizans* might with equal justification have been intro-
duced along with half cadences. One of them, the Converging cadence, is so named by
virtue of the way its two outer voices move toward each other, converging on the dominant
chord. Its bass shares many features with the half cadence, its core melody shares the intervallic pattern of the Prinner, and its ending is equivalent to the Comma. A simplified version is shown in example 11.35.

    A typical example of the Converging cadence appears at the end of the orchestral
introduction to Gluck's famous aria "Che farò senza Euridice?" (1762; ex. 11.36). Gluck
begins his short ritornello with a Meyer, whose second half closes with a Prinner. He treats
the Converging cadence's melodic moves from ❸ to ❷ and from ❶ to ❼ as opportunities
for appoggiaturas. As just mentioned, one could easily interpret the four main melodic
tones of Gluck's Converging cadence as part of a modulating Prinner—❻–❺–❹–❸ in the
key of G major. As discussed in chapter 2, the "usual Italian solfeggio" would have been the
same for both interpretations, *la–sol–fa–mi*. The ascending chromatic bass is similarly biva-
lent, with the final semitone F♯3–G3 being both ♯④–⑤ in C major and ⑦–① in G major.

EX. 11.35   A simplified Converging cadence

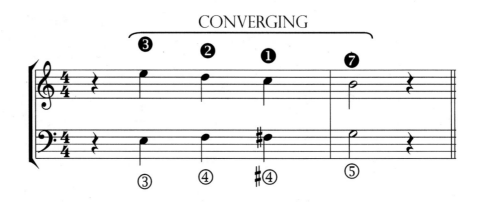

EX. 11.36   Gluck, "Che farò senza Euridice?" m. 1 (1762)

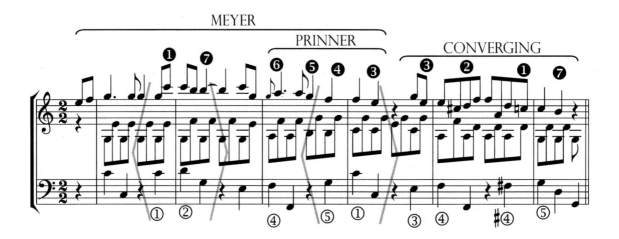

Again, in an eighteenth-century context, both interpretations would have the same solfeg-gio—*mi–fa*. Because a Converging cadence sets up the possibility for a modulation to the dominant key but does not guarantee that modulation, I will mark its scale degrees in the context of the original key (♯④–⑤ instead of ⑦–①). This favors one meaning but in no way excludes the other. In Gluck's aria, immediately after this Converging cadence Orfeo begins to sing in the key of C major.

The Converging cadence was an exceedingly popular schema and developed several subtypes with characteristic features. Daube, writing about unusual cadences, provided the thoroughbass shown in example 11.37, which spells out the startling clash of a diminished octave between the bass and soprano parts (my realization in smaller noteheads):

EX. 11.37   Daube, *General-Bass in drey Accorden* (1762)

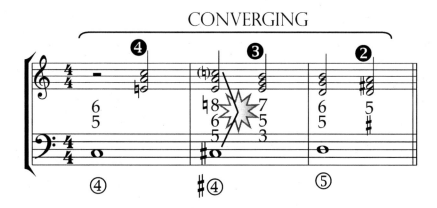

The normal converging melody is doubled a third higher to descend ❺–❹–❸–❷, a descent shared with many half cadences. Holding ❹ while the bass ascends from ④ to ♯④ causes the striking dissonance and cross relation of ❹ against ♯④, a diminished octave. Given the number of passages in which this occurs, it is likely that the effect was intentional. As to the thoroughbass "5" at the moment of the dissonance, it is either a misprint for "3" or an intrusion of Daube's own peculiar theory of harmony (more on this later). A fastidious composer like J. C. Bach could choose to avoid the direct clash by inserting into the melody a discreet rest (shown in brackets, ex. 11.38), although the impression of a cross relation remains rather strong:

EX. 11.38   J. C. Bach, Opus 12, no. 6, mvt. 2, Andante, m. 15 (Paris, 1773–74)

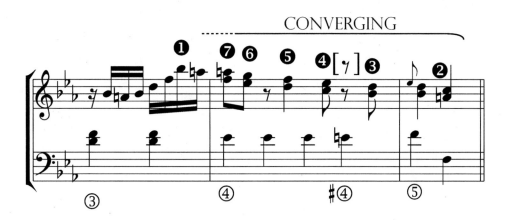

Referring to his thoroughbass examples of the clashing Converging cadence and the Jommelli schema, Daube remarked, "Nowadays these last two passages are considered well known and common, despite the fact that they were seldom regarded as legitimate in past times, in particular when the twelve modes were still popular. Now they are utterly essential and appear in all categories of composition. They have proven their worth. Therefore, beginners must know them."[17]

Some presentations of the Converging cadence feature an analogue of the High ❷ Drop. As was discussed in chapter 5, the High ❷ Drop is a fall from ❷ to ❹–❸, and it signals an approaching close. The same syllables *re–fa–mi* could be applied to a descent from ❻ to ❶–❼, a "High ❻ Drop" as shown in the following two, florid examples:

EX. 11.39   Cimarosa, Sonata in C (C56), Allegro, m. 9 (ca. 1780s)

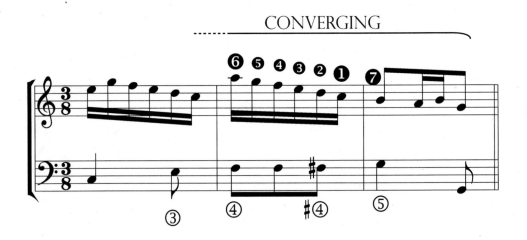

EX. 11.40   Clementi, Opus 5, no. 2, mvt. 2, Presto, m. 118 (ca. 1780s)

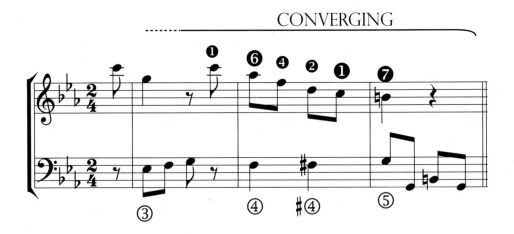

Johann Joachim Quantz (1697–1773), in his treatise on playing the flute (1752; see chap. 28), mentions that this descending ❻-to-❶ pattern "occurs very frequently before caesuras."[18] Regarding the Converging cadence, the above two examples closely match Quantz's precepts for decorating a "plain" High ❻ Drop. Cimarosa's cadence, example 11.39, conforms to Quantz's dictum that "six notes proceeding by step may be used to fill out this interval,"[19] "interval" meaning the drop from ❻ to ❶. Another of Quantz's recommendations for embellishing the High ❻ Drop—descending by thirds[20]—describes example 11.40 by Clementi.

My final species of *clausula cantizans* was employed to introduce a cadenza. The most common form contrasts a sustained ❶ in the melody against a rising scale with raised fourth degree in the bass. When the bass reaches ⑤, metered time ceases and the soloist begins to extemporize. Eventually, with a trill on ❷, the soloist will signal his or her readiness to return to metered time, and the accompanist will proceed as if concluding a standard cadence. In an example from 1737 by Locatelli, a violin virtuoso, the cadenza for violin solo was written out. I have placed in parentheses the obligatory 6/4 chord, something that was self-evident at the time:

EX. 11.41   Locatelli, Opus 6, no. 11, mvt. 1, Adagio, m. 7 (1737)

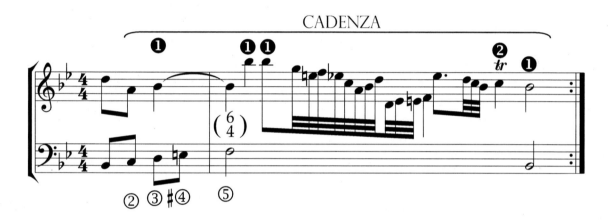

A similar example by Giovanni Battista Viotti (1755–1824) from almost fifty years later shows the stability and continuing utility of this tradition. Following the Converging-cadence bass, the bravura passagework is here left to the performer's discretion:

EX. 11.42   Viotti, Opus 4, no. 1, mvt. 3, Adagio, m. 40 (ca. 1785)

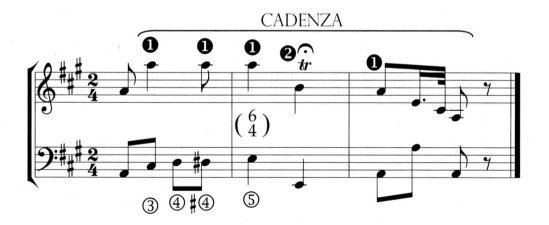

THE ②–① CLAUSULAE: *Clausulae tenorizans*
(CLOSES CHARACTERISTIC OF A TENOR)

For the medieval monks and clerics who established the precepts of counterpoint, a descending step to the final tone of a Gregorian chant was so prevalent a closing gesture that it would have been surprising had they *not* used this gesture as a point of reference. By their rules, if one voice sang the chant and descended a step at the close, the counterpointing voice should complement that gesture by *ascending* a step. If the chant descended by a whole tone, the counterpointing voice should ascend by a semitone, and vice versa. The voice "holding" the long tones of the chant was called the *tenor* (Lat., "to hold"), the counterpointing voice "singing apart" from the tenor was called the *discant* (Lat., "sing apart"), and their coordinated movements established the discant-tenor framework that is at the heart of centuries of polyphony. By the eighteenth century, the discant-tenor framework had become a melody-bass framework. Clausulae that still featured a descending step at the close fell under Walther's rubric of *clausulae tenorizans*, which is to say "small closes" that behave in the manner of the old discant-tenor framework. If the bass descends a whole step and the melody ascends a half step, the result was a *clausula vera*[21] or "true close," as in this example from a quartet by Galuppi (see chap. 15 for the complete movement):

EX. 11.43   Galuppi, *Concerto a quattro* in B♭ Major, mvt. 1, Grave sostenuto, m. 24 (ca. 1750s)

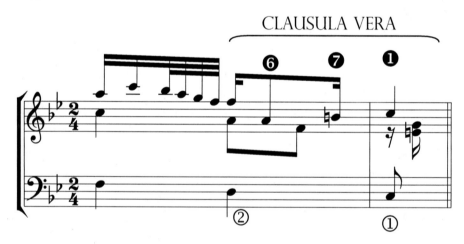

Galuppi was in charge of all music at Saint Mark's basilica in Venice, and his predecessors in that illustrious position included masters of Renaissance counterpoint like Willaert, Rore, and Zarlino. For them, the above cadence would have been a C-cadence, as the scale-degree markings indicate. But by Galuppi's time the meaning of the cadence had altered, and it was used to close on a dominant chord within a larger tonic key. Thus while the above Clausula Vera represents a moment's pause and focus on the C-major chord, it shares with the half and Converging cadences its balance between two closely related hexachords or keys—tonic and dominant, or the "natural" and "hard" systems. A ②-to-① bass is the local and older meaning, a ⑥-to-⑤ bass the global and newer meaning.

The other type of discant-tenor cadence would occur when the tenor descended by a half step and the discant ascended by a whole step. The result is a form of the Clausula Vera better known today as a Phrygian cadence, by reference to the older type of scale that featured a half step between ② and ①. Like the standard Clausula Vera, the Phrygian cadence has a dual focus, locally on the octave to which the voices expand, and globally on the key in which that octave is the dominant. Both the Clausula Vera and its Phrygian variant can be seen in the excerpt below by Durante (ex. 11.44). Modern ears find it very difficult to hear the C chord at the end of Durante example as a keynote, so I have marked the scale degrees of the Phrygian cadence in terms of the global key of F minor, and in particular as involving the two lower bass tones of the Phrygian tetrachord.

EX. 11.44   Durante, *Studio* no. 5, m. 7 (Naples, 1747)

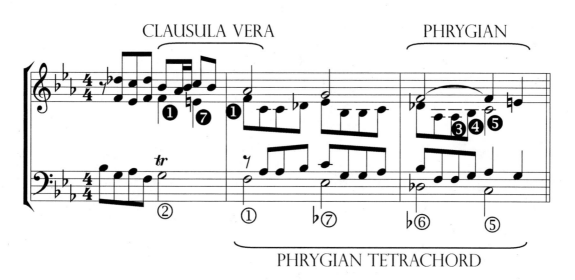

The stepwise descent of the bass through a Phrygian tetrachord, with the upper voice descending in parallel a tenth higher, was often used as a minor-mode analogue of the modulating Prinner. In the case of Durante's passage, even though his Phrygian cadence ends with a C-major chord (which modern ears will likely hear as the dominant chord in the key of F minor), he sets the ensuing phrases in the key of C minor. Again, the tonal plasticity of the galant schemata was great, especially earlier in the century.

If the discant voice of the Phrygian cadence, just before ascending to the octave, is chromatically raised a half step, its distance from the bass becomes an augmented sixth, which is the name for the third type of *clausula tenorizans*. A partimento by Durante's student Fedele Fenaroli (1730–1818) provides a good comparison between the Augmented Sixth variant of the Phrygian cadence and, in the relative major key (B♭), the normal Clausula Vera.

EX. 11.45   Fenaroli, *Partimenti*, book 2, no. 2, m. 1 (ca. 1770s)

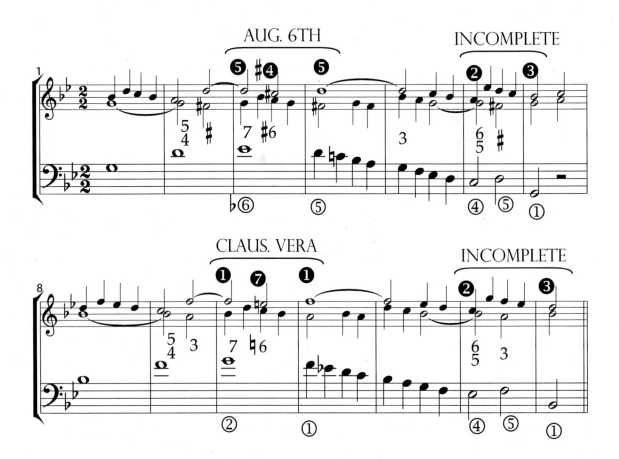

The different sets of scale degrees indicated for the Augmented Sixth and the Clausula Vera result from a modern, single-key-center perspective. In the eighteenth century these two cadences are identical in all but the size of their sixth and the choice of which voice will move a semitone in expanding to the octave. All the tenor clausulae—Clausula Vera, Phrygian cadence, and Augmented Sixth—had similar functions and, as the above examples by Durante and Fenaroli testify, were treated as analogues of one another.

Fenaroli's bass also indicates a standard cadence at the end of each line. In realizing these cadences, I chose the "incomplete" form where the melody ends on ❸ rather than ❶. Harmony books typically label such cadences "imperfect," an unfortunately literal translation of the Latin *imperfecta* ("incomplete," "unfinished").

THE ④–③ CLAUSULAE: *Clausulae altizans*
(CLOSES CHARACTERISTIC OF AN ALTO)

A descent in the bass from ④ to ③ often preceded a stronger cadence. A deflection downward before reversing into the upward stepwise ascent of the standard bass seems to have been a preferred strategy. The theme by Salieri shown earlier (ex. 11.8) presented the first two stages of a Prinner, with its ④–③ bass, before launching into a final Mi-Re-Do cadence. Haydn used the same strategy in the theme of his set of variations presented in chapter 10.

If the upward thrust of the cadential bass signified forward, goal-directed motion, the ④–③ descent could by contrast seem a step backward, what I term a Passo Indietro (It., "a step to the rear"). The most strongly characterized form of the Passo Indietro carried the pair of thoroughbass figures 6/4/2 and 6/3, usually shortened to 4/2 and 6. In a *siciliana* for flute, violin, and thoroughbass by Quantz, we can see the Passo Indietro preceding each of three attempts at a complete cadence. Flute and then violin first try to close separately, but their way seems blocked by the so-called Neapolitan sixth (D♭, marked as ♭6 in the thoroughbass). Their third, combined attempt ultimately succeeds after surmounting a deceptive cadence:

EX. 11.46   Quantz, Trio Sonata in G minor, mvt. 3, Siciliana, m. 22 (ca. 1750s)

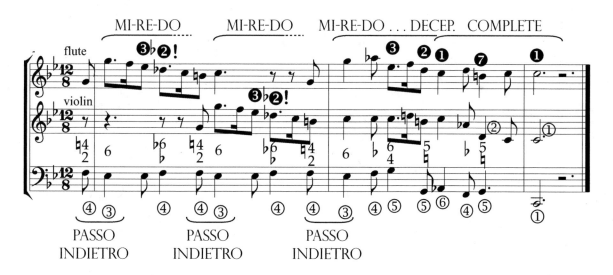

From Walther's point of view, at the end of this passage the melody-bass framework provides the "most complete close" or *clausula perfectissima* while the discant-tenor framework (here, flute-violin) provides a simultaneous Clausula Vera or *clausula tenorizans*.

STILL MORE CLAUSULAE

For its final cadence, the minuet by Somis (ex. 5.2) employed a rhythmic variation on the standard cadence. In place of two measures that would normally scan | 1 2 3 | 1 2 3 | Somis wrote a passage that scans | 1 2 | 1 2 | 1 2 |, an effect known as *hemiola* (from the Greek word for the ratio 3:2). Hemiola cadences occur only in triple meters and predominantly in the first half of the century. Only the standard cadence seems to have been refitted to the hemiola scansion.

As more and more techniques were explored to extend, evade, avoid, elude, and generally put off the closure of a strong cadence at the end of an important musical section, composers risked confusing their audiences. The Cudworth cadence had been a reliable cue of the end of a major section, but the addition of small codas and cadential echoes could undermine its finality. Whether for this or for other reasons, galant composers drew instead upon a final, unadorned melodic fall to serve as a musical "stop sign." The endings of the first and second halves of a famous Mozart keyboard sonata present the two most common variants of the Final Fall (ex. 11.47; see chap. 26 for the whole movement). The first is the more galant, and involves a fall from ❸ to ❶ (in the local tonic, here G major). The second, which closes the second half of this movement, falls an octave from ❶ to ❶ in C major. Nineteenth-century musicians appear to have favored the octave version of the Final Fall, and it can be heard at the end of many Romantic concert works for piano.

EX. 11.47   Mozart, Sonata KV545, mvt. 1, Allegro, mm. 27–28, mm. 72–73 (1788)

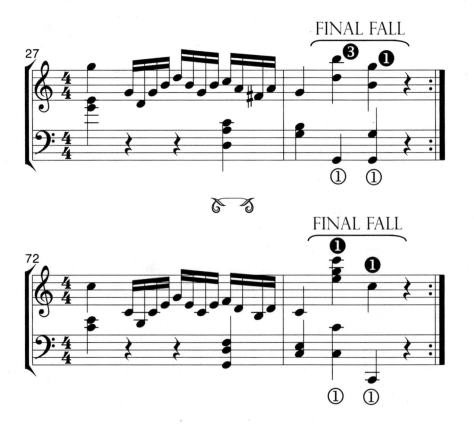

In chapter 7, the discussion of the Monte Romanesca taught by Mozart to Thomas Attwood made mention of a *cadenza doppia* or "double cadence." The "simple," "compound" (see ex. 11.3), and "double" cadences were the three types expressly named and taught to students of partimenti (see also appendix B, ex. B.1). Example 11.48 shows the two standard forms of the Cadenza Doppia, the first one the basic type and the second one characterized by the addition of a dominant seventh (F5).[22]

EX. 11.48   The Cadenza Doppia, plain and with the dominant seventh

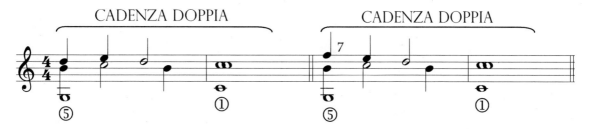

Historically, this cadence was old even in the eighteenth century, retained largely for pedagogical or sacred works. Generally reserved for the final cadence, the Cadenza Doppia made an appearance at the end of almost every partimento. This meant that as the student worked his or her way through a large collection of partimenti, the Cadenza Doppia would be played over and over again. By dint of repetition each of its voices became emblematic of cadencing, and traces of those voices can be found in many of the lighter galant clausulae. If one takes the soprano and alto voices from a version of the Cadenza Doppia with the dominant seventh and removes its pedal-point bass, one can replicate the soprano-bass combination of a Comma followed by a Mi-Re-Do cadence with the standard bass (ex. 11.49). Several examples of this type were shown earlier in examples 11.6, 7, and 13.

EX. 11.49   Homologies between the Cadenza Doppia and more galant clausulae

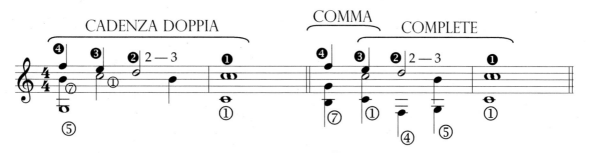

Walther's four categories of clausulae, which recognize the partly independent meanings and histories of the individual voices, were differentiated only by the final two tones in the bass. The subcategories shown in this chapter were sometimes differentiated by how the bass arrived at those final two tones. The Comma and Long Comma, for example, differ in having ⑦–① and ⑥–⑦–① basses, respectively. Sala made a distinction between the common types of standard cadences and what he termed a "long cadence" (*cadenza lunga*).[23]

EX. 11.50   Sala, the Long cadence (ca. 1790s)

   Sala's Long cadence features two falling thirds in the bass—①–⑥–④—that precede
the *clausula perfectissima*. Cadences that follow a Romanesca will have a bass whose downbeats fall on ①–⑥–④ before the penultimate dominant chord. Indeed, the ordering of
Paisiello's partimenti in a 1782 print[24] suggests that this maestro took the Romanesca as a
point of departure for more modern phrases that emphasized the falling thirds in the bass:

EX. 11.51   Paisiello, *Regole*, various partimenti (St. Petersburg, 1782)

Example 11.51 aligns five phrases from five of Paisiello's partimenti, with all but the last serving as opening gambits. His first example presents an obvious Romanesca with Prinner riposte, but his later examples move strongly toward the Falling Thirds schema. Notice also that in the later examples he begins to vary the types of cadences that follow the Falling Thirds, thus stretching out and redirecting the expected close. It would seem, from the evidence of these excerpts, that Paisiello's collection of partimenti not only inculcated the many schemata of galant practice, but also presented them in a general historical progression from older manners toward newer ones.

The partimento tradition represented an intense nonverbal form of instruction originally intended for poor boys learning a trade. The well-to-do amateur desired something more literate, concise, and easily digested. Daube's treatise was directed toward this latter audience, and its title (translated) of *Thoroughbass in Three Chords* presages the sort of handy "how-to" book that would become a middle-class staple. In his treatise he provides a concise table of cadences to cover all the ways suitable for modulating from G major to D major, its dominant. There is considerable overlap between Daube's "Twelve Ways" to modulate and the cadences discussed in this chapter. In the table presented on the following page (ex. 11.52), I have annotated Daube's chart to bring out the correspondences among Daube's examples, Walther's clausulae, and the various cadences discussed throughout this chapter.[25]

Daube considered his first ten ways "natural" and the last two artificial (they introduce a note, G♯, foreign to either key). He provided only basses for these cadences, and I found it difficult to provide realizations of them that respected his thoroughbass figures while still being characteristic of the galant style in Stuttgart. His treatise was written to show that three basic chords could serve for any musical situation. That is a gross simplification and explains why there is something "artificial" about all his examples. Without belaboring the details, perhaps the point can be made most simply by noting that, as quoted in chapter 3 (ex. 3.13), the Neapolitan maestro Saverio Valente recommended using the modulating Prinner "for a departure to the fifth of a key in the major mode."[26] Such is the musical situation for each of Daube's twelve ways. Yet not one of them takes Valente's path of least resistance. That is, not one of his examples allows the bass to descend stepwise from G4 to D4 (the bass of a modulating Prinner). Though the specifics of Daube's theory (rather than the regularities of galant practice) seem to have constrained his creation of examples, his table nonetheless covers the clausuale of all four of Walther's voice-types, and it touches upon many of the special clausulae described earlier in this chapter.

Vincenzo Manfredini was mentioned earlier for having compared various strengths of musical clausulae with different types of punctuation (see the discussion of the *clausulae cantizans*). Like Daube, Manfredini was a professional musician who chose to write for an amateur audience. In 1797 he issued a second edition of his *Regole armoniche* [Rules of Harmony]. In it he vigorously promoted the same three basic chords described by Daube (see my chap. 20) as the answer to all questions of harmony and modulation.[27] One of his

EX. 11.52   Daube, *General-Bass in drey Accorden*, twelve ways of modulating (1756)

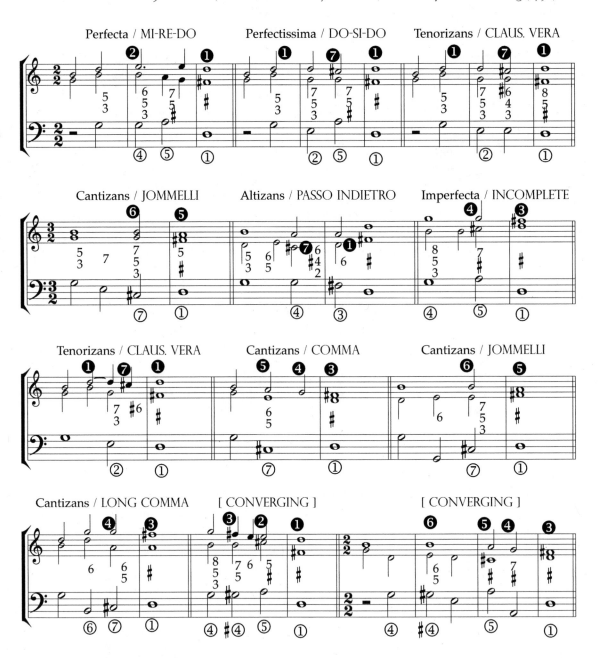

many examples begins with a Long Comma, and he indicates how that particular bass can be harmonized with (1) a 6/4/3 above ⑥, (2) a 6/5 above ⑦, and (3) a 5/3 above ①. The problem is that the Long Comma was not harmonized that way. The chord above ⑥ could take the figures 6, 6/5, 6/5/3, or even 7, but not Manfredini's implied 6/4/3.[28] Example 11.53 compares Manfredini's harmonization with the galant norm. His false chord above ⑥ was a requirement of his theory, not of Italian galant traditions. His small violation might have been apparent to professional musicians, but likely not to amateurs.

EX. 11.53 Manfredini, *Regole armoniche* (Venice, 1797) versus galant norms

Manfredini

Tradition

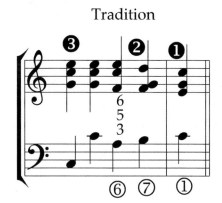

Manfredini's and Daube's theory-driven representations of eighteenth-century compositional practice, however well-intentioned, were harbingers of what was to come in the following centuries, with the end result being a thoroughly bourgeois reinterpretation of an esoteric courtly art. In terms of communication theory, what these documents reveal is the beginning of a shift from a "ritual" mode, with its required years of inculcation in the rites of partimenti and solfeggi, to a "transmission" mode, with the harmony textbook becoming the simplified vector of grand generalizations.[29] The Daube-Manfredini version of "harmony simplified"[30] became normative in the later nineteenth century, so much so that "harmony" and "cadence" became almost synonymous. We should not, however, mistake a triumph of popularization with an advance in understanding. Viewed through this new lens of harmony, a great many of the distinctions once important to galant clausulae became blurred and unrecognizable.

The preceding discussion of Falling Thirds cadences and too-strong theories of harmony began with a cadence by Sala (ex. 11.50). I would like to give Sala the last word (or tone) as well. Sala came to Naples in 1732 (the year of Haydn's birth) and entered the Conservatorio di Santa Maria della Pietà dei Turchini, where he remained in various capacities until 1799, retiring as *primo maestro* (principal master). As a student of Nicola Fago (1677–1745) and Leonardo Leo, his classmates included Jommelli and Gregorio Sciroli (1722–1781, teacher of Aprile). Sala taught generations of students, including early in his career the singer Farinelli and near his retirement the opera composer Gaspare Spontini (1774–1851). What follows is the final cadential passage from a large fugal partimento (ex. 11.54, beginning at m. 161!). A partimento of this scope and level of difficulty was for insiders only. Its discourse takes for granted knowing how to knit together a number of small performance traditions into a continuous whole. Its Falling Thirds schema entails understanding the proper resolutions of a suspended "2" and "7" within the larger context of the Romanesca, its Passo Indietro entails the presentation of an ensuing standard cadence in one of the

EX. 11.54   Sala, partimento in C minor, m. 161 (Naples, ca. 1790s)

approved subtypes, and its evaded cadences (at the exclamation points) entail knowing
how to arrange for the greater closure of the eventual complete cadence. Sala's cadential
passage is thus much more than proper counterpoint matched with sonorous harmony. It
is a master performer's closing soliloquy, a "usual scene" given life through the qualities of
its presentation. The potsherd of Sala's bass becomes whole again through a collaborative
process of reconstruction: Sala's bass, preserved by the editor Alexandre Choron (1808),[31]
probably figured by the Fenaroli student Vincenzo Fiocchi (1767–1843), and elaborated by
my upper voices in imitation of Quantz's Siciliana (cf. ex. 11.46).

      Is that reconstruction authentic? Certainly the figuring of the Falling Thirds passage
is explicit enough to constitute a nearly complete specification of the intended counterpoint. But the cadential series that follows (mm. 167–72) could be realized in a number of
very different ways. Sala himself seems to have favored similarly ornate and dramatized
cadences. One of his solfeggi, shown in ex. 11.55, begins with almost the same tones that
opened Galeazzi's example of cadences as punctuation (ex. 11.30). For ease of comparison,
Galeazzi's letters (A, B, C, D) are marked on Sala's music:

EX. 11.55   Sala, solfeggio in C major, Largo, m. 1 (Naples, ca. 1780s)

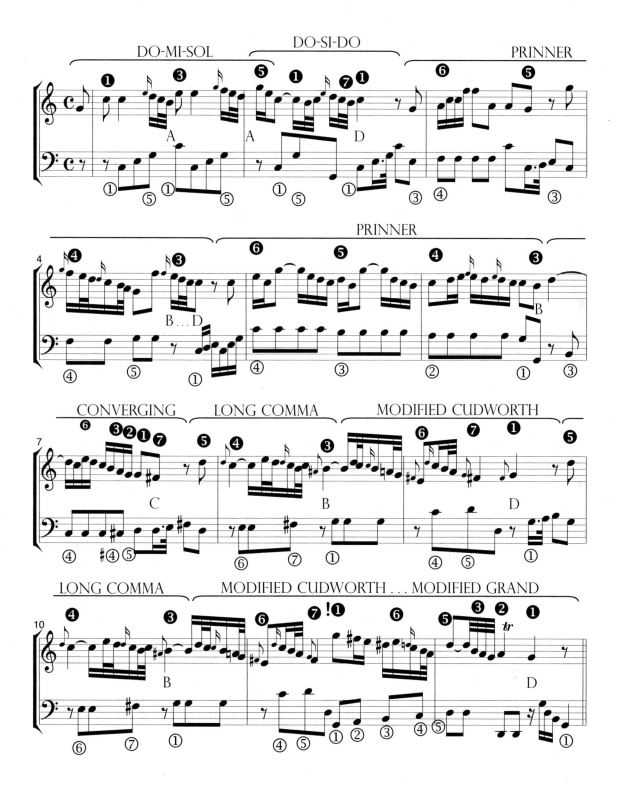

Sala's solfeggio begins by presenting, as mentioned, Galeazzi's Do-Mi-Sol in a bravura style. The Prinner riposte in measures 3–4 and especially the modulating Prinner in measures 5–6 seem to attenuate the energy of the opening, and the melodic motion rests following the Converging cadence in measure 7. Measure 8 begins the drive to the final cadence with the Long Comma, a very common preparatory schema. It leads into what is marked a "Modified Cudworth." That is, many distinctive features of the Cudworth cadence are present, but Sala has reworked its melody to rise ❻–❼–❶ in response to the preceding ⑥–⑦–① in the bass of the Long Comma. Sala then repeats the Long Comma and Modified Cudworth. Almost at the point where the Modified Cudworth would have concluded (m. 11) Sala shifts the expected ❶ an octave higher to begin the definitive descent to the final Mi-Re-Do cadence. This dramatic gesture rides roughshod over the details of the Grand cadence (note the dissonances between treble and bass in the second half of measure 11) but manages to conclude with the requisite ❸–❷–❶ and the telling trill on ❷. This *clausula perfectissima* ends the first half of Sala's solfeggio (a Fonte follows, as might be expected).

Galeazzi's letters (A–D), representing his analogues of punctuation, were applied to Sala's passage based on the behavior of the melody. But the behavior of the bass can undercut the degree of melodic closure. The type-D clausulae in measures 2 and 12, for instance, are reinforced by the strong closure on ① in the bass, whereas the same melodic clausulae in measures 4 and 9 are weakened by the bass quickly moving to a prominent ③. Galant music, with its pas de deux of treble and bass, can often defeat attempts to ascribe to it unitary clausulae. One should evaluate the combined effect of the separate clausulae in the context of the coordinated treble-bass behaviors that make up the repertory of typical closes.

Examples like Sala's solfeggio, which were intended to inculcate norms, demonstrate the sensitivity of galant composers to the subtle distinctions of clausulae. Just as properly executed curtsies and bows both articulated social discourse and embodied a recognition of the social order, so gradations of conventional clausulae articulated the musical flow and reinforced the impression of respectful, proper musical behavior. To paraphrase Norbert Elias, cadential "etiquette proves, if one respects the autonomy of the structure of court society, an extremely sensitive and reliable instrument for measuring the prestige value" of a galant musical utterance. Higher-status utterances, such as themes or large sections, received the "most complete" closes. Lower-status utterances, such as Commas before a complete cadence, received only weak articulations. Sensitivity to status was, of course, always a requirement for success at court.

12

AN ANDANTE

BY

CHRISTOPH WILLIBALD GLUCK

Sonatas for Two Violins and a Thoroughbass, no. 5, mvt. 1, 1746

AN EARLY SET OF TRIO SONATAS BY GLUCK (1714–1787), written perhaps in Milan but published in London, gives a good account of his excellent training in the Italian galant. In the Andante from the fifth sonata, presented below, little happens harmonically beyond a single use of the hermaphrodite Fonte. But the smooth succession of schemata, the good-natured exchange of the melody between first and second violins, and the subtle use of small clausulae of varying strengths all show a composer of refined technique and musical sensibility. When compared with Gluck's later operas, which achieved grand success in Paris and Vienna, this Andante may seem almost trifling. Yet many of the famous arias from those later works retain the same galant discourse.

Gluck wrote the first and second violin parts to trade motifs back and forth, generally with the first leading and the second echoing. He set the basso continuo to support them unobtrusively. All three parts maintain a pervasive rhythmic pattern of three or more eighth notes initiated between the main beats. From measure 5 to the end of the first section, Gluck wrote a series of increasingly strong clausulae. The series begins with a half cadence followed by a Comma. The first complete cadence has the weak ❻–❼–❶ melody. Its repetition ends deceptively and leads into a small Prinner. The second violin then makes the first try at a ❸–❷–❶, Mi-Re-Do cadence, using only the *cadenza semplice*. The first violin, with its customary musical seniority, repeats the cadence to end the first section. For the close of the second section, Gluck begins with a ❶–❼–❶, Do-Si-Do *cadenza semplice*. He then writes the stronger ❸–❷–❶, Mi-Re-Do *cadenza composta*. This could have been the ending had the melody not evaded closure by "fleeing" (*sfuggire*) into a string of sixteenth notes and another Prinner. Finally an arpeggiated flourish leads to the definitive Mi–Re–Do *cadenza composta* played by the first violin with the confirming trill on ❷.

In the list below, *bis* (Lat., "twice") refers to an immediate repetition, often with the violin parts exchanged. The second schema of the second half, labeled "[Romanesca]," refers to Gluck's reuse of elements of the Romanesca opening theme, but without the Romanesca schema.

Section	Schema	Key
1st Half	Romanesca	E♭
	Meyer	E♭
	Prinner, modulating	E♭ ⇨ B♭
	Half cadence	B♭
	Comma	B♭
	Cadence, *bis*, deceptive	B♭
	Prinner	B♭
	Cadence, *bis*	B♭
𝄆𝄂𝄇		
2nd Half	Fonte, hermaphrodite	Fm ⇨ E♭
	[Romanesca]	E♭
	Prinner, circle-of-5ths	E♭
	Prinner, *bis*	E♭
	Cadence, Do-Si-Do	E♭
	Cadence, evaded	E♭
	Prinner	E♭
	Cadence, Mi-Re-Do	E♭
𝄇		

EX. 12.1   Gluck, Sonatas, no. 5, mvt. 1, Andante (London, 1746)

13

THE QUIESCENZA

THE NOSEDA COLLECTION OF THE MILAN CONSERVATORY contains a large two-volume manuscript in which several different hands have copied hundreds of partimenti by Zingarelli. The second of these volumes lists a number of rules of thumb (*regole*) for the student, and two of them pertain to pedal points on the keynote of the mode. The first rule is that "the pedal is formed from the chords of the fundamental bass."[1] The partimento written below the rule makes clear that the fundamental bass in question is an implied cadence of triads whose roots are C, F, G, and C (the bass and figures are Zingarelli's; the realization, in smaller notes, and the indications of scale degrees are mine):

EX. 13.1   Zingarelli, from a collection of partimenti and *regole* (Milan, ca. 1810–20)

The second rule, or rather suggestion, is that "one can give partimenti the minor seventh as if one were proceeding in the nature of the fourth of the key."[2] Again, the partimento written below this statement clarifies the intended meaning:

EX. 13.2   Zingarelli, from a collection of partimenti and *regole* (Milan, ca. 1810–20)

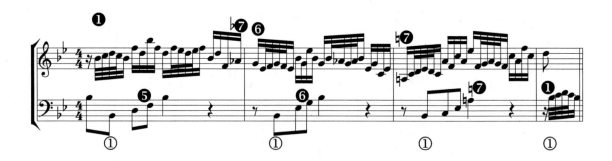

Early in the eighteenth century, the traditions of extemporized preludes, toccatas, *intavolature*, and *essercizi* frequently called for an opening passage that would, like an expanded cadence, move toward the subdominant ("the fourth of the key") and then toward the dominant before returning to the tonic. In his B♭-major invention for keyboard (ca. 1720), one of his lighter, more galant works, J. S. Bach presented this sort of broad, expository, key-setting passage. The phrase contains elements of both of the pedal points described by Zingarelli. A version of the first type, with a diatonic rise of ❺–❻–❼–❶, can be heard in the tenor range, and a version of the second type, with the chromatic ♭❼ leading to ❻, can be heard in the melody:

EX. 13.3   J. S. Bach, Invention in B♭ Major, m. 1 (Cöthen, ca. 1720)

Domenico Scarlatti, Bach's contemporary, had wide-ranging experiences in many of the great centers of galant music. He too wrote similar passages, but often performed them twice in succession in what seems to have been the fashion. Here is an example from a keyboard work in C major (K. 250). The passage appears immediately after an opening flourish and makes obvious its chromatic ♭❼–❻–♮❼–❶ melody:

EX. 13.4   D. Scarlatti, Sonata K. 250, m. 1 (ca. 1740s)

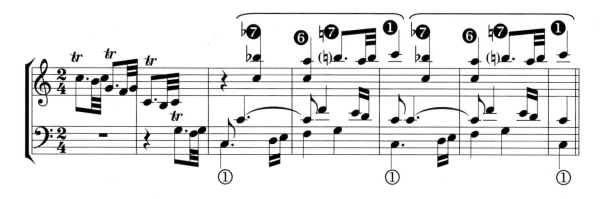

Given Scarlatti's roots in Naples, one might expect this pattern to have figured prominently in the partimenti from Neapolitan conservatories. It did not, and one reason seems to be that these partimenti had their own highly stereotyped endings, which favored pedal points on a penultimate ⑤, like the Cadenza Doppia. Zingarelli's comments about pedal points are thus a late addendum to that tradition, filling in a lacuna.

By midcentury this cluster of traits—a ♭❼–❻–♮❼–❶ melody, a tonic pedal point, the associated sonorities, and a double presentation—had stabilized as a stock schema employed for closing rather than opening passages. I call it "the Quiescenza" (It., "a state of repose or inactivity") by analogy with "cadenza." Just as a cadenza exploits a pause within an important cadence to show off the performer's taste, invention, and virtuosity, bringing the forward progress of a movement temporarily to a halt as a result, so a Quiescenza exploits a moment of quiescence *following* an important cadence, likewise holding back the further progress of the movement or delaying its ultimate close.

The ending function of the Quiescenza was made clear by Bach's son Carl Philipp Emmanuel (1714–1788) in his book on the proper playing of a keyboard instrument. Near the conclusion of the second volume (1762), C. P. E. Bach included his own partimento upon which the reader could extemporize a *fantasia*. Immediately after its final cadence, Bach indicates the standard thoroughbass figures of the Quiescenza:

EX. 13.5   C. P. E. Bach, *Versuch über die wahre Art das Clavier zu spielen*, vol. 2, p. 123 (Berlin, 1762)

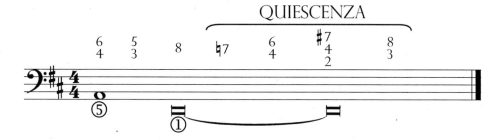

C. P. E. Bach's Quiescenza is unusual only by virtue of its single presentation. In Paris, double presentation had already become the norm. For instance, the passage from Gossec's Requiem mass discussed in chapter 9 featured a Pastorella leading to a strong Mi-Re-Do cadence. Example 13.6 illustrates how Gossec followed that cadence with a double presentation of the Quiescenza. The three staves in the example correspond to the three strata of his Quiescenza. The bottom staff shows the reiterated tonic note in the cellos and basses; the middle staff shows the characteristic chromatic form of the Quiescenza melody in parallel thirds and sixths played by the violins; and the top staff shows the two soprano soloists performing a decorative type of melodic commentary.

EX. 13.6   Gossec, *Missa pro defunctis*, mvt. 15, [Andante], m. 26 (Paris, 1760)

Gossec's memorable passage was written at a time when the Quiescenza was rapidly emerging as a Parisian commonplace. A passage by L'Abbé le Fils (ex. 13.7) appeared in Paris in 1763. L'Abbé uses the diatonic version of the Quiescenza whose four stages feature a four-note melodic ascent from ❺ up to the octave ❶. His diatonic Quiescenza follows a strong cadence signaled by the half-note trill on A5 (❷ in m. 77). The Quiescenza confirms the importance of the preceding cadence and provides a short period of relative stability before the running scale that leads up to a Cudworth cadence and Final Fall.

EX. 13.7   L'Abbé, Opus 8, no. 3, mvt. 1, Allegro, m. 77 (Paris, 1763)

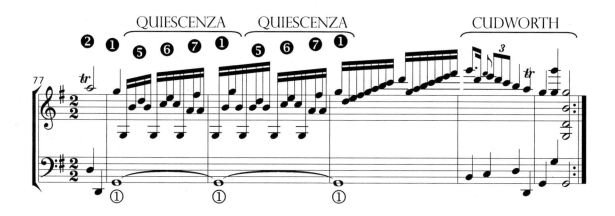

L'Abbé le Fils was, as mentioned, a pupil of Leclair and talented enough as a violinist to perform with the *Wunderkind* Pierre Gaviniés, who was to become a dominant figure in French musical life. Gaviniés approached the Quiescenza much as did L'Abbé, repeating the diatonic version of the schema. In the following example Gaviniés does, however, introduce a brief ♭❼:

EX. 13.8   Gaviniés, Opus 3, no. 5, mvt. 3, Tempo di Minuetto, m. 25 (Paris, 1764)

The galant French violinists produced many of their finest works as "solo sonatas," a misleading term describing duos for violin and continuo. The bass part was frequently unfigured and so required the keyboard player to infer the proper harmonization from the context. This was not always easy. The iterated or tied ① in the bass of a Quiescenza, for example, gave no overt clues to the different chords intended. When, as in example 13.8 by Gaviniés, the violin played double stops that clarify each chord, the keyboard player could have read the harmony from the violin part. But in many other instances that might not be possible. For example, a late solo sonata by Gaviniés includes a Quiescenza that, if the four stages presumably last for one quarter-note each, requires the keyboard player to introduce the ♭❼ and ♮❼ in advance of the violinist. In other words, the accompanist would need to know this "usual scene" beforehand in order to anticipate the harmonies. The version shown below is a likely realization with an added tenor voice. The complete printed tempo indication—*Allegro con fuoco ma non troppo presto*—hints that the work's galant schemata are being pressed into service for a more dynamic, Napoleonic-era musical aesthetic.

EX. 13.9   Gaviniés, *Trois sonates pour le violon*, no. 1, mvt. 3, Allegro . . . , m. 61 (Paris, 1801)

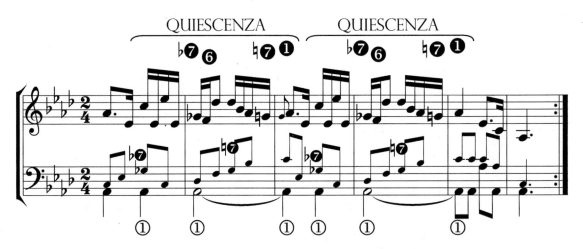

A galant composer could, of course, follow the example of Simon Leduc (*l'aîné*; 1742–1777), a pupil of Gaviniés. Leduc also wrote solo sonatas with unfigured basses, but at the opening of his Opus 4 (1771) he placed the characteristic chromatic line of the Quiescenza in the bass so that the schema could not be missed (see ex. 13.10). The accompanist would still need to infer an inner voice, which could include an iterated ❶ for stages one, two, and four (the third stage—the chord over G♯3—requires a ❷ in place of ❶ because the Quiescenza's unique third-stage sonority of the dominant seventh chord above a tonic pedal is one that often cannot be successfully inverted). Leduc's presentation of a Quiescenza as an opening schema could be viewed either as very modern for its day (1771) or as very old fashioned and in the style of sixty years earlier. I suspect that "very modern"

is the correct assessment, especially since the practice flourished throughout the 1770s and 1780s. In this later period, the use of a Quiescenza to open a movement seems associated with broad, pastoral expositions, and perhaps Leduc's performance indications of *dolce* and *cantabile* support that association.

EX. 13.10   Leduc, Opus 4, no. 1, mvt. 1, Cantabile, m. 1 (Paris, 1771)

It was in Vienna that the Quiescenza became so common as to seem almost a cliché. The string quartets of Johann Wanhal, for example, show a rapid evolution toward the stock form of this schema. During his absence from Vienna for a tour of Italy from 1769 until 1771, Wanhal wrote a set of six quartets that were published in Paris in 1771, the same year as the previous example by Leduc. The closing bars of the first and last movements from his F-major quartet (F6 in the Bryan catalogue) contain two early Quiescenzas:[3]

EX. 13.11   Wanhal, Quartet in F Major (F6), mvt. 1, [Allegro moderato], m. 110 (Paris, 1771)

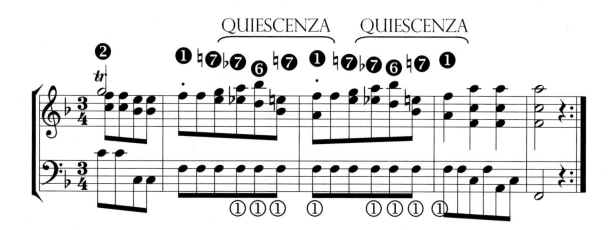

EX. 13.12   Wanhal, Quartet in F Major (F6), mvt. 3, Presto, m. 83 (Paris, 1771)

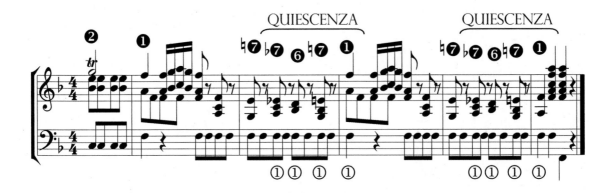

As was common in Paris, a trill on ❷ followed by an iterated bass on ① signals the beginning of Wanhal's early Quiescenzas. Example 13.11 presents the ♭❼-to-❻ dyad in the alto voice instead of in the melody. And both that passage and the very similar one shown in example 13.12 are unusual in having ♮❼ precede ♭❼. One might say that he understood the function and placement of the schema but was either uncertain of or experimenting with the details of the norm.

During the next two years, Wanhal seems to have arrived at a mature understanding of the Quiescenza, whether from actual study or just from his broadened experiences and travels. In 1773, he wrote what became one of his most popular quartets (C1). At the end of its first movement he provided a broad, flowing Quiescenza, one that resembles the diatonic exemplars of L'Abbé le Fils and Gaviniés:

EX. 13.13   Wanhal, Quartet in C Major (C1), mvt. 1, Allegro, m. 163 (1773)

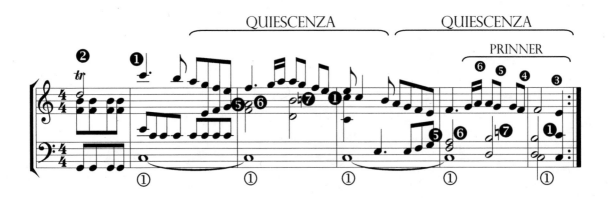

Note that the rising ❺–❻–❼–❶ melody has retreated into the alto voice, leaving the soprano voice—the first violin—to provide melodic commentary, including a small melodic Prinner at the close. Gossec's Requiem (ex. 13.6) had provided an early Parisian model not only for this scoring, but also for the calm mood. For the slow movement of this quartet, Wanhal provided a Quiescenza in the minor mode with the standard pairings of ♭❼-to-❻ and ♮❼-to-❶, modifying the tenor voice to become E♮–F and D–E♭:

EX. 13.14   Wanhal, Quartet in C Major (C1), mvt. 3, Adagio, m. 69 (1773)

The mature forms of the Quiescenza remained a staple in Wanhal's repertory. As a final example of his style, let us look at a G-major quartet written around 1780 (G8). The Quiescenza's ♭❼-to-❻ *proposta* is gently stated by the second violin, and its ♮❼-to-❶ *riposta* politely provided by the first violin's florid melodic commentary:

EX. 13.15   Wanhal, Quartet in G Major (G8), mvt. 4, Adagio, m. 91 (1780)

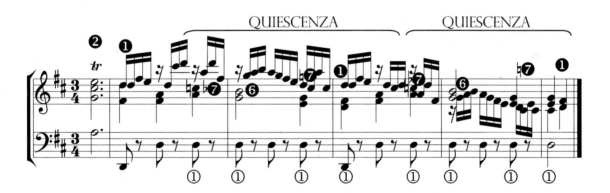

Wanhal's manner of treating the Quiescenza is quite representative of the Viennese scene. For comparison we might look to a protégé of Gluck, Antonio Salieri, who was appointed chamber composer to the imperial court of the Hapsburgs in 1774, the year after the publication of Wanhal's popular C-major quartet. In the first year of his new appointment, Salieri penned a lovely Quiescenza to close the slow movement of a double concerto for flute and oboe in C major (ex. 3.16). The two soloists signal the end of their cadenza with a double trill on ❷ and ❼. The soloists then rest while the strings present the Quiescenza with the cellos setting out the ♭❼–❻ to be answered by the second violins'

♮**❼**–**❶**, all supporting the first violins' discant. A chain of Final Falls, slowing down like an old clock, brings the movement to completion:

EX. 13.16   Salieri, Double Concerto in C Major, mvt. 2, Andante, m. 55 (1774)

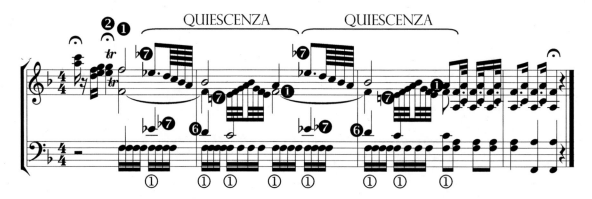

A decade earlier, in 1763, the seven-year-old Mozart had reached Paris on his tour as a child prodigy. In a work copied in his father's hand (and later published in Paris as part of his Opus 2), Mozart wrote his first unmistakable Quiescenza:

EX. 13.17   Mozart, Sonata KV8, mvt. 1, Allegro, m. 63 (1763)

He had already written many small pieces, but his Opus 2 sonatas for Paris, which he scored for keyboard with an optional violin part, were the first of his compositions large

enough to warrant the framing function of the Quiescenza. Everything that one might
expect of a Quiescenza is in place: the ♭❼–❻–♮❼–❶ melody, a tonic pedal point, the
requisite sonorities, double presentation, and location after a major cadence. The figure
of his father, Leopold, looms large over these works, but other manuscripts from this period
in the son's hand suggest that the young Mozart understood the Quiescenza on his own.

Mozart embraced the Quiescenza in subsequent works, of which his mature keyboard sonatas are representative. A set of six sonatas was written in Munich early in 1775,
perhaps with the purpose of impressing the concertmaster Christian Cannabich (1731–
1798), who had studied with Jommelli in Rome. The closing rondo movement of the
sonata in B♭ major (KV189f; ex. 13.18) presents a pair of Quiescenzas, with trilled ❼s that
signal the end of the rondo's first contrasting episode. The same type of simple, direct
Quiescenza also ends the first half of the opening movement of his G-major sonata from
the same set (KV189h; ex. 13.19):

EX. 13.18   Mozart, Sonata KV189f, mvt. 3, Allegro, m. 38 (1775)

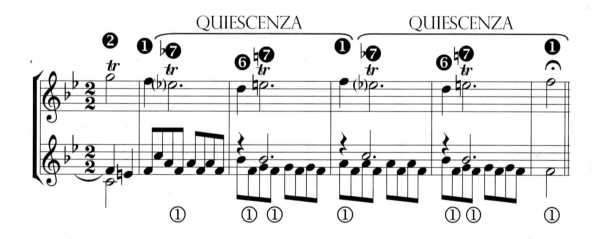

EX. 13.19   Mozart, Sonata KV189h, mvt. 1, Allegro, m. 51 (1775)

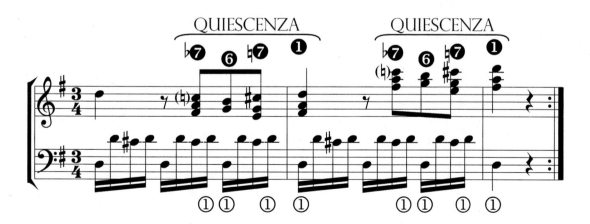

On Mozart's return to Paris in 1778 he wrote an A-minor sonata, KV300d, with a middle movement in F major. Its first half ends with a pair of Quiescenzas that, like contemporary works in Vienna, posit the ♭❼–❻ in an inner voice to be answered by the melody's ♮❼–❶. These Quiescenzas are among Mozart's first without an active bass.

EX. 13.20   Mozart, Sonata KV300d, mvt. 2, Andante cantabile, m. 29 (1778)

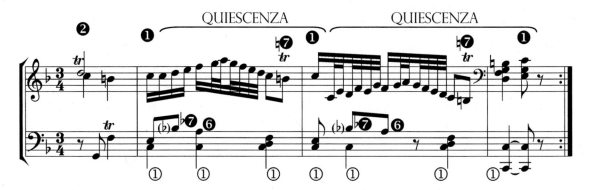

Good examples of Mozart's later style can be found in a B♭-major sonata written in Linz and Vienna between 1783 and 1784 (KV315c). All three movements end with the schema in question. In the first Quiescenza at the end of the sunny first movement, Mozart introduces a patch of darkness with a brief excursion to B♭ minor (note the starred tones D♭ and G♭ in the example below). But that darkness dissipates in the second Quiescenza, which abandons the tonic pedal and substitutes a cadential bass:

EX. 13.21   Mozart, Sonata KV315c, mvt. 1, Allegro, m. 163 (1783–84)

This darker version of the Quiescenza was openly taught by the partimento master Mattei, Mozart's contemporary and someone whom he had probably met in Bologna.[4] The passage quoted here completes a section that is securely in C major, notwithstanding the F-major key signature:

EX. 13.22   Mattei, from his *Piccolo basso*, m. 25 (Bologna, ca. 1780s)

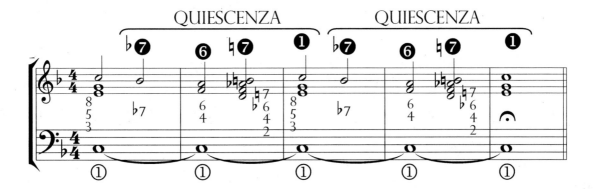

Mattei, a pupil and close associate of the great maestro Padre Martini (1706–1784), would go on to teach Donizetti and Rossini in the first few years of the nineteenth century. That is the same era that saw Beethoven's "Spring" sonata for violin and piano (see ex. 13.23). Both halves of Beethoven's movement conclude with the double presentation of a Quiescenza, preceded by the cue of a trill on ❷ (in the piano part). One finds the exact chordal pattern of Mattei's partimento combined with the Viennese tradition of florid melodic commentary. What sets the first of Beethoven's Quiescenzas apart from those of his predecessors is his apparent violation of a basic precept of galant syntax: one should avoid having both tones of an important dyad sounding simultaneously. In measure 196, for instance, ♭❼ in the piano part (E♭5) still sounds as ❻ enters on the downbeat in the violin part (D4). To be sure, the volume of sound that could be sustained on early pianos was not great, so the piano's tones may have almost died away by the time the violin changes the schematically crucial tone. The decay of keyboard tones would have been even more rapid on the instruments played by Mozart and Haydn, yet it is difficult to imagine them committing quite so bald a violation of galant musical propriety. For Beethoven the piano and violin parts were each internally correct—they merely articulate the shift to the second event of the Quiescenza (❻) at slightly different moments.

Let us give Mozart the last word on the Quiescenza. He concludes the third and final movement of his mature B♭-major sonata (K315c) with a large rondo, whose ending features two broad, epilogue-like statements of a Quiescenza (ex. 13.24). As with the passage from Salieri's double concerto (ex. 13.16), there is a trill on ❷ followed by a tonic close. The melody then sets out the ♭❼, but the direct ♭❼–❻ connection falls to the tenor voice,

EX. 13.23   Beethoven, Opus 24, "Spring," mvt. 1, Allegro, m. 193 (1802)

as in Salieri's example. The melody eventually provides the closing ♮❼–❶, again as in
Salieri's example. But a trait that clearly distinguishes the mature Mozart from Salieri is the
simultaneous presentation of more than one schema. Mozart manages to embed a Fenaroli
(see chap. 16) between the ♭❼–❻ and the ♮❼–❶ of the Quiescenza. The Fenaroli, a schema
often used to increase activity and forward momentum, has that effect here by accelerating
the harmonic rhythm. While the Quiescenza changes chords every measure in this

EX. 13.24   Mozart, Sonata (KV315c), mvt. 3, Allegretto grazioso, m. 212 (1783–84)

example, the embedded Fenaroli alternates dominant and tonic chords every quarter note. Mozart seems to have delighted in this sort of play, and some connoisseurs of his time doubtless found the effect stimulating. But the complexity was not to everyone's taste. We will revisit this problem and the general subject of Mozart's late style in chapters 26 and 30. Chapter 25 will show how a propensity toward a musical *ars combinatoria* was evident even in his earliest works.

14

THE PONTE

ACCORDING TO RIEPEL, the Italian word *monte* meant "a mountain to climb up onto," *fonte* meant "a well to climb down into," and *ponte* meant "a bridge to cross over."[1] I have already discussed the rising pattern of the Monte in chapter 7 and the descending pattern of the Fonte in chapter 4. Here I will discuss Riepel's several interpretations of the "bridge" created by the Ponte.

Riepel's archetypal Ponte, like his Monte and Fonte, can be found immediately following the double bar in a minuet, which would be the ninth measure in Riepel's many minuet examples. As we have seen before, he presented only a melody for his prototype:

EX. 14.1   Riepel, a Ponte melody, to begin at m. 9 in a minuet (1755)

This melody emphasizes the tones of the dominant triad in C major (or possibly the tonic triad in G major) in measures 9 and 10. Descending appoggiaturas in measure 11 help lead the melody down from the High ❷ of D5 to the ❹–❸ of F4 and E4 in measure 12, resulting in a small cadence in the main key of C major.

Any number of basses could accompany this melody. Indeed, the point of Riepel's frequent and extended demonstrations of the *ars combinatoria*—meaning the seemingly infinite variation and recombination of preexisting patterns—was to reinforce the motto that he printed at the end of each of his books: "Music is an inexhaustible sea."[2] From these limitless possibilities I offer the following bass, written in smaller notes to show that it is not by Riepel. While it is just one of many possibilities, this bass is very close to the default case presented in numerous galant minuets:

EX. 14.2   Riepel's prototype of the Ponte melody with a likely bass

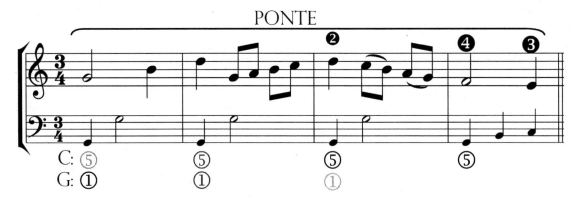

Beneath this score, two separate annotations suggest a fading sense of the bass as ① in the previous context, G major, and a growing sense of the bass as ⑤ in the following context, C major. The same change of tonal orientation is implied in the upper voice. Modulation of this type is implicit rather than explicit, and depends almost entirely on the listener's experience and expectations.

After mastering the basic schemata of the Monte, Fonte, and Ponte, Riepel's student volunteers to try his hand at the *ars combinatoria*. The student begins by exploring variations on the Monte and Fonte. Then he announces his intention "to play around a bit with the Ponte as well."[3] The result is a series of twelve melodic examples. I will present each one in combination with its presumed bass and annotate its pertinent features. The student offered the following melody as his first variation on the Ponte:

EX. 14.3   The student's first Ponte variant

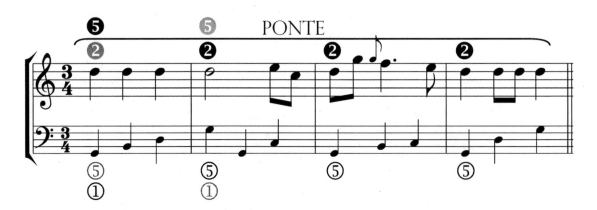

In place of the prototype's rising melodic triads, the student establishes a melodic axis on D5, which is likely perceived as ❺ in G major initially and later as ❷ in C major. He also transfers the harmonic rhythm of the prototype's last measure (a strong dominant chord on the downbeat followed by a weak tonic chord on the third beat) to both measures 10 and 11 of his new Ponte.

In considering the first variant, the student remarks that to avoid having two cadences on the dominant "one after the other"[4] (the first would be the cadence just before the double bar), he would close his second Ponte with a tonic cadence:

EX. 14.4   The student's second Ponte variant

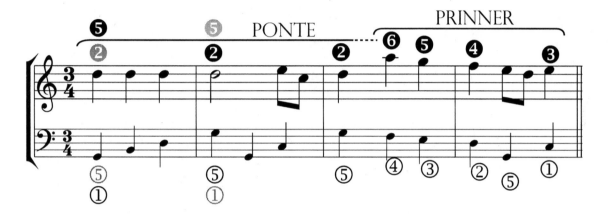

As one can see, the Prinner fit his aims nicely, providing a weak tonic chord on the last beats of measures 11 and 12. The student declares his foregoing example "also good"[5] and promptly proceeds to write a third Ponte:

EX. 14.5   The student's third Ponte variant

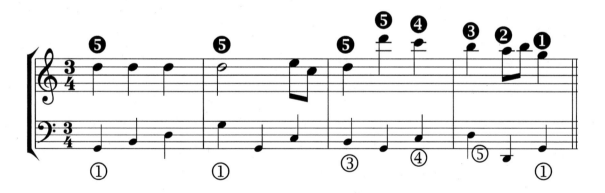

Measures 9 and 10 are identical to the previous example. But in measure 11, the previous melodic leap up a fifth has been extended to a full octave, from whence a stepwise descent leads to a cadence in G major. In evaluating his third Ponte variant, the student admits that it is "not nearly as good as the previous one."[6]

At this point in the dialogue the teacher enters to praise his student's efforts. The student, flattered and encouraged, responds with *nine* more Pontes. Be forewarned that Riepel's concept of "Ponte" becomes more perplexing with each new example. The student's first new phrase, fourth overall, begins with that same emphasis on a repeated D5:

EX. 14.6   The student's fourth Ponte variant

Two important features have changed, however. One is the form—the Ponte's two halves now closely resemble each other, as indicated by the horizontal braces. The other is the harmonic rhythm—it is slower, with weak tonic measures replacing weak tonic beats. Moreover, these two changes will permit an inner voice to iterate ⑤ as an internal pedal point, which will bring the student's fourth Ponte very close to the Fenaroli schema (see chap. 16). Without going into the details of the Fenaroli here, that schema's overall "feel" is often of sequential ascents, frequently in canonic imitation. Riepel's student seems to have that tradition in mind as he proceeds to compose his fifth and sixth Pontes.

For his fifth Ponte, the student now makes the second half of his melody an exact transposition of the first half, which would enable him to form a canon between the soprano and alto voices. Again, only the melody is given in the treatise; the bass and alto parts are my reconstructions of a typical galant texture:

EX. 14.7   The student's fifth Ponte variant

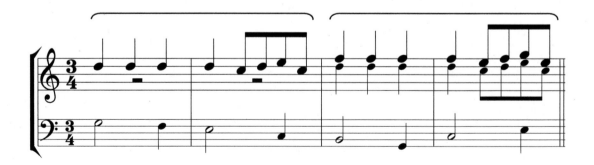

This fifth Ponte sets up a strong expectation for upward motion every two measures at the interval of a third. That is, the melodic ❷ in measure 9 (viewed in C major) leads up to the ❹ in measure 11, which strongly implies a ❻ in measure 13. The student's continuation (ex. 14.8) validates that implication and rises all the way to the octave C6 before descending to the minuet's final cadence in C major:

EX. 14.8   The melodic continuation of the student's fifth Ponte variant

The student's sixth Ponte, with its sequence of three tied notes, looks rather different from the previous two variants. It is, nevertheless, built on the same design:

EX. 14.9   The student's sixth Ponte variant

This sixth Ponte leads into exactly the same continuation and cadence shown earlier for the fifth Ponte. But whereas the student's fifth Ponte had a sequence of ascending *two*-measure modules, his sixth has a sequence of *one*-measure modules. The explicit suspensions of the tied notes and the more obvious and earnest rising sequence suggest some styles of church music. Riepel, as author, has his fictional student propose ever new examples of Pontes. In imagining these new styles, it is quite possible that Riepel needed to think beyond the chamber style of his minuets. If one adds to the above melody a bass similar to those given to the fourth and fifth Pontes, an explicit inner pedal point on ⑤ in the tenor voice, and a series of 2–3 suspensions caused by a sequentially rising alto voice (a Corellian "leapfrog" passage), the resulting four-part texture would not be out of place in a mass or motet by any number of galant chapel masters (ex. 14.10).

EX. 14.10   The student's sixth Ponte variant set in a sacred style

Having perhaps temporarily exhausted the possibilities of the Fenaroli-style Ponte, the student moves on to still other combinations. For his seventh effort, he follows his initial repeated D5 with a tonic version of measure 10 adapted from his teacher's prototype, leading then into another Prinner:

EX. 14.11   The student's seventh Ponte variant

For his eighth Ponte he returns to the idea of a two-measure module:

EX. 14.12   The student's eighth Ponte variant

But instead of single measures alternating between dominant and tonic harmony, he writes two measures of primarily dominant harmony followed by two measures of primarily tonic harmony. Note that measures 11 and 12 now are only one step higher than measures 9 and 10.

Ascending triadic motion on dominant harmony was an important feature of the teacher's prototype (ex. 14.1). The student borrows that idea for his ninth Ponte, but instead of beginning on G4, he begins on his favorite D5, as he has done in all his previous Pontes. The student also reintroduces the prototype's High ❷ Drop and ensuing Comma:

EX. 14.13   The student's ninth Ponte variant

The prototype's implied pedal-point bass on ⑤ (ex. 14.2) would also fit nicely with the ninth Ponte, further strengthening the example's close connection with the teacher's model.

The student then remarks that he could vary the preceding Ponte so that it ends with a half cadence, "depending on whether it pleases or pains the ear."[7] The result is his tenth Ponte:

EX. 14.14   The student's tenth Ponte variant

He follows this with an eleventh Ponte that retains the half cadence (in C major), begins even higher (on G5 instead of D5), presents a Do-Re-Mi opening (in G major), and closely copies the ascending eighth-note scale from the second measure of the teacher's model (see ex. 14.15). Indeed, if one equates Do-Re-Mi as the first three steps of the scale with Do-Mi-Sol as the first three "steps" of the triad, then the first three measures of this Ponte are a very close copy of the teacher's prototype.

EX. 14.15   The student's eleventh Ponte variant

The student's twelfth Ponte begins even higher, on B5, retains echoes of a Do-Re-Mi opening, but shifts the High ❷ Drop earlier to measure 10 and closes with a Prinner:

EX. 14.16   The student's twelfth Ponte variant

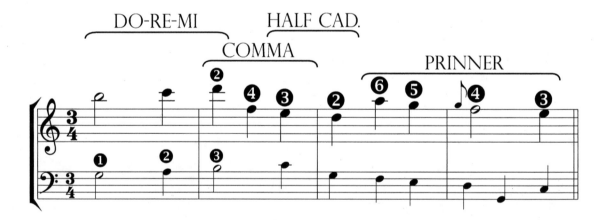

At this point the teacher cries "CEASE!" ("Höre doch auf!").[8] The student, undaunted, offers to write some bad examples in order to demonstrate his ability to distinguish good from bad. Bad Montes and Fontes appear first, followed by one bad Ponte. The examples seem to be judged primarily by whether they repeat, in measure 12, the G cadence that ended the minuet's first half, which is a fault in Riepel's opinion. Here is the "bad" Ponte, whose beginning matches the student's ninth Ponte and whose ending matches his first:

EX. 14.17   The student's "bad" Ponte

Following this deprecated Ponte, the student proposes an example that seems "quite good, notwithstanding the fact that it belongs to neither the Monte nor the Fonte nor the Ponte":[9]

EX. 14.18   The student's melody claimed to be neither Monte, Fonte, nor Ponte

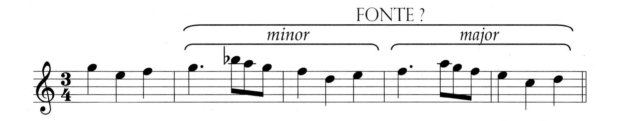

When I first read this passage and saw the example, I fully expected Riepel, in his fictional role as teacher, to interrupt and correct his student. I thought he would tell the student, "Your example begins in the main key but goes on to present a perfect Fonte." But Riepel does not intervene. Instead, the student is allowed to reinforce his assertion by showing how the teacher's three cardinal patterns should properly begin the second half of a minuet. Note that, for a proper Ponte, the student reverts to the prototypical ascent through the tones of the dominant triad:

EX. 14.19   The student's prototypes for beginning a Monte, Fonte, and Ponte

The student goes on to demonstrate that even the introduction of embellishing variations (ex. 14.20) does not detract from the correctness of the way each pattern begins. For the Ponte we see a further emphasis on the tones of the dominant triad.

EX. 14.20   The student's openings for an elaborated Monte, Fonte, and Ponte

The matter rests there for several pages of dialogue. When the student returns again to the Ponte, he writes one that is almost an exact copy of the original minuet's opening theme, transposed to the dominant key:

EX. 14.21   The student's new Ponte

In measures 10 and 11 this Ponte shares with many of the student's "Fenaroli" examples an alternation between strong dominant chords and weak tonic chords. But those earlier examples did not include a melodic F♯, and their phrases, not explicitly "in" G, were instead possibly "on" G. That is, the previous examples began on a G chord in what quickly becomes the context of the key of C major, while this example reinforces the sense of being in the key of G major. One wonders what has become of the "bridge" (It., *ponte*) function.

In a later section on the expansion of phrases, the student reverts once more to a close copy of his teacher's prototype for a point of departure:

EX. 14.22   The student's model for an expandable Ponte

He then expands this phrase through a combination of extensions, repetitions, variations, and insertions:

EX. 14.23 The student's expanded Ponte

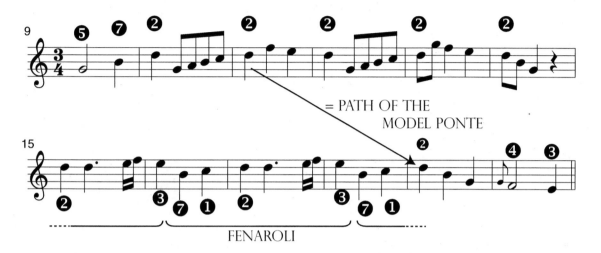

Measures 9 and 10 are unchanged from the model (cf. ex. 14.22). Measure 11 extends the upward motion of measure 10 and leads back to a repetition of measure 10 in measure 12. A further upward extension in measure 13 leads to a half cadence in measure 14. After a brief rest, the student begins anew with a Fenaroli-type Ponte like those he had developed in his first Ponte exercises. He repeats measures 15–16 in measures 17–18 and then closes with the exact High ❷ Drop that ended his model. The expansion and extension remain in C major, not G major.

Much later in the same treatise, the relationship between Ponte and key is given a further twist when the fictional teacher identifies the following phrase as a Ponte:

EX. 14.24 The teacher's Ponte in a minor-mode minuet

The student, perplexed, remarks that this Ponte seems "borrowed from C major,"[10] and the teacher agrees with him. The phrase begins the second half of a small Andante in the key of A minor. In its first half, the movement modulates from A minor to C major. The Ponte, which begins with its trademark ascending triad, then might build a "bridge" from the key of C major back to the main key of A minor. The addition of a bass voice (ex. 14.25) can help to clarify how such a modulation would have been possible.

EX. 14.25   A harmonization of the teacher's minor-mode Ponte

Riepel, unfortunately, does not make clear how he, or his fictional interlocutors, heard that passage. If he heard no modulation, then once again the function of the Ponte as a bridge between keys would be in doubt.

Considered as a group, Riepel's numerous examples of the Ponte seem to represent two principles occasionally at odds with each other. On the one hand, he presents the abstract idea of a bridge that links two keys. The first key occurs just before the real or imagined double bar, and the second key returns at some point during or immediately after the Ponte. In that sense the Ponte has no intrinsic key itself and no necessary structure. Whether a given Ponte is *in* or *on* the dominant would be immaterial as long as its bridging function remained. On the other hand, the great majority of Riepel's Ponte examples strongly emphasize the dominant triad or seventh chord of the main key, often with rising movement. This is especially true in the initial measures.

When, in the next treatise in his series, Riepel begins by reminding the student of the three cardinal patterns, he presents a Ponte that returns to the prototypical emphasis on the tones of the dominant triad or seventh chord. But he also introduces a likely Converging cadence that, while related to the student's examples with closing Prinners, is unique among Riepel's Pontes. I have added a bass to clarify the Converging cadence:

EX. 14.26   The teacher's Ponte in a later chapter

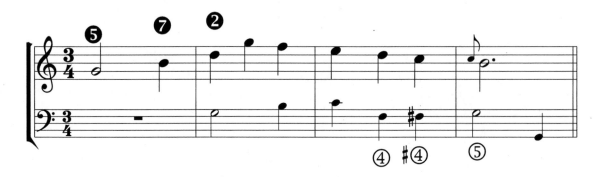

One has the impression that, given Riepel's "inexhaustible" invention, each new presentation of the Ponte would be likely to include some new feature or relationship. When Riepel ventures into his chapter on "deceptive" composition,[11] even the seemingly more stable schemata of the Fonte and Monte begin to dissolve in a deep sea of variation and transformation. At times, it seems that all that remains of a schema is a characteristic opening gesture or cue. That observation, of course, is not without importance for understanding galant music and the categorizations of one of its practitioners. The setting up of musical expectations was crucial, whereas those expectations could be realized, frustrated, delayed, or deflected according to artistic strategies that varied considerably in different locales and contexts. Yet rather than follow Riepel to the far shores of schema dissolution, let us ourselves exclaim "CEASE!" and turn back to examine two small repertories for more empirical evidence concerning Riepel's "three cardinal patterns."

Two Repertories

At the location following the double bar in a minuet or similar movement, how well does Riepel's prescription for a threefold choice of Monte, Fonte, or Ponte conform to actual eighteenth-century practice? To evaluate that question with reference to the first half of the eighteenth century we can turn to our galant Everyman—Wenceslaus Wodiczka. As mentioned in chapter 4, there are five minuet movements distributed among the six sonatas of his Opus 1. Let us take them as our sample of probabilities toward the end of the 1730s.

The first minuet opens in the key of C major and then modulates to G major by measure 8, just as in Riepel's model minuet. In measure 9, following the double bar, Wodiczka writes a clear four-measure Fonte:

EX. 14.27   Wodiczka, Opus 1, no. 2, mvt. 3, Menuetto, m. 9 (Paris, 1739)

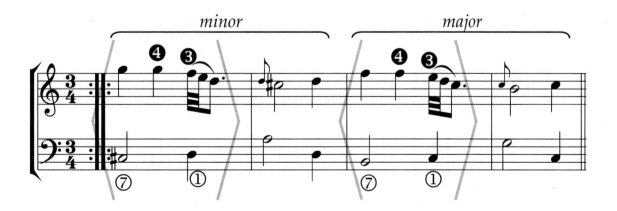

All the features of the common Fonte are present: the opening in D minor, followed "one step lower" by the same passage in C major; the ❹–❸ melodic dyads; the support of two ⑦–① basses, and the characteristic minuet scansion of the dyads crossing the weak metrical boundary between beats two and three.

His third sonata contains two minuets, one in the major mode and one in the minor mode. The first begins in the key of G major and modulates to D major by measure 8. In measure 9, following the double bar, Wodiczka writes a clear four-measure Monte:

EX. 14.28   Wodiczka, Opus 1, no. 3, mvt. 3, Menuetto I, m. 9 (1739)

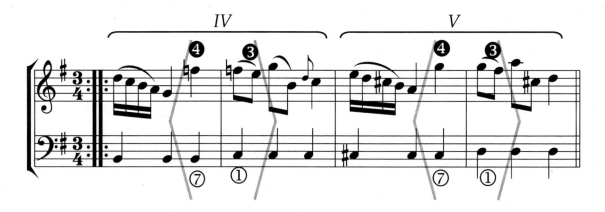

Note that this Monte, with local foci on C major and D major, is highlighting IV and V in the main key of G, not in the immediately prior key of D.

The second of this pair of minuets begins in the relative minor (E minor) and modulates to G major by measure 8. In measure 9, following the double bar, Wodiczka writes an extended eight-measure Fonte:

EX. 14.29   Wodiczka, Opus 1, no. 3, mvt. 3, Menuetto II, m. 9 (1739)

The minor-then-major keys of the Fonte are in relation to the "second" key of G major, not the main key of E minor. Or as Riepel's student would put it, the Fonte is "borrowed" from the major mode.

In Wodiczka's fifth sonata, a minuet begins in the key of A major and modulates to E major by measure 8. In measure 9, following the double bar, Wodiczka writes a clear four-measure Fonte that returns to A major:

EX. 14.30   Wodiczka, Opus 1, no. 5, mvt. 4, Menuetto, m. 9 (1739

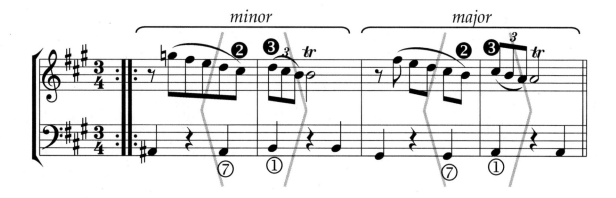

In his final sonata, a minuet begins in the key of F major and modulates to C major by measure 8. In measure 9, following the double bar, Wodiczka writes what I believe Riepel would have considered a Ponte. As with the student's eighth Ponte, this phrase begins with a repeated initial melodic tone that is ❺ in the preceding key and ❷ in the main key:

EX. 14.31   Wodiczka, Opus 1, no. 6, mvt. 3, Menuetto, m. 9 (1739)

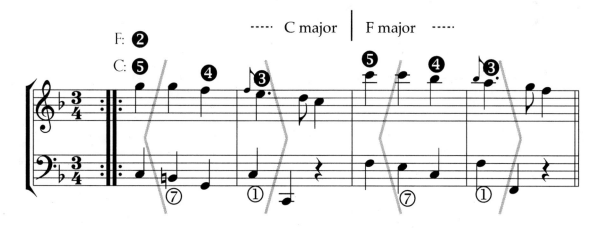

The melody of example 14.31 begins by sounding all the tones of the dominant triad; it features two measures of primarily dominant harmony followed by two measures of primarily tonic harmony; and it forms a bridge between the preceding key of C major and the following main key of F major. Though it is some distance from Riepel's own prototype, this Ponte would seem to validate Riepel's general prescriptions. That is, the choices made by Wodiczka corroborate the utility of Riepel's "threefold example." Moreover, Wodiczka's usage provides a reasonable general estimate for the relative frequency of these schemata in that particular context: there are three Fontes, one Monte, and one Ponte. Wodiczka's phrases also confirm Riepel's notion that a Monte, Fonte, or Ponte should, in a minor-mode movement that modulates to the relative major before the double bar, take its tonal bearings from that relative major key. This is in contrast to a major-mode movement, where these schemata take their tonal bearings from the main key of the movement. In galant music, "major" became the norm and the standard of reference.

To evaluate the situation in the second half of the eighteenth century we should perhaps look to a more mature and cosmopolitan composer for a sample repertory. In a letter to the Baron d'Hermenches, her secret male correspondent, Isabelle de Charrière asked him to obtain some music for her. "What I especially love are fine trios or quartets in the style of Campioni and Pugnani."[12] Even today these works can be difficult to obtain. But Gaetano Pugnani (1731–1798), an important pupil of Somis who became famous in both Paris and London, did write a set of violin sonatas during the later 1760s or early 1770s that have been reprinted, and they contain a number of movements that are like minuets in form and style (though titled *Amoroso* or *Andante esprezzo*).

In Pugnani's second sonata, an Amoroso begins in the key of C major and remains in C major through measure 8. In measure 9, following the double bar, Pugnani writes a clear four-measure Prinner with a High ❷ Drop:

EX. 14.32   Pugnani, Opus 8, no. 2, mvt. 3, Amoroso, m. 9 (Amsterdam, ca. 1771–74)

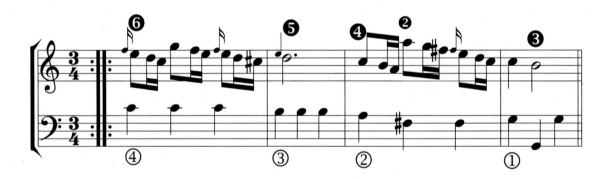

Can a modulating Prinner be considered a Ponte? The phrase bears scant resemblance to Riepel's prototype Ponte, though the student's Pontes did include smaller Prinners.[13] Yet this modulating Prinner does serve as a bridge from the previous key, C major, to the new key that follows, G major. Of course the situation where the first half of a movement does not modulate is one that Riepel had never envisioned.

In Pugnani's third sonata (ex. 14.33), an Amoroso begins in the key of D major and modulates to A major by measure 16. In measure 17, following the double bar, Pugnani writes two four-measure statements of a Ponte, though not of a type specifically notated by Riepel. Its two phrases are definitely *on* the dominant chord of D major, with a drumlike pedal point on ⑤, an alternation of tonic and dominant measures, and a melody that descends from ❺ to ❷. This eight-measure Ponte corresponds to the larger dimensions of this Amoroso, whose double bar, as noted, does not appear until the end of measure 16.

EX. 14.33   Pugnani, Opus 8, no. 3, mvt. 3, Amoroso, m. 17 (ca. 1771–74)

In Pugnani's fourth sonata (ex. 14.34), an Amoroso begins in the key of E major and modulates to B major by measure 8. In measure 9, following the double bar, Pugnani writes a four-measure Fonte with the typical melodic descents of ❻–❺–❹–❸:

EX. 14.34   Pugnani, Opus 8, no. 4, mvt. 3, Amoroso, m. 9 (ca. 1771–74)

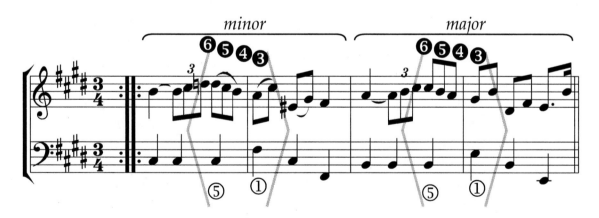

His fifth sonata (ex. 14.35) presents an Andante esprezzo instead of an Amoroso. The movement stays in the key of A major for the first twenty-four measures. In measure 25, following the double bar, Pugnani writes an ornate four-measure modulating Prinner complete with the *la*-to-*sol* flourish and an ornate extension of the High ❷ Drop.

EX. 14.35   Pugnani, Opus 8, no. 5, mvt. 3, Andante esprezzo, m. 25 (ca. 1771–74)

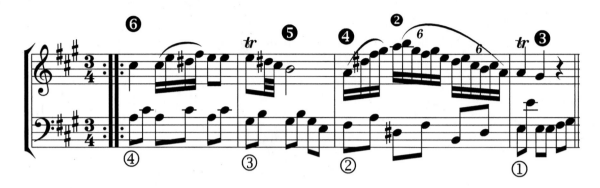

In his sixth and final sonata, Pugnani reinstates an Amoroso. The movement begins in the key of B♭ major and modulates to F major by measure 11 (Riepel would have objected to the odd number). In measure 12, following the double bar, Pugnani writes a hermaphrodite Fonte (note the starred flat), with the normal roles of bass and soprano inverted:

EX. 14.36   Pugnani, Opus 8, no. 6, mvt. 3, Amoroso, m. 12 (ca. 1771–74)

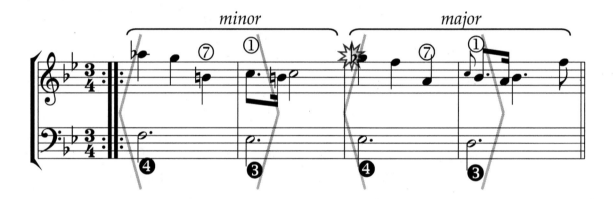

In this small repertory, Pugnani does not use the Monte. Indeed, by the 1770s the Monte was showing its age, with Riepel and others mentioning its possibly pejorative nickname "cobbler's patch" (*Schusterfleck*).[14] Pugnani does use the Fonte in its more colorful guise, and he does use the Ponte, at least once. But whether one also ought to think of Pugnani's modulating Prinners as Pontes depends on how one interprets Riepel. If one favors Riepel's most abstract notion of a bridge, then these Prinners do function as bridges between keys. If one favors Riepel's prototypes as his true intention, then a Prinner is a Prinner, not a Ponte.

I have presented so many instances of the Ponte not so much because of its intrinsic importance—it usually fulfills a subservient role—but because of the light it sheds on faultlines in Riepel's discourse, between viewing a phrase in terms of what it *does* and viewing it in terms of what it *is*, however that might be defined. As mentioned before, Riepel and other eighteenth-century music scholars had difficulty conceiving of a phrase as a composite of other patterns. His preference was to describe a phrase as a unitary Ponte, rather than as, say, "a triadic ascent on tones of the dominant triad followed by reference to the Fenaroli, leading to a High ❷ Drop and a tonic cadence." Nevertheless, the examples by Wodiczka and Pugnani show that, for much of the eighteenth century, Riepel's "threefold example" of Monte, Fonte, and Ponte was very much on target as a description of general practice within a specific musical context. Because Riepel's experiences were concentrated in the earlier part of the eighteenth century, it is hardly surprising that his schemata—his abstractions of those experiences—fit the earlier Wodiczka somewhat better than the later Pugnani. If Monte and Fonte have their roles and construction tightly bound together, the Ponte, as described through the voices of Riepel's idealized teacher and student, shows that different constructions can serve the same role. In keeping with the general approach of this book, I will favor structure, labeling as "Ponte" those phrases that highlight a dominant pedal point and the tones of the dominant triad or seventh chord. Yet as we will see in the following chapter, where Galuppi introduces a tonic Ponte, the structural emphasis can at times oversimplify actual practice. Such cases help us to appreciate Riepel's dilemma as a writer on galant practice and to value his prolix but rich explication of what he held to be a schema of great significance. His inventory of Pontes, whether or not one believes them to fit a single schema, constitutes the largest corpus of phrases to have been categorized by an eighteenth-century musician. That he was a successful, long-serving *maestro di capella* at one of the wealthiest courts in Europe gives his opinions added weight.

15

A GRAVE SOSTENUTO

BY

BALDASSARE GALUPPI

Concerto a quattro, B♭ Major, mvt. 1, Venice, ca. 1750s

HAD THERE BEEN OPINION POLLS IN THE EIGHTEENTH CENTURY, Baldassare Galuppi (1706–1785) would have been among the most frequently named as "greatest composer." Not only were his operas and sacred works tremendously popular, but he enjoyed great esteem among musicians owing to the obvious high quality of his work. For over forty years the great courts of Europe vied for the services of the lauded chapel master of St. Mark's in Venice, and young musicians everywhere carefully studied his scores. How then did it come about that Galuppi's music is known today only to specialists and antiquarians?

Part of the problem may be the lack of a complete edition of Galuppi's works. Many of his greatest compositions exist only in manuscript. And part of the problem may also be that some of the genres in which he excelled—*opera seria* and sacred motets—were themselves eclipsed by newer genres like the symphony and the string quartet. But I believe the central problem is that while Galuppi's art rewards the listener who knows and enjoys galant schemata, it frustrates the listener who wants an experience more in line with Romantic musical values. A case in point may be the opening slow movement of Galuppi's *Concerto a quattro* in B♭ major. Galuppi's movement, still unpublished, derives from an arcane genre that predates the string quartet. For an impatient listener, this music may seem to go nowhere. And yet for the devotee of galant music, it contains in abundance what Galuppi himself described as the hallmarks of musical excellence: "beauty, clarity, and fine modulation" ("vaghezza, chiarezza, e buona modulazione"). I take *modulazione* in the older sense of the flow of melody, the smooth connection of schemata, and the pacing of events.[1]

The list below lays out an expansive, frequently digressive movement employing many different schemata. They are generally presented with such *chiarezza* (clarity) that the reader may wish to test his or her knowledge of galant schemata by first listening to the movement without looking at the score provided here. The very slow tempo of this movement makes it experientially long even without the repetition of each half, although the order of schemata conforms to what would be found in a double-reprise movement. Were each half to be repeated, the double bar would have been placed in the neighborhood of measure 31. The movement's tonal design is quite flexible and aligned with the older practice of touching on most of the "tones" in the hexachord. That is, in the chart's third column, you will find the names of all six tones of the hexachord on B♭: B♭, C, D, E♭, F, and G.

Section	Schema	Key
1st Half	Meyer	B♭
	Prinner	B♭
	Fonte	Fm ⇨ E♭
	Fonte	Cm ⇨ B♭
	Prinner, modulating	B♭ ⇨ F
	Fonte	Cm ⇨ B♭
	Monte, diatonic	B♭ ⇨ F
	Clausula Vera	C
	Ponte	F
	Cudworth	F
	Quiescenza, diatonic, *bis*	F

(𝄆 𝄇)

2nd Half	Quiescenza, diatonic, *bis*	B♭
	Monte	Cm ⇨ D
	Ponte	Gm
	Cudworth	Gm
	Clausula Vera	F
	Meyer	B♭
	Ponte, tonic	B♭
	Monte/Converging cad.	E♭ ⇨ F
	Fonte	Cm ⇨ B♭
	Fonte	Fm ⇨ E♭
	Monte, diatonic	F ⇨ B♭
	Clausula Vera	F
	Ponte	B♭
	Cudworth, deceptive	B♭
	Cadence, Mi-Re-Do	B♭

𝄇

Even though the bulk of this movement contains the most common schemata of the galant style presented in almost prototypical fashion, some passages are "custom tailored." The fact that I place no brackets or labels over a measure or two does not mean that the passage is in any way inferior. It means only that for one or two measures Galuppi may have gone beyond the simplest types of schemata, may have reverted to a more note-to-note contrapuntal style, or may have blended schemata in ways that defy easy categorization. My goal is not to replace the tyrannies of modern musical analysis with a tyranny of galant schemata. Not everything was taken "off the shelf," and many passages remain sui generis even if one has broad experience with this music. While I believe that the recognizing and savoring of common schemata was part of the galant patron's aesthetic experience, I would never claim that it was all of that experience.

The score presented in example 15.1 is a reduction and adaptation of a recorded performance given by the Quartetto Aglàia.[2] Many galant slow movements, whether preserved in scores or in individual vocal or instrumental parts, give a bare-bones impression on the page that is quite misleading. The written music was intended merely as a working script to be elaborated and embellished in the act of performance by talented artists.

EX. 15.1   Galuppi, *Concerto a quattro* in B♭ Major, mvt. 1, Grave sostenuto (ca. 1750s)

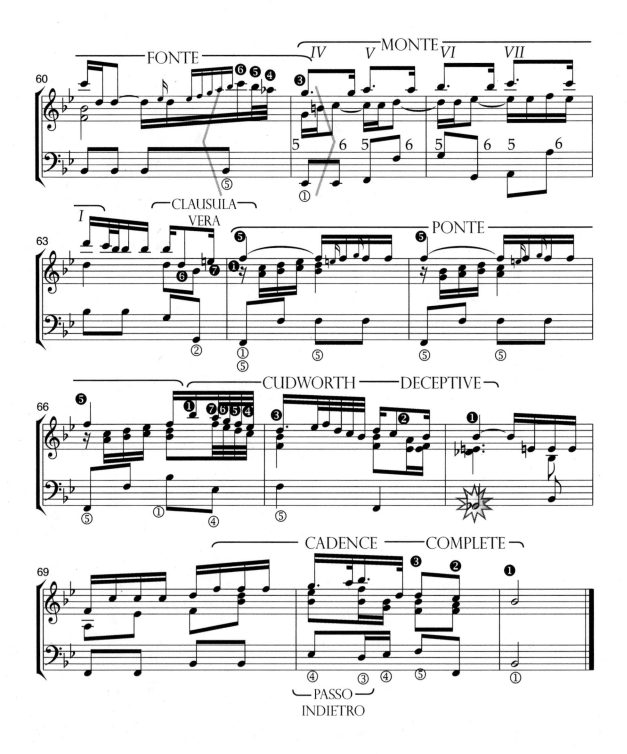

16

THE FENAROLI

TWO OF THE EARLY NEAPOLITAN MASTERS OF THE GALANT STYLE, Francesco
Durante and Leonardo Leo, were viewed by later generations of Italian musicians as having
established important artistic lineages. Conservatory lore in Naples described two camps—
the *Durantisti* and *Leisti*[1]—with different approaches to the art of composition. Modern
scholars, however, have found it difficult to substantiate this divide.[2] Perhaps the relevant
eighteenth-century distinctions were contingent on very specific contexts. That is, perhaps
they represented conflicting preferences for how to handle the details of a given schema.

In his *Sei Sonate per cembalo divisi in studii e divertimenti* (ca. 1747–49), Durante
included the following canon at the octave in C minor:

EX. 16.1   Durante, *Studio* no. 1, mvt. 1, m. 1 (ca. 1747)

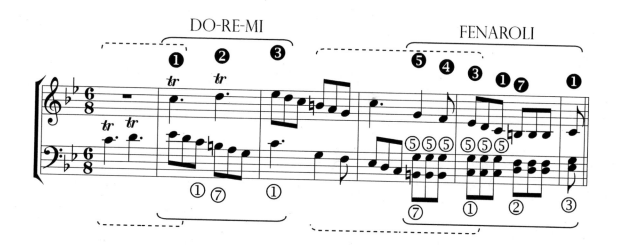

The canon begins with a Do-Re-Mi (dotted horizontal braces indicate the bass as *dux* or leader, anticipating the treble as *comes* or follower). Then, in the second half of the fourth measure, where a third voice enters by repeating the dominant ⑤, the two outer voices combine in a pattern that coalesced as a popular schema. The rising scale ⑦–①–②–③ in the bass is a crucial feature, but the upper voice's descending ❺–❹–❸–❶–❼–❶ is also important as a countermelody. Also worth noting are (1) the sense of one voice chasing another, guaranteed by the canon, and (2) the anchor provided by the repeated ⑤s.

Durante's importance as a font of galant tradition stems in part from his widely admired sacred works, in part from his many partimenti, and in part from the enormous pedagogical reputation of his student Fedele Fenaroli (1730–1818). Fenaroli wrote *the* famous collection of partimenti that, after about 1790, was used by generations of Italian and French musicians. As late as 1871, Fenaroli's partimenti received praise from no less a figure than Giuseppe Verdi.[3] Fenaroli thus served as a bridge between the eighteenth and nineteenth centuries, passing on the Neapolitan repertory of galant schemata. To recognize his role in the inculcation and transmission of this important tradition, I call the above schema "the Fenaroli."

The twenty-eighth of Durante's fifty-seven *partimenti numerati*, or "figured" partimenti, opens with a twofold presentation of this Fenaroli schema (ex. 16.2). The bass staff shows Durante's partimento, and the treble staff, in smaller notes, shows my conjectured realization. The repeated ⑤s of example 16.1 are replaced in example 16.2 with a pedal point in the soprano (F5). Durante's countermelody in example 16.1 is replaced with a canonic countermelody that lags behind the bass by two tones:

EX. 16.2   Durante, *partimenti numerati*, no. 28, m. 1 (Naples, ca. 1730s–40s)

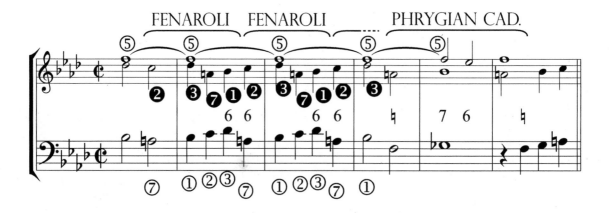

J. S. Bach, Durante's contemporary, was aware of the Neapolitan's music and his high status. Bach had even copied one of Durante's masses for his own use (BWV Anh 26, 1727). In Bach's sonata for flute and harpsichord (BWV 1030) we can recognize a similar twofold presentation of the Fenaroli schema (ex. 16.3). Bach places the repeated ⑤s in the sustained tones of the flute. He employs the same type of canonic countermelody, though animated in sixteenth notes that leap between the tenor and alto ranges. The leap down from ❷ to ❹–❸ is the much favored High ❷ Drop.

EX. 16.3   J. S. Bach, flute sonata, BWV 1030, mvt. 1, Andante, m. 1 (Leipzig, ca. 1736)

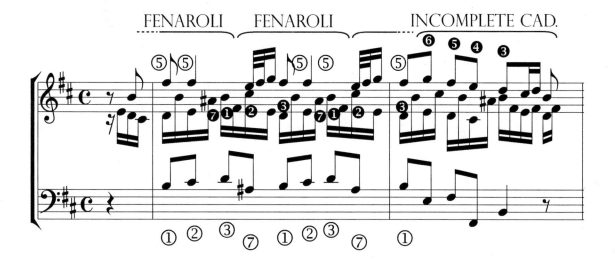

Durante's student Fenaroli wrote his own partimenti, originally in manuscript and then printed (ca. 1800) and reprinted for more than a century as a set of six books (*libri*). Though based on Durante's models, Fenaroli's partimenti were organized more like a modern textbook. That is, they start simply but become increasingly difficult as one advances through the collection. The first book treats the harmonization of ascending and descending scales in whole notes, guided by the "Rule of the Octave,"[4] and includes the "simple," "compound," and "double" cadences (see chap. 11). The second book introduces more musically representative basses of medium difficulty, still provided with some thoroughbass figures. Example 16.4 presents the twelfth partimento from the second book (the annotations are mine, the figures Fenaroli's). Note that, for a younger composer like Fenaroli, the Fenaroli schema was no longer used as an opening gambit.

All the components of a small movement—a minuet, for instance—are present in this partimento. An opening schema of some type begins the movement in the key of E minor, with a following cadence played twice (the "ABB" form common to opening themes from the 1740s and 1750s, more Durante's era than Fenaroli's).[5] Then in measure 6 a modulation to the key of G major leads in measure 8 to two statements of a Fenaroli. The half note G3 in measure 12 ends the first half of the movement where, were it a minuet, one would find the double bar (the double bar line shown above the staff following measure 12 is not present in the partimento).

EX. 16.4   Fenaroli, *Partimenti*, book 2, no. 12 (ca. 1770s?)

As Riepel might have predicted, a Fonte begins the second half of the movement, followed by a Monte in measure 17 that climbs to the main key of E minor. In measure 20 there begins the first of two statements of the Fenaroli in E minor. They lead to the cadence and final half note on E3 in measure 25, ending the second half of the movement. In terms of a nineteenth-century notion of sonata form, the Fenaroli would be the "second theme," which occurs first in the "second key" and then is later transposed back to the main key. What Joel Lester described as the cyclical quality of "second themes,"[6] with their regular alternation between tonic and dominant chords, is perhaps due, at least in part, to the legacy of the many Fenarolis used in that location.

    In attempting to reconstruct the full polyphonic fabric of the Fenarolis in example 16.4, we could begin with the fact that the pedal point on ⑤ is already written into the bass part as a second "voice" (the repeated D3s). For a third voice, we could use the descending countermelody of Durante (cf. ex. 16.1), or we could choose to imitate, in canon, the rising scale in the bass. Were we to investigate Durante's many manscripts of solfeggi, we would see that he himself had already set a pattern quite similar to the above Fenarolis as a canon for bass voice and partimento. The voice leads and the partimento follows (the local key is G major, in spite of the D-major key signature):

EX. 16.5   Durante, *Solfeggi*, Noseda Collection, MS F.42, p. 93, m. 3 (ca. 1740s)

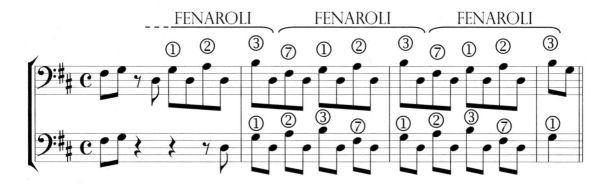

The Fenaroli schema seems to have been easily incorporated into other, larger patterns. For example, in the eighteenth partimento of the same book, Fenaroli presents the descending Durante countermelody (cf. ex. 16.1) in each half of a large Fonte, with the Fenaroli melody to be inferred by the student:

EX. 16.6   Fenaroli, *Partimenti*, book 2, no. 18, m. 45 (ca. 1770s?)

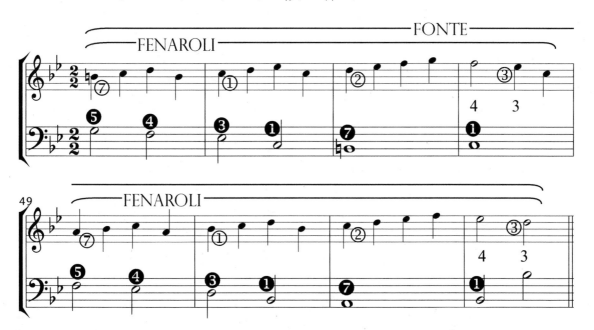

Fenaroli's reputation as a teacher was ensured by the success of his students, among them Domenico Cimarosa and Niccolò Zingarelli, who was mentioned in chapter 3 as a teacher of Isabelle de Charrière and Bellini. Cimarosa worked in illustrious circles. For various high courtiers he composed many small keyboard works that are almost ideal realizations of the schemata sketched in the partimenti of Durante and Fenaroli. Cimarosa seems to have preferred setting the descending Durante countermelody in the bass when employing the Fenaroli schema:

EX. 16.7   Cimarosa, Sonata C24, m. 8 (ca. 1780s)

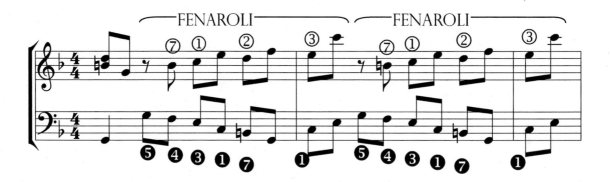

The above excerpt, from a sonata in F major, presents the two Fenaroli's in the "second key" of C major. Like his teacher, he could also set a Fenaroli in each half of a Fonte:

EX. 16.8   Cimarosa, Sonata C51, Allegro, m. 19 (ca. 1780s)

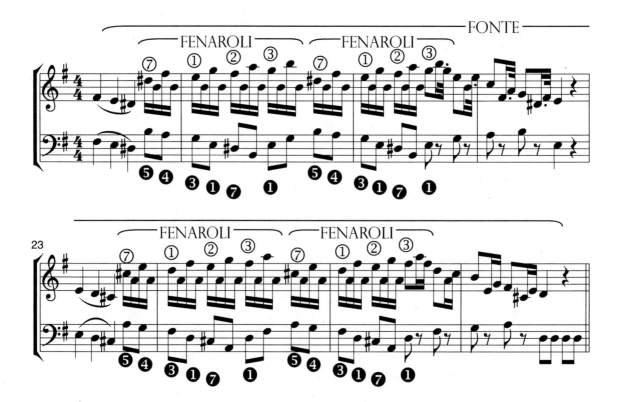

Note the double presentation of the Fenaroli, first twice in minor and then twice in major. Cimarosa follows the tradition of Durante and Fenaroli by interleaving tones of the Fenaroli melody with tones of the dominant pedal (the B4 sixteenth notes), and he includes his personal touch of adding a third above each of the core tones of the Fenaroli, as he did with the Do-Re-Mi (cf. ex. 6.8).

Cimarosa could also set a Fenaroli in each half of a Monte, in this case choosing only a single presentation before the rising modulation:

EX. 16.9   Cimarosa, Sonata C31, Allegro, m. 40 (ca. 1780s)

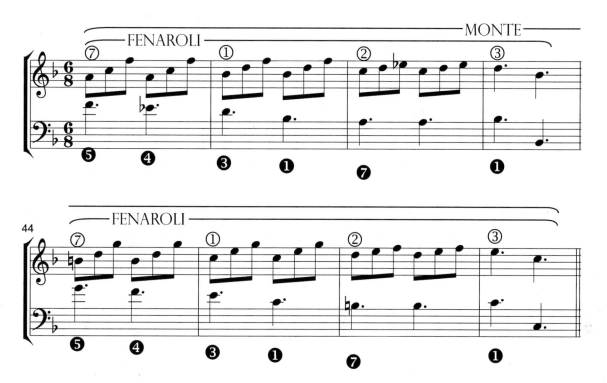

As these examples confirm, Cimarosa preferred to write a Fenaroli with the descending Durante countermelody as the bass. Even if he reduced the countermelody to its bare essentials, ❹–❸–❼–❶, Cimarosa would still set it in the bass voice, as shown in example 16.10. Notice that he gives reiterated pedal points on ⑤ to both the tenor and the soprano voices.

Giovanni Paisiello studied with Durante the year before the master's death in 1755. Much later, during Paisiello's tenure at the court of Catherine the Great of Russia, he published a collection of partimenti (1782) dedicated to the future Tsarina Maria Feodorovna, then Grand Duchess of All the Russias.[7] In example 16.11 I have provided an extended excerpt from the middle of one of Paisiello's more advanced partimenti. It presents the Fenaroli six times in succession, the first three in a sequence of descending thirds and the last three in a sequence of descending fifths. I have marked the probable entry of

EX. 16.10   Cimarosa, Sonata C57, Allegro, m. 18 (ca. 1780s)

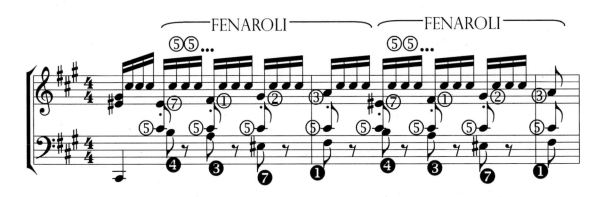

each of the six Fenarolis and indicated the relevant scale degrees. Save for a "♯4" and *"Imitazione"* in measure 26, the original partimento was devoid of words or figures:

EX. 16.11   Paisiello, *Regole*, p. 36, m. 20 (St. Petersburg, 1782)

In the tradition of partimenti, "*imitazione*" was a hint to set a recent motif—here presumably the Fenaroli sixteenth notes—against the written bass. The thoroughbass "♯4" meant that an E♮ should sound above the B♭ in the bass. A third clue is given by the rapid leapfrogging between soprano and bass clefs, signaling the entry of a high voice, most likely the pedal point ⑤. With those clues, and a knowledge of the Fenaroli schema, a three-voice realization of the partimento becomes possible:

EX. 16.12   A realization of Paisiello's partimento from example 16.11

Understanding this schema dramatically simplifies the task of realizing the partimento. Instead of deciding on 106 voice-pairings above 106 separate bass notes, one can focus on choosing appropriate registers for the pedal point and the countermelody of each Fenaroli. Worth noting is the elegant way that Paisiello manages to incorporate both the Durante countermelody and a canon in each of the Fenaroli's six presentations.

Paisiello seems to have been more comfortable with setting the Fenaroli bass in the bass voice than was Cimarosa. One account of technical differences between the Durantisti and Leisti concerned whether or not one should treat the interval of a fourth above the second degree of the scale as a consonance.[8] In the key of C major, that would allow a G above a bass D, as for example when continuo players freely added G to a plain "6/3" chord above ②. For the Fenaroli schema, this type of fourth could occur at its third stage if the bass sounds ② while an inner or upper part sounds the pedal point's ⑤. Perhaps a composer like Cimarosa represented one camp in preferring to avoid that interval of a fourth by placing the "bass" in the treble range, while Paisiello represented the other camp by being willing to treat that fourth as a type of consonance. The idea that these two preferences might not depend solely on who studied with whom could help explain why attempts to tie lineages of students to different styles have proven difficult. Comparing two distinct practices within the context of a single schema does help to bring out differences between what, at a distance of two and a half centuries, sound like very similar styles. As with Jonathan Swift's eighteenth-century description of the "schism" between Lilliput and Blefuscu over table manners,[9] the technical distinctions between imagined Durantist and Leist practices may come down to some very small things. Still, small things can matter. When Riepel, writing in the Bavarian city of Regensburg, wished to make a point about an acceptable use of a fourth, one sanctioned by "several famous maestros," he presented a canonic Fenaroli (repeated) and marked that very interval—part of what harmony texts call a "passing" 6/4—with a Maltese cross:[10]

EX. 16.13   Riepel, from a discussion of an allowable fourth (1757)

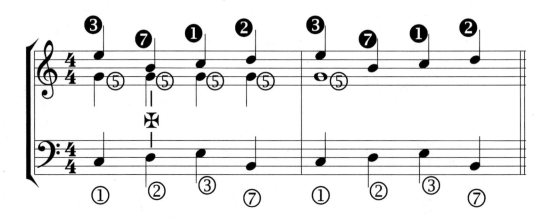

Whether for a Durantista, a Leista, or a galant musician far removed from the Italian scene, a schema like the Fenaroli was so well known and overlearned that either of its outer voices could act as a cue for the other. In one of the many compositional exercises that he wrote in the *zibaldone* of his pupil Barbara Ployer, Mozart provided the following melodic cue:

EX. 16.14   Mozart, an assignment for Barbara Ployer, p. 41 [mod. ed.], m. 6 (1785–91)

Ployer, who was among Mozart's most talented pupils, seems to have recognized a common variant of the Fenaroli bass, ⑦–①–④–③, in the first four half-notes of her assignment. She responded by adding a note-perfect Durante countermelody that leads smoothly into a Converging cadence:

EX. 16.15   Ployer, completion of Mozart's assignment, p. 41 [mod. ed.], m. 6 (1785–91)

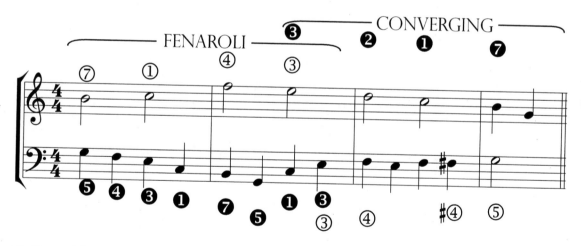

Had her task been one solely of "harmonizing" the melody, any of a hundred basses might have resulted. Instead, she recognized or intuited the schematic contexts and responded with one of the handful of solutions that would demonstrate her fluency in the galant style. In the courtly sense, her musical behavior was impeccable.

To be sure, the young Ployer had one of the supreme galant stylists for a maestro. Mozart, when eight or nine years old in London (1764–65), had been set a similar task. The report of Daines Barrington (1769) states that "he had a thorough knowledge of the fundamental principles of composition, as, upon producing a treble, he immediately wrote a base under it, which, when tried, had very good effect."[11] During the 1780s, the time of Ployer's apprenticeship, Mozart continued to pass on, through his teaching and through the examples of his own compositions, the "fundamental principles" of galant composition. Take, for instance, the following excerpt from one of his late "Prussian" string quartets, KV575:[12]

EX. 16.16   Mozart, String Quartet, KV575, mvt. 3, Trio, Allegretto, m. 12 (Vienna, 1789)

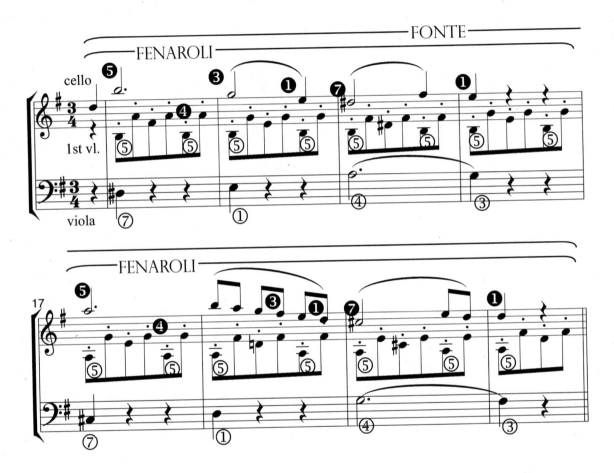

Its location is just after the double bar in the Trio, where Mozart provides the typical Fonte schema. In each half he embeds a Fenaroli with the variant bass, ⑦–①–④–③. A simplified version of the Durante countermelody is obvious in the minor-mode section (mm. 13–16), and a florid variant of that countermelody can be discerned in the major-mode section (mm. 17–20). Choosing to make this a Trio in the old meaning of the word, he wrote only three voices: (1) the Fenaroli bass played in the low register of the viola, (2) the Durante countermelody played in the high register of the cello (shown, for visual clarity, an octave higher than it sounds), and (3) a busy, staccato inner voice, played by the first violin, that provides both the pedal point on ⑤ and the broken-chord or tremolo figuration typical of the Fenaroli. We earlier saw the Fenaroli schema embedded within a Fonte in example 16.8 by Cimarosa. Fenaroli himself was teaching this combination of schemata (cf. ex. 16.6), and the same combination of patterns occurs in the famous opera *La buona figliuola* (1760) by Durante's favorite student, Niccolò Piccinni (1728–1800) (see ex. 25.9). Mozart's practice is thus almost indistinguishable from that of the best-known representatives of the Neapolitan conservatories. On the small but telling point of how to treat the fourth above ② — a reputed Durantist/Leist fault line — Mozart deftly avoided the problem by substituting ④ for ② (m. 15).

It has never been difficult to imagine Mozart — who signed his name on early works as "Signore Wolfgango Mozart," who proudly wore the pontifical decoration *Cavaliere dello Sperone d'Oro* (Knight of the Golden Spur), who was a member of the Bolognese Academica Filarmonica, and who was a master of both *opera seria* and *opera buffa* — as a composer of "the Italian school." The same cannot be said of Beethoven. Generations of biographers have depicted him as so archetypically *the* German musician that his deep roots in the Italian galant style have been easy to overlook. Even a cursory description of his complex development as a composer would go far beyond the scope of this volume. But perhaps a single example from an early piano sonata can suggest how faithfully he had absorbed the traditions of the galant schemata, even as he was dilating and dramatizing them in unexpected ways.

Before turning the page to view this example, imagine if you will the choices that a galant composer might consider for a transition to the "second key" of an Adagio in the major mode. If the movement were planned to be expansive, a direct modulation through the modulating Prinner might be too rapid. One might instead arrange for a digression by way of a Fonte. Then a cadence on the dominant of the new key could be tantalizingly stretched out through a Ponte. For the "second theme" itself, two presentations of the Fenaroli could suffice if they were set forth broadly enough to match an expansive opening theme. The second presentation could then have the customary addition of some melodic embellishments. The preceding commentary in fact describes the slow movement of Beethoven's piano sonata Opus 10, no. 1 (see ex. 16.17). As commonly played today, the example lasts almost a full minute, with as much as seven or eight seconds between the stages of the Fonte (approaching the practical limits of short-term memory). One can almost imagine characters from the commedia dell'arte slowed down into living statuary.

Still more complex were the relationships between the first generation of avowedly Romantic composers and a repertory of galant practices that formed a significant part of their musical heritage. Galant practices remained vital for quite some time in Italy, France, and Eastern Europe (Italian masters had been brought to St. Petersburg and other eastern capitals in the eighteenth century, and the careers of their students stretched well into the nineteenth century). In opera, partimento-trained Italian composers like Bellini, Donizetti, Rossini, and Spontini dominated the scene. Their influence on the melodic style of someone like Fryderyk Chopin (1810–1849) was obvious at the time. Franz Liszt (or his consort Princess Carolyne von Sayn-Wittgenstein), commenting on the operatic sources of

EX. 16.17   Beethoven, Opus 10, no. 1, mvt. 2, Molto adagio, m. 17 (Vienna, ca. 1795–97)

Chopin's highly decorative melodies, wrote that "he gave to this type of ornament, origi-
nating solely in the *fioritures* of the great and venerated school of Italian song, the ele-

ments of surprise and variety beyond the capacity of the human voice which, until then, had been slavishly imitated by the piano in stereotyped and monotonous decoration."[13] Liszt's use of the word "stereotyped" is characteristic of a Romantic rhetorical disdain for past formalisms. Yet consider this example from Chopin's arch-Romantic Scherzo No. 2:

EX. 16.18   Chopin, Opus 31, Scherzo No. 2, Sostenuto, m. 306 (Paris, 1837)

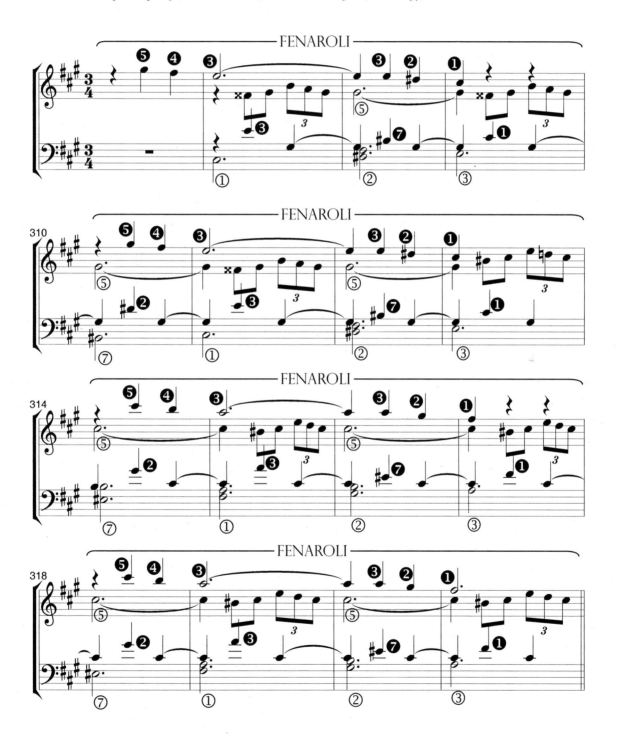

Obviously the negotiations and accommodations of Liszt's generation vis-à-vis galant tradition could be more involved than their rhetoric might suggest. The above example from Chopin's second Scherzo presents the galant Fenaroli down to the smallest detail. It has a canon between bass and tenor (⑦–①–②–③), elements of the Durante countermelody in the soprano part (❺–❹–❸), a rearticulated pedal-point ⑤ in the alto, and the double presentation so characteristic of this schema. Appearing first in the key of C♯ minor, the schema then shifts to F♯ minor for a second double presentation. The passionate effect of the whole passage is thoroughly Romantic. The schema on which it was built, however, is securely galant.

17

$\begin{array}{c}\mathcal{E}\mathcal{E}\end{array}$

AN ALLEGRO

BY

Carl Ditters von Dittersdorf

Quintet No. 6 in G Major (K. 190), mvt. 1, Allegro, 1789

IN SIZE AND SCOPE, the Allegro from Dittersdorf's sixth string quintet far surpasses the movements presented in previous chapters. More notes are played in its first eight bars than in all of the Somis minuet in chapter 5. Yet Dittersdorf's writing is still largely grounded in the Italian galant. It was his "mother tongue," taught to him from about age twelve by Giuseppe Bonno (1711–1788), who had been sent to Naples by Charles VI to study with Durante and Leo. So Dittersdorf, like Haydn, was a direct product of what the French came to describe as *l'école d'Italie*[1]—the Italian School.

In the opening movement of his quintet, Dittersdorf selects all the common galant schemata. His first theme group is made up of Do-Re-Mi's with a Prinner riposte (see the list below). A Fonte then digresses from the original key of G major and leads to the new key, D major. There a large Fenaroli helps build up energy for the drive to the main cadence. Anyone familiar with the galant style should feel completely at home up to this point. It is following this main cadence, where the galant tradition would recognize completion of the first half of the movement, that Dittersdorf slightly adjusts his style. I have labeled this new section "coda" (mm. 31–46), using a nineteenth-century nomenclature but meaning no more than "something tacked on to the end." I might note that the melodic prominence of the lead cello in this coda may have less to do with the art of composition than with Dittersdorf's skill as an ingratiating courtier. The first cello part was probably directed toward a royal devotee of the cello, King Friedrich Wilhelm II of Prussia (r. 1786–97). Given Dittersdorf's visit in 1789 to Friedrich's court, made with (unrealized) hopes of employment, it was only practical to favor the new king with music that matched his tastes and special interests.

Dittersdorf composed this coda with a bass line that seems locked in a long series of alternations between tonic and dominant tones. His melody repeats its initial phrase four times, with the melodic terminations of **❹–❸** and **❷–❶** serving to distinguish between relatively open and closed endings, respectively. Eventually the melodic content dissolves, and the alternation of tonic and dominant harmonies accelerates to one chord per quarter note (mm. 45–46). This "liquidation" at the end of a major section became an important marker in late eighteenth-century and early nineteenth-century music. It formed part of the Beethovenian tradition and was described by Schoenberg as a feature of classical form in general.[2] It was not, however, typical of the galant style. In Dittersdorf's movement these two styles are juxtaposed without being reconciled. The galant tradition provides the real content and forward progress, while the newer, post-galant style provides a decorative and rhetorical contrast. This contrast is at its sharpest in measure 54, where the tremendous energy of the two E-minor Fenarolis (mm. 46–53) completely dissipates in the almost static passage of measures 54–62.

Section	Schema	Key
1st Half	Do-Re-Mi	G
	Do-Re-Mi, paired, *bis*	G
	Prinner	G
	Grand cadence, *bis*	G
	Fonte	Em ⇨ D
	Fenaroli, *bis*	D
	Cadence, *bis*	D
	Coda	D
	Ponte	D ⇨ G
:‖:		
2nd Half	Fenaroli	Em
	Echo of Coda	C
	Monte	C ⇨ D ⇨ E ⇨ F♯
	Circle of 5ths	F♯ ⇨ B ⇨ E ⇨ A
	Ponte	D ⇨ G
	Do-Re-Mi	G
	Do-Re-Mi, paired, *bis*	G
	Prinner	G
	Grand cadence, *bis*	G
	Grand cadence, *bis* ★	C
	Fonte	Am ⇨ G
	Fenaroli, *bis*	G
	Cadence	G
	Fenaroli, *bis*	G
:‖	Coda	G

In measure 93, after the return of the main theme in the main key, Dittersdorf follows a Grand cadence in the tonic key of G major with the same cadence in the subdominant key of C major (at the star in the list above). Even though specialists in eighteenth-century music long ago noted this practice,[3] it remains surprising to students and casual observers. In this movement, as in many others, the modulation to the subdominant had a decidedly practical purpose. If one moves to a position five tones below the tonic, one can then simply copy out the ensuing, analogous passages from the first half of the movement. Passages that modulated up a fifth from tonic to dominant in the first half of the movement will now modulate up a fifth from subdominant to tonic in the second half. Moving to the subdominant thus obviates the need to recompose the previous material. A composer could shift to the subdominant and then direct a music copyist to finish the rest of the movement through simple transposition.

As mentioned, Dittersdorf's Prinner in measures 11–14 (see ex. 17.2) functions as a traditional riposte to the opening Do-Re-Mi's. But Dittersdorf was demonstrating more than just where to place the Prinner. He was also demonstrating a particularly rich and complex Neapolitan version of the Prinner that featured (1) a chain of 2–3 suspensions between soprano and alto voice, and (2) a special bass that supports 6/5-to-5/3 progressions. Allowing for transposition, Dittersdorf's version is a close copy of a vocal duet exercise that Porpora had written for students in Naples perhaps sixty years earlier (ex. 17.1). Dittersdorf's own teacher Bonno had himself studied singing in Naples in the late 1720s, and Bonno may have known Porpora's solfeggi. Whether or not so direct a connection existed, it is nevertheless clear that this intricate pattern was openly taught, transmitted, and reproduced many times by many musicians (cf. ex. 6.5 by Leclair). We will examine an even more complex variant of the Porpora model in chapter 30, where the discussion focuses on its use by Leo, Pergolesi, J. C. Bach, Haydn, and Mozart.

EX. 17.1   Porpora, *Solfeggi*, no. 18, Allegro moderato, m. 6 (Naples, ca. 1730s)

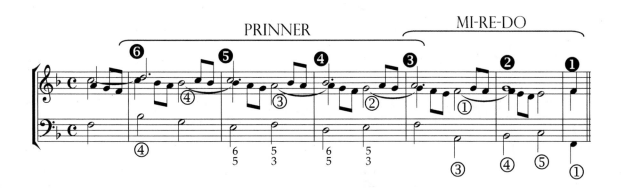

EX. 17.2   Dittersdorf, String Quintet No. 6 (K. 190), mvt. 1, Allegro (1789)

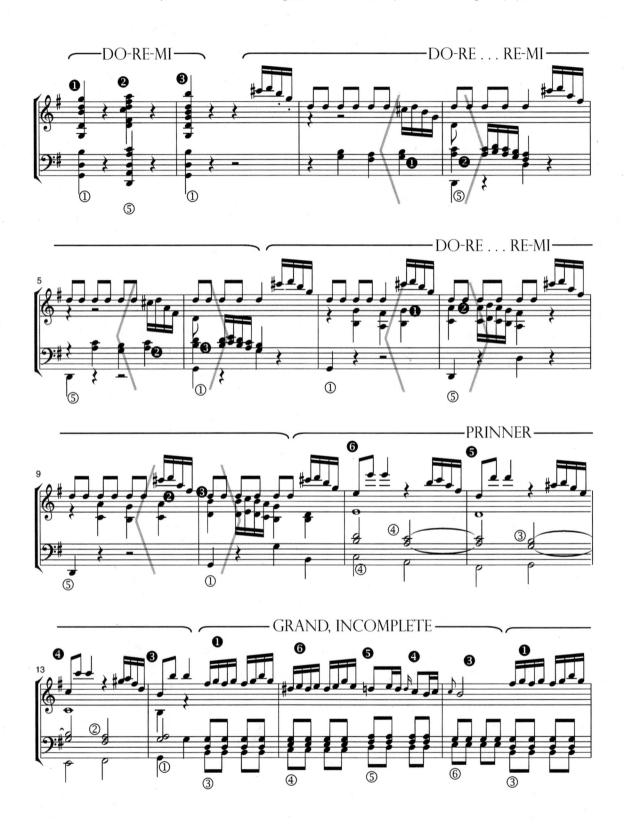

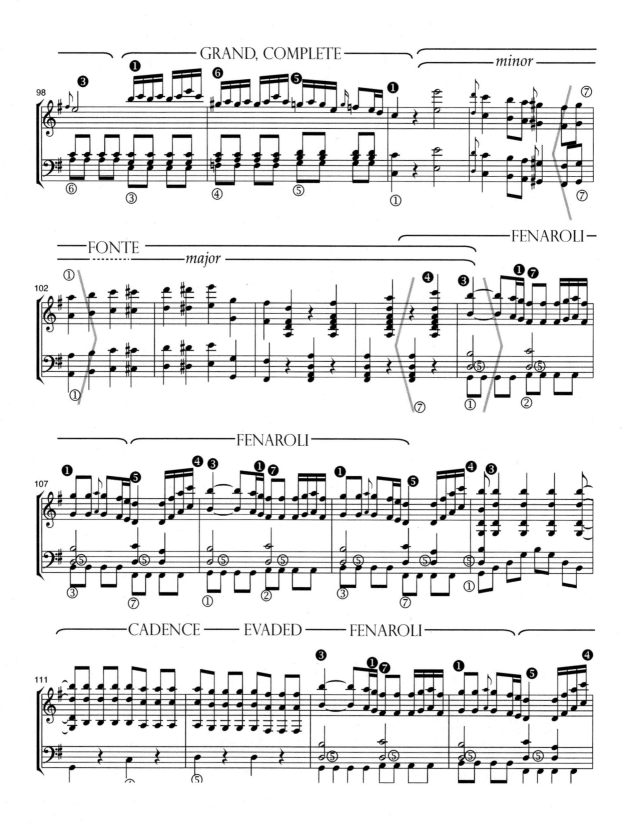

18

∽

THE SOL-FA-MI

A FRENCH MANUSCRIPT FROM DIJON contains a setting by Galuppi of *Confitibor tibi Domine* (Psalm 111, known in English as "I will praise the Lord with all my heart").[1] Galuppi's sacred music is every bit as graceful as his secular music, and full of elegant details. Two versions of the music that opens this motet are shown below. The first version is from the soprano's initial entrance and features a melodic Sol-Fa-Mi linked to a Long cadence that supports elements of a Do-Re-Mi and a Prinner.

EX. 18.1   Galuppi, *Confitibor tibi Domine*, mvt. 1 (ca. 1740s)

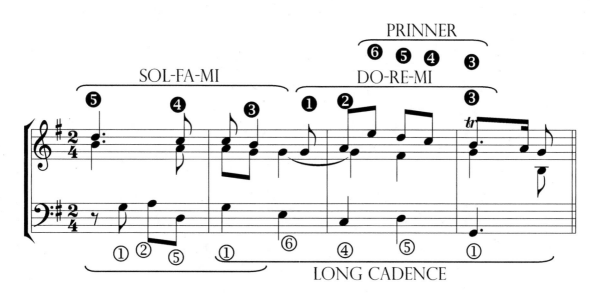

The second stems from the first instrumental interlude, in which the small orchestra plays a similar melody but substitutes a bass with elements of the Romanesca leading into a standard bass cadence. The upper voices are nearly the same as in example 18.1:

EX. 18.2   Galuppi, *Confitibor tibi Domine*, mvt. 1 (ca. 1740s)

Though these are charming passages, it was a fact of galant practice that Sol-Fa-Mi, as a simple three-stage schema, was never as prevalent as, for example, Do-Re-Mi. Descending stepwise melodies, especially when in parallel thirds, were more likely to form constituents of a proper Romanesca or of various cadences. And both of the Galuppi basses shown here (exs. 18.1–2) suggest that four, rather than three, stages may have been intended. That is, the bass's leap down from A3 to D3 (②–⑤) implies two separate chords under the melodic Fa (❹). At roughly the same time that the four-stage Do-Re-Mi became common (as Do-Re . . . Re-Mi, see chap. 6), the four-stage Sol-Fa-Mi emerged as a preferred schema for important themes.

A four-stage Sol-Fa-Mi has a concluding ❹–❸ dyad (*fa–mi* in major) in common with the Prinner, the Meyer, the Pastorella, and both halves of the typical Fonte and Monte. So one can expect to see the same High ❷ Drop that often signals the ensuing ❹–❸ in all of those schemata. That is certainly the case with example 18.3 by Giuseppe Tartini (1692–1770), the acknowledged *primo violino* in Padua for almost half a century. Tartini begins with a two-measure, four-stage Sol-Fa-Mi that features a High ❷ Drop in the second measure. He then continues with a modulating Prinner into which he nests a small Meyer. Both the Prinner and the Meyer converge and close on the same ❹–❸ dyad, signaled by another High ❷ Drop.

A minor chord over ② at the second stage of the Sol-Fa-Mi was not required—a dominant chord would also have worked well. But galant composers seem to have preferred the minor chord there, especially in slower movements like Tartini's Adagio. There could at times be special technical circumstances that would preclude a minor chord at

EX. 18.3   Tartini, Opus 6, no. 4, mvt. 1, Adagio, m. 1 (Paris, ca. 1748)

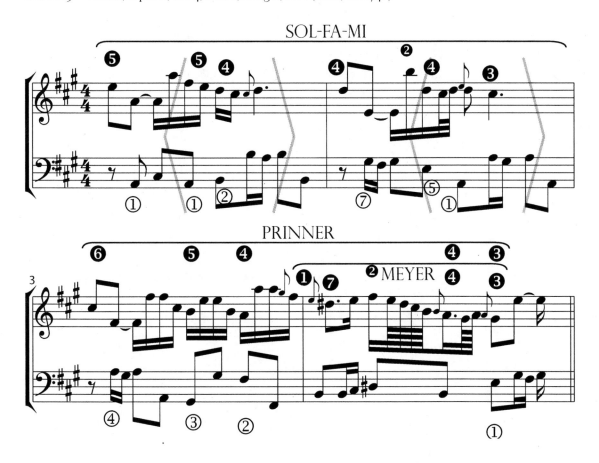

the second stage. For example, when Anton Stamitz (1750–1789/1809), who grew up in the whirl of court music at Mannheim (his father directed its famous orchestra), wrote a Sol-Fa-Mi with rising chromatic appoggiaturas (see ex. 18.4), a ② in the bass at the second stage (m. 2) would have created a horrible clash (C3 against both B♮4 and D5). So he used a ⑤ (F3) instead, ornamented from below by E♮.

EX. 18.4   A. Stamitz, Opus 11, no. 2, mvt. 1, Allegro, m. 1 (ca. 1775)

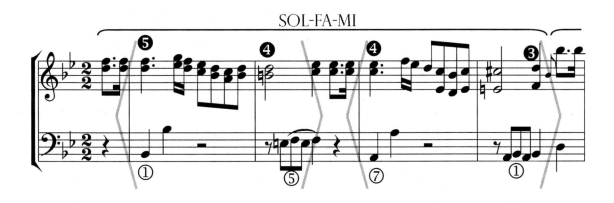

Luigi Boccherini (1743–1805), in a movement that nineteenth-century publishers touted as his "Celebrated Minuet," also employs a ⑤ for the bass of the second stage. The fame of this movement, which at various times in the twentieth century stood as one of the best-known galant works, even having a role in film,[2] may rest partly on its syncopated melody and partly on its delightful texture. The unique combination of violin 1 *con sordino*, violin 2 *con sordino* on alternating E_4 and E_5 sixteenth notes, and violas/cellos *pizzicato* cannot, unfortunately, be replicated on the two-staff reduction shown below:

EX. 18.5   Boccherini, Opus 11, no. 5, mvt. 3, Minuetto, m. 1 (1771)

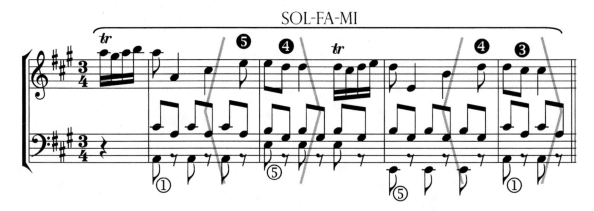

In spite of variants like those favored by Stamitz and Boccherini, Tartini's 1740s blueprint for a four-stage Sol-Fa-Mi proved to be remarkably stable, even when, in later decades, the schema doubled or quadrupled in length. In 1771, for instance, the French violinist Leduc wrote a four-measure Sol-Fa-Mi very much along Tartini's lines, with a ② supporting a minor chord at the second stage, a High ❷ Drop, and a closing melodic Prinner (ex. 18.6). He then followed this with an eight-bar (!) Prinner, not shown.

EX. 18.6   Leduc, Opus 4, no. 2, mvt. 1, Moderato, m. 12 (Paris, 1771)

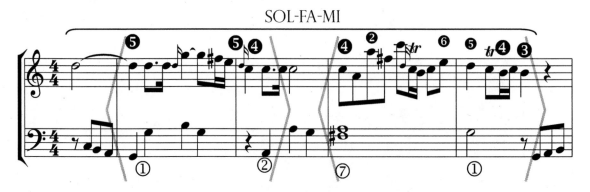

In the same decade, Salieri wrote an *eight*-measure Sol-Fa-Mi, *allegro molto*, which features the short melodic interjections characteristic of comic opera. Salieri's passage

races on through an eight-measure Monte and three Fenarolis before catching its breath
on a grand pause seventeen measures after the end of the Sol-Fa-Mi.

EX. 18.7   Salieri, Sinfonia from *La fiera di Venezia*, mvt. 1, Allegro molto, m. 96
(Vienna, 1772)

The small triangle of scale-degree numbers in Salieri's measure 108 is meant to high-light the overlapping contexts that impinge on the notated B5. In the spirit of Tartini's "usual Italian solfeggio," that tone would be B *la-mi-re*—*la* in relation to the overall D-major key, *mi* in relation to the G-major focus just established by the first part of the Monte, and *re* or High ❷ in relation to the imminent A-major focus of the second part of the Monte. Because the bass line in measures 105–11 forms a rising chromatic line—F♯3, G3, G♯3, A3—the B5 in measure 108 serves not only as High ❷ for the move to the ensu-ing A-major dominant chord, but also as High ❻ of a Converging cadence. Salieri's prac-tice is typical of an increasing reluctance during the 1770s and 1780s to write com-pletely regular and predictable Montes. As mentioned, the more frequent use of the term *Schusterfleck* (Ger., "cobbler's patch")[3] to describe such sequences is another indicator of the Monte's decline in esteem.

The late nineteenth-century founders of the modern Olympic movement devised a motto—*citius, altius, fortius* (Lat., "fastest, highest, strongest")—that neatly encapsulates a Romantic notion of excellence. Connoisseurs of galant music were not immune to the allure of ostentatiously fast and showy performances, and bourgeoise audiences found them irresistible. Indeed, the speed and élan of Salieri's passage does foreshadow many trends that came to dominate music in the decades following the French Revolution. But to an eighteenth-century court of the ancien régime, excellence in music meant some-thing more. It often meant "sensibility," a trait highly valued in galant society. Sensibility could be musically demonstrated through elegant details rather than through sheer speed, range, or loudness.

Chromatic decoration was one of the obvious musical marks of sensibility. As was discussed in chapter 8, Riepel's imaginary student had mentioned that the following mel-ody "seems like a workaday Fonte":[4]

EX. 18.8   Riepel, the student's "Fonte" or Sol-Fa-Mi

The imaginary teacher neither agreed nor disagreed but noted "some composers ornament it as follows":[5]

EX. 18.9   Riepel, the ornamented "Fonte" or Sol-Fa-Mi

Riepel appears to be acknowledging, without describing it as such, the nexus between diatonic and chromatic versions of the Fonte and the Sol-Fa-Mi, which all share a global ❺–❹ . . . ❹–❸ core melody.

The type of ornamentation suggested by Riepel can be seen clearly in the following two Sol-Fa-Mi's by Leduc. The first four measures show Leduc's diatonic theme, a paired Sol-Fa-Mi. Then, after a four-measure interlude (not shown), the theme returns with added chromatic ornamentation and a slightly different character, having lost its playful eighth-note "escape tones" (cf. mm. 47, 49):

EX. 18.10   Leduc, Opus 4, no. 2, mvt. 1, Moderato, mm. 46–49, 54–57 (1771)

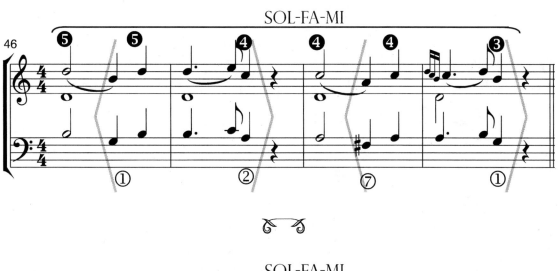

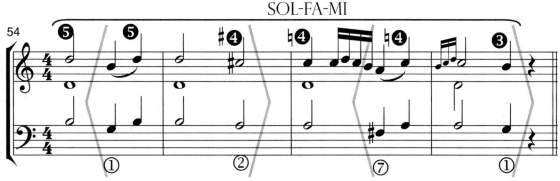

Just a few years later, in one of his movements titled Amoroso (one presumes that music with an "affectionate" or "loving" character ought to exhibit considerable sensitivity), Pugnani likewise employed the paired Sol-Fa-Mi with the ornamental chromatic descent. Moreover he seems to have recognized and exploited the implication for continuing the chromatic descent beyond ❺–♯❹ and ♮❹–❸ to ♭❸–❷:

EX. 18.11   Pugnani, Opus 8, no. 2, mvt. 3, Amoroso, m. 1 (ca. 1774)

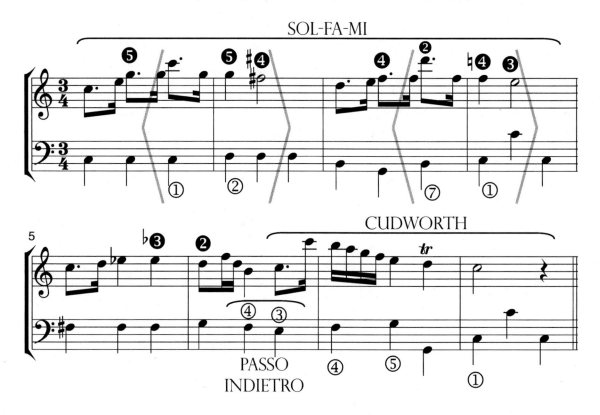

Giovanni Battista Viotti (1755–1824), the most famous student of Pugnani (who was in turn a pupil of Somis), often expressed sensibility through chromatic appoggiaturas that approach the chord tone from below. Those tones and similarly strong diatonic dissonances are starred in example 18.12, selected from one of Viotti's solo sonatas for violin. He employs extensive chromatic decoration in his first cadence, which is a relatively short adaptation of the Grand cadence. He then inserts the Fonte and returns to a larger, more conclusive Mi-Re-Do cadence that largely eschews chromaticism in favor of rapid scalar runs. Viotti's Fonte, which itself could be viewed as a chromatic variant of his Sol-Fa-Mi, has its melody a third above the normal, global ❺–❹ . . . ❹–❸, thereby fostering the expressively more salient sonorities of dissonant seventh chords at the first and third stages of the schema (each half of his Fonte matches the Jommelli variant of the Comma; cf. ex. 11.34). This melodic excerpt, though it does not venture beyond first position on the violin's E string, represents the height of sensitivity in late galant instrumental music.

Many presentations of the Sol-Fa-Mi were also given in the minor mode. In most cases few changes were made to the basic schema, even though a dissonant triad results at the second stage (e.g., in A minor: B, D, F). There was, in fact, a fashion for a type of minor-mode Sol-Fa-Mi that included an even stronger dissonance at the second stage—a 6/4/2 chord and the resulting 2–3 suspension. An example by Gaviniés originated in the *minore* section of a minuet (see ex. 18.13). The bass holds ① through both the schema's

EX. 18.12   Viotti, Opus 4, no. 1, mvt. 3, Adagio, m. 9 (ca. 1785)

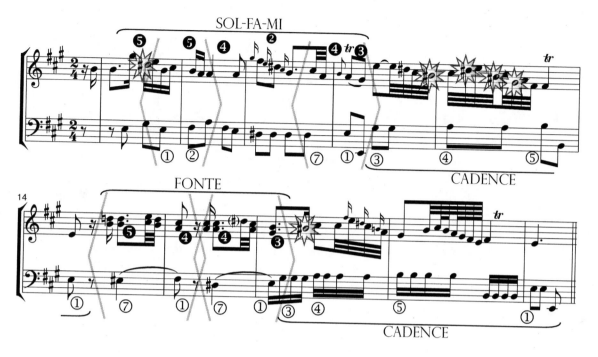

first and second stages, then resolves down to ⑦ at stage three. Note the affectively charged leap up to the High ❷ in the second measure following the *agitato* syncopations of the first measure. Though the effect is quite different in the minor mode, Gaviniés's syncopations are almost exactly the same as Boccherini's (cf. ex. 18.5).

EX. 18.13   Gaviniés, Opus 3, no. 5, mvt. 3b, Tempo di minuetto, m. 1 (1764)

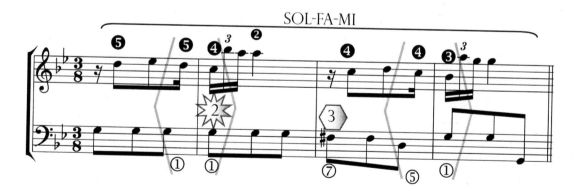

Gaviniés's pupil Leduc produced a similarly sensitive Adagio on the same template. The added tenor voice in the original print suggests that either Leduc or his printer decided to make the 2–3 suspension explicit, since it is easily missed by the keyboard player in these unfigured basses. The marking of *rinforzando* (It., "strengthening") at the start of the Prinner melody in measure 3 reinforces the inference of heightened "affection" (ex. 18.4).

EX. 18.14   Leduc, Opus 4, no. 3, mvt. 2, Adagio, m. 1 (1771)

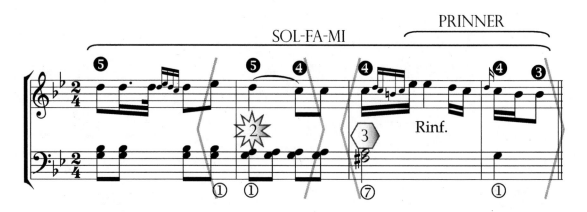

If one were to combine the affective charge of the Sol-Fa-Mi's written by these French violinists with the size and dynamism of the orchestral Sol-Fa-Mi by Salieri (ex. 18.7)—thus pairing French melodic sensitivity with Viennese orchestral élan—the result might resemble the famous opening of Mozart's G-minor symphony (1788). This deservedly famous theme is, in my opinion, no less arresting for having been built on the stock schematic template of the paired Sol-Fa-Mi:

EX. 18.15   Mozart, Symphony in G Minor (KV550), mvt. 1, Allegro, m. 1 (1788)

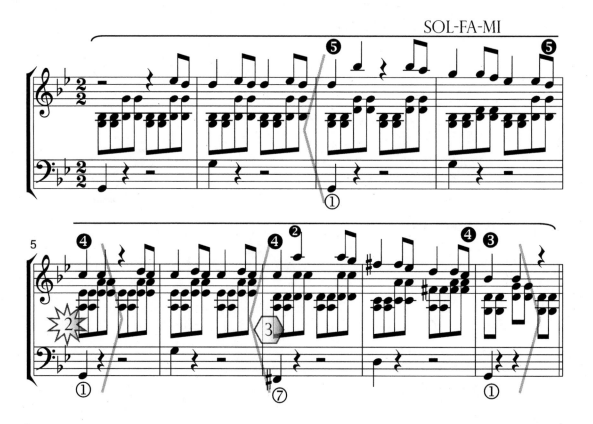

19

AN ANDANTE

BY

JOHANN CHRISTIAN BACH

Opus 12, no. 6, mvt. 2, Andante, Paris, 1773–74

GIVING FATHERLY ADVICE ABOUT THE ART OF COMPOSITION, Leopold Mozart wrote to his son Wolfgang:

> The small is great, when it is natural—fluent and lightly scored and solid in its composition. To compose like that is more difficult than to write all the artificial harmonic progressions *incomprehensible to most people*, and melodies *difficult to perform*. Did Bach lower himself by this? Never! Good writing and the ordering of things, *il filo* [the thread]—this distinguishes the master from the bungler, even in trifles.[1]

Leopold was seeking to influence his son by invoking a name that the younger Mozart held in high esteem. "Bach," however, meant Johann Christian Bach (1735–1782), Italian trained, Catholic like the Mozarts, and master of music to Queen Charlotte of England. And though Mozart did eventually acquaint himself with some music by Bach's less well known older brother (C. P. E.) and deceased father (J. S.), he always viewed the Bach who had written operas for Naples as the great model, the man whose style he worked to emulate more assiduously than any other during his early years.

In trying to explain how one could distinguish, from the internal evidence of texts, between those produced in oral and literary traditions, Albert Lord wrote:

> Formula analysis, providing, of course, that one has sufficient material for significant results, is, therefore, able to indicate whether any given text is oral or "literary." An *oral* text will yield a predominance of clearly demonstrable formulas, with the bulk of the remainder "formulaic," and a small number of nonformulaic expressions. A *literary* text will show a predominance of nonformulaic expressions, with some formulaic expressions, and very few clear formulas. . . . Analyses of different kinds of enjambment in different styles are

likewise helpful. We have seen that nonperiodic enjambment, the "adding" style, is characteristic of oral composition; whereas periodic enjambment is characteristic of "literary" style.[2]

This chapter presents the Andante slow movement of Bach's B♭ sonata from his late collection of keyboard pieces, Opus 12 (Paris). If Galuppi or Dittersdorf represents a type of oral tradition characterized by the chaining together of stock material and a minimum of inter-figure overlap, enjambment, or cross-reference, Bach represents a more literary style. One hesitates to point out indications of calculation and conscious construction in a movement that succeeds so well in conveying the "noble simplicity" and naturalness that was an avowed aesthetic goal in the later 1770s. Yet naturalness is an artful impression and not necessarily indicative of the mode of construction. Bach seems to have treated even the most trivial musical material as a candidate for arbitrary manipulation. For instance, the accompanimental figure in the bass of measure 1 features an accented lower neighbor tone followed by a pattern of rising chord tones (see ex. 19.1). He uses this figure three times in succession (mm. 1–3). Beginning in measure 7, he slightly changes its contour for three more statements, and then from measure 13 he seems to echo this pattern in sixteenth notes for the twofold presentation of a decorative melodic figure.

EX. 19.1   Motivic associations in Bach's Andante

One could argue that the neighbor-note-with-arpeggio motive of example 19.1 was part of Bach's main theme and thus likely to be used repeatedly in the course of the movement. But the same could not be said of the small *Eingang* (Ger., "lead-in") in measure 11 that introduces a new theme in the key of B♭ major (see ex. 19.2). Ten measures later, this same generic little pattern is played upside down and backwards (retrograde inversion) to introduce a different theme. Recherché variation of this type, more characteristic of seventeenth-century court poetry than of light, galant sonatas, would have been appreciated better by Mozart the son than by Mozart the father.

EX. 19.2   Bach's mirroring of a small *Eingang*

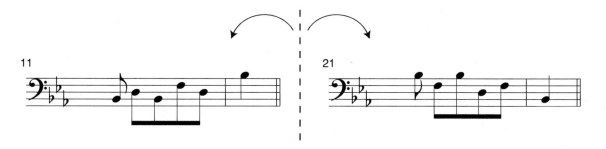

Musical similarity is in the ear of the beholder, and more instances of motivic similarity in Bach's sonata could be found if one were committed to the effort. His several different uses of the Sol-Fa-Mi schema, for instance, would naturally have many features in common. My point in drawing attention to these practices is not to claim that they result in superior compositions, or that Bach was building a bridge to Beethoven and Brahms. But Bach's working methods do seem to reflect a German orientation to galant composition, one that proved to be a significant influence on Mozart in his early years, and one that can still speak to modern listeners without requiring as much translation as might be needed for the works of his Italian contemporaries. Because Bach draws so heavily on internal relationships and references, his work can be appreciated more easily by outsiders, whereas the references in works by Galuppi or Dittersdorf are more to the galant tradition as a whole, which favors insiders with broad knowledge of the courtly repertory. These two approaches are not opposites, but rather different weightings of (a) similarity perceived within a work, and (b) similarity perceived between works. Both approaches employ rich networks of relationships, the one more internalized, the other more externalized, the one more solitary, the other more social.

As the list on the following page shows, this long movement barely departs from the scales of tonic and dominant, the one exception being the hint of the hermaphrodite Fonte (the "wrong," lowered ❻ being the C♭ in m. 44). This work's fluid diatonicism and delicate, well-subordinated chromatic embellishments can easily conceal how carefully Bach strove to elide, run together, and generally undermine the normal scansion of the galant schemata. Even the opening theme departs significantly from what a courtier might have learned to expect from a Sol-Fa-Mi. Instead of the melodic dyad *sol–fa* being answered by the dyad *fa–mi*, Bach proceeds directly to *mi*, accompanied by a move in the bass much like a deceptive cadence (❺–❻). I say "much like" because there are also strong hints of the Romanesca in Bach's opening bass (mm. 1–3). The ensuing cadence is evaded, and the closure of the "complete" cadence that follows is itself lessened by the entry in the bass of the motive shown earlier in example 19.1 (as m. 7). Only with the end of the Prinner, and its extension to the half cadence in measure 12, is there a real caesura. When the strong cadence of measure 25 finally "finishes" the first half of his movement, Bach embarks on a large, increasingly bravura digression with roots in Italian opera sinfonias.

Section	Schema	Key
1st Half	Sol-Fa-Mi	E♭
	Cadence, evaded . . . complete	E♭
	Prinner	E♭
	Meyer	B♭
	Passo Indietro	B♭
	Converging cadence	B♭ ⇨ F
	Sol-Fa-Mi	B♭
	Cadence, evaded . . . complete	B♭
	(triadic ascent)	B♭
	Cadence, evaded . . . complete	B♭
	Quiescenza, *bis*	B♭
:‖:		
2nd Half	Sol-Fa-Mi	B♭
	Cadence, evaded . . . complete	B♭
	Fonte, hermaphrodite	Fm ⇨ E♭
	Prinner	E♭
	Ponte	E♭
	Sol-Fa-Mi	E♭
	Prinner	E♭
	Sol-Fa-Mi	E♭
	Cadence	E♭
	(triadic ascent)	E♭
	Cadence, evaded . . . complete	E♭
	Quiescenza, *bis*	E♭
:‖		

While each passage in this movement repays careful examination, I want to draw attention to just a few that relate specifically to the topics of preceeding chapters. One is the use of the Quiescenza to end each half of the movement. Chapter 13 described the diatonic and chromatic versions as different types of the same schema. That seems to have been Bach's conception as well, since he ends the first half of the movement with the diatonic version and the second half with the possibly more emphatic, more noticeable chromatic version. Chapter 11 described the Passo Indietro as often being performed just before the beginning of a significant cadence. Bach uses the Passo Indietro in measure 15 and quite properly follows it with a large Converging cadence. Chapters 3 and 9 presented dozens of examples of the Prinner and Meyer with High ❷ Drops. Bach follows that tradition throughout this movement. But he also introduces a relocation of the Prinner in the movement's second half. After the double bar, instead of appearing as riposte to the opening theme, the Prinner is replaced by a Fonte (m. 43). The Prinner that served as riposte to the opening gambit in the movement's first half only returns late in the movement (m. 57) as riposte to a "second theme," itself a Sol-Fa-Mi just like the opening gambit. While in its first appearance that Prinner riposte was accelerated to close with a half cadence (m. 11), in its second, delayed appearance Bach allows it the normal scansion (m. 57). Mozart later copied this manner of delaying and relocating the Prinner riposte in the slow movement of his great G-minor symphony (see the final section of chap. 9). Bach's Andante, by galant standards a challenging, "literary" movement, sometimes takes the galant repertory of schemata only as a point of departure. His compositional style, nonetheless, remained thoroughly grounded in that repertory.

EX. 19.3   J. C. Bach, Opus 12, no. 6, mvt. 2, Andante (Paris, 1773–74)

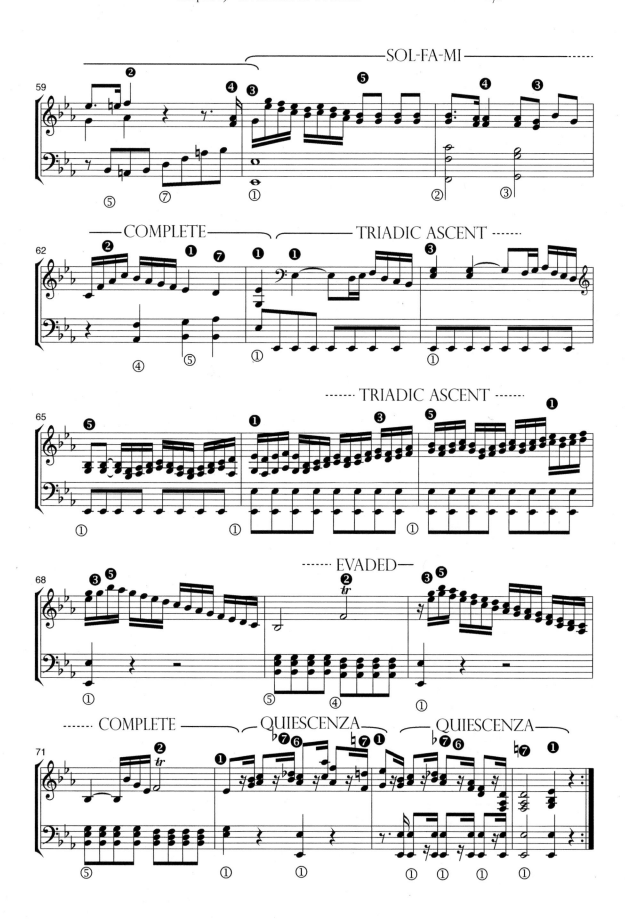

20

THE INDUGIO

COURT MUSICIANS IN CENTRAL EUROPE wrote several major treatises during the 1750s and early 1760s. Those of Riepel (1752, 1755, 1757, 1765) are still significant for their descriptions of compositional practice.[1] The flute treatise of Quantz (1752), the keyboard treatises of C. P. E. Bach (1753, 1762), and the violin treatise of Leopold Mozart (1756) are important for detailing performance practice.[2] And the thoroughbass treatise of Johann Friedrich Daube (1756) is valuable as a sign that galant simplifications of musical syntax had begun to influence conceptions of the tonal system.[3] Daube's *General-Bass in drey Accorden* [Thoroughbass in Three Chords] drew attention, as Rameau had earlier in France (1722), to the central roles of three distinct sonorities: a 6/5 chord above ④ in the bass, a seventh chord above ⑤, and a simple triad above ①. Though Daube oversimplified galant practice for his readership of amateur musicians, as we saw in chapter 11, it is nevertheless true that one can produce a typical galant cadence using only these three sonorities:

EX. 20.1   Daube's "three chords" (1756) set as a cadence

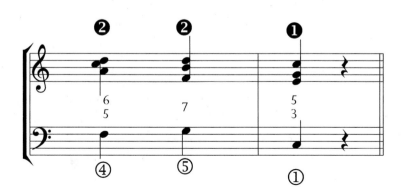

Among the schemata introduced in previous chapters, the Ponte could be characterized as an extension of, and a focus on, the second type of sonority (a seventh chord on ⑤), and the Quiescenza could be described as an extension of, and a focus on, the third type (a simple triad on ①). What I call "the Indugio"—so named because it signals a playful tarrying or lingering (It., *indugiare*) that delays the arrival of a cadence—was a schema for extending and focusing on the first type of sonority, a 6/3 or 6/5/3 chord on ④.

To show the Indugio in a typical setting, I have selected a passage from one of the many undated keyboard works by Cimarosa (ex. 20.2). The movement in question began in B♭ major but at this point has already modulated to the dominant key, F major:

EX. 20.2   Cimarosa, Sonata C78, Allegro brioso, m. 21 (ca. 1780s)

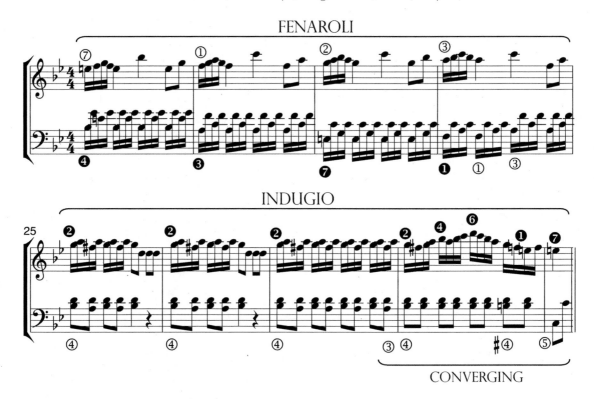

Cimarosa first presents a four-measure Fenaroli in F major. In the Fenaroli's last measure (m. 24), its bass moves from ① to ③, which often indicates the beginning of a cadence. Measure 25 would thus likely have begun a one- or two-measure cadence had not an Indugio delayed the cadence for several extra measures (mm. 25–28). Moreover, the Indugio leads into a Converging cadence on C, which can be heard either as the new tonic key or as the dominant of F major. Cimarosa's example presents many of the hallmarks of the Indugio. There is the initial and prominent melodic ❷ (m. 25), the rapid, ultimately rising sixteenth-note figures that touch on ❷, ❹, and ❻ (mm. 25–28), the sound of the minor mode (G minor), chromatic lower neighbor-notes (the A♮s in the bass and F♯s in the soprano of mm. 25–28), and the chromatic rising bass of the Converging cadence (mm. 28–29). Just as important is the perception that the strong forward progress of the Fenaroli gets sidetracked by the Indugio. Measure 26 repeats measure 25 exactly, the first half of measure 27 repeats the first half of measure 26, and the second half of measure 27 repeats the first half of the same measure. In short, the listener is forced to linger in a busy stasis until the Converging cadence reestablishes a sense of goal-directed motion.

Gaviniés, though twenty years senior to Cimarosa, nonetheless shared with him many of the same strategies for employing the Indugio. Example 20.3 is taken from the slow movement of his violin sonata in G major. Like the movement of Cimarosa, this movement modulates to the dominant key of D major and then begins a Fenaroli. Cimarosa went from a Fenaroli directly to an Indugio. Gaviniés takes a more leisurely route. A full cadence follows the Fenaroli (mm. 15–16) and closes the first half of the movement. The second half begins with a chromatic Fonte (mm. 17–20). The Fonte's melodic descent of D5–C♯5–C♮5–B4 leads down to A4 as ❷ in measure 21, where Gaviniés lingers on the Indugio.

EX. 20.3   Gaviniés, Opus 3, no. 3, mvt. 2, Adagio cantabile, m. 11 (1764)

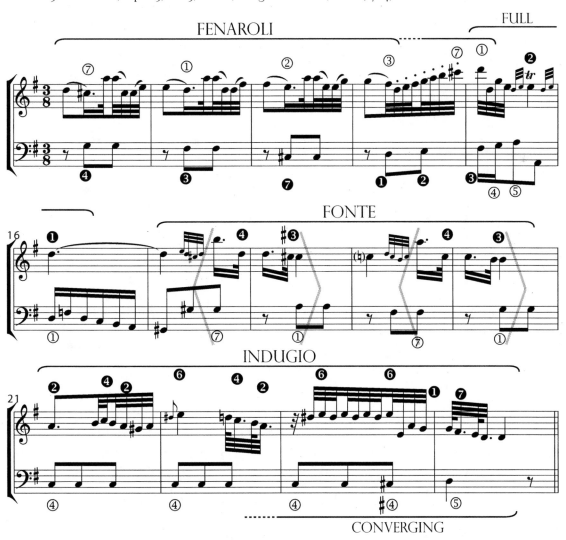

An important variant of the Indugio features a bass with stepwise ascents and descents between ④ and ⑥, while the melody parallels that movement by going up and down between ❷ and ❹. The combination of an inner-voice pedal point on the tonic ① with the passing tones in the outer voices produces a passing 6/4 chord over ⑤. Each of the two examples by Cimarosa shown below demonstrates this practice. The first one, in D♭ major, notates all three voices and may thus be easier to recognize as the passing-6/4 variant. It features the common *agitato* syncopations in the melody:

EX. 20.4   Cimarosa, Sonata C70, Andantino, m. 8 (ca. 1780s)

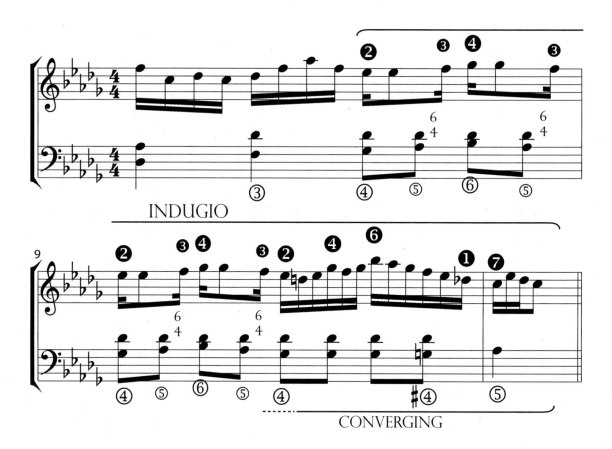

The second one, in B♭ major (ex. 20.5), presents only the two outer voices, with the inner-voice pedal point implied. This Indugio is likewise slightly syncopated and includes a chromatic leading tone (B♮) to ❷. As in the previous example, I have added the figures "6/4" to highlight the placement of that sonority—the figures are not present in the early manuscripts or prints. This second example of the passing-6/4 variant also shows the less common option of the Indugio not proceeding to a Converging cadence. Instead the phrase comes to a complete cadence in the key of B♭.

EX. 20.5   Cimarosa, Sonata C72, Allegro, m. 19 (ca. 1780s)

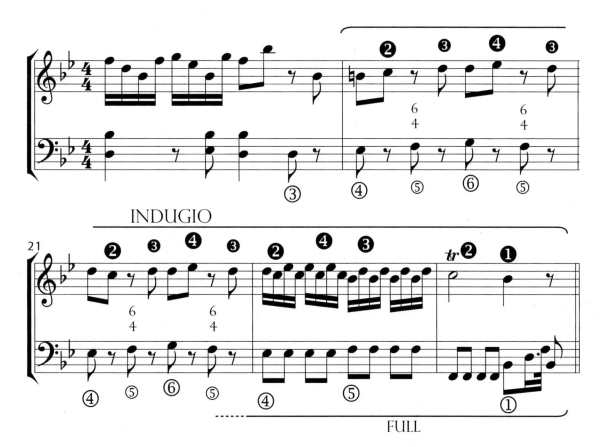

In the partimento tradition, the passing-6/4 variant of the Indugio was sometimes figured without an overt "6/4," but in a way that better conveyed the movement of voices. In
an example by Tritto one can see the tonic inner-pedal figured as "5 —" (meaning "sound
the fifth above and hold it") and the melody-bass parallelism figured as "6 6 6 6." The
partimento shows an Indugio occupying the third stage of the Long cadence, as defined
by Sala (see chap. 11):[4]

EX. 20.6   Tritto, partimento in G major, m. 46 (ca. 1810–15)

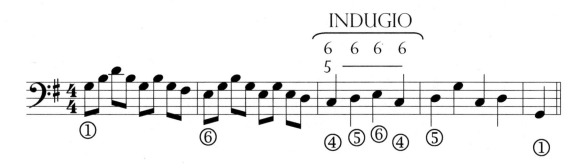

Unlike the Indugios of the last two examples, a typical Indugio will generally conclude with a Converging cadence. These cadences strike a balance between the keys of the tonic and dominant, allowing for either to be heard. Only a slight push is needed to upset that balance and force a single interpretation. In another Indugio by Gaviniés, the early arrival of C♯ in both bass and melody (m. 21) puts D major squarely in the foreground:

EX. 20.7   Gaviniés, Opus 3, no. 5, mvt. 1, Allegro, m. 19 (1764)

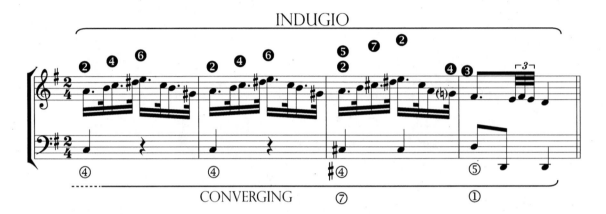

As is true of most galant schemata, the Indugio had a number of incidental variants, due perhaps to local traditions and personal preferences. In Vienna, for example, Wanhal frequently put the Converging cadence's bass of ④–♯④–⑤ in the tenor voice. Two such examples from his string quartets feature a modulating Prinner that precedes the Indugio. The first, example 20.8, adds a Ponte and fermata after the Indugio to further the delay of E major, the new tonic harmony.

The second, example 20.9, is also preceded by a large modulating Prinner, which in this case has a common type of Meyer embedded in its second half. As in Wanhal's previous example, the ❻–❺–❹–❸ descent of the Prinner leads smoothly down to the ❷ of the Indugio, making a long general descent that continues through ❶ and ❼ at the close of the Converging cadence.

The contractual arrangements that tied court musicians to their noble patrons were sometimes onerous, sometimes generous. Though Mozart, Haydn, and many others frequently chafed under these agreements, they did so as free men. Wanhal, by contrast, began life actually owned by a nobleman. Legally he was a serf, someone's chattel. He reached an important milestone when he became successful enough to buy his own freedom. He never subsequently became lackey to any court, and made a good living as a writer of keyboard and chamber music to be printed and sold to the middle class. This bourgeois music still draws heavily on the repertory of galant schemata, but subtle changes arise in how the schemata are presented. At times, the musical discourse seems to become more obvious, almost didactic.

EX. 20.8 Wanhal, Quartet in A Major (A4), mvt. 1, Allegro mod., m. 16 (ca. 1784)

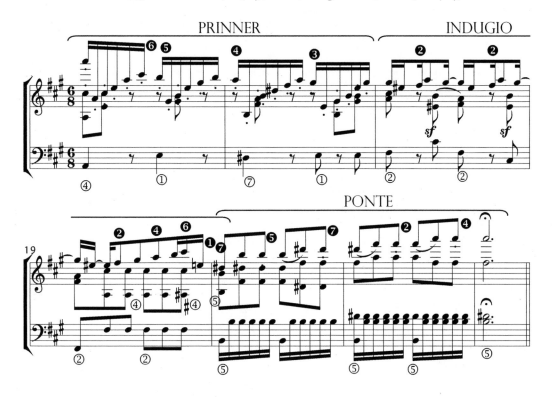

EX. 20.9 Wanhal, Quartet in C Major (C1), mvt. 1, Allegro, m. 18 (1773)

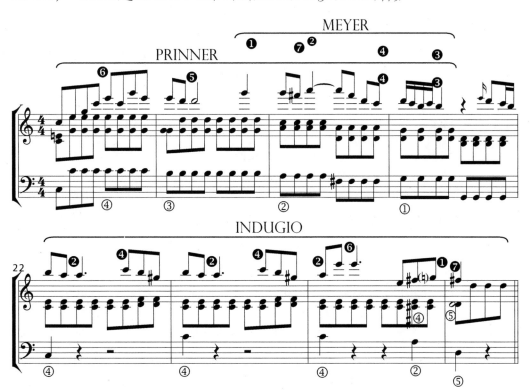

Three examples provide a glimpse into the development of this repertory, the larger story of which falls outside the scope of this book. The first is taken from Wanhal's early C-minor quartet (1768–69). Galant practices are still very much in evidence. A flowing cadential four-bar phrase in E♭ major ends with a deceptive cadence in measure 24 as the first violin plays an appoggiatura and the second violin completes a melodic Prinner. As the phrase is repeated, an ornate Indugio leads to the standard Converging cadence:

EX. 20.10   Wanhal, Quartet in C Minor (c2), mvt. 1, Allegro mod., m. 21 (1768–69)

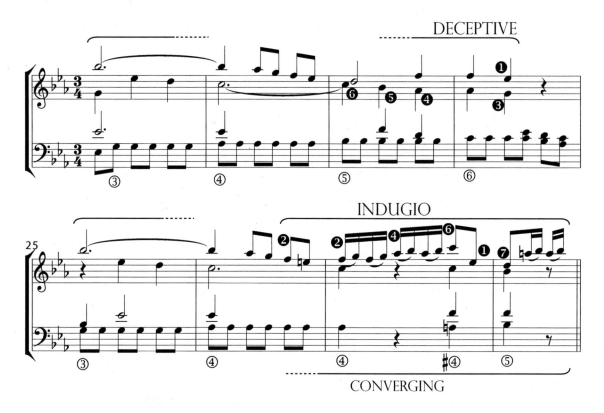

In the second example, from his G-major quartet of around 1780 (see ex. 20.11), the first phrase hints at an Indugio in measure 143; the second phrase then realizes that potential by adding two extra measures, some of which is silence (m. 143 becomes mm. 147–49).

The third and final passage (ex. 20.12) comes from Wanhal's E♭ string quartet of the mid 1780s (1785–86). As in the previous two examples, Wanhal presents a model phrase followed by an altered copy. The model phrase is very "four-square"—no appoggiaturas, no Prinner, no deceptive cadence. Only the hint of an Indugio at the melodic ❷ in measure 7 (note the associated syncopations) helps to delay the full cadence until the middle of measure 8. The second phrase is an extended copy of the first. The extension begins at the melodic ❷ in measure 11 and turns into a large Indugio complete with an embedded, canonic Fenaroli in F minor. When the complete cadence arrives in measure 14, it falls squarely back on the downbeat.

EX. 20.11   Wanhal, Quartet in G Major (G8), mvt. 1, Allegro molto moderato, m. 142
(ca. 1780)

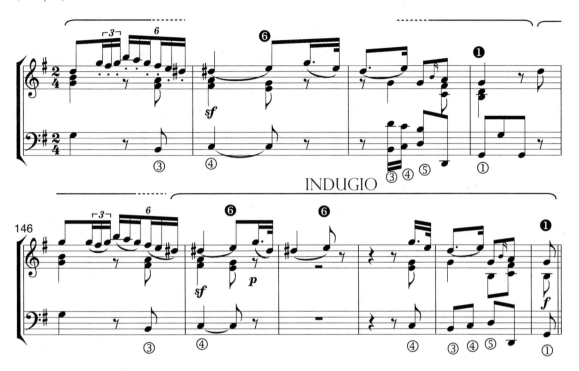

EX. 20.12   Wanhal, Quartet in E♭ Major (E♭ 11), mvt. 1, Allegro con fuoco, m. 4
(1785–86)

In the previous three excerpts one can see a stylistic progression in which musical meaning becomes more internal to the single work. That is, whereas a courtly audience could be expected to understand an Indugio whenever and wherever it occurred, one senses that Wanhal was giving his more bourgeoise audience internal clues to the schema's meaning. He was, in part, teaching them. In each excerpt he presents a model (the first phrase), then inserts an Indugio to lengthen the copy (the second phrase). The meaning of each extension can be inferred from the internal evidence of its corresponding model, and thus someone without extensive musical experience of the courtly style could still get the point of the Indugio. I recognize that the transition toward a musical art that was more self-referential and less formulaic is generally ascribed to the "heroic" acts of composers like Beethoven. But perhaps changes in the audience and the economics of being an independent composer were equally important. If we accept Norbert Elias's contention that some of Mozart's problems stemmed from his being a nascent "bourgeois artist in court society," then perhaps Wanhal's success was in recognizing how to function as a bourgeois artist in bourgeois society.[5]

Beethoven, as one might expect, took matters somewhat further. The opening of his E♭ piano sonata from 1802 (ex. 20.13) presents the Indugio as an opening schema. This unusual tack can still elicit comment long after the Indugio ceased to resonate as a courtly schema. The program notes for a 2003 London recital by Artur Pizarro broadcast on the BBC mention that "the Sonata opens with a striking harmonic idea that begins on an ambiguous added-sixth chord and does not reach the tonic until the sixth bar."[6] The courtly schema thus fades into a harmonic curiosity.

EX. 20.13   Beethoven, Opus 31, no. 3, mvt. 1, Allegro, m. 1 (Vienna, 1802)

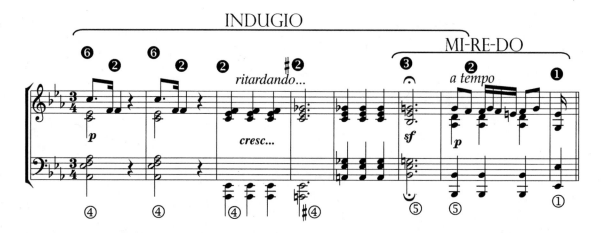

The gradual transition from a galant to a more bourgeois music culture accelerated during the final decades of the eighteenth century. Obviously the revolution of 1789, which led to a crisis for French aristocrats and the bishops of the Church, created a concomitant crisis for the many musicians whom they supported. The unfortunate Anton Stamitz, one of Louis XV's resident musicians ("ordinaire de la musique du roi"), is believed to have gone mad—he was never seen again in public. The ensuing Napoleonic Wars made matters worse across the continent, since a court musician, who had little choice but to work for whoever was in power, could suddenly become persona non grata following a change of regime. In Naples, for example, the regime changed five times in the decade from 1798 to 1808. As early as 1794, Piccinni had been placed under house arrest for unfounded Jacobin leanings, being released only in 1798. The following year saw Paisiello investigated for sedition and Cimarosa imprisoned under sentence of death, though later pardoned. Cimarosa and Piccinni never really recovered from these shocks. The far more agile Paisiello managed to become chapel master to Napoleon himself.

If famous, well-connected composers had difficulties, imagine what it was like for an ordinary musician. In her memoire of the revolution, Grace Elliot, one of the most exalted courtesans of the time, mentions that on Sunday, July 12, 1789,

> I went, with the Duke of Orléans, Prince Louis D'Aremberg, and others whose names I do not recollect, to fish and dine at the Duke's château of Raincy, in the Forest of Bondy, near Paris. We returned to Paris in the evening, meaning to go to the *Comédie Italienne*. We had left Paris at eleven o'clock in perfect tranquillity; but on our return at eight o'clock at the Porte St. Martin (where the Duke's town-carriage was waiting for him, and my carriage for me), my servant told me that I could not go to the play, as the theaters were all shut by orders from the police; that Paris was all confusion and tumult.[7]

In the course of her *fête galante* everything had changed. History records that the great duke would later be executed, and that the beautiful courtisan was arrested and would only narrowly escape the guillotine. Yet we ought not to forget the thirty or so musicians who worked at the Comédie Italienne. They all lost their jobs.

21

A CANTABILE

BY

SIMON LEDUC

Opus 4, no. 1, mvt. 1, Paris, 1771

AS A NOTED PUPIL OF GAVINIÉS, Simon Leduc (1742–1777) had already become one of the premier musicians in Paris when the child Mozart made his first tour there in 1763–64. Mozart's father, an acknowledged authority on violin performance, wrote approvingly of Leduc's playing, and given the style of Leduc's compositions it would be difficult to believe that Wolfgang did not also find much to admire and emulate in Leduc's elegant melodies.

Leduc wrote highly refined music for small aristocratic gatherings in chambers and salons. The fluency and perfection of his style was matched by few others, and almost every one of his phrases features a galant schema presented in a way that exploits its traditions and expressive opportunities. Take, for instance, the Indugio. He included three different Indugios in the violin sonata that serves as the focus of this chapter. The first gives a representative combination of the Indugio with the Converging cadence:

EX. 21.1   Leduc, Opus 4, no. 1, mvt. 1, Cantabile, m. 9 (Paris, 1771)

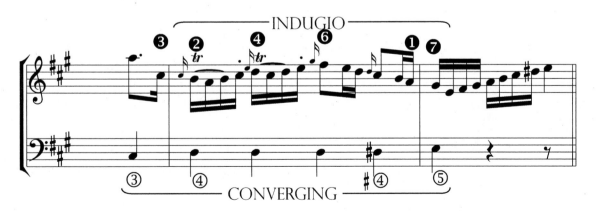

The movement's second Indugio, with a diatonic bass, emerges when a tentative Prinner stalls and fails to develop:

EX. 21.2   Leduc, Opus 4, no. 1, mvt. 1, Cantabile, m. 16 (Paris, 1771)

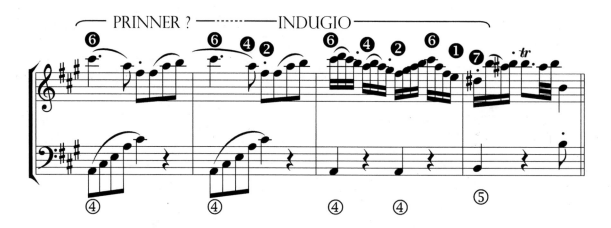

And the movement's third Indugio presents a clear case of the passing-6/4 variant, along with more of the melodic embellishment characteristic of the schema:

EX. 21.3   Leduc, Opus 4, no. 1, mvt. 1, Cantabile, m. 69 (Paris, 1771)

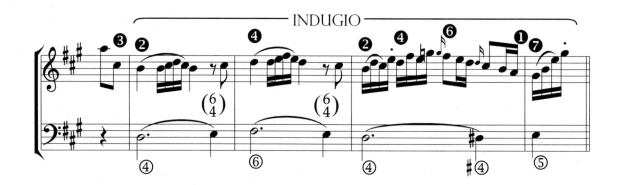

Such a movement could easily have emanated from Naples, given the extent of its correspondences with Italian practice. In particular, Leduc's style has affinities with that of his slightly younger contemporary Cimarosa. Example 21.3, for instance, shares many features with an Indugio by Cimarosa discussed in the previous chapter (ex. 20.4).

The next two examples illustrate the many similarities in how Cimarosa (ex. 21.4) and Leduc (ex. 21.5) present double statements of a stepwise Romanesca. Though these passages are roughly contemporaneous, difficulties in dating Cimarosa's instrumental works make it difficult to say which was written first:

EX. 21.4   Cimarosa, Flute Quartet, no. 1, mvt. 1, m. 77 (ca. 1770s)

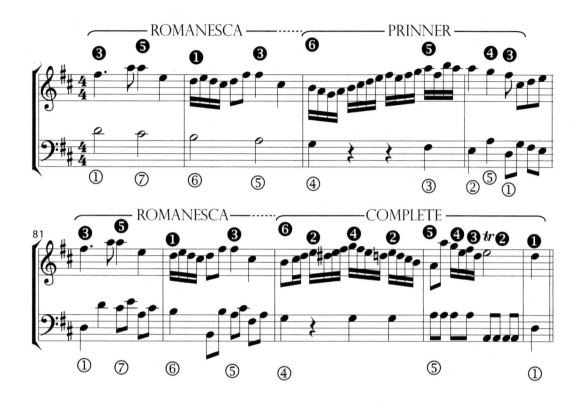

EX. 21.5   Leduc, Opus 4, no. 1, mvt. 1, Cantabile, m. 100 (Paris, 1771)

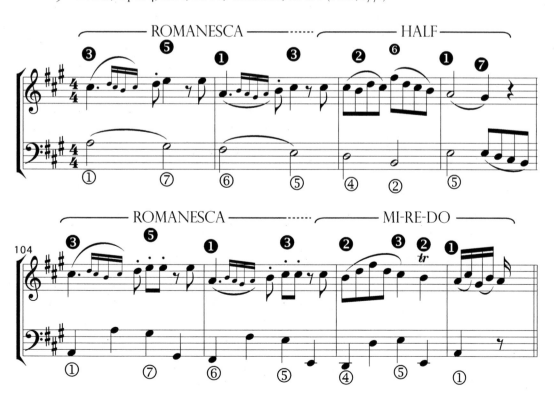

In both cases one hears the same stepwise descending Romanesca and a varied repetition including a more active bass. I very much doubt that either composer borrowed directly from the other. They were both drawing upon the galant tradition, looking into their *zibaldone* for something appropriate and, because the musical situations were similar, making similar choices. Cimarosa is still more Italian in style than Leduc, given his choice of a Prinner riposte for the Romanesca. Both, however, adopt the very similar strategies of using the Romanesca as a type of Falling Thirds preparation for a weak cadence, which then entails a varied repetition that ends with a strong cadence.

Leduc's ingenuity in drawing out the endings of each half of his movement is impressive, with, depending on how one counts, as many as six opportunities for a cadence before the definitive Cudworth cadences. He, like Cimarosa (see chap. 11, ex. 11.21), frequently evades strong closure not through avoidance of the tonic tones, but by fleeing (*sfuggire*) the expected moment of repose, in Leduc's case often with a flurry of sixteenth notes (see ex. 21.6, mm. 37ff.).

Section	Schema	Key
1st Half	Quiescenza, *bis*	A
	Prinner	A
	Indugio	A ⇨ E
	Sol-Fa-Mi	E
	Indugio	E
	Half cadence	E
	Long cadence	E
	Evaded cadence, *ter*	E
	Romanesca, chromatic	E
	Converging cadence	E ⇨ B
	Romanesca, *bis*	E
	Evaded cadence, *ter*	E
	Falling Thirds	E
	Long Comma	E
	Cudworth cadence	E
:‖:		
2nd Half	Quiescenza, *bis*	Em
	Converging cadence	F♯m
	Comma, *bis*	F♯m
	Fenaroli, *bis*	Bm
	Fonte	Em ⇨ D
	Prinner	A
	Indugio, passing 6/4	A

Comma, x4 (pre-Cadenza)	A/E
Augmented 6th	A
Ponte / Cadenza	E ⇨ A
Quiescenza, *bis*	A
Prinner	A
Indugio	A ⇨ E
Long cadence	A
Evaded cadence, *ter*	A
Romanesca, chromatic	A
Converging cadence	A ⇨ E
Romanesca, *bis*	A
Evaded cadence, *ter*	A
Falling Thirds	A
Long Comma	A
Cudworth cad., deceptive	A
Cudworth cad., complete	A

François Fayolle, in his *Notices sur Corelli, Tartini, Gaviniés, Pugnani et Viotti* (Paris, 1810), made it clear that the "mainstream of music," to use Donald Francis Tovey's once famous phrase, ran from Italy to France. Tovey's own mainstream, which might have had the title *Notices sur Haydn, Mozart, Beethoven, Schubert et Brahms*, flowed in German-speaking lands. To judge by common opinion among the devotees of classical music, Tovey's mainstream trumped Fayolle's. But Tovey's mainstream is like a huge canal dug by a determined corps of historical engineers with the intention of redirecting the natural streambed. Composers like Cimarosa and Leduc coursed down the principal channel, not some obscure tributary. In Leduc's Cantabile one will find galant music of real quality, possessing, in the Earl of Chesterfield's phrase, "a superior gracefulness" conveyed through "engaging, insinuating, shining" musical manners.

EX. 21.6   Leduc, Opus 4, no. 1, mvt. 1, Cantabile (Paris, 1771)

22

🙥 🙦

A LARGHETTO

BY

LEONARDO LEO

from *L'Olimpiade* (libretto by Metastasio), Naples, December 19, 1737
Act 3, Scene 6, Aria of Cleisthenes, King of Sicyon

THE WORDS CAME FIRST IN GALANT OPERA. To an expert on early eighteenth-century music, that is obvious. Yet since relatively few readers of this volume may have that expertise, permit me to continue with a series of similar statements that, while obvious to a few, are yet worth repeating given the long reign of *opera seria* as the absolute ruler of the galant musical world. Leonardo Leo (1694–1744), assistant chapel master in Naples, would have received the following two stanzas of six-syllable verse (*senarii*) from the court poet Metastasio to set to music for the aria of King Cleisthenes (the translation is mine and closely follows, at some cost to the meaning and rhyme, the scansion of the original):

Stanza	Line	Original Text	Translation
A	1	Non so d'onde viene	I know not the source of
	2	Quel tenero affetto:	That tender affection,
	3	Quel moto che ignoto	That motion which surges
	4	Mi nasce nel petto:	Unknown in my bosom,
	5	Quel giel che le vene	That chill which now seizes
	6	Scorrendo me và.	My soul through and through.
B	7	Nel seno a destarmi	Conflicting emotions
	8	Sì fieri contrasti,	Arise now within me,
	9	Non parmi, che basti	I fear that they never
	10	La sola Pietà.	To pity will yield.

One can infer much about serious Italian arias from any similar text. The content is obviously about the character's inner feelings. That is, the text does not tell a story to

advance or explicate the plot. The two contrasting stanzas—call them A and B—describe
different moods and will likely be set to contrasting music. The regular, strong-weak line
endings (lines 1–5, 7–9: *versi piani*) will likely be set as melodic appoggiaturas, and the two
final, strong-only line endings (lines 6 and 10: *versi tronchi*) will likely fall on a strong beat
without an appoggiatura. A recapitulation of the first stanza (more florid at the performer's
discretion) will complete the overall ABA form. Leo honored all these conventions and
assigned the various poetical lines to a string of galant schemata, every one of which
should now be familiar.

The list below details the correspondences between lines and schemata. The two
initial statements of stanza A form the heart of the aria, and I have placed repeat signs in
parentheses to highlight the similarity between them and the two halves of a minuet or
sonata. Pedagogically, it may be efficient to compare arias and concertos to minuets, as
Riepel did.[1] Historically, however, the aria was the more esteemed and highly developed
standard of form. Somis's minuet of 1734 (see chap. 5) seems almost a trifle alongside Leo's
aria of only three years later. Writing minuets or sonatas was often an incidental activity for
a galant composer. The job of real consequence concerned writing vocal music for the
church and the court theater. In the context of the previous chapters, an initial reaction to
the list of Leo's schemata might be amazement at its size and complexity. On closer
inspection, however, one can see the concatenization of a number of smaller, simpler sections. Each appearance of the *ritornello*, for instance, functions as an independent instrumental interlude between the sung portions of the aria.

Section	Line	Schema	Key
Ritornello R1		Opening gambit	E♭
		Prinner riposte	E♭
		Half cadence	E♭
		Pulcinella cadence	E♭
		Comma	B♭
		Evaded cadence, *ter*	E♭
		Complete cadence	E♭
𝄋			
Stanza A1	1	Opening gambit	E♭
	2	Prinner riposte	E♭
	3–4	Prinner, modulating	B♭
	4	Half cadence	B♭
	5	Monte	E♭ ⇨ F
	6	Comma	B♭
	. . .	Pulcinella cadence	B♭
	. . .	Comma	F

	6	Evaded cadence, *ter*	B♭
	6	Complete cadence	B♭
(:‖:)			
Ritornello R2		Opening gambit	B♭
		Meyer	E♭
		Half cadence	E♭
Stanza A2	1	Comma	B♭
	2	Fonte	Fm ⇨ E♭
	3	Prinner, 1st half	E♭
	4	Converging cadence	E♭
	5–6	Monte	A♭ ⇨ B♭ ⇨ Cm
	. . .	Prinner	Cm ⇨ E♭
	. . .	Pulcinella cadence	E♭
	. . .	Comma	B♭
	5	Comma	E♭
	6	Evaded cadence, *ter*	E♭
	6	Cadenza	E♭
Ritornello R3		Meyer	E♭
		Cudworth cadence	E♭
(:‖)			
Stanza B	7–8	Do-Re-Mi, paired	Cm
	9	Prinner / Passo Indietro	Gm
	10	Evaded cadence, *bis*	Gm
	10	Cadenza	Gm
Ritornello R4		Opening gambit	E♭
		Prinner riposte	E♭
		Complete cadence	E♭

Dal Segno

Leo became a central figure in the musical life of Naples. He held important posts in the conservatories, eventually was appointed chapel master of the royal court, and early in his career vied with J. A. Hasse (1699–1783) and Leonardo Vinci (ca. 1696–1730) for dominance as the city's premier composer of opera. He had dozens of students who would later have significant careers at courts all over Europe. Important for this book is his student Jommelli, whose opera duet from *Demofoonte* will be presented in chapter 24.

EX. 22.1   Leo, *L'Olimpiade*, act 3, scene 6, aria of Cleisthenes (Naples, 1737)

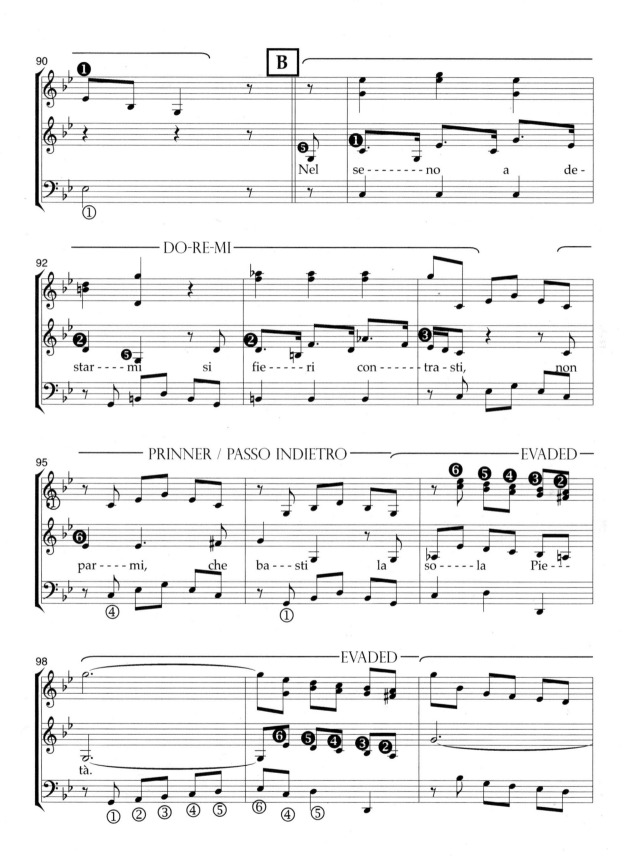

23

AN ANDANTINO

BY

BALDASSARE GALUPPI

from *La diavolessa* (libretto by Goldoni), Venice, November 15, 1755
Act 2, Scene 10, Aria of Dorina, Ingenue

THE TEAM OF GOLDONI AND GALUPPI once dominated musical comedy in the eighteenth century as Gilbert and Sullivan would later in the nineteenth. Carlo Goldoni wrote the words and Galuppi the music for their *La diavolessa* ("The She-Devil"), a spoof on upper-class posturing and lower-class avarice. In the following text, Goldoni has Dorina, the gold-digging ingenue, sing in Venetian dialect to Don Poppone, an elderly gentleman, a scene typical of commedia dell'arte banter between the Dottore and perhaps Fravoletta or Pimpinella:

Stanza	Line	Original Text	Translation
A	1	Sior omo generoso,	O kind and gentle mister,
	2	El cuor vu me offerì?	Why pledge your heart to me?
	3	Cossa m'importa a mi	What purpose would there be
	4	De sto regalo?	For such a present?
B	5	Co no gh'avè de meggio	And have you nothing better
	6	Con mi per farve onor,	By which to do you proud?
	7	Tolè sto mio conseggio,	Take heed of my suggestion,
	8	No stè a parlar d'amor;	Please never talk of love;
	9	Tegnivelo, godevelo,	Please keep it, sir, enjoy it, sir,
	10	Salvevelo, pettevelo,	Preserve it, sir, contain it, kind
	11	Sior generoso, el cuor.	And gentle sir, your heart.

In the jargon of modern film criticism, Goldoni makes this song "diegetic"—part of the story itself. That is, the ingenue refers to this "little song" (*canzonetta*) and then proceeds to sing it for Don Poppone, creating the type of performance within a performance so characteristic of musical comedy. Unlike the aria from Leo's *opera seria* (chap. 22), this aria from Galuppi's *opera buffa* does in fact advance the plot.

The musical setting of this song is considerably simplified if one takes the full-blown arias of *opera seria* as the standard of comparison. Galuppi still uses the stock schemata of the courtly style, but presents them as short, self-contained units. Gone are the many measures of melismas on single syllables, replaced by a relatively rapid declamation of the witty lines of text. And gone is the contrasting mood of a separate B section. Instead, the two stanzas of text are apportioned to what would be the first and second halves of a sonata (see the repeat signs in parentheses below). Like a popular song, this *canzonetta* has multiple verses. When Dorina finishes the first verse, the ritornello returns to lead into her performance of the second verse (not shown); and when the second verse concludes, a few measures of cadence serve to close out the number (also not shown). Goldoni's characters were obvious adaptations of the stock roles of the commedia dell'arte. Galuppi's music was an adaptation of the courtly galant style. Goldoni adapted from below, Galuppi from above, with the result being famously entertaining.

As the following list demonstrates, the standard sequence of schemata is very much in evidence. A Romanesca-Prinner pairing plays its "usual scene" as the aria's theme. The Fonte plays its normal role as a digression early in the second half of the form. The comedic wordplay of lines 9–10 (*Tegnivelo, godevelo, Salvevelo, pettevelo*), perhaps the theatrical high point of the aria, is set to a rising sequence atypical of the courtly style, though common in comedic opera. As the singer reaches her melodic high point (D5), she launches into a series of Cudworth cadences once again securely grounded in the courtly style.

Section	*Line*	*Schema*	*Key*
Ritornello R		Romanesca	D
		Prinner riposte	D
		Passo Indietro ?	D ⇨ A
		Complete cadence	A
Stanza A	1	Romanesca	D
	2	Prinner riposte	D
	. . .	Half cadence	D
	3–4	Prinner, modulating ?	D ⇨ A
	4	Cudworth	A

(𝄆𝄁𝄇)

Stanza B	5	Ponte	A ⇨ D
	6	Prinner	D
	. . .	Half cadence	D
	7	Fonte	Em ⇨ D
	8	Converging cadence	D
	9–10	. . .	D
	11	Prinner	D
	11	Cudworth, evaded, *bis*	D
	11	Cudworth, complete	D

(:‖)

Ritornello R	[as above]	D

Second verse . . .

EX. 23.1   Galuppi, *La diavolessa*, act 2, scene 10, aria of Dorina (Venice, 1755)

24

AN ANDANTINO AFFETTUOSO

BY

NICCOLÒ JOMMELLI

From *Demofoonte* (libretto by Metastasio), Stuttgart, February 11, 1764
Act 2, Scene 10, Duet of Timante and Dircea, Lovers

BIRTHDAY CELEBRATIONS FOR CARL EUGEN, DUKE OF WÜRTTEMBERG, were crowned with *opera seria*. As a connoisseur of music, having studied the clavier with no less than C. P. E. Bach, the duke expected the very best. Indeed he spared no expense to ensure that his court opera was the equal of any in Europe. For his ballet master he engaged the famous Parisian Jean-Georges Noverre (1727–1810), for his head chapel master the Neapolitan Jommelli. Great violinists like Antonio Lolli (ca. 1725–1802) and Pietro Nardini (1722–1793) played in his orchestra (the theorist Daube sat as second flute). For the celebrations of 1764 the renowned tenor Arcangelo Cortoni would sing the role of Demofoonte, King of Thrace (and allegorical stand-in for the duke). The loving spouses— Timante and Dircea—were sung by the famous castrato Giuseppe Aprile (Naples-trained author of the solfeggi discussed in chaps. 2 and 9) and the prima donna Maria Masi-Giura. One of the highlights of the evening would be their duet "La destra ti chiedo."

A duet in *opera seria* was an opportunity not only to display the virtuoso talents of two such acclaimed singers but also to showcase the ability of the court composer to create a compelling musical rendering of the duet's central message: that two separate identities can join together in love and unshakeable fidelity. As mentioned, the two singers represent Timante, a prince and son of King Demofoonte, and Dircea, Timante's beloved but secret wife. Condemned to death through no fault of their own, they lament their fate. Each singer performs a separate stanza to the same music. Then, in the third stanza, they cry out to each other before combining their voices in extended bravura display. Timante, the castrato role, is written in the mezzo soprano range, allowing him to join Dircea in long roulades of parallel thirds and sixths. These three stanzas form a grand "A" section, which is sung twice before the traditional "B" stanza follows with contrasting music.

Singer	Stanza	Line	Original Text	Translation
Timante	Aa	1	La destra ti chiedo,	I ask for your hand now,
		2	Mio dolce sostegno,	My solace and comfort,
		3	Per ultimo segno	As one final gesture
		4	D'amore, e di fè.	Of love and of faith.
Dircea	Ab	5	Ah questo fu il segno	Ah, this was the sign of
		6	Del nostro contento:	Our dearest contentment:
		7	Ma sento, che adesso	I sense that from now on
		8	L'istesso non è.	It won't be the same.
Timante	Ac	9	Mia vita, Ben mio . . .	My dearest, my only . . .
Dircea		10	Addio, Sposo amato.	Farewell now, my consort.
Both		11	Che barbaro Addio!	What barbarous parting!
		12	Che Fato crudel!	What pitiless fate!
Both	B	13	Che attendono i rei	What terrors and torments
		14	Dagli astri funesti,	Await all the wicked,
		15	Se i premi son questi	If thus is rewarded
		16	D'un' alma fedel?	A virtuous soul?

Jommelli, the central musical figure at the Stuttgart court and one of the most influential of all Naples-trained composers, was to set Metastasio's text to music four times (1743, 1753, 1764, 1770). This duet from the version of 1764 lays out a vast musical canvas that calls for singers of extraordinary endurance and flexibility, as the music ranges from quiet tenderness to resigned pathos to defiant exultation. In terms of schemata, Jommelli adapts the familiar Romanesca-Prinner pairing as a stable thematic anchor, followed by extensive passagework and cadential bravura (see the list opposite). Jommelli was reported to have carefully studied Leo's scores.[1] Because librettos by Metastasio were set by almost every composer of opera, a young musician could study how earlier masters had handled the same, or similar, dramatic situation and how they musically embodied the emotional moment. The scope and dynamism of this aria aside, one should not overlook its elegant and sensitive touches. Especially fine, in my estimation, is the moment when, in measure 65, the two lovers' voices come together during the Romanesca theme. They musically embrace in the "passion" of a 2–3 suspension whose resolution begins a train of sensuous parallel thirds.

In contrast to the broad lyricism of the A section, the B section is densely canonic, with the two singers rapidly chasing each other through a thicket of short, repeating patterns. Both main sections place exceptional demands on the singers, and since Jommelli has largely dispensed with extended ritornellos, there are few moments for the singers to catch their breath. Perhaps to address that problem, he wrote a short interlude that appears at the end of A1 and of B. Designed on the question-and-answer, digress-and-return frame of the Fonte, the interlude is almost like accompanied recitative, and the singers address each other in short utterances almost as in speech. In a nice compositional touch, the final event of this Fonte—delayed by a fermata to increase expectation—falls on the opening tones of the next stanza, A2a.

As one might imagine, Jommelli was fond of the eponymous Jommelli schema. In this grand duet he employed it as an intensified version of the Comma, almost always preceding a stronger cadence like the Cudworth.

Section	Line	Schema	Key
Stanza A1a	1	Romanesca	G
	2	Prinner	G
	2	Cadence, Mi-Re-Do	G
	3–4	Prinner, modulating	G ⇨ D
	4	Jommelli	D
	4	Cudworth	D
Stanza A1b	5	Romanesca	G
	6	Prinner	G
	6	Cadence, Mi-Re-Do	G
	7–8	Prinner, modulating	G ⇨ D
	8	Jommelli	D
	8	Cudworth	D
Stanza A1c	9–10	Quiescenza? *bis*	D / Gm
	10	Quiescenza	DM / Dm
	11		D
	11–12	Falling 3rds / Romanesca	D
	12	Jommelli, *bis*	D
	12	Cudworth	D
	9–10	Quiescenza? *bis*	D / Gm
	11		D
	11–12	Falling 3rds / Romanesca	D
	12	Jommelli, *bis*	D
	12	Cudworth, evaded	D
	12	Jommelli	D
	12	Cudworth, evaded	D
	12	Jommelli	D
	12	Cudworth, complete	D
Ritornello R1		Converging / Monte	G ⇨ A
		Cadence, deceptive	D
		Cadence, complete	D

(:‖:)

Interlude	9–10; 1	Fonte	Am ⇨ G

𝄋

Stanza A2a	1	Romanesca	G
	2	Prinner	G
	2; 5	Cadence, Mi-Re-Do	G
Stanza A2b	6; 9	Romanesca	G
	6; 9	Prinner	G
	6; 9	Cadence, Mi-Re-Do	G
Stanza A2c	10; 9	Comma, *bis*	C ⇨ F
	9–10	Cadence, deceptive	C
	9–10	Augmented 6th	Cm
	11		G
	11–12	Falling 3rds / Romanesca	G
	12	Jommelli, *bis*	G
	12	Cudworth	G
	7	Monte	C ⇨ D
	11	Jommelli, *bis*	Gm
	11		G
	11–12	Falling 3rds / Romanesca	G
	12	Jommelli, *bis*	G
	12	Cudworth, evaded	G
	12	Jommelli, *bis*	G
	12	Cudworth, evaded	G
	12	Jommelli	G
	12	Cudworth, complete	G
Ritornello R2		Prinner	G
		Cadence, evaded	G
		Cadence, complete	G

(:‖)

Stanza B	13–14	Do-Mi-Sol, canonic	C
	14	Comma	G
	14	Half cadence	G
	15	Fonte, 1st half	Am
	15		Am ⇨ C
	15–16	Sol-Fa-Mi, canonic	C
	15–16	Fonte	Dm ⇨ C
	16	Cadence, Mi-Re-Do	C

	15–16	Sol-Fa-Mi, canonic	F
	15	Comma	F
	15	Comma	C
	15–16	Sol-Fa-Mi, canonic	C
	15–16	Fonte	Dm ⇨ C
	16	Cadence, evaded	C
	16	Sol-Fa-Mi, *bis*	C
	16	Comma / Jommelli	C
	16	Cadence, evaded	C
	16	Sol-Fa-Mi	C
	16	Comma	F
	16	Comma / Jommelli	C
	16	Cadence, evaded	C
	16	Jommelli	C
	16	Cadence, complete	C
Ritornello R3			C
		Indugio / Fauxbourdon	C ⇨ G
Interlude	9–10; 1	Fonte	Am ⇨ G
Dal Segno			

EX. 24.1　Jommelli, *Demofoonte*, act 2, scene 10 (1764)

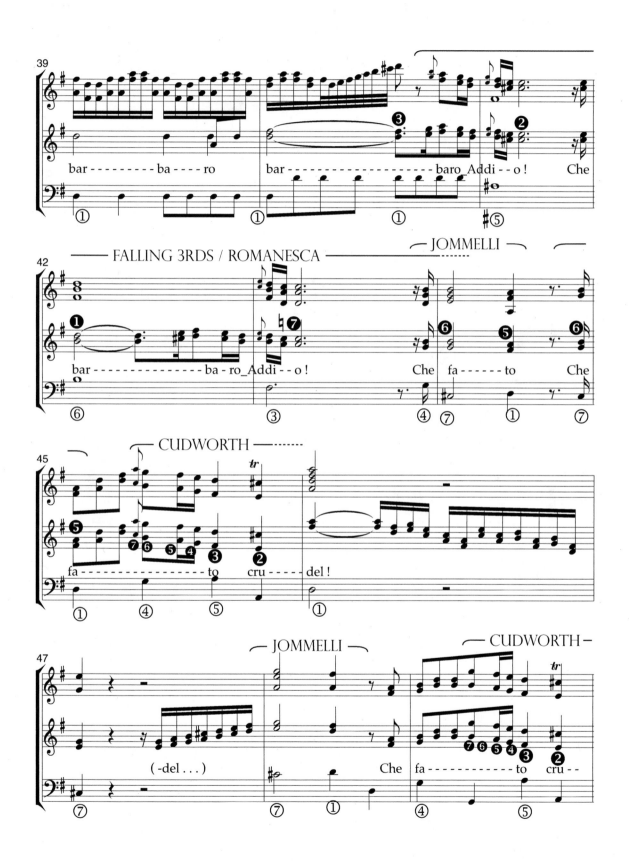

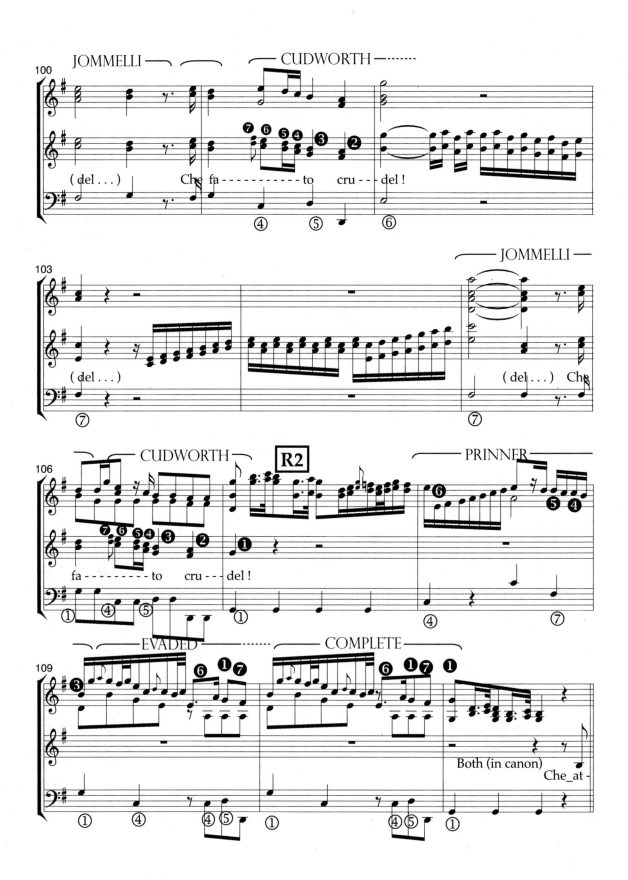

25

THE CHILD MOZART

THE EARLIEST COMPOSITIONS OF WOLFGANG AMADEUS MOZART (1756–1791) reflect both the private and the public faces of the Mozart family. Some of them resemble individual leaves in a childhood album—an internal family record of the boy's musical growth, complete with music-grammatical errors and awkward expressions. Others suggest the transcription of a studied musical performance—a written documentation of the boy's precocity and professionalism intended to impress potential patrons or sponsors. All of them were produced under the careful eye and ear of his father, an esteemed court musician in his own right. These early manuscripts are in the father's hand because Wolfgang, like a child in any language, learned to "speak" before he learned to write. That is, he learned to recognize and replicate phrases of adult music before he learned musical notation. The possibility of a kind of dual authorship of father and son cannot therefore be fully excluded. Moreover, Mozart's first published works—Opera 1 and 2 (Paris)—could have been variously redacted by a gauntlet of adults: his father, the copyist, the publisher, and the engraver. A little boy, fully dependent on adults, cannot be considered an autonomous artist, and we should expect adult influences to color these compositions at every step. Indeed, that is why these small works are so interesting and important. They document the rapid assimilation of adult patterns of musical "speech" by a precocious child. If, as I maintain, a galant musician needed to learn a repertory of phrase schemata in order to "speak" music at court, then the preserved corpus of Mozart's juvenilia should document his acquisition of that knowledge. Because these pieces are preserved from the "kindergarten" period of Mozart's life, we should be able to chronicle the entrance of new schemata into his working musical vocabulary and to describe how he first used them in simple contexts. The presence or absence of sanctioned modes of variation and recombination should help us to distinguish whether the boy was merely parroting adult behavior or whether he was actually acquiring a working knowledge of the schemata and their appropriate usage.

During the 1956 bicentennial celebration of Mozart's birth, scholars were able to examine some long-lost pages from what was presumably the music notebook of Mozart's sister. These pages contain four small compositions in Leopold Mozart's hand, attributed to "Little Wolfgang" (Wolfgangerl) and date from the spring to the early winter of 1761, when Mozart was five years old. The strong provenance of these compositions, together with the explicit dating, puts them first in the Köchel numbering of Mozart's works: KV1a–d. The earliest, KV1a, is demonstrably the most childish (ex. 25.1). It begins in one meter, 3/4 time, and then switches to a different meter, 2/4 time, just four measures later. Such a shift might seem tame in the world of Bartók or Stravinsky. But in the world of the Mozarts it would, at best, have been viewed as endearing childhood gibberish.

EX. 25.1   Mozart, KV1a (1761; age 5)

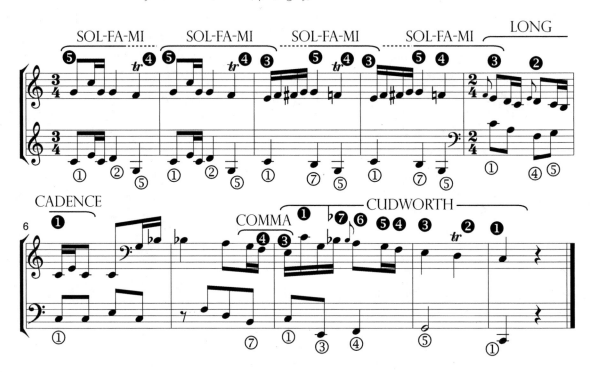

This metrical switch, which looks so definite and planned on paper, was likely a result of Leopold's best effort at transcribing Wolfgang's idiosyncratic performance. The boy may not yet have acquired what a specialist in child development might describe as "metrical constancy," the knowledge that a stable metrical framework should persist throughout a movement. It is also possible that this piece represents quite literal imitations of different exemplars. One, in 3/4 time, is recalled by babbling short fragments based on the Sol-Fa-Mi schema. From a technical perspective, the first two iterations (mm. 1–2) show the melodic ❺ as a stable consonance that becomes unstable and descends to ❹ after the bass

ascends from ① to ②. In the second two iterations (mm. 3–4) the melodic ❺ is reached
from below, which would create bad counterpoint if the bass once again ascended from ①
to ②. So Mozart changes his bass and descends from ① to ⑦, indicating possibly a sensitivity to variants of this schema or early training in the basics of counterpoint. Other exemplars, in 2/4 time, are recalled through two standard cadences, a Long cadence (mm. 5–6)
and a Cudworth (mm. 8–10). The small passage between these cadences is ungrammati-
cal, fitting easily into no single galant schema and including a combination of contrapuntal infelicities (m. 7) typical of the rank beginner. It would appear that the boy knew each
cadence well but was unable to link them effectively. His use of the older, "Mixolydian"
form of the Cudworth cadence (m. 8; note the flatted ❼) may reflect the very conservative
style of pieces that, on the evidence of his sister's musical notebook, were being taught in
the Mozart household.

In his second composition, KV1b, the metrical constancy is no longer a problem. The
curious babbling iterations of an opening schema seen in KV1a are now replaced by a
broader, somewhat more coherent discourse, and the incorporation of a deceptive cadence
followed by a full cadence shows a recognition of the proper linkage of schemata:

EX. 25.2   Mozart, KV1b (1761; age 5)

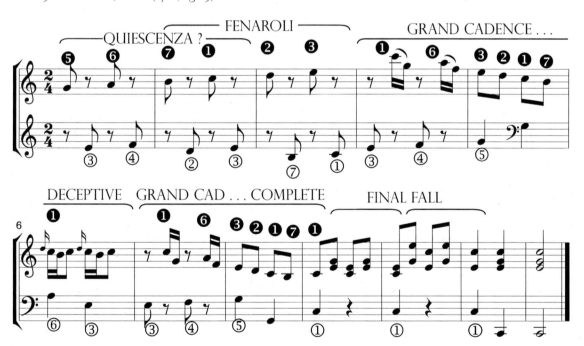

The opening gambit grafts aspects of a Quiescenza onto the traits of a Fenaroli. Given the
unadorned two-voice texture, which initially sounds only one note at a time (mm. 1–3),
both schemata are underdetermined. That is, they lack the unambiguous cues and ancil-
lary features that would solidify their reference. The diatonic Quiescenza without a tonic
pedal point, for example, can only be called such by conjecture, and a Fenaroli without a

dominant pedal point would be unusual. Later in his life Mozart would embed a Fenaroli within a Quiescenza (see ex. 13.24), but the dovetailing of a Quiescenza into a following Fenaroli violates the normal functions of both schemata. If the boy's musical discourse is nevertheless now much clearer than in KV1a, the proportions of this tiny work are little improved. Fully three-fourths of the movement is involved with a single extended act of cadencing. Measures 4–6 present the initial cadence, which ends deceptively. Measures 7–9 repeat the cadence an octave lower with the expected full close. Measures 9–12 constitute a small coda with Final Falls and closing iterations of the tonic chord. In a normal galant movement, these nine measures of cadencing would end a work of perhaps eighty to a hundred measures. So although young Mozart cannot yet construct a movement of that scope, he would appear to be listening to full-sized works and learning to replicate important parts of them.

Being able to control various schemes of repetition was a necessary skill for crafting galant music. In KV1a Mozart repeated the Sol-Fa-Mi, but not in any approved manner. In KV1b he nicely handled the repetition of the cadence, yet the ubiquity of deceptive-to-authentic pairing of cadences was such that the boy might merely have been replicating a passage that he learned as a single entity. Only in KV1c, whose date of December 11, 1761, may place it as much as eight months later than the previous two works, do we see the repetition scheme of the double-reprise form that defined the adult norm for small instrumental movements:

EX. 25.3   Mozart, KV1c (1761; age 5)

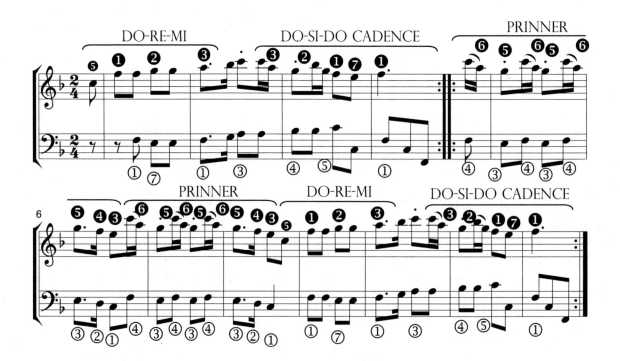

This work signals a marked advance in Mozart's ability to present a well-crafted movement. The previous two works began with awkward or ambiguous opening gambits. KV1c
begins with an obvious Do-Re-Mi. The previous two works had cadences out of all propor-
tion to their movements as a whole. KV1c matches a two-bar cadence to the two-bar Do-
Re-Mi. The previous two works had no Prinner ripostes as foils to their opening gambits.
KV1c includes a Prinner, though on the "wrong" side of the double bar and functioning
instead as a type of Ponte. The previous two works did not modulate. KV1c modulates
implicitly through its Prinner, although the Prinner lacks the inner-voice B♮ that would
make patent the modulation to C major. And whereas the previous two works never
returned to their opening material, KV1c closes with a restatement of the opening schema
and its matching cadence.

The "Menuetto" of KV1d was notated a scant five days after KV1c:

EX. 25.4   Mozart, KV1d (1761; age 5)

This Menuetto (KV1d) was Mozart's first work to be attributed to a genre. Genre had great significance in galant music because of its close connection with social function. Whereas the previous small pieces were for an unknown, presumably internal purpose, the Menuetto makes an explicit reference to an external purpose. This is not to say that anyone would have ever danced to it. But at least it was an imitation of music with adult functions and associations. Its two-measure, six-beat unit of the dance step is clearly evident in the composition's unbroken series of two-bar phrases.

The Mozarts owned a copy of Riepel's treatise, the first three volumes of which appeared during the 1750s. Riepel would no doubt have approved of Wolfgang's early focus on the minuet because Riepel considered it fundamental to the larger genres. Indeed, once initiated in this genre, Wolfgang continued with a series of minuets that explored Riepel's "three master examples" of Monte, Fonte, and Ponte. KV1d, above, introduced Mozart's first Ponte, his first Converging cadence, his first Passo Indietro, his first Comma, and overt modulations not only to C major with the melodic B♮ in measures 6–7, but also to a fleeting G major with an F♯ in measure 5. We can thus see in this Menuetto a significant expansion of his schematic vocabulary (with each new schema used appropriately), the first real three-voice texture (mm. 1–2), the first octave played by one of Wolfgang's small hands (m. 1), and perhaps the first sign of Wolfgang's interest in the recherché manipulation of thematic material.

The strangely hectic, oddly accelerating third measure of the Menuetto has no counterpart later in the movement. If follows the far more serene quarter-note descent of measures 1–2 and leads into a similarly calm measure 4. Could that peculiar melody have been a byproduct of the boy's fascination with an unusual type of *ars combinatoria*? That is, did he desire to fashion the bass of measures 3–4 from the melody of measures 1–2 played backwards? I have added gray beams to measures 1–4 of example 25.4 in order to highlight this possible relationship. Listeners are generally unable to recognize the retrograde version of a melody, so this type of esoterica, if intentional, would be done for personal satisfaction or to impress a professional like Leopold. Ordinarily one does not look to galant minuets for technical manipulations more typical of fugues. But such manipulations do reoccur in Mozart's early works, and throughout his adulthood they seem to remain a private pleasure or possibly a gift to the *cognoscenti*. Haydn's *Minuetto al rovescio* (Hob. XVI:26), where the minuet is played forwards and backwards, would be another case.

Mozart's second minuet, also in F major, appeared in January of 1762, the month of his sixth birthday (ex. 25.5). If KV1c was based on two-measure units, and the minuet of KV1d on two-measure units occasionally pairing to span four measures, then KV2 shows a complete reliance on four-measure units. The obvious Fonte after the double bar even combines two four-measure halves into an eight-measure whole, the boy's longest utterance to date. This Fonte is also constructed from the motives of the opening cadential phrase, a degree of integration not seen before in these early works. The prominence of ❹–❸–❼–❶ in the Fonte melody, as well as the hint of a canon (⑦–① in mm. 8–9 answered by ❼–❶ in mm. 10–11) are suggestive of the Fenaroli schema.

EX. 25.5 Mozart, KV2 (1762; age 6)

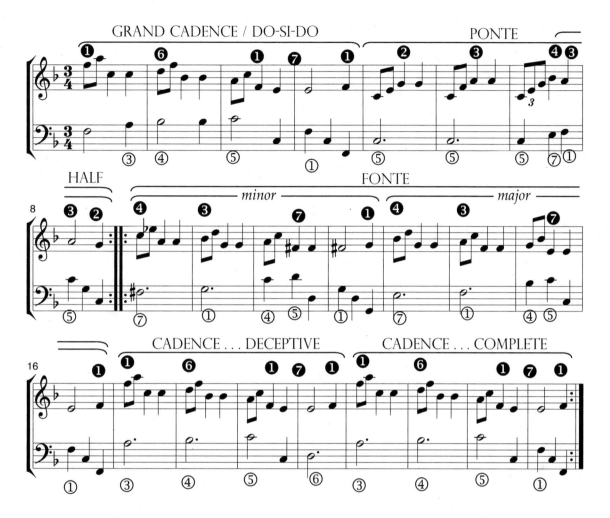

On March 4, 1762, the six-year-old played, and the father transcribed, the thirty measures of KV3 (see ex. 25.6). The small, initial Do-Re-Mi is unremarkable, though following it with a double presentation of the diatonic Quiescenza (minus the pedal point) is unusual. This work properly positions its Prinner ahead of the double bar and makes explicit the Prinner's modulation (note the melodic E♮ in m. 7). It also makes explicit the close connection between the Fenaroli, the Do-Re-Mi, and each half of a Fonte. There were, as mentioned, hints of this relationship in the Fonte of KV2, but in KV3 one can hear the melodic ascent of the Fenaroli "bass" ⑦–①–②–③ (mm. 14–16), the Do-Re-Mi ①–②–③ (mm. 15–16), and a close copy of the Durante countermelody ❺–❹–❸–❼–❶ (mm. 14–16). The eighth-note rest that separates the Fenaroli's ⑦ from the ①–②–③ is likely due to Mozart's again matching the motives of the Fonte to those of the opening theme. Because the theme presents a descending pattern of thirds, an eighth-note rest, and then an ascending stepwise pattern (mm. 1–4), Mozart gives each half of his Fonte the same general profile (mm. 13–16, 19–20).

EX. 25.6   Mozart, KV3 (1762; age 6)

Mozart continues in this same vein with his next two minuets, KV4 and KV5, from May and July of 1762 (KV5 in Wolfgang's own hand). The two works are so similar in their sequence of schemata as to be almost the same piece written twice, each featuring Mozart's first Montes. KV4, Mozart's third attempt at a minuet, is given as example 25.7. At twenty-four measures long, it is the first of these early works to be shorter than its predecessor. Furthermore, with the exception of the new Monte, it represents something of a step back

EX. 25.7   Mozart, KV4 (1762; age 6)

from the high rate of novelty in the preceding pieces. It seems almost a resumé of his previously learned schemata, a chance to revisit the old material so as to use it more artfully.
The minuet begins with a Do-Re-Mi (mm. 1–2), first heard in KV1c in the same key, and
cadences with a variant of the Cudworth cadence (mm. 3–4) first heard in KV1a. In measure 5, the very notes that began the Fonte of KV3 now introduce a Passo Indietro with its
attendant modulation to the dominant key of C major, the same combination used in the

same key and in the same measure in KV1d. A repetition of the Passo Indietro leads into the final cadence of the first half of the movement, which features descending triads whose upper tones outline the first three stages of a Prinner.

The second half of the movement (m. 11) begins with the opening motive of this minuet and continues, in measure 12, with the exact notes of the Do-Re-Mi that began KV3. The hint of a Fenaroli within the Monte, that is, the weak connection between the bass ⑦ of measure 11 and the ①-②-③ of measure 12, will be reworked into a clear Fenaroli in KV5, described below. This first Monte ends in measure 14 of KV4 and is followed by the two-bar Do-Re-Mi of the opening. Mozart repeats this passage an octave lower, a procedure that he tried originally in KV1b, and then varies the repetition of the Passo Indietro (mm. 21–22), also transposing it an octave (though an octave *higher*). From there Mozart replays the same cadence that ended the first half of the movement, transposed of course to the home key of F major. The extent to which he reused literal quotes of his earlier works is, to my mind, indicative of a fascination with the combinatorial possibilities of these galant schemata and their constituent parts. His love of combining his "toys" in every possible way has been shared by many little boys, though in the twentieth century the focus of that attention was more likely to be directed toward Tinker Toys, Erector Sets, and Legos than toward Montes, Fontes, and Pontes.

In Mozart's fourth minuet, KV5 (ex. 25.8), he assembled almost the same schemata that he used in KV4, but he varied their melodic motives and figurations in such a way that the two movements' underlying similarity is not immediately apparent. A simple correlation of schemata with measure numbers nevertheless reveals that these works are nearly identical: Do-Re-Mi (mm. 1–2); Cudworth cadence (mm. 3–4); Passo Indietro or Fenaroli, repeated (mm. 5–6, 7–8); cadence of triplet descending thirds (mm. 9–10). The Passo Indietro of KV4 and the Fenaroli of KV5 (mm. 5–6) share the same descending bass G3–F3–E3 and the same B♮4–C5 melody, so Mozart could substitute the one for the other. Perhaps it was the prominence of the Fenaroli in measures 5–8 that suggested emphasizing, in KV5's Monte, the embedded Fenaroli that was only implied in KV4. It is in KV5 that the Fenaroli emerges as an independent entity in Mozart's vocabulary. His double presentation of this schema as the first pattern in the key of the dominant is further evidence of a careful emulation of adult galant norms.

All in all, these two minuets are perhaps best understood as transcriptions that, in different months, froze in time two slightly different images of the same evolving performance. Mozart's choice, for example, to restate the opening gambit in the second half of the minuet was a performance option (KV4, yes; KV5, no), not a fundamental difference of "form." The same can be said of the option of using the deceptive-authentic pairing of cadences (KV4, no; KV5, yes). It cannot, of course, be easily determined if the six-year-old Mozart made these decisions alone, or if these transcriptions represent final states suggested and approved by his father. What is indisputable is that later the same year the boy was to embark with his father and sister on the first of a series of European tours that would have him improvising keyboard music at the greatest courts of the age. Through his music

EX. 25.8   Mozart, KV5 (1762; age 6)

he "spoke" publicly and by all accounts impressed both the casual listeners and the connoisseurs. In the words of Friedrich Melchior, Baron von Grimm, a German diplomat
who heard him in Paris in 1764 and became one of the family's sponsors:

What is incredible is to see him play off the top of his head for a full hour. He abandons himself to the inspiration of his spirit and to a wealth of ravishing ideas, ideas which he nevertheless knows how to place one after the other with taste and without confusion. The most consummate music director could not be more profound than him in the science of harmony and of modulations which he knows how to lead down paths lesser known but always precise.[1]

In the early 1760s one of the "most consummate" music directors was Niccolò Piccinni (1728–1800). His *La buona figliuola*, a comic opera based on Goldoni's adaptation of the English novel *Pamela*, went from a hugely successful Roman premiere (1760) to stagings all over Europe. Its charming, heartfelt arias became among the best known of the decade and, like Jean-Jacques Rousseau's novel *Julie, ou la nouvelle Heloïse* (1761), helped fuel the vogue for things "sentimental." Mozart's two Fenarolis in KV5, for instance, share many traits with the Fenarolis in Piccinni's aria "Una povera ragazza" ("A Poor Girl"). That is, they both dwell at length on ⑦s in the upper voice before ascending ①–②–③ on consecutive beats (ex. 25.9). Both also present a version of the Durante countermelody in the lower voice. Of course Mozart's phrases are small, brief, and relatively simple, whereas Piccinni's have real breadth, an ornate inner voice, and a more complex presentation as part of a large Fonte (cf. exx. 16.6 and 16.14).

EX. 25.9   Piccinni, *La buona figliuola*, act 1, scene 12, Andantino, m. 28 (Rome, 1760)

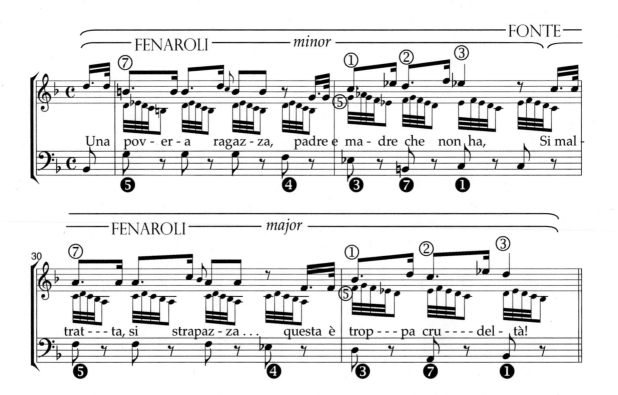

Baron von Grimm's observations, even allowing for hyperbole, suggest that the boy was fluent in the galant style by age seven or eight. His first publication, known then as his Opus 1 (= KV6 and KV7), contains two multimovement sonatas for keyboard with optional violin accompaniment. These works, while not equal to the art of a Piccinni, Galuppi, or J. C. Bach, are nonetheless on a par with compositions by, for instance, an assistant chapel master at a small court. Mozart continued to show musical growth and to refine his technique. In the slow movement of KV6, for instance, he wrote his first attempt at a Quiescenza in its normal position following a main cadence, basing it on the Prinner:

EX. 25.10   Mozart, Opus 1 (KV6), mvt. 2, m. 42 (1762–64; age 7)

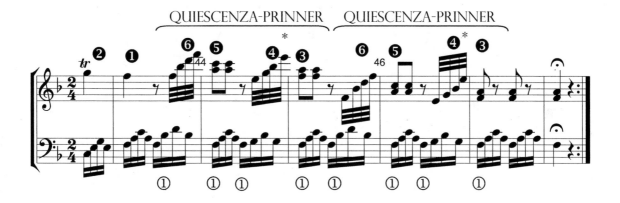

While this was an adequate, even charming effort, it had technical shortcomings. The thirty-second-note high E6 of measure 44 (at the asterisk) and the corresponding E5 of measure 46, for example, are left hanging at the top of the register without really connecting to a tonic F. But just a month later, in the opening movement of KV8, Mozart produced (or reproduced) a proper Quiescenza with all the standard features (see chap. 13, ex. 13.17).

His overreliance on the Prinner was apparent as early as KV1c, when he used it in place of a Ponte. Almost two years after KV1c, in the first of the two minuets from KV7, he showed that he could write a Ponte that bears comparison with Riepel's prototype. To aid that comparison, I notate Riepel's prototype in the same key as Mozart's Ponte, that is, in the local A-major dominant of a global D-major context (ex. 25.11). Mozart matches not only the technical features of Riepel's Ponte, but even its heavy accentuation of each successive downbeat.

As Mozart learned where not to put a Prinner, he also learned how, in its proper position, a Prinner should be expanded and ornamented. You may remember that his very first Prinners, in KV1c and KV3, were only four beats long (discounting repetitions). That was fine for such little pieces but would not serve the larger movements found in KV6 and beyond. In the opening movement of KV6, Mozart tried his hand at a full-sized Prinner (ex. 25.12). He incorporated a simplified version of the *la-to-sol* flourish in the melody

EX. 25.11   Riepel (1755?) and Mozart, KV7, mvt. 2, m. 11 (1762–63? age 7)

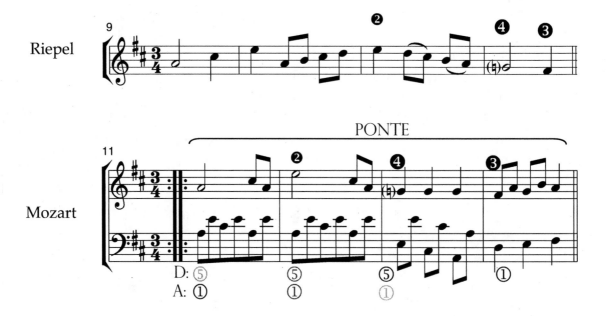

(the rise from ❻ up to the tonic and then back down to ❺) and employed an Alberti bass as accompaniment. Inasmuch as the movement's opening theme was four measures long with a two-measure extension, this two-measure Prinner was still not quite large enough. Mozart thus repeated it (mm. 7–8, not shown) to achieve a rough parity between opening gambit and riposte.

EX. 25.12   Mozart, KV6, mvt. 1, m. 7 (1762–63? age 7)

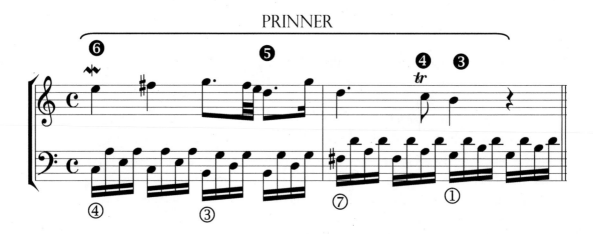

In the opening movement of KV9, Mozart refined his presentation of the four-bar Prinner. His opening theme had been only two bars in length, with a busy Alberti bass. He matched that with the first two bars of his Prinner, also with an Alberti bass and a mature form of the *la*-to-*sol* flourish, and then concluded the Prinner by shifting the sixteenth-note activity to the melody:

EX. 25.13   Mozart, KV9a, mvt. 1, m. 3 (1763–64? age 8)

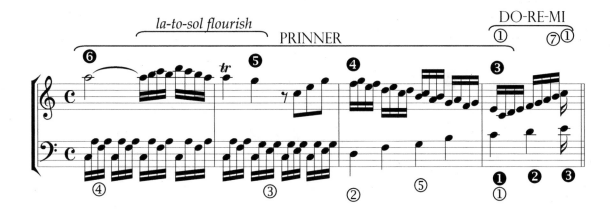

The first half of his Prinner, which puts the ④–③ bass in an inner, tenor voice, may have been in imitation of the Parisian keyboard virtuoso Johann Gottfried Eckard (1735–1809; see chap. 26, ex. 26.1). The second half of his Prinner bears comparison with a slightly more compact passage from one of Cimarosa's keyboard works (ex. 25.14). I am not suggesting any direct influence or copying between Mozart and Cimarosa—in 1764 they were both just boys far removed from each other, with Mozart eight and Cimarosa fifteen. Moreover, Cimarosa likely wrote his sonata much later. But the passages do show how two musicians from the same generation could come up with similar solutions to similar problems if they both began with the same repertory of stock schemata.

EX. 25.14   Cimarosa, Sonata C48, Allegro, m. 2 (ca. 1780s)

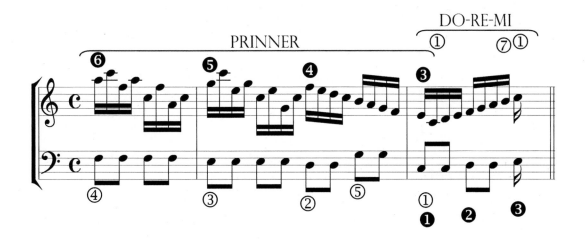

The maestros in Naples had been imparting such Prinners to their students for quite some time, demonstrating how the various parts could be combined in different ways. Giacomo Insanguine (1728–1795), a student of Durante, taught the following two variants in his solfeggi for bass voice—the first a modulating Prinner with a simplified *la-to-sol* flourish and a root-position bass, the second a Prinner riposte with a triadic flourish and the tonic in the bass:

EX. 25.15   Insanguine, Solfeggi nos. 24 and 25 (Naples, ca. 1770s?)

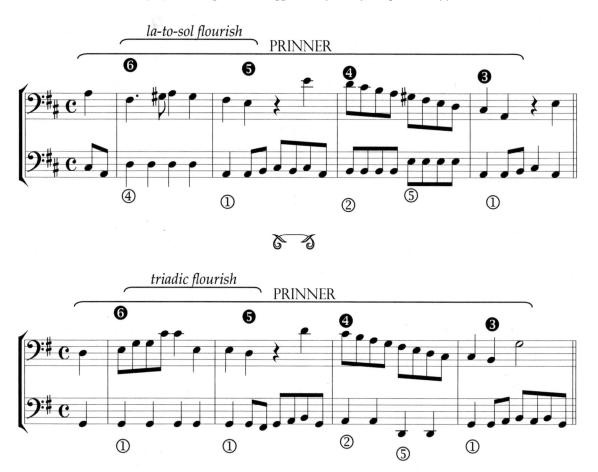

Similar constructions of the four-bar Prinner can be found in the solfeggi of Sala, a student of Nicola Fago (1677–1745) and Leo, and the solfeggi of Aprile (cf. ex. 9.15), who was a student of Gregorio Sciroli (1722– ca. 1781), himself a student of Fago and Leo. These Leisti taught nearly the same variants as a Durantisto like Insanguine, suggesting a common currency. Aprile in turn taught Cimarosa, so the lineage of Cimarosa's Prinner can be determined with some specificity. The same cannot be said for Mozart. It remains unclear whether he learned the galant schemata solely from hearing other compositions or whether, at some point, he encountered the widely disseminated didactic works emanating from Naples and other centers of musical training.

Mozart's musical world expanded tremendously as the family toured Europe. He heard a broader and more fashionable repertory than was played in Salzburg, and he met with musicians of greater talent and experience than he had encountered at home. It was during this period, especially 1764–65, that his schematic vocabulary came more fully into alignment with the practices of galant musicians as a whole. The Romanesca, for example, was a staple of the Italian masters but absent from Mozart's earliest pieces. Mozart's first try at what appears to be a Romanesca occurred in the small minuet of KV8:

EX. 25.16   Mozart, KV8, Menuet I, m. 1 (1763–64? age 8)

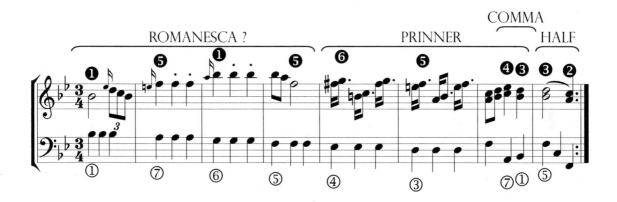

The fourth stage of a Romanesca in C major (m. 4) would normally have an E3 bass with a C-major harmony, or a G3 bass with E-minor harmony. Mozart's phrase has the G3 bass but with G-major harmony, not quite comme il faut. Indeed, the G-major harmony of measure 4, coupled with the F♯ grace note of measure 2, suggests that measure 3 would have been harmonized with the tones A, F♯, and C, a chord more appropriate to the modulating Prinner or the Clausula Vera than the Romanesca. That is, this phrase has a Romanesca-like melody but an accompaniment better suited to schemata that shift their tonal focus toward G major.

While harmonizations like that in KV8 do occur in works by other galant composers, and while they conform to the "Rule of the Octave" (see appendix B), they were not the norm as an opening gambit, especially when given a Romanesca-like melody as in KV8. Nearly identical melodies by Pasquale Cafaro and Fulgentius Peroti (shown in the following chapter as exx. 26.2, 26.3), for instance, both employ the standard Romanesca bass. In his next work, KV9, Mozart demonstrated that he had learned the standard Romanesca (ex. 25.17). He now makes a clear distinction between its harmonization and that of a modulating Prinner. He followed his Romanesca with a pair of cadences, the first deceptive, the second complete. In the deceptive cadence he presents an embedded Prinner in the main key of C major. After the complete cadence, he then offers a pair of modulating Prinners in the key of G major, complete with High ❷ Drops.

EX. 25.17   Mozart, KV9, m. 1 (1763–64? age 8)

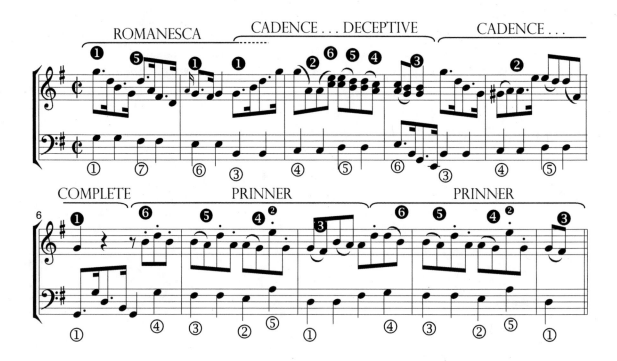

Leopold, of course, may still have had a hand in Wolfgang's works destined for public presentation, such as Opus 1 and Opus 2 (= KV6–7 and KV8–9). Wolfgang's London sketchbook of 1765, however, shows few if any traces of Leopold's editorial influence. The sketchbook was created in part during a period when Leopold was ill in London and Wolfgang was more or less confined to their hotel room for weeks on end. These personal, unexpurgated musical "doodlings" reveal that the young Mozart had fully internalized the normal Romanesca opening (see ex. 25.18). Mozart's placement of the deceptive cadence second instead of first in a pair of cadences is typical of the idiosyncracies that abound in this private sketchbook. A comparison of examples 25.17 and 25.18 with example 3.17 by L'Abbé le Fils will show the extent to which Parisian models helped shape Mozart's evolving compositional practice.

Whether through the conservative influence of his father, frequent exposure to the simple pieces played by his sister, knowledge of the repertory played in Salzburg, or the effects of early training in the "strict" style of counterpoint, Mozart did not decorate his earliest works with elaborate "graces." That is, the Salzburg pieces lack indications of the conventionalized and highly ornamental melodic tracery that was considered fashionable and indicative of a "heightened sensibility." That all changed when the Mozarts came to Paris in 1764. Melodic graces were something of a French specialty, and it would have been impossible to impress the Parisians without demonstrating considerable skill at ornamentation.

EX. 25.18 Mozart, KV15ii (London Sketchbook), m. 1 (1765; age 9)

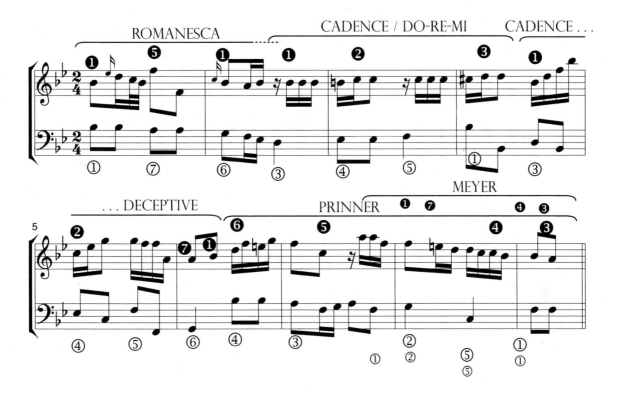

For the study of French ornamentation, the music of Johann Gottfried Eckard would have seemed an obvious choice. Though of German birth, Eckard spent his professional life in Paris, where he was renowned as a brilliant keyboard performer whose playing and compositions were singled out for praise by Baron von Grimm, by the Englishman Charles Burney, and most importantly by Leopold Mozart. In Eckard the young Mozart encountered someone who could spin out highly ornamented versions of the basic schemata of galant music such that twenty or thirty notes might separate their individual stages. So ornate is Eckard's manner that an example from 1763 takes an entire page of notation to present only its Jupiter opening gambit and a Prinner riposte with embedded Meyer (ex. 25.19). Notice that the ❹–❸ dyads of these schemata are played twice, the first time closing more weakly and the second time more strongly.

The effect on young Mozart must have been significant, for his subsequent works quickly began to show a variety of Parisian traits. After leaving Paris, the Mozart tour continued on to London, where as mentioned Mozart worked on his sketchbook. He also composed six more sonatas for violin and keyboard that were eventually published as Opus 3. They were dedicated to the young Queen Charlotte, who had met the Mozarts and heard both children play. She was the same Charlotte Sophia whose "accomplishment" in music had helped advance her marriage to George III in 1761 (see chap. 1). The queen's Master of Music was, of course, J. C. Bach.

EX. 25.19   Eckard, Opus 1, no. 6, mvt. 1, Con discretione, m. 1 (Paris, 1763)

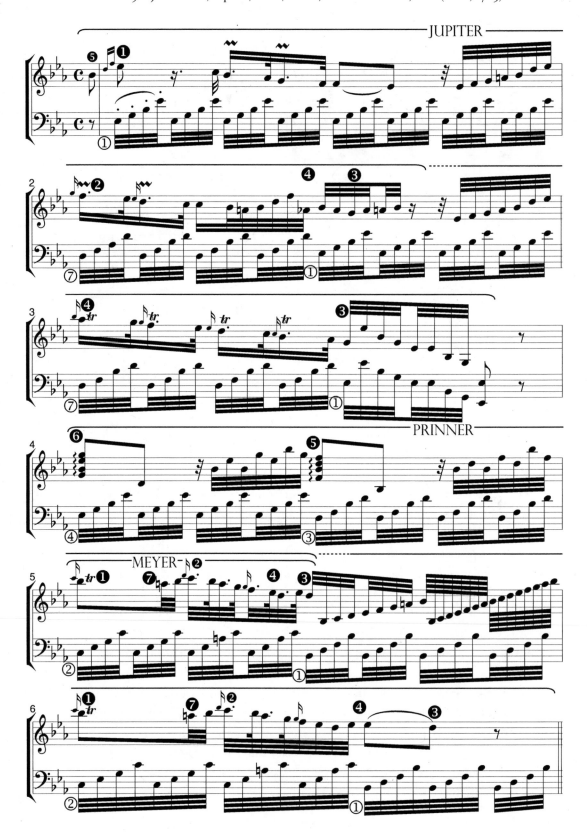

One of these sonatas, KV12, documents an early stage in Mozart's assimilation of Eckard's style. In its first movement (ex. 25.20), we can compare an opening Jupiter and a Prinner riposte to the same schemata in the preceding example by Eckard. The boy has adopted chromatic appoggiaturas in the melody and a thirty-second-note run, but the overall effect is still somewhat mechanical and four-square. The Prinner that begins in measure 5 contains the standard *la*-to-*sol* ornament between stages one and two of the schema. In retrospect, its first half, with the ④–③ bass, functions like a gentle form of the Passo Indietro (cf. mm. 5–6 of the theme for Haydn's variations in chap. 10). The second half of the Prinner was thus replaced by a cadence, here a Converging cadence. Characteristic of Mozart's precocious understanding of how these schemata can be interchanged and recombined, the Converging cadence has the same melody as a modulating Prinner. That is, the tones E5–D5–C5–B4 (mm. 6–8) can be heard as either ❸–❷–❶–❼ in C major (as shown) or as ❻–❺–❹–❸ in G major. Neither representation alone does justice to the merged meaning that I believe they had in Mozart's time.

EX. 25.20   Mozart, KV12, mvt. 1, m. 1 (1764; age 8)

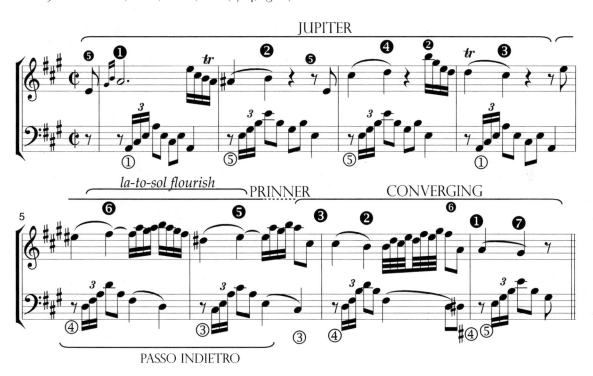

After spending over a year in London, the Mozarts began their return journey by way of the Hague, the most illustrious court in the Netherlands. Six additional sonatas, Wolfgang's Opus 4, were published there in 1766, and in the opening movement of KV27 (ex. 25.21) he showed that he had mastered and perhaps exceeded the art of Eckard. A Meyer serves as opening gambit, with a smaller Meyer as echo leading to a Prinner riposte. At six measures in length, the Prinner matches the extended opening gambit.

EX. 25.21   Mozart, KV27, mvt. 1, Andante poco adagio, m. 1 (1766; age 10)

In a movement like this, the ten-year-old Mozart achieves an adult level of sophistication. He has, to be sure, copied much from Eckard's style. In addition to all the borrowed tracery like the thirty-second-note ascending scale of measure 4, Mozart has learned to emulate the pacing of Eckard's "delivery." For example, Eckard presented his Jupiter in two measures, but echoed its last half in order to add an additional measure, three in all. He then began a broad Prinner, giving one measure to each of the first two stages before quickening the pace with an embedded Meyer. Those same proportions hold for Mozart's movement, though the count of measures is doubled. Mozart begins with a four-measure Meyer (mm. 1–4), which is echoed by a two-measure Meyer (mm. 5–6), six measures in all. He then begins a broad Prinner, giving two measures to each of the first two stages (mm. 7–10). The end of Mozart's Prinner is likewise accelerated so that the last two stages take only one measure each (mm. 11–12).

While this movement shows ornamentation and form well in hand, it also shows a mature understanding of combinations and subtle contingencies between and among schemata. A simple example would be the embedding of a Prinner within the second half of a Meyer (mm. 2–4), something that we have seen done by adult composers like Graun and Haydn (see chap. 9). More subtle would be the relationship between the ❹–❸ termination of a Meyer, Jupiter, or similar schema and the beginning of a following modulating Prinner. A common practice was to end the opening gambit on ❸ in a middle register and then to begin the modulating Prinner an octave higher on what becomes ❻ in the key of the dominant. In Eckard's movement, the ❸ falls on E4 in measure 3, and the ensuing ❻ in the key of the dominant is the E5 in measure 4. In Mozart's movement the same E4 is ❸ in measure 6; then, in measure 7, E5 an octave higher becomes ❻ in the key of the dominant. This was a very traditional move, one already practiced by Leo in the 1730s (see chap. 22), yet it might not be evident to someone who had only learned each pattern by rote.

As a last mark of his rapidly maturing craft, I might cite the way in which Mozart draws out, through the extension of the first two stages of his modulating Prinner, an association with the Fonte. By using the less-common A-minor harmony for the Prinner's first stage, and a G-major harmony for the second stage, he provides a minor-then-major, one-step-down analogue of the Fonte, which serves here as a Fonte-like digression from, and then return to, the more goal-directed activity. As Baron von Grimm said, "The most consummate music director could not be more profound than him in the science of harmony and of modulations which he knows how to lead down paths lesser known but always precise." A ten-year-old boy might seem an unlikely candidate for the "consummate music director," but only well-trained adults could match the level of skill shown in KV27.

One can, of course, imitate subtlety without understanding it. The Parisian Leduc wrote similar passages, and the boy might have been mimicking Leduc's procedures (cf. his Opus 4, no. 2, mvt. 1, mm. 17–20, not shown). He might also have been mimicking the opening aria of *La buona figliuola* (see ex. 25.22), with its two Meyers and broad Prinner-as-Fonte.

EX. 25.22   Piccinni, *La buona figliuola*, act 1, scene 1, Andantino, m. 25 (Rome, 1760)

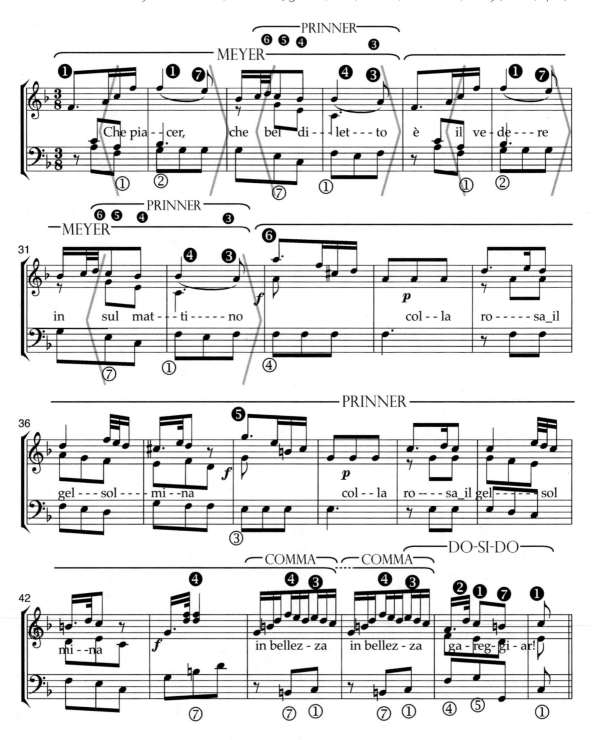

Piccinni, who was indeed a "most consummate music director," devoted ten measures to the minor-then-major contrast of his modulating Prinner (mm. 33–44; he aided his listeners by marking *forte* the widely separated core events). When examined closely, however, Mozart's Andante poco adagio of KV27 appears more like a synthesis of certain aspects of Eckard, Leduc, Piccinni, J. C. Bach, and others. The weight of evidence from all of his juvenilia suggests that imitation progressed quickly to assimilation. As he absorbed a variety of prototypes and exemplars, Mozart internalized their various traits, structures, meanings, and contingencies, becoming a fluent speaker of galant musical "prose" by perhaps age eight and a minor artist of galant musical "poetry" by perhaps age ten.

26

AN ALLEGRO

BY

Wolfgang Amadeus Mozart

KV545, mvt. 1, June 26, 1788

"FOR BEGINNERS" (FÜR ANFÄNGER) was a phrase once attached to the sonata KV545, though few beginners play it well. The subtitle does, nevertheless, hint at the infantilization of galant music by later generations. Mozart's Allegro, which by galant standards was a remarkably sophisticated and advanced composition, seemed childishly simple to Romantic pianists more accustomed to the physically demanding works of Schumann, Liszt, or Rubenstein. No longer hearing a discourse of courtly schemata, their attention turned to the movement's lack of bravura, chromatic harmonies, remote modulations, and perceived drama or narrative. While still allowing for Mozart's continued high status and for the work's origin at roughly the same time as his most revered symphonies, the Romantics reconceived his Allegro as propaedeutic—one of the worthy "steps to Parnassus" to be climbed by the apprentice pianist. Its many ascending and descending scales in sixteenth notes no doubt echoed the earnest "methods" for the training of young players. The work scrupulously avoids physical demands that would have exceeded the ability of a talented child executant—much of the time only a single note is played in each hand, and smaller hands need only stretch to the occasional octave. At no time do more than three notes need to played in a chord, and then only within the span of a seventh.

From a galant perspective, one might better subtitle this work "The Art of the Prinner." Mozart presents five different types of Prinner in the course of the movement, each showcasing a different technique or style. He sets the first, in measures 3–4 (see ex. 26.6), as a two-measure riposte to the two-measure opening gambit. The Prinner's normal inner voice appears in the bass, echoing the Parisian style of Eckard or the Neapolitan style of Aprile. Here is the analogous Prinner from one of Eckard's keyboard works (note his *la*-to-*sol* flourish connecting ❻ to ❺ and then echoed as ❹ to ❸; cf. ex. 9.15 by Aprile).

EX. 26.1   Eckard, Opus 1, no. 2, mvt. 1, Allegro con spirito, m. 25 (Paris, 1763)

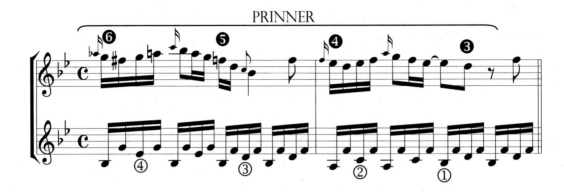

Mozart sets his second Prinner, measures 5–8 (see ex. 26.6), as a florid riposte to measures 1–4. This well-known passage, the Waterloo of many young pianists, was something of a set piece for a Prinner riposte. Both the famous Neapolitan maestro Pasquale Cafaro (1715/16–1787) and the little-known Padre Fulgentius Peroti (fl. 1750s) used the same scales in Prinner ripostes. Cafaro's passage, following a Romanesca, comes from a collection of his solfeggi, and was thus truly intended to be didactic:

EX. 26.2   Cafaro, solfeggio in C major, Allegro, m. 1 (ca. 1770s?)

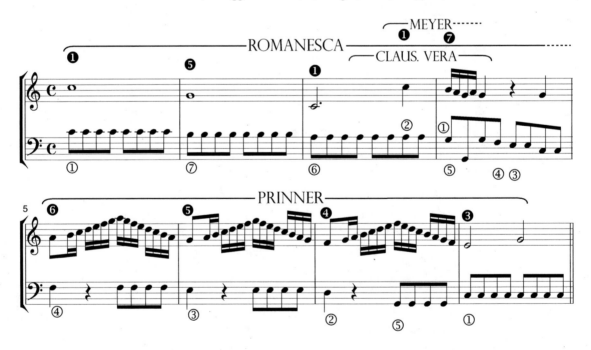

Note how in measures 3–4, when an implied inner voice might ascend E–F♯–G to complete a Clausula Vera, the melody sounds the ❶–❼ dyad of a Meyer, to be answered by the ❹–❸ close of the ensuing Prinner.

Peroti's work was published in 1756 by the Nuremberg lutenist Johann Ulrich Haffner (1711–1767). Haffner's publications were widely disseminated, and Leopold Mozart had asked for some of Wolfgang's early pieces to be sent to Haffner. Note how, in measures 3–6, Peroti prefaces his large Prinner (mm. 7–10) with two statements of the same type of small, simple Prinner used by Mozart at the analogous location (ex. 26.6, m. 3):

EX. 26.3   Peroti, Sonata in B♭ Major, mvt. 3, Allegro non tanto presto, m. 1 (ca. 1750s)

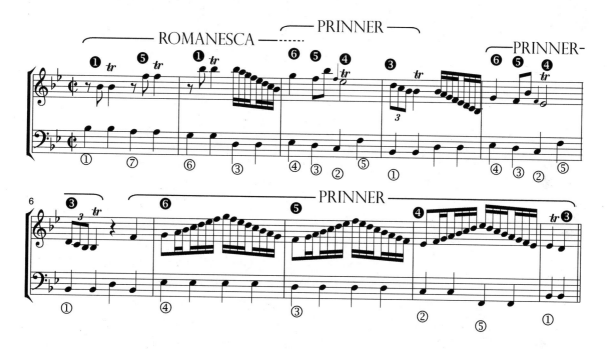

Unlike Cafaro and Peroti, Mozart does not allow his Prinner to close quite so completely. He continues the scalar figure for a fourth measure, on ❸, which carries the melody down to ❷ and the beginning of an Indugio (ex. 26.6, mm. 9–11).

Mozart's third Prinner, measures 18–21, serves as a four-measure riposte to the two preceding two-measure statements of the "second theme" in the key of G. Both of these two-measure statements (mm. 14–15, 16–17) are "open" syntactically, ending with the ❶–❼ dyad of a Meyer or Aprile (cf. ex. 26.2 by Cafaro). As with Cafaro's passage, the ❹–❸ close of the ensuing four-measure Prinner serves to realize and complete those implications. Mozart's third Prinner echoes a technique used by Dittersdorf in one of his keyboard concertos, where each stage of the Prinner is preceded by a less stable 6/3 chord (see ex. 26.4). Mozart and Dittersdorf may both have had Italian models in mind, like the excerpt from a Galuppi sonata (ca. 1750s) shown in example 26.5. Galuppi presents four measures of a Monte before continuing with the four-measure Prinner. His model shares with the passages by Mozart and Dittersdorf the alternation of 6/3 and 5/3 chords, and the melodic descents of a sixth from the 6/3 chords to the 5/3 chords. The last of these descents matches ornamental versions of the standard High ❷ Drop.

EX. 26.4   Dittersdorf, Concerto in A Major (la32), m. 36 (1779)

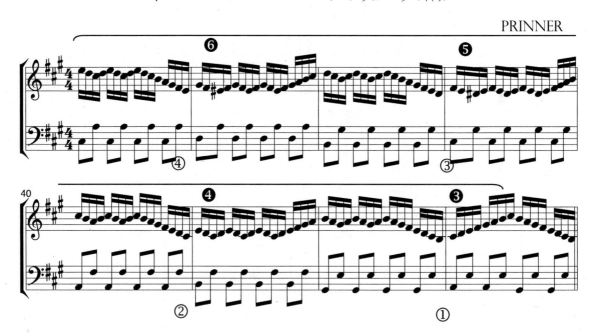

Mozart places his fourth Prinner, measures 37–40, in the minor mode (A minor) and arranges its standard two parallel voices in a canon at the lower fifth. The previous large Prinners had all been extended so that their melodies continued descending to ❷. Here that would have been B♮4 in measure 41. In a deft harmonic-melodic sleight-of-hand, Mozart flats the ❷, suggesting the very dark sound of the Neapolitan 6th, only to quickly reinterpret the B♭ as ❹ in the key of F major.

His fifth and last new Prinner, measures 50–53 (see the starred Prinner in the list of schemata, p. 364), was technically unnecessary. He had set the return of the opening theme (mm. 42ff.) in the key of F major, the subdominant. He could have subsequently let the movement "play itself out" in the sense that the Indugio of measures 54–56 could have modulated back to C major, just as it had facilitated a modulation up a fifth in the first half of the movement (mm. 9–11). Instead, Mozart follows the repeat of his second type of Prinner (mm. 46–49) with a modulating Prinner created by exchanging the parts. That is, the prior bass becomes the melody and the prior melody becomes the bass. This exchange of voices, however, is accomplished without inverting the schema. The Prinner's core melodic tones remain in the melody and the core bass tones remain in the bass. Mozart even works in the convention of beginning a modulating Prinner by shifting *mi* an octave higher (the old ❸ becomes a new ❻), as was seen previously in Leo (ex. 22.1, mm. 22–23), Eckard (ex. 25.19, mm. 3–4), and one of Mozart's own early works (ex. 25.21, mm. 6–7). For a devotee of the galant style, this added Prinner might have been received as a mannerist gesture that calls attention to its compositional virtuosity. Indeed, the whole movement demonstrates what one might term the High Galant, but in a piece of modest dimensions and with modest demands on the performer.

EX. 26.5   Galuppi, Sonata in D Major, m. 66 (ca. 1750s)

Of all the complete movements presented in this volume, this is the only one to be designed so that the material following the double bar fits nicely into the nineteenth-century concept of a "development section." For a large sonata, as opposed to a small minuet, the galant norm called for the material right after the double bar to restate the first theme, but in the key of the dominant. Though Leonard Ratner began pointing this out in a series of widely circulated publications from the late 1940s onward,[1] the facts of galant norms have never made much headway in the face of the Romantic ideal of a three-part sonata of "exposition, development, and recapitulation." For Mozart, sonatas like this one were something of a departure from his training and long experience. These newer procedures began to be widely adopted and eventually constituted a new norm. Yet one can hardly speak of a "common practice."

Section	Schema	Key
1st Half	Opening gambit	C
	Prinner riposte	C
	Prinner	C
	Indugio	C ⇨ G
	Ponte	G
	?, *bis*	G
	Prinner	G
	Indugio	G
	Mi-Re-Do Cadence	G
	Coda, *bis*	G
	Final Fall	G

:||:

Section	Schema	Key
2nd Half	Coda, *bis*	Gm
	Meyer	Dm
	Coda, *bis*	Dm
	Meyer	Am
	Prinner	Am
	(modulation)	Am ⇨ F
	Opening gambit	F
	Prinner riposte	F
	Prinner	F
	Prinner ★	F ⇨ C
	Indugio	C ⇨ G
	Ponte	C
	?, *bis*	C
	Prinner	C
	Indugio	C
	Mi-Re-Do Cadence	C
	Coda, *bis*	C
	Final Fall	C

:|

EX. 26.6   Mozart, Sonata in C Major (KV 545), mvt. 1, Allegro (1788)

27

IL FILO

A POCO ADAGIO

BY

JOSEPH HAYDN

Opus 20 (Hob. III/33), no. 3, mvt. 3, 1772

LIKE GALUPPI'S FAMOUS HALLMARKS OF MUSICAL EXCELLENCE, "beauty, clarity, and fine modulation" ("vaghezza, chiarezza, e buona modulazione"),[1] Leopold Mozart's hallmarks of a master composer, "good technical composition and the arrangement of material: *il filo*" ("der gute Satz, und die Ordnung, *il filo*"),[2] can be difficult to translate into the language of our time. I, for instance, read Leopold as describing two concepts, with the second named in both German and Italian, while Emily Anderson, the enormously talented translator of Mozart's letters, took Leopold's laconic remark to have three parts—"good composition, sound construction, *il filo*."[3] The English words "composition" and "construction" seem insufficiently distinct. In my view, Leopold's use of *Satz* refers to the craft of musical composition, with all its rules and preferred procedures, while *Ordnung* refers to the choices made in the serial disposition of musical material. Placing things in a suitable order creates the cognitive thread (*il filo*) that, like Ariadne's thread which led Theseus through the labyrinth, guides the listener through a musical work. One might have wished for Leopold to expand on *il filo*, since it appears to have had an accepted meaning among the Mozarts and perhaps among musicians of that time generally. Like so many musical terms of the eighteenth century, whether *adagio, concerto, crescendo,* or *fonte*, it was Italian in provenance and probably disseminated through both Italian musicians working in the north and northern musicians studying in Italy.[4] As a metaphor the term is, of course, open to many interpretations. In this chapter, I will approach it from four perspectives—schemata, paths, partimenti, and sketches—in the hope of establishing a more prosaic definition, one that nonetheless is important for understanding how the Mozarts and other galant musicians conceived of the art of composition.

In the conservatories of Naples there was a pragmatic orientation to the training of young composers. A maestro needed to impart the specifics of a living praxis. When asked a difficult "why" question of the type that beginners love to pose, the great maestro Durante is said to have replied,

> My dears, do it this way because this is the way it is done. It must be this way because the true and the beautiful are one, and in this I am not mistaken. I cannot tell you the reasons that you ask of me, but you may be sure that the maestros who come after me will find them, and of the precepts that I give you now, they will make many axioms that will develop into infallible rules.[5]

Durante (1684–1755) was succeeded at the conservatory of Sant'Onofrio da Capuana by Carlo Cotumacci (ca. 1709–1785), who was in turn succeeded by his student Giovanni Furno (1748–1837). When Furno's student Francesco Florimo (1800–1888) recalled Furno, in the same situation, saying "Do it this way, and as I tell you, for this is how my teacher Cotumacci taught me to do it,"[6] we hear the continuity, even the obstinacy of Neapolitan tradition. The situation appears to have been much the same in Bologna. Of his teacher Stanislao Mattei, Gioachino Rossini recalled that "when I asked Mattei for explanations, he always replied: 'This is the way it has been done.'"[7] Durante, Cotumacci, Furno, and Mattei were not, however, Old Testament prophets awaiting a New Testament revelation of harmonic principles from a Fétis, Riemann, or Schenker. The Italian emphasis on the emulation of models, the internalization of frequently occurring schemata, and the training of the musical imagination through partimenti and solfeggi was, in fact, the very sort of regimen that experts in the learning sciences might recommend today.

A generation of Neo-Romantic idealists active in the later nineteenth and early twentieth centuries was at pains to ground its deeply felt engagement with classical music in the quasi-magical properties of harmonically tonal forces and the Hegelian mysteries of sonata form. Given that none of the world's other musics appeared governed by those forces or privy to those mysteries, they held classical music as a thing apart, as a zenith of musical development attained by only one people. The early study of ethnomusicology, for instance, was directed toward all musics except the classical heritage of Europe. Yet if one adopts the perspective of twenty-first-century ethnomusicology, eighteenth-century galant musicians in Naples, Dresden, Versailles, or London do not look so very different from eighteenth-century court musicians in Tehran, Dehli, Yogyakarta, or Seoul. All these artisans worked in preindustrial cultures where highly trained, often hereditary musicians catered to the refined tastes of noble patrons. Training in any of these traditions took years and required the memorization of huge amounts of musical vocabularly and repertory. Apprentices learned how traditional melodic figures and motifs could be fit within frameworks of scales and meters, and which music should be chosen for various moods, occasions, and ceremonies. In styles that favored improvisation, young musicians practiced how to select strings of patterns that helped to fashion larger formal or narrative designs:

They develop flexibility in the use of initially limited stores of vocabulary, devise a systematic way of relating vocabulary patterns one to another, and absorb the aesthetic principles that guide vocabulary usage.[8] . . . Once thoroughly absorbed into a storehouse, new patterns take their place beside the multitude of other set patterns—the precise shapes from which musical thoughts are fashioned. There, within the artist's imagination, they lead a rich existence, continuously transformed in relation to other vocabulary patterns. . . . As soloists call the figures repeatedly into action and redefine their relationships, however, they sometimes find that the figures occur to them more frequently in some settings than others, interact more comfortably with certain other individual patterns, and even evolve increasingly consistent forms of usage with specialized syntactic functions.[9]

The above quotation might equally well describe how to select from the musical storehouse of *radif* for a performance of classical Persian music, or how to string together galant schemata to create a *fantasia*. The actual source is the ethnomusicologist Paul Berliner describing the employment of learned "licks" by jazz improvisers.

Oral traditions have much in common no matter what the culture, century, or medium involved. Berliner's concepts of frequency of occurrence and evolving syntactic function through co-occurence are amplified and formalized in Domenico Pietropaulo's description of commedia dell'arte banter as a Markov chain of serial probabilities:

Improvisation is a text-building process . . . , a collaboration among the cast for the purpose of conjoining signs drawn from the repertoires of the individual actors and harmonised into a plot-creating strategy. It is, in other words, a process of composition—aiming, that is, at the formation of composite units by the addition of discrete parts. . . . Given the stimulus produced by one character, the process of improvistion must determine the textually appropriate response of his interlocutor, which is then regarded as another stimulus, itself awaiting a response in the evolving script. . . . A perfectly co-ordinated company . . . may be described as a system of interrelated parts which, from an initial state of rest at the beginning of a scene, goes through a series of transformations that take it from a state, in which it is dominated by an actor performing a segment of his repertoire, to another, in which a second actor claims the spotlight, and so on, until one of them engenders a verbal or gestural expression which cannot be further elaborated. . . . Because at any given time the possible states that the system can enter are all items in actual repertoires, they must have all occurred in various combinations in the theatrical tradition prior to the performance in question, and this means that their formal history as second elements in composite units of communication can be expressed as relative frequencies of occurrence in the verbal and gestural language of the commedia dell'arte. Relative frequency, however, is just another name for probability.[10]

We understand today that auditory learning depends very much on the probability distributions of the sounds we hear. Whether a child learns, say, Dutch or German vowel sounds depends on the probabilities of the exact vowels heard, not on some universal principle. In the same way, the probabilities of one schema following another account for much of what Durante described as "the way it is done" in the galant style. If one takes the complete movements presented in this volume as a small but representative sample of galant music,[11] one can then compute the probability of any schema leading to any other schema. There are over three hundred such pairings in this small sample. All of them are represented in the graph below (fig. 27.1), with the darkness of each square representing the probability of the schema named on the left leading into the schema named along the top. In this small repertory, for example, the Jupiter has a 100 percent chance of leading into a Prinner, as shown by the black box in the extreme lower left of the chart. Likewise the deceptive cadence is certain to lead to a complete cadence. The dotted line on the diagonal indicates a schema followed by itself. For the Fenaroli and the Quiescenza, immediate repetition is the most likely outcome. Though a graph like this is not easy to assimilate visually, it contains a wealth of information. One can find important asymmetries that help to reveal a schema's function. The vertical column "Prinner," for instance, shows that this schema is most likely to follow themes like the Romanesca, Do-Re-Mi, or Jupiter, while the horizontal row "Prinner" shows that it can lead to more than a dozen

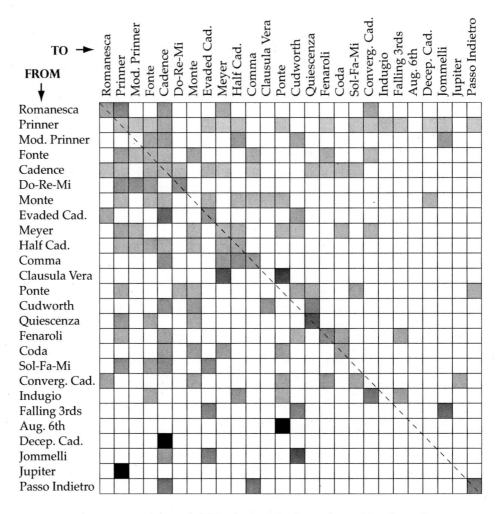

FIGURE 27.1   The probability of progressing from schema A to schema B

other schemata, with only a slight edge given to a following cadence. Thus a Prinner is often strongly implied, but itself has weak implications for a following schema. Similarly the Indugio is most likely to lead to a Converging cadence, and the Cudworth cadence to a Quiescenza, but not the reverse.

For the strong probabilities, one can legitimately speak of expectations or implications. For the many weak probabilities it may be better to speak of permitted successions. If one were to examine the numerical data, the Prinner, for instance, would have a 30 percent chance of leading into a cadence, a 12 percent chance of repeating itself, and low-single-digit chances of leading to a dozen other schemata. A pairing of two schemata that occurred just once in forty or fifty opportunities could hardly be described as "expected," though one might want to distinguish such occasional combinations from pairings that never occur at all.

The above matrix of "transitional probabilities" is based on too small a repertory to be fully representative of galant music as a whole. The graph is nevertheless sufficiently detailed to suggest some preferred paths through a composition. If one were to choose "Romanesca" as a starting point, the following series would be highly probable: Romanesca ⇨ Prinner ⇨ Cadence ⇨ Fonte ⇨ Prinner ⇨ Cadence. Allowing for some minor adjustments, that series would come close to the basic thread of the minuet by Somis in chapter 5. In other words, a highly probable path may outline a prototypical composition. These probabilities—what a linguist might term a "finite state grammar"—capture only some of the knowledge of galant musicians. Successful musicians also possessed technical knowledge of contrapuntal and harmonic patterns internal to a given schema, and strategic knowledge of how to arrange the schemata to achieve certain aesthetic effects and to fulfill the requirements of particular moments in the course of specific musical genres. That said, an understanding of the normal *dispositio* of schemata formed an important background to the judging of compositions. In our own time, the failure to understand this basic type of musical phrase grammar may explain why many computer-composed works "in the style of Mozart" seem to have tangled or broken threads that rarely sound like Mozart to experienced listeners.

Applications of schema theory to music, as developed by Leonard B. Meyer, Eugene Narmour, and myself, focus on a listener's evolving interactions with a stream of musical events.[12] As suggested above, the actual complexity of those real-time interactions, in which a listener attempts to relate each new sensation to learned regularities and remembered exemplars, may go far beyond verbal description. But if one focuses only on highly probable, idealized successions of events, then it may be possible to present at least an outline of a modern schema theory as it relates to musical patterns.

Central to the experience of a listener familiar with galant music would be the recognition of musical events that imply subsequent events, and of later events that suitably realize those earlier implications. Let me review basic schema theory by first imagining a simple, abstract schema of two parts: an implication *I* and a realization *R*. A listener may learn to associate *I* with *R* to form a recognizable whole that we may call schema A:

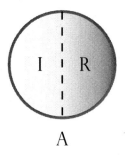

FIGURE 27.2   An implication *I* and realization *R* combined in a schema *A*

This schema is not a preordained whole or unity. There need be nothing about *I* that intrinsically or essentially points to *R* other than the statistics of their frequent co-occurrence. A single implication could become associated with different realizations to form different, though related, schemata. In figure 27.3, implication *I* could associate with at least three different realizations to form three different schemata: *A*, *B*, and *C*.

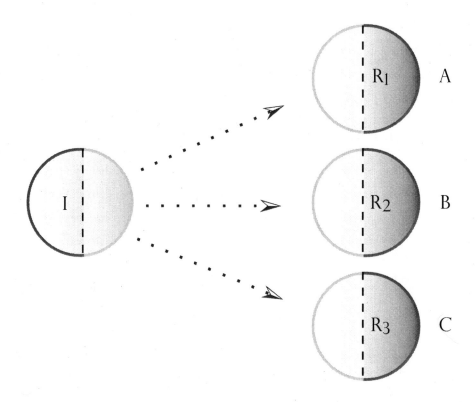

FIGURE 27.3   An implication *I* can join with various realizations R_1, R_2, R_3 . . .

In galant music, a number of musical events or configurations are strongly implicative. Thoroughbass norms, for example, hold a 6/5 chord to be implicative of a subsequent

realization. The characteristic passages shown below in example 27.1 take the identical
6/5-chord implication (shown in a rectangle) and realize it in three different, though
related, keys—F minor, B♭ major, and G minor. Note that the designations of scale degrees
only become stable in retrospect as each combination of implication and realization (or
further implication) clarifies the context. The F-minor passage, for instance, achieves a
measure of perceived closure and stability as a two-event schema. The B♭-major and G-
minor passages, by contrast, remain implicative as notated and would require at least one
more event to stabilize as a memorable whole.

EX. 27.1   A musical implication with three different realizations

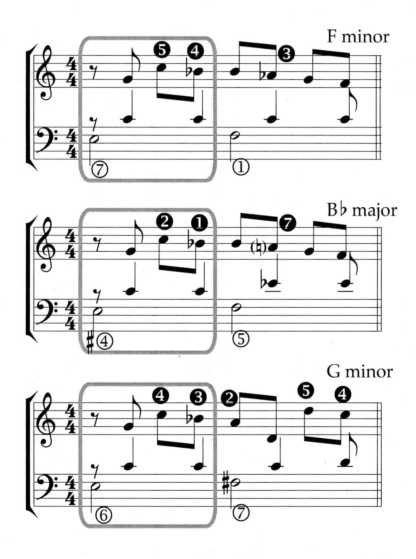

A series of schemata could be imagined as beads on a mental string or cognitive
thread—*il filo* (see fig. 27.4). This thread represents an impression of continuity, which
can arise from simple succession, from various kinds of higher-level schemata, or from the

quite low-level but nevertheless significant effects of musical meter and the stepwise movement of parts. Simplistic ways of thinking that might be fallacies in formal logic—for example, believing that because two events occur in sequence, the prior one caused the later one—can have a strong influence on the human interpretation of musical logic and continuity. As Carl Dahlhaus observed, it can be very difficult to make two passages played in succession seem unrelated.[13]

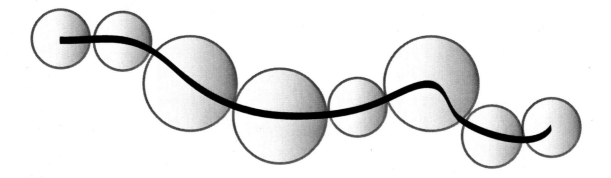

FIGURE 27.4   A string of schemata—*il filo*

If higher-level schemata can give a sense of continuity to a succession of lower-level schemata, then clearly it must be possible to superimpose schemata of different dimensions:

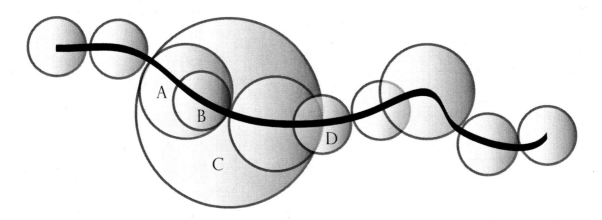

FIGURE 27.5   A string of nested and overlapping schemata

In figure 27.5, schema A is not only nested within schema C but also contains schema B. These are abstract examples of complete nesting where one schema is wholly contained, or wholly contains, another schema. Simple overlaps are also possible, as where schema D begins near the end of schema C.

Highly contrapuntal works like fugues often feature overlapping schemata. A new entry of the fugue subject, for example, may begin before a previous context has fully concluded, and a *stretto* is defined as a series of such overlaps. Works in the galant style, by contrast, are the *loci classici* of nested schemata. For instance, the previous musical example featured an implicative 6/5 chord followed by three possible continuations. The first of these, as a two-event schema interpreted in the key of F minor, could itself form the implicative event in larger schemata, which in turn might have different realizations leading to still different keys:

EX. 27.2   The first schema of example 27.1 embedded within a Fonte and a Monte

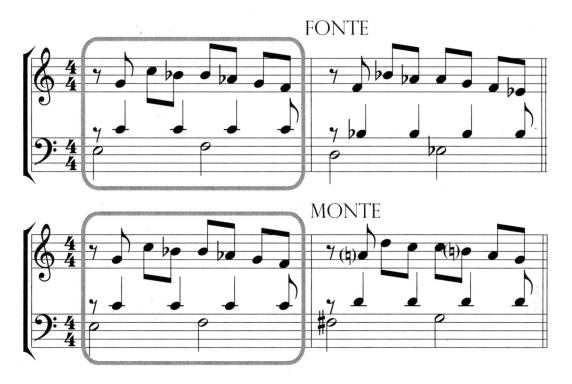

That F-minor, 6/5-to-5/3 schema (shown in the rectangle above)—what I termed a Comma in the chapter on clausulae (chap. 11)—can nest comfortably within either a Fonte or a Monte. The context of the larger schema alters the retrospective significance of the scale degrees and harmonies of the embedded 6/5-to-5/3 schema, just as the 6/5-to-5/3 schema itself helped determine an interpretation of the 6/5 chord. So the overall key of the Fonte is likely perceived in E♭ major, and that of the Monte in C minor, even though both are initiated by a smaller schema that, heard alone, would be perceived in F minor.

Because it is based on the statistics of music heard, and on human learning, memory, and other cognitive abilities, schema theory does not insist on either a canonical set of schemata (certain patterns and no others) or a canonical set of relationships. It is descriptive rather than prescriptive. It accepts that connoisseurs may be able to recognize a large

number of highly differentiated schemata with quite specific implications, while neo-
phytes may apply a coarser, all-purpose set with very general implications. Both types of
listeners may thus enjoy hearing the same composition, and neither may fully understand
the experience of the other.

In addition to the cases of (1) a thread of separate schemata and (2) a thread of nested
and/or overlapped schemata (two constructions often associated with oral and literary traditions, respectively),[14] there is the case of (3) clusters of associated schemata. For instance,
a florid melody may simultaneously match the features of a number of schemata associated with slightly different types of galant themes. The paired Do-Re-Mi, for instance,
shares features with other thematic schemata like the Jupiter and the Pastorella. All three
schemata may be activated simultaneously by a particular passage, as shown in abstract
form in figure 27.6. The three schemata, A, B, and C, are depicted next to each other like
consecutive documents in a file, but they represent either simultaneous alternatives or
superpositions for that location on the cognitive thread. Although schema B might seem
the most salient, schemata A and C could also be cognitively activated. In particular, a
different performance could change the relative salience of these schemata and result in
schema C, for instance, being the dominant frame of reference. Performers and listeners
hence play major roles in determining how a composition will be interpreted. For advo-
cates of exemplar models of categorization, figure 27.6 would still be relevant, though the
clusters of associated schemata would be replaced by associated exemplars.

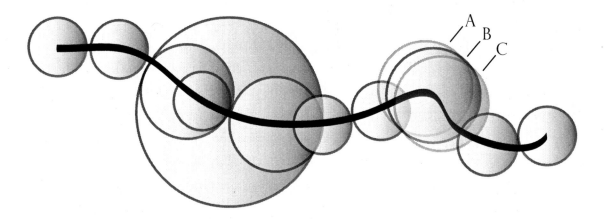

FIGURE 27.6   A cluster of three associated schemata, A, B, C

As mentioned, any study of implications and realizations will need to refer, even if
only generally, to the probabilities of implication I being followed by realization R. Some
combinations are highly probable, some are highly improbable, and others are somewhere in between. Within a given schema, there are also certain combinations of features
that are more or less probable to be its constituents. Likewise there are more and less probable successions of schemata. In common parlance, musicians use different terms to
describe unexpected events in these different contexts. They often describe improbable

realizations in terms of surprise ("a deceptive cadence"), improbable features in terms of oddity or transgression ("an altered chord"), and improbable sequences of schemata in terms of a metaphorical path ("a sudden turn toward . . .").

Baron von Grimm is worth quoting again for his use of the path metaphor in describing his first experience of hearing the child Mozart improvise at the keyboard.

> What is incredible is to see him play off the top of his head for a full hour. He abandons himself to the inspiration of his spirit and to a wealth of ravishing ideas, ideas which he nevertheless knows how to place one after the other with taste and without confusion. The most consummate music director could not be more profound than him in the science of harmony and of modulations which he knows how to lead down paths lesser known but always precise.[15]

The image of "ideas . . . place[d] one after the other" corresponds well with the image of *il filo* as a cognitive thread connecting a series of schemata. But the metaphor of "paths lesser known" suggests the existence of more than one thread. There is not only the thread spun out along the path actually taken, but also other threads that might have existed had the music proceeded down different paths. Thus there are forks in the road:

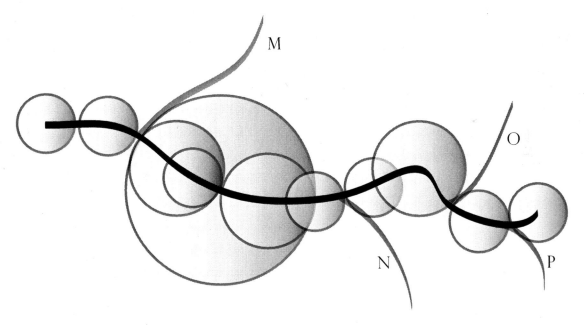

FIGURE 27.7   Alternative paths *M, N, O, P*

The path, or *the* thread, is the result of choices made at various forks. In figure 27.7, paths *M, N , O,* and *P* represent choices not made.[16] The musical import of those choices can vary considerably from listener to listener. Someone new to the galant style will hardly be aware of any of the paths not taken. A galant composer, by contrast, would have known several alternatives at each fork and understood their implications. Taking a roundabout path early in a movement, for example, could be a clue that the dimensions of all the subsequent sections will be enlarged. Taking a shortcut in the second half of a movement could be understood as a reasonable defense against listener boredom.

Composers were the musicians skilled enough at pathfinding and thread-spinning to warrant writing down their creative excursions. In speaking disapprovingly of an inexperienced instrumentalist who would try his hand at writing a solo sonata (soloist plus thoroughbass), Quantz commented, "If he lacks knowledge of the rules of composition, he has someone else write the bass."[17] The sense that a bass contained the essential trace of the musical path was widespread and explains to some extent why partimenti were so common in the training of future composers.

Learning and performing partimenti involved recognizing at each moment a suitable path. Elementary partimenti contained abundant road signs in the form of thoroughbass figures. More advanced partimenti rarely gave the student overt figures but did provide other clues to the intended path. In a fugal partimento by Durante (ex. 27.3),[18] I have marked the entries of the *proposta* (P) and *riposta* (R), or subject and answer. Note that, beginning in measure 4, each new entry is preceded by a change of clef:

EX. 27.3   Durante, a fugal partimento in A major

(new material)

The first entry of the riposta in measure 2 did not cause a change of clef because it was common to demonstrate how the continuation of the proposta and entry of the riposta should fit together. One might argue that the changes of clef were motivated by a desire to avoid ledger lines. Yet Durante could have notated this passage with only two clefs—treble and tenor—and still avoided ledger lines.

If clef changes signaled the thematically significant entries of distinct voices in the contrapuntal texture, the presence of a second voice often signaled a contrapuntal combination worthy of the student's special attention. Durante presented the opening combination in two voices and then reverted to the partimento norm of a single voice until measure 7. There a second voice and a new clef indicate a new contrapuntal combination (Long Comma and Cadenza Doppia; see chap. 11) that would recur several times later in this work. Once that new material was presented, Durante again returned in measure 9 to the norm of a single voice. In terms of information theory, more bandwidth seems required at the beginning of the work and at passages where new, less predictable combinations are intended. Less bandwidth is required where the partimento merely cues material already known or readily inferred. As a continuous, mostly one-voice blueprint for realizing a polyphonic composition, an advanced partimento shares many features in common with what scholars of composers' sketches often term a "continuity draft." Indeed, someone unacquainted with partimenti could easily mistake a manuscript copy of an advanced partimento for a composer's sketch.

Most galant composers left behind no sketches. For many of these musicians, rough drafts of new compositions were likely worked out only at the keyboard or in their imaginations. The case is different for Mozart and Haydn, whose fame encouraged the preservation of ephemera, and who both at times cultivated a more complex musical style that warranted sketching. Mozart's early study of the sacred music of Johann Ernst Eberlin (1702–1762), a respected composer in Salzburg, would have exposed him to basses that at times look very much like Durante's fugal partimenti. A copy in Leopold Mozart's hand (1769) of an Eberlin *Hosanna* presents a bass replete with clues from which almost the complete four-voice fugue can be unpacked. The first excerpt (ex. 27.4) begins in the manner of a fugal partimento, with the opening proposta (P) presented solo without figures. The riposta (R) in measure 6 is implied by the figures. Note the "8" in measure 6, which draws attention to itself for being redundant with regard to any chord, but which specifies the opening tone of the riposta. I have drawn circles around all the tones similarly specified, and one can thus see how the core tones of the riposta emerge.

EX. 27.4   Leopold Mozart, copy of Eberlin's *Hosanna*, m. 1 (1769)

After all four voices have sung either the proposta or the riposta, the bass returns with the proposta to end the first section of the work. Rapid modulations to G major, C major, and A minor ensue. During this modulatory passage the clef changes frequently in connection with the entries of voices. A large Cadenza Doppia then prepares the entry of the proposta in the minor mode. As seen in a second excerpt (ex. 27.5), the resulting bass strongly resembles a fugal partimento (I have annotated the local key, cadence, and entry of the proposta):

EX. 27.5   Leopold Mozart, copy of Eberlin's *Hosanna*, bass part, m. 24 (1769)

Young Mozart became quite comfortable with the partimento method of encapsulating a multivoice work in a single bass part. As an adult, he often sketched works on a single staff, using frequent clef changes either to signal the entries of new voices or to accommodate different instrumental or vocal ranges. Mozart did not restrict this technique to contrapuntal or sacred works, nor did Durante, who frequently used rapid changes of clef to indicate the call-and-response of treble and bass in an imaginary concerto-like dialogue. Example 27.6, for instance, comes from Mozart's incomplete comic opera *L'oca del Cairo* (*The Goose of Cairo*). The excerpt begins in soprano clef (m. 22) with the second part of an evaded-then-complete pair of cadences. The bass clef signals a modulation to F major (m. 23), following which Mozart presents a large Do-Re-Mi (mm. 24–28):

EX. 27.6   Mozart, sketch for a duet, *L'oca del Cairo*, Allegretto vivo, m. 22 (1783)

Treble clefs cue the core events of the schema (the "calls") while the interleaved comedic patter is cued by the bass clef (the "responses"). Because Mozart was sketching for himself, he notated only some of the clef changes, which made these sketches a challenge to read before their decipherment in a modern edition.[19]

The remainder of this chapter is devoted to the sketches for a slow movement by Haydn from the third of his Opus 20 string quartets of 1772. As you will see, in producing these sketches Haydn likewise seems to have retained many of the notational practices taught in advanced partimenti, learned perhaps from his Neapolitan maestro Porpora.

A diplomatic transcription of the sketches can be found in the modern edition of Haydn's complete works.[20] Haydn sketched the first half of the movement on one large sheet of paper ruled with staff lines, and did the second half on a second, similar sheet. These sketches exhibit a more or less consistent correspondence with the left-to-right and top-to-bottom progression of notation typical of a finished score, though some variants of passages are written near their models instead of where they will occur in the completed quartet. Reading these sketches can be difficult. Not only does one need to flip back and forth constantly between quartet and sketch, but one is also confronted with a number of musical paths, not all of which were chosen for the finished quartet. While there is no substitute for a careful comparison of every detail of the sketches with the corresponding part or parts of the quartet, I believe it is possible to gain a broader view of Haydn's working method by integrating the sketches and the quartet into a single score.

If *il filo* could be likened to a necklace of pearls, then Haydn's sketches would resemble that necklace laid in a small jewel box. To better view the necklace one would first need to remove it from the box and stretch it out. That is what I have done with his sketches. I have taken Haydn's four staves of fragmentary parts and aligned them, on a single staff where possible, in Haydn's ordering. For much of the sketched movement Haydn notated only a single staff, and he did not bother to sketch fully some repetitions and returns of earlier material. For the opening measures he notated all four parts, for more complicated combinations of voices he notated two parts, and for the movement's apex of complexity—a tour-de-force Monte in the minor mode—he again notated all four parts. The shifting of attention between the voices naturally involved changes in clefs, and so the end result of my adaptation looks very much like an advanced partimento. A young composer who had studied advanced partimenti would have learned all the essentials of how to create a continuity draft or sketch, and it is likely that these two domains of activity influenced each other. Someone taught to hear multiple voices from the cue of a single voice would only need to write a single voice as a cue for himself.

After adapting the notational form of the sketches, I adapted the notational form of the quartet. I reduced its four original staves to two. Not every note of every part could be preserved without creating a notational tangle, but I hope the loss of a few insignificant doublings and filler parts is compensated by the increased legibility of the result. I then placed the adapted sketches directly above each measure of the quartet. Blank measures in the sketches generally indicate repetitive material that Haydn did not deign to sketch, and blank measures in the quartet indicate sketched material that he omitted from the final version.

The sketches, as shown in example 27.7, present almost all the material found in the finished movement. Only a few passages indicate major divergences from the movement's final form. The first of these begins in measure 19, where Haydn had sketched a Monte (I have added in parentheses a minimal second voice to make the Monte Principale more audible). It was mentioned in earlier chapters that as the century progressed the Monte became less and less fashionable in the first half of a movement. For whatever reason, Haydn chose to leave this Monte out of the final version and drew a large X across it in the sketches. What seems significant for this chapter is the inference that Haydn's compositional choice involved deciding whether to add the entire schema to *il filo*—in other words, whether to add a whole pearl to his musical necklace. These four measures (mm. 19–22) were clearly treated as a conceptual unit.

The second major divergence involves the four alternate paths sketched for the approach to the final cadence of each half of the movement. Because it was not possible to show all four sketched paths above the quartet score, and because an understanding of Haydn's strategies will be facilitated by having just heard the final version of his movement, I defer presenting his network of alternate cadential paths until the end of this chapter.

A number of passages, here listed by beginning measure number, warrant special notice.[21]

m. 1	Haydn begins by sketching all four voices. There is considerable overlapping of schemata (a plain texture but complex relationships). All repeated material is sketched in only one voice.
m. 3	Leonard Meyer's phrase "grammatical simplicity and relational richness"[22] comes to mind in viewing Haydn's Prinner riposte. For its later reappearances I mark it simply as "Prinner." Yet his phrase is a nexus of references to other important schemata as well. The four notes of the bass, ④–③–⑦–①, match the reduced countermelody of a Fenaroli. The phrase's first half, with its ④–③ bass and ♯4/2 sonority on beat 2 matches the Passo Indietro, and its second half (m. 4) matches the Comma.
m. 13	A modulating Prinner begins a broad, ornate section (a complex texture but simple relationships) sketched in two voices.
m. 19	As mentioned, this is a Monte Principale not used in the final version.
m. 27	Haydn writes divergent paths toward the cadence (see below).
m. 74	Great complexity required sketching all four voices.
m. 81	The sketched bass shows the Falling Thirds / Romanesca pattern more clearly than the final version.

m. 85   I have circled Haydn's "et." (= etc.), which referred to the self-evident but unsketched second half of the Fonte. It makes sense that a pattern so common as the Fonte would not need to be sketched in full. A curved line leads to a sketch for measure 88.

m. 88   Haydn sketches only the lower voice of a Fenaroli, and he gives only one statement of it. The normal pair of statements appears in the final version. As the graph showed (fig. 27.1), double presentation of the Fenaroli was the most probable sequence. For Haydn, it seems to have been a matter of course.

m. 89   This is the last measure notated on the second page of sketches. Everything else was deemed self-evident.

m. 97   This variant of a cadence appears on the first page of sketches (see p. 396).

The following pages present the condensed score (bottom two staves) and reformatted sketches (upper staff or staves) of the slow movement from Haydn's string quartet, Opus 20, no. 3.

EX. 27.7   Haydn, Opus 20 (Hob. III/33), no. 3, mvt. 3, Poco adagio (1772)

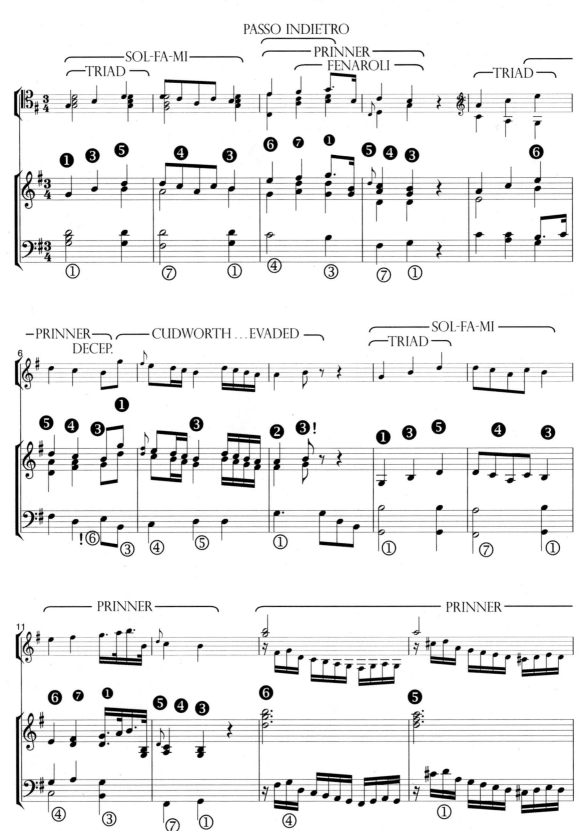

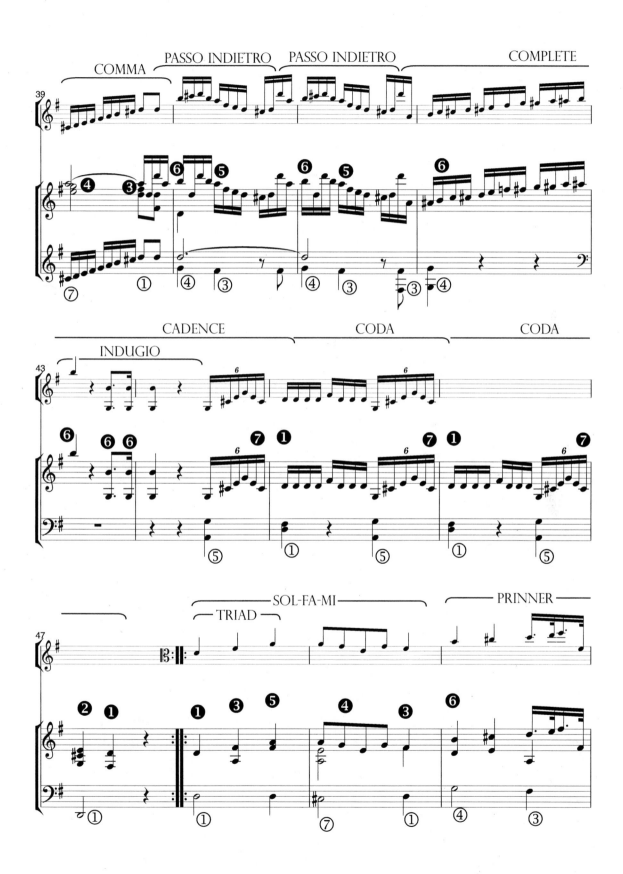

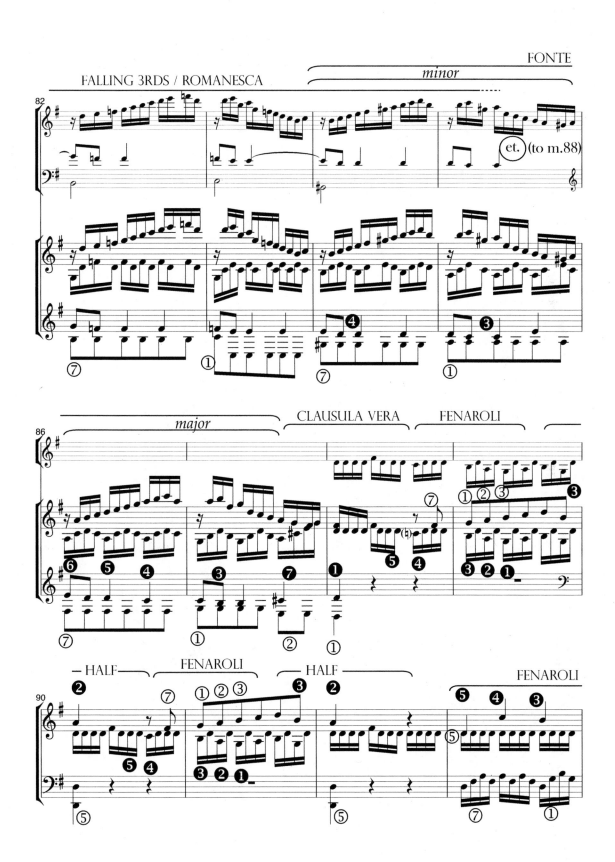

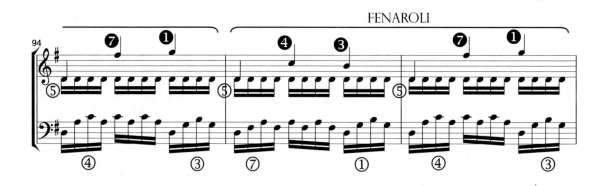

FENAROLI

PRINNER / PASSO DIETRO   CUDWORTH . . .

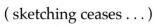

(sketching ceases . . .)

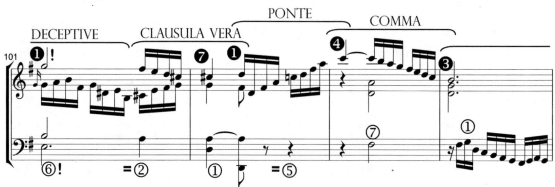

PONTE

DECEPTIVE   CLAUSULA VERA   COMMA

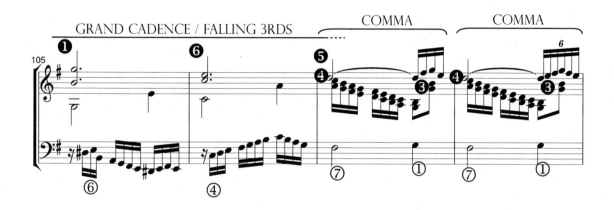

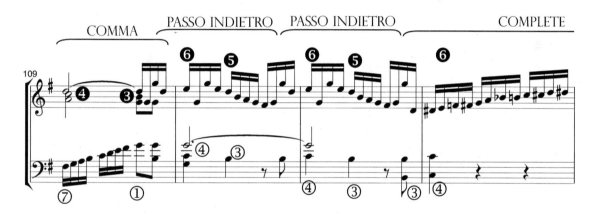

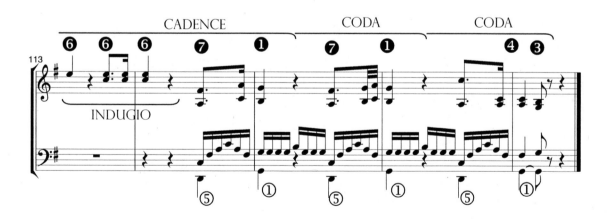

For Haydn, the alternate paths of *il filo* seem to have branched most luxuriantly in extended cadences. Example 27.8 shows Haydn's sketches for the paths of four related cadences. The first path, which was the most straightforward in simply launching into the cadence, was rejected and crossed out. Immediately below it was sketched the second path, which first detours through a Passo Indietro and then veers away from complete closure with both deception and evasion. This was the path chosen to end the first half of the quartet movement. For his third path, destined for the second half of the movement, Haydn expands the design of the second path by doubling the length of the *fioritura* over ③ in the bass. The fourth and final path, which was not incorporated into the finished quartet, adds the further detour of the Indugio. Note that in the second measure of this

EX. 27.8   Haydn, four sketches for a cadence; dotted lines highlight expansions

fourth path, Haydn overshot his mark with the rising *fioritura*. He crossed out his mistake and then resumed his course. In rejecting this fourth path, with its chromatic and rather hectic Indugio, he may have felt that he had also overshot his mark in terms of the character of the whole movement.

It should not be surprising that Haydn, who studied with a famous Neapolitan maestro, would create a partimento-like sketch. Nor should it be surprising that having mastered the Italian galant style as a young man he would use almost the full set of schemata introduced in this volume. Yet I do find it surprising that across two centuries of time and cultural distance one can nevertheless find the preserved traces of a particular type of schematic music-compositional thought. It seems clear that Haydn had the equivalent of a mental jewel box filled with musical pearls, the galant schemata. He could choose to add a pearl to *il filo*, or he could change his mind and take one off. One can almost hear him thinking, "A Monte would work nicely here, but . . . I'll just leave it out" or "The Fonte starts here" or "The Fenaroli works here. . . . I only need to notate the first one." When he envisioned paths branching off in several directions, his sketch branched as well, as if he were evaluating each alternative: "Standard bass . . . too simple. Passo Indietro followed by standard bass . . . good before the double bar. Passo Indietro with a florid extension leading into a Cudworth . . . good toward the end. Passo Indietro, florid extension, Indugio, Converging Cadence . . . too much!" There is no evidence, of course, that Haydn used any particular labels, or thought musically in terms of words at all. But his behaviors would be difficult to explain had he not learned the equivalent galant concepts and categories. His compositional craft, of which he was justly proud and for which he gave credit to Porpora, seems clearly grounded in knowing the proper features of each galant schema, and it demonstrates what Leopold Mozart would have called *der gute Satz* ("good technical composition"). Knowing how to string the schemata together, and how to judge their effects, required a companion skill at *die Ordnung, il filo* ("the arrangement of material: the thread"), and that depended on Haydn's highly developed musical taste.

28

A MODEL ADAGIO

BY

JOHANN JOACHIM QUANTZ

from his *Essay on Playing the Flute*, Berlin, 1752

THREE OF THE KEYS TO SUCCESS at an eighteenth-century court were held by Johann Joachim Quantz (1697–1773). He was a highly talented performer (on the flute primarily), he composed music that delighted his aristocratic audiences (in Dresden first, and later in Berlin), and he learned how to please powerful princes (the Elector of Saxony and, most importantly, Frederick the Great, King of Prussia). As simultaneously "composer for the royal court," "composer for the royal chamber," and "professor of flute for the king of Prussia," Quantz received ten times the salary of the king's harpsichord player, Carl Philipp Emanuel Bach (1714–1788), even though Bach was a musician of staggering abilities. Successful music at court was not about "art for art's sake," to use the Romantic phrase. Christian Gottfried Krause (1719–1770), a prominent Berlin lawyer and musical devotee at the Berlin court, described C. P. E. Bach as a musical Milton whose melodies required "thorough prior acquaintance" before they could please.[1] Not every courtier had the time or inclination for "thorough prior acquaintance." A winning strategy for a court composer was thus to create music that could be understood and enjoyed on first hearing, and Quantz played that game to perfection.

In Vienna Quantz studied counterpoint with Jan Zelenka, who would later be Riepel's own maestro. Then, after securing work as an oboist in Dresden and Warsaw, he was able to spend about two years studying in Italy, beginning in 1724. There he met the greatest singers of the day, including the castrato Farinelli, and he heard the music of many of the composers already discussed in previous chapters: Somis, Leclair, Domenico Scarlatti, Leo, Hasse, Marcello, Porpora, and Gasparini. Like Wodiczka, who would study there a decade later, Quantz learned to replicate all the fashionable schemata. The "textbook" presentations of the Romanesca-Prinner in his Siciliana from a G-minor trio sonata attest to Quantz's fluency in the Italian galant (ex. 28.1).

EX. 28.1   Quantz, Trio Sonata in G Minor, mvt. 3, Siciliana, m. 1 (ca. 1750s)

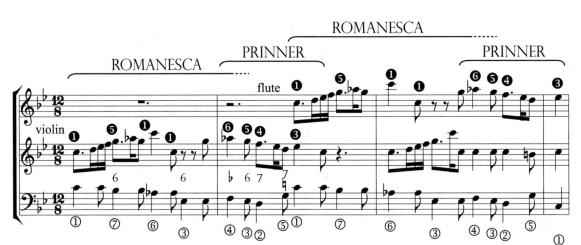

The Romanesca-Prinner pairing provided a secure framework on which he could add imaginative touches like the violin's close imitation of the flute in measure 3. His seemingly effortless ability to create singable melodies served him well in later life when he was called upon to produce hundreds of flute compositions for Frederick the Great (and one presumes that the many flute pieces ostensibly written by the king may have been heavily edited or ghostwritten by Quantz).[2]

The breadth and depth of Quantz's experiences were equaled by few other musicians: he began at the bottom of the ladder, a blacksmith's son apprenticed as a town musician, and rose to the very top; he learned to play several string instruments, trumpet, oboe, and flute; he studied abroad not only in Italy but also in France and England; he performed across the continent; he met the top musicians of the age; and he had the good fortune to have been employed by two of the royal courts most unstinting in their musical expenditures and most committed to musical excellence, those of the King of Poland (and Elector of Saxony) at Dresden and the King of Prussia in Berlin. At the peak of his career Quantz committed his experiences to paper, producing one of the greatest books ever written on eighteenth-century music. His 1752 *Versuch einer Anweisung die Flöte traversiere zu spielen* [Essay on Playing the Flute][3] is not just about making sounds on a flute. It covers the full range of issues that had engaged the mind of this famous musician during his long and successful career, and it provides guidance in areas that were likely beyond the understanding of its largely amateur readership.

Quantz writes at length about the art of embellishing a "plain air." The novice performer's problem was that an eighteenth-century manuscript or print of a slow movement generally gave only the bare bones of the melody. Some small embellishments could be added almost mechanically. For example, the notated interval of a falling third invited a filling-in by an intervening tone. Here are three of Quantz's seventeen increasingly complex suggestions for embellishing the interval from E5 to C5:

EX. 28.2   Quantz, *Versuch*, from his Fig. 22 (1752)

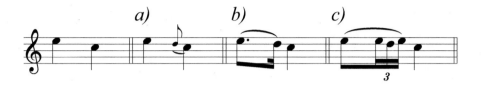

But other, more extensive embellishments required knowledge of particular musical contexts. To give his readers an overview of these contexts, Quantz supplied a chart of "the most common kinds of intervals"—meaning "plain" melodies of from two to six notes—"together with the basses appropriate to them," including their thoroughbass figures.[4] His Table VIII (see ex. 28.3, shown in the format that appears in his treatise), may be viewed as a master musician's chart of his galant schemata—his "compulsory figures." For purposes of comparison, below Quantz's examples I have placed in parentheses the names of corresponding schemata described in the preceding chapters of the present volume.

For several figure/schema pairings, the correspondence could hardly be better. Quantz's Fig. 2, for instance, matches the Do-Re-Mi, his Fig. 16 matches Riepel's diatonic Monte, and his Fig. 6 matches my Passo Indietro. In a few cases Quantz's "intervals" represent a combination of schemata. His Fig. 5, for example, matches the combination of a Prinner with a following half cadence. In many other cases Quantz's intervals represent just the opening or closing half of a larger schema. His second example of Fig. 8, for instance, would match the second half of a Meyer (as indicated), or a Fonte, Pastorella, Jupiter, Monte, Sol-Fa-Mi, or Prinner.

For a few of Quantz's figures I show no matching schemata. The problem is not the absence of similarity, but its diffusion across several possibilities. The final example of Fig. 8 is a case in point. At first glance its closing descent from G5 to E5 does not conform exactly to any of the schemata discussed in this book. But when one examines the "variations" that Quantz provides for that "plain air," it becomes clear that the closing third was intended to be filled in. He notated thirty-eight interchangeable variations for the examples of Fig. 8, almost all with a melodic termination of F5–E5.[5] In example 28.4 I have notated the six that he mentions as being especially pertinent to the final example of hiss Fig. 8 (the indications of scale degrees are mine, the letter names of variations are from Quantz). All of the variations except *q* end with a ❹–❸ dyad (and I suspect that a grace-note F5 was intended for version *q* and left off by the engraver); variations *o*, *q*, and *r* feature the High ❷ Drop; and variation *n* presents a small Prinner melody (the tempo is *adagio*). So although this final plain air given in Quantz's Fig. 8 *looks* atypical of galant schemata, his proposed variations reveal that it was meant to *sound* typical in performance. Moreover, he provided the stock melodic cues appropriate to the schemata into which this building block would likely be inserted. If Quantz the theorist might appear

EX. 28.3   Quantz, *Versuch*, Table VIII (1752)

EX. 28.4   Quantz, *Versuch*, from his thirty-eight ways of embellishing Fig. 8 (1752)

idiosyncratic at times (he was a novice writer in this his first publication), Quantz the musician was unfailingly mainstream. The musician's prolix variations help to explain what the laconic theorist had in mind. For Figs. 3 and 10, those variations were crucial in determining that Quantz had intended these plain airs in the contexts of G major and F major, respectively (the cautionary accidentals in Quantz's table are mine).

An examination of the literally hundreds of variations that Quantz provided for the many musical figures in his treatise would take us well beyond the scope of this book. Quantz himself may have recognized how difficult it might be to absorb such a mass of disconnected, intricate melodic fragments, for later in the treatise he attempted a *summa* of the art of "extempore variations" in the form of a complete Adagio for flute and thoroughbass. Not only does his Adagio include both the plain air and its recommended embellishment, but it also includes numerous cross-references to both the table of figures (Table VIII) and his hundreds of suggested embellishments. This Adagio is unquestionably the great tour-de-force in his treatise. Yet it is notable that the order of the figures in Quantz's table closely follows the order in which they occur in the Adagio, that rare patterns in the Adagio rate inclusion in the table, and that important patterns absent from the Adagio are absent from the table. I thus surmise that Quantz either used an existing Adagio and crafted his table around it, or wrote the Adagio and the table together. In any case, Quantz's careful cross-referencing of the "common kinds" of melody-bass pairings in his Adagio provides valuable points of comparison with the schemata described in this book.

Tracing the Adagio's more than 140 separate references back to either the table of figures or the many pages of embellishments might tire even the most diligent reader. To reduce this problem I will present his Adagio phrase by phrase, replacing Quantz's cross-references to the figures with reproductions of the corresponding melody-bass pairs (i.e., plain air plus bass). The cross-references to the embellishments are already embodied in the embellished voice displayed below the plain air. Here is the opening phrase:

EX. 28.5   Quantz, *Versuch*, Adagio, mm. 1–2 (1752)

Quantz's Fig. 9 corresponds to the "open" half of either schema, and his Fig. 8e corresponds to the "closed" half. Each of Quantz's figures depicts three abstract events: (1) an initial state or starting point, (2) the first event of an important dyad, and (3) the second event of the dyad. I say "abstract" because certain features like chord inversion appear generalized. For instance, his Fig. 9 presents two root-position chords (basses C3 and G3), whereas the Adagio presents the second chord in first inversion (bass B3, m. 1).

Following his opening gambit, Quantz presents and then repeats a modulating Prinner riposte (see ex. 28.6). As we have seen in many, many examples in previous chapters, this riposte could hardly be more normal and expected. Yet it posed a challenge for Quantz the theorist—a modulating Prinner begins in one key and ends in another. He ignores the C-major part of the first Prinner and instead references his Fig. 3, Sol-Fa-Mi in G major. As mentioned, I notate it with a key signature of one sharp (in parentheses) because although the original Fig. 3 has a C-major signature with F♯ provided in the thoroughbass, Quantz's table of variations on Fig. 3 has an overt G-major key signature.[6] Note that in the embellished air of the first Prinner, the F♮5 grace note gives a slightly Mixolydian cast to the phrase, whereas in the second Prinner more traditional figurations appear, including the High ➋ Drop. The repeat of the Prinner could be conceived entirely in G major, so Quantz now recognizes the Prinner's opening, Fig. 7, as leading into Fig. 3. This Fig. 7 may be something of an expedient to accommodate the modulating Prinner, inasmuch as it never appears again in his parsing of the Adagio. Quantz's table of figures does contain clear Prinners in Figs. 5 and 15, but he shows them in C major. When the Jupiter/Pastorella opening gambit returns in the second half of this Adagio, it is followed by a large Prinner in C major (see ex. 28.16). At that point Quantz references the Prinner of his Fig. 15, with Figs. 7 and 3 nowhere to be seen.

EX. 28.6   Quantz, *Versuch*, Adagio, mm. 3–4 (1752)

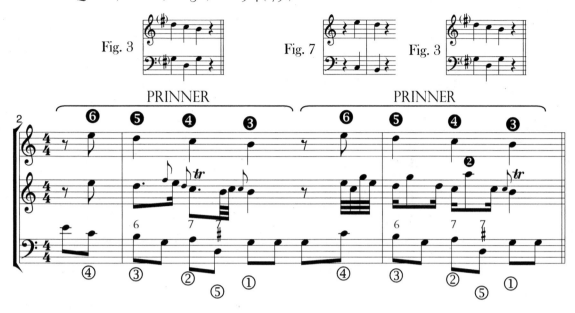

As is shown in example 28.7, Quantz then wrote two statements of the Passo Indietro, which corresponds closely with his Fig. 6:

EX. 28.7   Quantz, *Versuch*, Adagio, mm. 5–6 (1752)

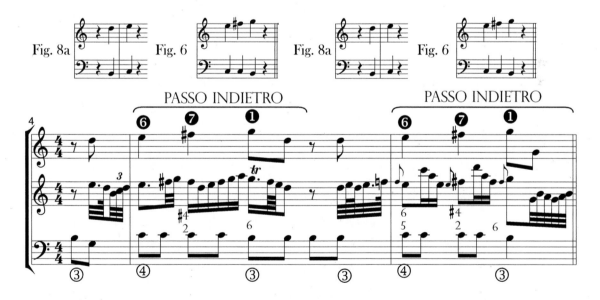

The Passo Indietro schema implies a cadence in G major, which indeed ensues (see ex. 28.8, mm. 6–7). The particular combination of Comma and Mi-Re-Do cadence serves as a lighter derivitave of the more august Cadenza Doppia (see chap. 11). Quantz does not connect the cadence to any of his melody-bass figures.

EX. 28.8   Quantz, *Versuch*, Adagio, mm. 7–8 (1752)

The above Do-Re-Mi corresponds to Quantz's Fig. 2, in the key of D minor. Of course Fig. 2 from Table VIII was in C major, but Quantz endorsed transposing his figures: "Although, to avoid prolixity, these examples have been set for the most part only in major keys, they are also to be used in minor keys; thus it is necessary that you familiarize yourself with the keys in which you wish to play them, so that you are immediately able to imagine the sharps or flats that must be prefixed in each key, without confusing whole tones with halves or halves with wholes in the transpositions."[7]

The Adagio continues with a variant of the Fonte (see ex. 28.9). Because its phrasing is at odds with harmonic resolution (each phrase-half ends "open"), Riepel's fictional student might well have said again that it "belongs to neither the Monte nor the Fonte nor the Ponte" (cf. ex. 14.18). The return to the tonic C-major harmony only comes at the start of a new phrase in measure 11 (ex. 28.10). Yet notwithstanding the unusual scansion, all the features of the Fonte are present, including its function as a tonal digression. It is somewhat curious that Quantz references his Fig. 8a for the end of the minor half of his Fonte (the end of m. 9 and beginning of m. 10), but does not reference the same figure at the analogous place at the end of the major half (cf. ex. 28.10, mm. 10–11). Since these references were for the purpose of providing contexts to guide embellishments, and since the end of the second half of his Fonte is only minimally embellished, Quantz may have felt that no such contextualization was necessary.

After the Fonte's digression and return, Quantz sets a series of small cadences to facilitate a move toward the key of A minor (see Ex. 28.10). His Fig. 5 refers to a Prinner extended to a half cadence, which in the Adagio seems present only in the most abstract sense. That is, one can identify tones that proceed down a hexachord from F5 to A4, but the bass and harmonization of Fig. 5 are nowhere in evidence. The Adagio bass is more

EX. 28.9 Quantz, *Versuch*, Adagio, mm. 9–10 (1752)

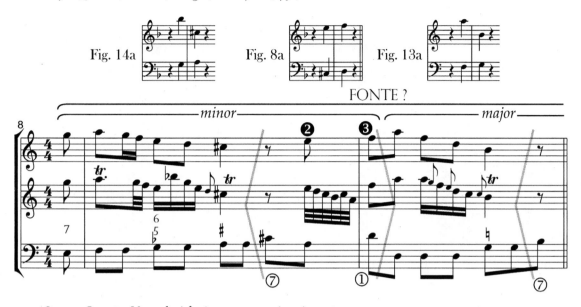

EX. 28.10 Quantz, *Versuch*, Adagio, mm. 11–12 (1752)

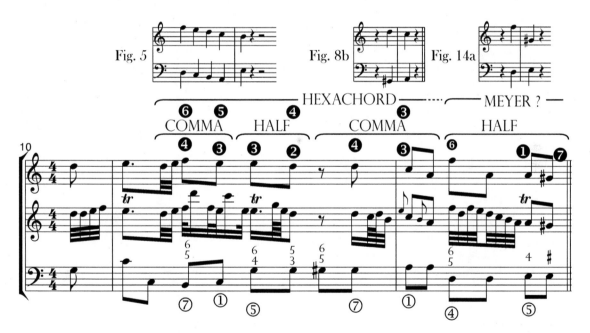

typical of the Converging cadence. Moreover his figures show no echo of the strong paral-lelism of the Comma-to-half-cadence pattern first in the major mode and then a third lower in minor.

The half cadence in A minor (m. 12) is distantly answered, as if by the second half of a Meyer, by the first of two large Commas (mm. 13–14, see ex. 28.11). The florid version of these Commas shows that Quantz treats the first statement as weaker and more perfunc-tory, the second as stronger and more emphatic (note the High ❷ Drop).

EX. 28.11   Quantz, *Versuch*, Adagio, mm. 13–14 (1752)

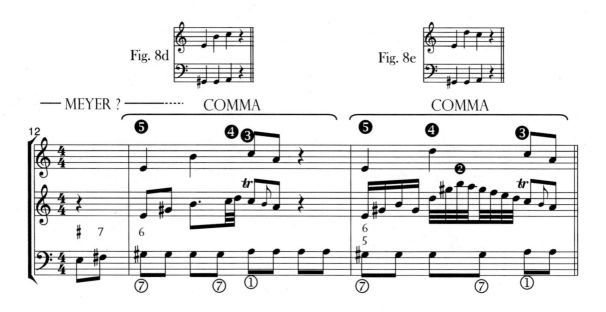

Commas generally precede strong cadences, and that is the case here, where they lead into the intricate close of this A-minor section. Note in particular how Quantz coordinates the melodic hexachordal descent with various schemata of increasingly strong closure:

EX. 28.12   Quantz, *Versuch*, Adagio, mm. 15–16 (1752)

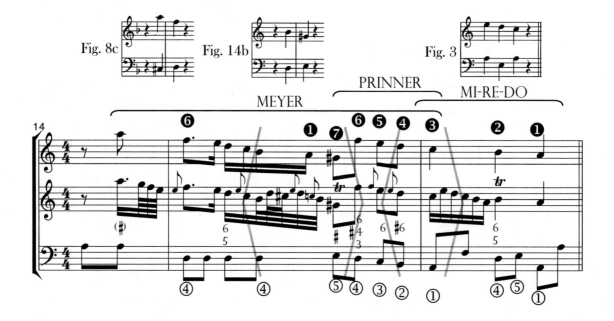

A stock Durante countermelody ushers in a typical Fonte. Quantz references the Fonte's two similar halves with different figures (Nos. 11 and 8). The difference seems to be that Fig. 11 begins "closed" whereas Fig. 8 begins "open" in its local key:

EX. 28.13   Quantz, *Versuch*, Adagio, mm. 17–18 (1752)

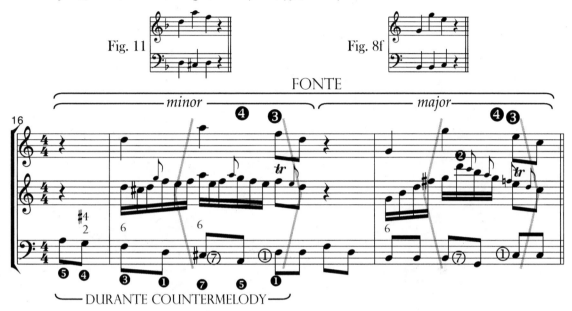

He follows the Fonte with a very clear Prinner that begins the melodic descent of the hexachord. The Indugio extends that descent, beginning on ❷ and ultimately continuing through ❶ and ❼ (or through ❹ and ❸ in the hexachord on G):

EX. 28.14   Quantz, *Versuch*, Adagio, mm. 19–20 (1752)

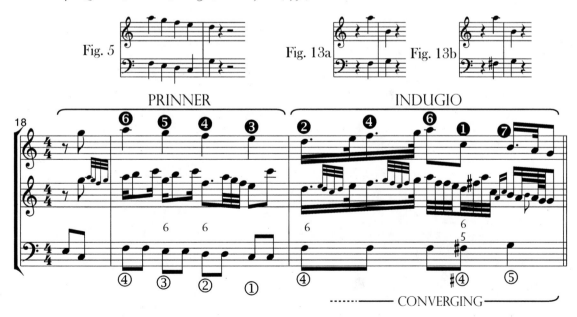

After the fermata Quantz restates his opening theme with, in the embellished part, diminutions in sixteenth-note triplets. In contrast to his analysis of the opening measures (mm. 1–2), he here adds a reference to Fig. 1. That reference seems a measure late, though it might indicate how to treat a static tone in the melody (F5 in m. 22) as the bass moves through a stepwise dissonance, in this case B2 (⑦) of the Long Comma:

EX. 28.15   Quantz, *Versuch*, Adagio, mm. 21–22 (1752)

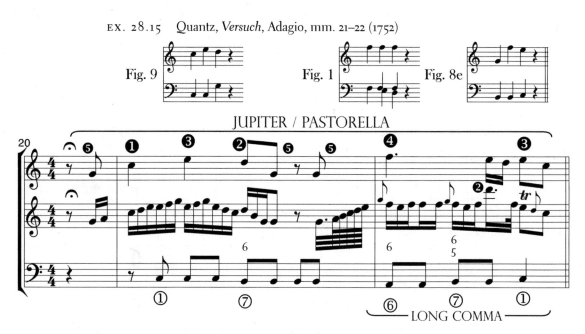

In place of the two modulating Prinners of measures 3–4, Quantz substitutes a nonmodulating Prinner that appears as a hybrid of his two ideal types, Figs. 15a and 15b. That is, its first half features the descending stepwise bass and 7–6 suspensions of Fig. 15a, while its second half features the leaping, circle-of-fifths bass of Fig. 15b:

EX. 28.16   Quantz, *Versuch*, Adagio, mm. 23–24 (1752)

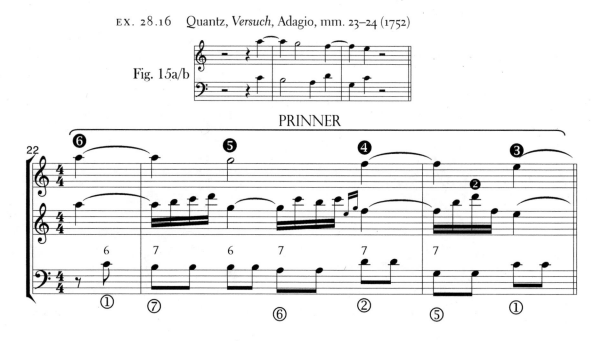

Quantz connects the end of this Prinner to the beginning of a complex of schemata that could easily be the final cadence did it not close a bit too "easily," lacking the emphasis of a Cudworth cadence or the extension of the Long and Grand cadences:

EX. 28.17   Quantz, *Versuch*, Adagio, mm. 24–25 (1752)

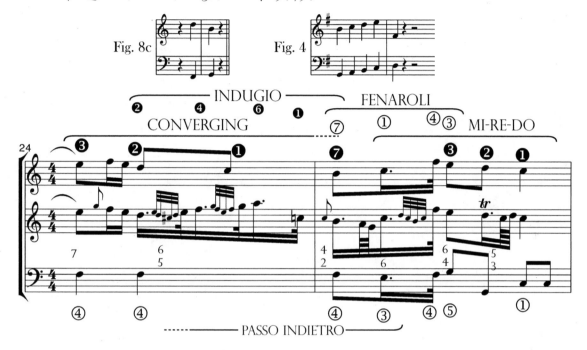

After the "early" cadence, he sets two perfunctory Meyers in the same way a later galant composer might set two Quiescenzas:

EX. 28.18   Quantz, *Versuch*, Adagio, mm. 26–27 (1752)

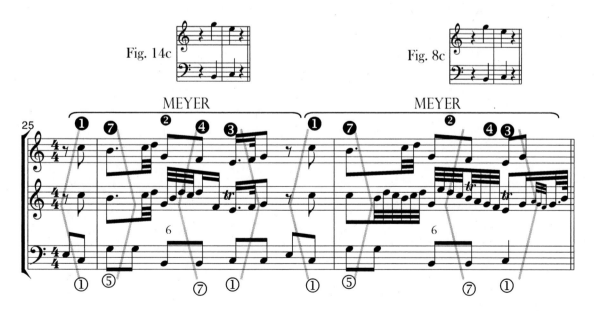

In measure 28 Quantz begins a five-part diatonic Monte whose rising bass extends all the way up to the tonic (①). The last stages of that rise overlap a Long Comma, which is followed in quick succession by a regular Comma and a half cadence:

EX. 28.19   Quantz, *Versuch*, Adagio, mm. 28–30 (1752)

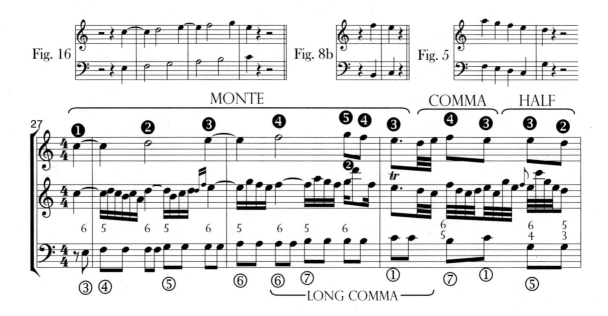

Quantz then uses a Prinner as part of an elaborate preparation for the final close, which arrives in the full panoply of the Cudworth cadence, as shown in his florid version (ex. 28.20).

Given his long experience first in Dresden and then in Berlin, where conservative tastes prevailed, it stands to reason that Quantz selected or composed an Adagio that may seem rather old-fashioned and fussy for the 1750s, the time of his treatise. The schemata presented in this book are generalizations of galant practice as a whole, with a special focus on the most fashionable Italian practice. One would not expect the Italian practice to match in every respect the musical habits of an older musician at a German court. And yet there is a very high degree of correspondence between Quantz's figures and the galant schemata. Galant practice was so widely disseminated, and so carefully taught through partimenti, solfeggi, and other rituals, that one can easily speak of an international musical style. Quantz, like Jommelli or Mozart, uses a Jupiter as a theme, a Prinner as a riposte, a Fonte for a digression, a Monte for rising tension, a Comma or Passo Indietro to prepare for a stronger cadence, and so forth. These were the paths down which galant music coursed, and court musicians everywhere appear to have felt at home in this landscape.

One of Quantz's aims in presenting this model Adagio was to give performers a context for the choices that they faced in embellishing a "plain air." He grounded his notion of context on the "most common kinds of intervals." The modern player interested in the

EX. 28.20   Quantz, *Versuch*, Adagio, mm. 31–32 (1752)

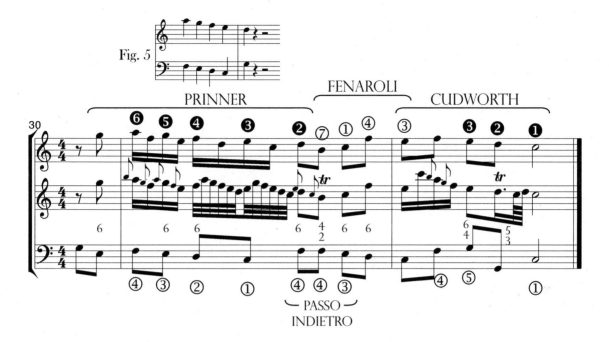

fine points of historically informed performance should note that while different "intervals" may be involved in different contexts, the intervals themselves are not fully determinative of their context. The Indugio, for instance, is a context with a tradition of characteristic embellishments (see chap. 20). Those embellishments appear in Quantz's music but elude his concept of "interval." Reexamining his techniques of embellishment in light of the specific contexts of the galant schemata can thus suggest the most appropriate norms for embellishment. The schemata supplement omissions in Quantz's first attempt (*Versuch*) at theory, reinforcing the richer vein of Quantz's justly lauded practice.

29

A MODEL ALLEGRO

BY

FRANCESCO GALEAZZI

from his *Elementi teorico-pratici di musica . . .* , Rome, 1796

FRANCESCO GALEAZZI (1758–1819) WAS BORN IN TURIN. There the tradition of violin playing at the court of Savoy was perhaps the finest in Europe. Its great maestro G. B. Somis had studied with Corelli. Somis in turn trained first Leclair and later Pugnani, who in turn trained Viotti. Galeazzi grew up in that tradition, studying violin in the 1770s surrounded by many of these great musicians. He would, however, be almost completely unknown today had not Bathia Churgin, in an often-cited article from 1968,[1] drawn attention to a small section of a large treatise that Galeazzi published in 1796.[2]

The section in question seems to discuss "sonata form," though Galeazzi never actually uses the term. Someone unacquainted with the traditions of late nineteenth- and twentieth-century conservatories and collegiate music departments would likely be astonished at the way "form," and "sonata form" in particular, developed into fetish objects. Parallels would be difficult to find. Collegiate students of literature appear to worry very little about identifying "novel form" in each novel that they read. Collegiate art majors seem unconcerned about the presence or absence of "still-life form" in every still life that they view. But collegiate music students seem to consider identifying the presence or absence of the delineaments of sonata form their first order of business when asked to "analyze" an instrumental work from the eighteenth century. Inasmuch as most such works *are* sonatas, with the exceptions openly announced on the printed score ("rondo," "theme and variations," "fantasia"), one might justly wonder what all the fuss is about.

As I suggested in the introduction, many inherited approaches to eighteenth-century music are perhaps best understood as descendants of nineteenth- and early twentieth-century attempts to reinterpret the galant tradition—a tradition that, although in many ways antithetical to the bourgeoise art of Romanticism, was nevertheless claimed by the Romantics as a crucial part of their patrimony. Galant music became the childhood of

Romantic music, meaning that the galant was thought to be both childlike and suitable for children. An adult galant musician like Clementi, capable of great range and profundity, became known almost exclusively for tiny pieces used to teach beginning piano students in Victorian middle-class households. Galant musicians, thus viewed as genial children, were judged to lack an understanding of "higher" form. At best, they seemed to stumble toward sonata form, with only Haydn and Mozart finally getting it right.

The French Revolution (1789) had begun a long series of dislocations and upheavals that weakened the galant social order. Napoleonic armies overturned, bankrupted, or threatened almost every court in Europe, including the Church. When nearly thirty years of instability ended with the Treaty of Vienna (1818), prerevolutionary life was but a distant memory. Perhaps the Romantic reinterpretation of galant music was thus unavoidable. Having lost touch with galant society and its web of interdependent meanings, gestures, and modes of communication, the Romantics could do little else but reflect their own musical preoccupations onto an earlier music that was now cut loose from the culture that had nurtured it. The once highly contingent, socially located musical behaviors of court musicians came to be received in some quarters as just pleasant patterns of sound. In a nutshell, the Romantics eviscerated galant content and named the hollow corpse "form."

Other authors have attempted to narrate the complex history of "form" as a central preoccupation of early musicological discourse. Carl Dahlhaus, for instance, noted the homologies between the Romantic passion for taxonomies of flowers, butterflies, or birds, and their taxonomies of musical forms: "first rondo form," "second rondo form," and so forth.[3] That history is largely a history of nineteenth-century authors, and much of the attention given to Galeazzi's description of a double-reprise *melodia* has been due to its being one of the first accounts to conform with what became the paradigmatic Romantic prescription of a sonata's "themes and keys." Since many modern readers come to Galeazzi with that paradigm in mind, the fact that Galeazzi's description resonates with the Romantic paradigm is often taken as a partial validation of the paradigm's applicability to Classical music, as a confirmation of its cognitive force some thirty or forty years before the German and French treatises that finalized the nineteenth-century codification of sonata form. As the title of Churgin's article proclaims, a reader inculcated in the Romantic paradigm will encounter "Francesco Galeazzi's description of sonata form."

By 1796, Galeazzi had long since left the Savoy court to seek his fortune in Rome, where the treatise was published. In April of that same year, Napoleon, seeking a fortune with which to pay his destitute legions, invaded Savoy to begin the conquest of the peninsula. His forces entered Rome less than two years later, deposed the pope, and sent some five hundred wagonloads of plundered art back to France. The publication of Galeazzi's treatise thus coincided neatly with the end of one era of Italian history and the beginning of another. If Galeazzi could be seen as a transitional figure, as someone more Janus-faced and less merely a harbinger of the future, then his treatise should still resonate with galant traditions. The *melodia* with which he illustrated his ideas should, presumably, contain strong echoes of the phrase schemata that were so central to the tradition in which he was nurtured at Turin. It might showcase a newer notion of form, to be sure, but perhaps not without honoring a remembered content as well.

The first two columns in the list below show the correspondences between Galeazzi's *melodia* as parsed by him according to the terms used in his treatise (col. 1) and by this author according to the galant schemata discussed here in previous chapters (col. 2). Measure numbers refer to example 29.12, where the full *melodia* can be seen along with a bass that I have added to clarify the schemata.

Galeazzi's Term	*Schema*	*Key*	*Measure*
Principal Motive	Do-Mi-Sol . . .	C	1
2nd Motive / Depart. from the Key	Prinner, modulating	C ⇨ G	10
Characteristic Passage	Fenaroli, *bis*	G	17
Cadential Period	Falling Thirds	G	21
——	Cudworth	G	23
Coda	Quiescenza, *bis*	G	24

:‖‖:

Motive / Modulation	Fonte	Dm ⇨ C	29
——	Converging cad.	Am	33
——	Fenaroli	Am	34
——	Augmented 6th	Am	36
——	Ponte	Am	37
——	Passo Indietro	Am	38
——	Complete cadence	Am	39
Reprise	Do-Mi-Sol . . .	C	42
——	Indugio	C	50
Rep. of the Characteristic Passage	Fenaroli, *bis*	C	53
Rep. of the Cadential Period	Falling Thirds	C	57
——	Cudworth	C	59
Repetition of the Coda	Quiescenza, *bis*	C	60

Leaving aside for a moment the opening gambit ("Do-Mi-Sol . . ."), Galeazzi's series of schemata—Modulating Prinner, Fenaroli (repeated), Falling Thirds, Cudworth cadence, Quiescenza—hardly seems revolutionary. If anything it seems old-fashioned, more like movements from the 1760s or 1770s. The typical schemata of the galant style occur in the typical order. A Fonte following the double bar could hardly be more traditional. As the discussion in chapter 14 demonstrated, a Fonte in that position was the first choice for an earlier composer like Wodiczka and for a later one like Pugnani. The minuet in chapter 5 by Pugnani's teacher Somis, written in Turin sixty years before Galeazzi's treatise, used the Fonte in exactly the same way.

Galeazzi would likely have approved of Leopold Mozart's term *il filo*. According to Galeazzi, the best composers concerned themselves more with the flow and sequence of things than with the character of a single motive or phrase. As he put it, "The art, then, of the perfect composer does not consist in the invention (*trovare*) of galant motives (*galanti motivi*), [or] of agreeable passages, but consists in the precise behavior (*esatta condotta*) of an entire piece of music."[4] The emphasis on the *esatta condotta*, which could also be translated as "exact conduct" or "correct behavior," is not a reference to a reified global form or design. The perception of musical "behavior" is dynamic, and depends on moment-to-moment evaluations. Thus while being able to invent "galant motives" based on recognized schemata was a necessary prerequisite for composition, merely stringing them together without care was not sufficient for perfection in composition. Galeazzi's subsequent focus on "laying out the melodies"[5] highlights the same skills that, in Leopold's words, distinguished "the master from the bungler."[6] A treatise nearly contemporaneous with Galeazzi's, the third volume of *Versuch einer Anleitung zur Composition* [An Introductory Essay on Composition; 1793] by Heinrich Christoph Koch (1749–1816), shows this very same focus in its subtitle: "On the Connecting of Melodic Parts."[7] If many of the "parts" (*Theile*) in question are the "compulsory figures" of the galant style (with *galanti motivi*), then one should expect to find Koch's descriptions of musical functions or manipulations likewise exemplified by well-known schemata.

In a discussion of musical "parenthesis," he described how one could insert a "complete part" between repetitions of a passage. The passage in question was a four-bar, paired Sol-Fa-Mi with strong elements of the Do-Re-Mi as well. His first choice for a "complete part" to insert between the Sol-Fa-Mi and its repetition was the venerable Fonte (ex. 29.1):[8]

EX. 29.1   Koch, *Versuch*, "parenthesis," vol. 3, p. 221 (1793)

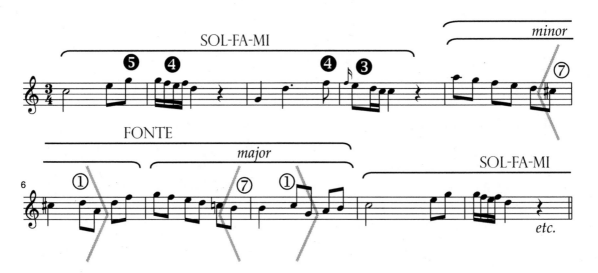

A Fonte was almost always a good choice for a parenthetical insertion, since it can digress from, and then return to, the same key. But Koch's choice also exhibits a sensitivity to larger-scale melodic coherence. The ❺–❹ . . . ❹–❸ descent of the Sol-Fa-Mi's core melodic tones would, if projected forward, reach a ❷ in measure 6. That would be D5, the ① of the minor half of the Fonte, which, continuing the progression, leads to a global ① "one step lower" in the major half (m. 8). So here "precise behavior" is a combination of a likely sequence of schemata with a sensitivity toward how emerging melodic implications might be smoothly realized.

Koch's second choice, a further "expansion" of the previous parenthetical insertion, involved placing complete Fenarolis within each half of the Fonte. This eight-measure "part" was then extended even further by a Converging cadence (ex. 29.2). Again the global ❷, D5, is reached in measure 6. But since the Fenarolis serve to double the length of each half of this Fonte, the global ①, C5, is not reached until measure 10. Continuing this broader progression, a global ❼, B4, is reached right on schedule in measure 14. As the leading tone, ❼ then makes a good connection back to the return of the Sol-Fa-Mi. Koch's "thread," while hardly the mythical *Urlinie*, completes a simple but satisfying course that still meets Galeazzi's demand for "precise behavior."

EX. 29.2   Koch, *Versuch*, "parenthesis," vol. 3, p. 222 (1793)

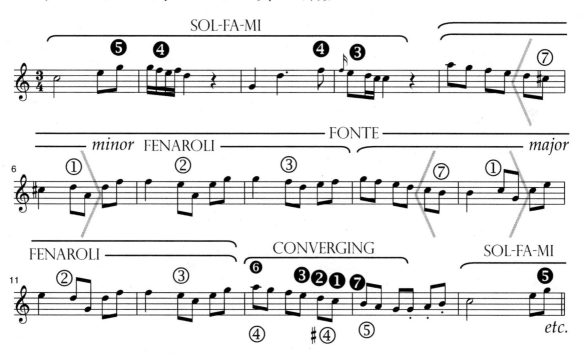

Though Koch wrote obvious Fontes and acknowledged the influence of Riepel, he did not use the terms *fonte*, *monte*, or *ponte*. Curiously, aside from tempo indications, Koch used almost no Italian terms, avoiding even the solfège syllables. Perhaps as chapel master of the small Protestant court at Rudolstadt in Thuringia, he wanted to avoid the impression of describing a Catholic practice. But Koch's musical examples are nonetheless always in general accord with the Italian practices described by Riepel's "three-fold example."

Koch's clear understanding of the normative details of the standard schemata can be observed in his discussion of "progressions."[9] He began by describing progressive repetitions of a small motive on successively descending scale degrees and gave the following phrase for illustration:

EX. 29.3   Koch, *Versuch*, a "progression," vol. 2, p. 431 (1787)

In the key of G major, the tones that fall on the downbeats (E5, D5, C5, B4) sound out the Prinner melody. Koch seems to have made the same association. He remarked that because of the "underlying harmony," it might be necessary to adjust some of the intervals. To illustrate his point he offered a more galant example, on which he marked two "modified" intervals with Maltese crosses. As shown below, the phrase that he provided, now in D major, presents a prototypical instance of the galant four-bar Prinner, complete with High ❷ Drop and a concluding half cadence:

EX. 29.4   Koch, *Versuch*, a modified "progression," Allegretto, vol. 2, p. 432 (1787)

"Harmony" alone does not fully explain the choices of Koch's modified tones, inasmuch as several alternatives were equally "harmonic." Only the tones actually chosen were exact matches to the Prinner schema replicated countless times in the galant repertory. From the viewpoint of schema theory, it is revealing to witness Koch implicitly equating the older, "mechanical" pattern of the circle-of-fifths Prinner (ex. 29.3), which was Riepel's "seventh-progression," with the newer, galant type (ex. 29.4).

Koch's sense for the proper concatenation of schemata—the "connecting of melodic parts"—is at times grounded on the stepwise progression of core tones, at times based on harmonic expectation, and at other times motivated by simple patterns of repetition. Example 29.5 shows his basic version of the modulating Prinner, introduced by the phrase "modulation through the transposition of a part to a new key."[10] The example begins with a Comma followed by a half cadence (both treble and bass are by Koch). The stepwise melodic descent ❹–❸–❸–❷ links these two schemata, as does a traditional association based on older, more elaborate clausulae like the Cadenza Doppia. The appearance of the modulating Prinner begins a new descent in the new key, D major. The Prinner and ensuing Converging cadence lead the melody down through the complete D-hexachord, ❻–❺–❹–❸–❷–❶—one step per measure—to close with an accelerated descent from ❶ to ❼ and beyond in measure 8:[11]

EX. 29.5   Koch, *Versuch*, "modulation through the transposition of a part to a new key," vol. 3, p. 209 (1793)

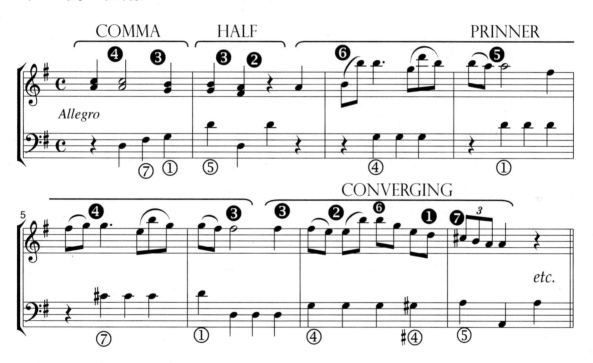

The location at the beginning of measure 7 (ex. 29.5), where the melody reaches ❷ and the bass sounds ④, is one shared by a number of schemata. It is a place where a galant musician would recognize *il filo* as potentially leading off in a number of different directions. One could chose to take one of those divergent paths, or just allude to one with a characteristic figuration. In example 29.5, for instance, Koch already hinted at the Indugio. In example 29.6, he went further in that direction by allotting to his Converging cadence the sixteenth-note figurations strongly associated with the Indugio.[12]

EX. 29.6   Koch, *Versuch*, a modulating Prinner leading to a Converging cadence, vol. 3, p. 365 (1793)

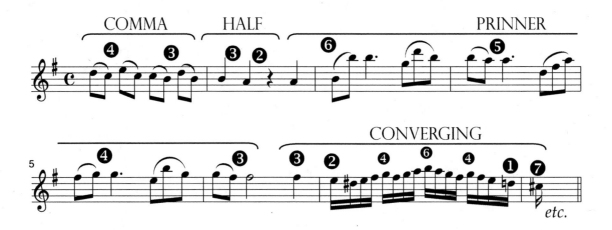

In example 29.7, he stepped fully onto the path of the Indugio, inserting a complete two-measure extension of the basic Converging cadence:[13]

EX. 29.7   Koch, *Versuch*, a modulating Prinner leading to an Indugio, vol. 3, p. 219 (1793)

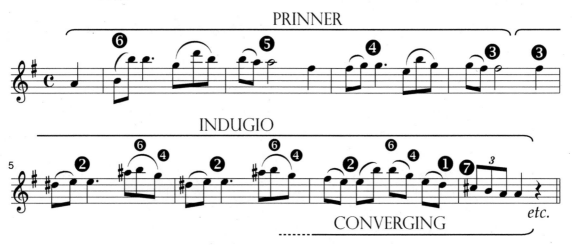

His two versions of characteristic Indugio figurations (exx. 29.6–7) are very similar to those that Mozart employed for the first movement of his C-major keyboard sonata of 1788 (see ex. 26.6, mm. 9–10, 22–23).

As Koch discusses various musical genres, it becomes clear that each involves different selections and arrangements of the same set of "parts" and procedures—an *ars combinatoria*. The difference between the first and second ritornellos of a concerto or aria, for instance, rests on the need to modulate to the key of the dominant in the second ritornello. In his example of a second ritornello (ex. 29.8), he matches the requirement (a modulation to the dominant) with the generic, formulaic "part" of the modulating Prinner, indeed one almost identical to those shown in examples 29.5–7. In all these cases he respects the old precedent of ending the preceding part in a low register before leaping up an octave to begin the modulating Prinner (cf. ex. 22.1, m. 23, by Leo; ex. 25.19, m. 4, by Eckard; or ex. 25.21, m. 7, by Mozart). His modulating Prinner, unimpeded by an Indugio (the path not taken), moves directly to the Converging cadence, which then leads into two statements of a busy Fenaroli, complete with a rapidly repeating pedal-point ⑤, in the new key of D major:[14]

EX. 29.8   Koch, *Versuch*, the modulation in a second ritornello, vol. 3, p. 426 (1793)

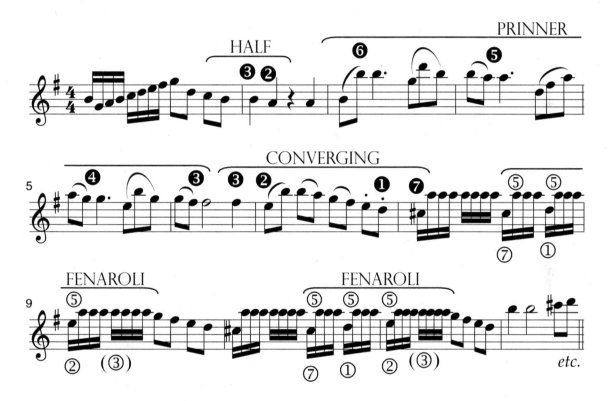

Galeazzi faced a similar situation after the close of the first "period" of his *melodia*, and he responded by choosing the same basic parts with nearly the same procedures (see ex. 29.9).[15] After a complete cadence in the tonic key of C major, a modulating Prinner extends to a complete cadence on the dominant of the new key of G major ("V of V"), to be followed by two statements of a Fenaroli (the normal ⑦–①–②–③ voice would be in the bass).

While Koch's choices were made in "concerto form" or "aria form," Galeazzi's were made in "sonata form." Since the same general choices were made in both instances, the reasonable inference arises that "form" had relatively little influence on the "connecting

EX. 29.9   Galeazzi, *Elementi*, the modulation in a "second motive" (1793)

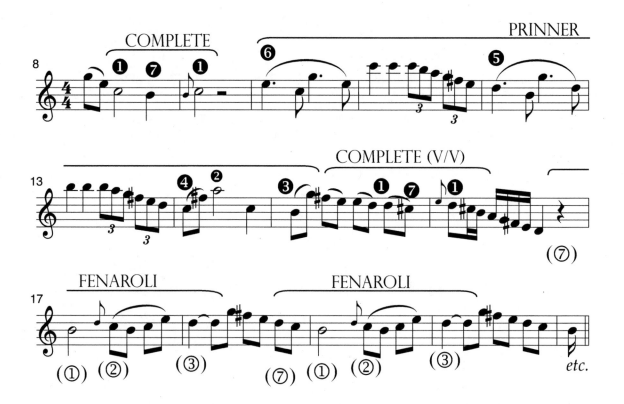

of parts." Rather than failing to understand form, and being unable to articulate its "deeper" secrets, galant composers and writers about music understood it very well. They understood the practical abilities of listeners to follow schemes of repetition, digression, or return, to attend to the rise or fall of melodic or bass progressions, and they understood that the real art of composition lay in guiding their patron's and audience's moment-to-moment experiences. Galant composers could succinctly describe the overall form of movements in different genres because the craft of managing *il filo* depended very little on the different formal schemes. One only needed to be aware of a few important forks in the road. To be sure, Galeazzi transforms the *character* of the Fenaroli, and his treatise describes this "characteristic passage" as "dolce, espressivo, e tenero" ("sweet, expressive, and tender")[16] in a way that strongly resonates with Romantic definitions of a lyrical second theme. But navigation by the perceived contrast of character, which became an important listener strategy as nineteenth-century compositions grew in both length and complexity, would lie outside a galant concept of "form."

As mentioned, for many students the formal analysis of an eighteenth-century movement still involves finding the development, the second theme, and other nineteenth-century markers of sonata form. The twentieth century has added a professional level of analysis in which the goal is to assign every tone to its place in a vast "tonal hierarchy."

One might ask "Why?" The typical answer is that the tonal hierarchy demonstrates the organic unity of the musical artworks produced by a small set of master musicians. Surely this is a metaphysical solution to a self-inflicted problem. Since music, in the full sense of the word, takes place in the human brain rather than in a metaphysical world of tonal "spirits" and "wills," we should be interested in a cognitive hierarchy, which is typically a mental structure that outlines levels of abstraction or "chunking." Take, for example, Jane Austen's novel *Pride and Prejudice*.[17] A reader or listener (early novels were often read aloud) hears sounds (phonemes) that make up parts of words; the words make up clauses, which make up sentences, which in written texts make up paragraphs, then chapters, and finally the book as a whole. At each level of this cognitive hierarchy the elements are somewhat different in kind. The gist of a chapter, for instance, is not the text of any individual paragraph, nor is the gist of the novel as a whole the text of any one of its chapters. In a tonal hierarchy, by contrast, it would seem that the elements of each level are exactly the same as the elements above or below. To take an absurd but actual example, the claim would be that the gist of the finale of Beethoven's Ninth Symphony would be the tone D that sounds at its conclusion. The analogous claim might hold the gist of *Pride and Prejudice* to be its final word: "them."

The more closely one studies the craft of eighteenth-century court music, the less the "organic unity" of the musical artwork seems "a truth universally acknowledged," to echo the opening line of Austen's novel. There was a galant musical hierarchy, to be sure. Tones made up parts of figures, which made up parts of phrases, which in instrumental music combined into sections, movements, works, and finally a published opus. But within each quite distinct level of the hierarchy there was considerable freedom and latitude. Replacing a D with a C♯ in a small melodic figure would not cause the whole musical house to collapse, nor would replacing a Sol-Fa-Mi with a Romanesca. As the cognitive scientist Herbert Simon pointed out more than thirty years ago,[18] the hierarchies of complex systems are usually "partially decomposable," meaning that each level in the hierarchy has a measure of independence. What he labeled "loose coupling" refers to the relative weakness of interactions between levels and the relative strength of interactions within a given level. The "precise behavior" of *il filo* was crucial at the level of phrases and cadences, but of minor significance at the level of overall form.

The master musicians were the ones most able to recognize the contingent nature of any particular musical thread. They were the ones who chose to follow a particular path in the schematic road, and in doing so had to forgo the alternate paths. Jane Austen, it appears, looked at *Pride and Prejudice* in much the same way. Upon its publication she wrote teasingly to her sister:

> Upon the whole . . . I am well satisfied enough. The work is rather too light, and bright, and sparkling; it wants shade; it wants to be stretched out here and there with a long chapter of sense, if it could be had; if not, of solemn specious nonsense, about something unconnected with the story: an essay on writing, a critique on Walter Scott, or the history

of Buonaparté, or anything that would form a contrast and bring the reader with increased delight to the playfulness and general epigrammatism of the general style.[19]

Austen, a master writer if ever there was one, described a need for "stretching out" the work "here and there," and focused on the need for "anything that would form a contrast." She may have exemplified her points facetiously, but it was a writer's discourse on writing. Galeazzi's concerns were similar. He described "the most interesting part of modern music" as involving "drawing out the melodies" ("tirare le Melodie").[20] And he advocated beginning the second half of a double reprise with the contrast of "an idea that is quite new and foreign," preferably in a different key to achieve a "greater surprise."[21] Austen's and Galeazzi's discourse reflects artists' careful evaluations of the effects that various compositional options may have on a listener or reader. In 1845, A. B. Marx (1795–1866) described Mozart's style as a succession of many "small structures that lack any stonger connection than that derived from the general mood. This gives his compositions the charm of the ever changing, the ever new, nimbly seeking further."[22] Marx, from the generation of Franz Schubert, had sought to contrast Mozart's style, somewhat negatively, with the dynamism and "inner necessity" of Beethoven's. Marx did not advocate a Mozartean style for his contemporaries, and in the 1920s Heinrich Schenker excoriated Marx ("mistakes thrive like rats in the canals of ignorance") for failing to understand Mozart's organic "sonata-synthesis."[23] Thus, concerning the galant *sprezzatura* (nonchalance) in the linking of "small structures," one can mark a gradual progression from approving description (Koch, Galeazzi, Austen) to accepting remembrance (Marx) to disbelief and condemnation (Schenker).

In the list shown earlier, in which Galeazzi's *melodia* is parsed by different taxonomies, an obvious difference between the first two columns is the greater detail in the "schema" column. Galeazzi was aware of omissions and mentioned that his "small, extremely simple" example did not contain every possible detail. But there is another reason for the difference: his intended readership. His title page makes explicit the orientation toward "beginners, dilettantes, and violin teachers." In other words, rather than being a technical specification of *melodia* for the training of aspiring composers, Galeazzi's terms are more a list of impressions or characteristics that might be recognizable to someone without professional training (I believe he intended "violin teachers" to serve as proxies for their untrained students). Like Riepel and Koch, he used mostly melodic examples described in generic, functional terms. As mentioned earlier, the vast nonverbal knowledge that professional musicians gained through years of studying partimenti, solfeggi, and famous scores under the guidance of a maestro contrasts markedly with what could be imparted through words to amateur musicians. It might not be too strong an interpretation to describe these widely read eighteenth-century music treatises as "translations" from a ritualized, preindustrial, nonverbal culture to a commercial, modern, verbal one.

Perhaps the most modern aspect of Galeazzi's *melodia* was, as mentioned, his treatment of the opening theme:

EX. 29.10   Galeazzi's opening theme realized with a bass and inner voices

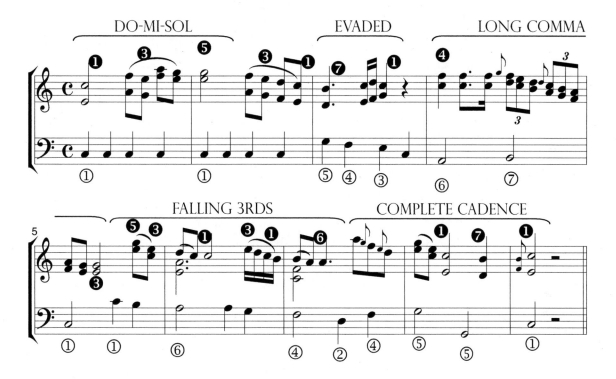

This opening section is discursive in the way it "draws out" the melody, eschewing any single organizing schema. Galeazzi begins with a small Do-Mi-Sol melodic triad. His "thread" wanders through an evaded cadence (cf. the Passo Indietro), a Long Comma, and a Falling Thirds sequence before reaching the complete cadence of measures 7–9. This was never a common succession of schemata, and one senses a lack of direction in what he termed his "principal motive" (mm. 1–9). Inasmuch as he admired Haydn, Boccherini, Wanhal, and other major composers active in the 1790s, he may have been trying to emulate the ways in which they created large opening "periods," to use his term. Perhaps Galeazzi meant the second system of this example to present a large form of Sala's Long cadence. In my added bass, the downbeats of measures 5–9 do present the ①–⑥–④–⑤–① pattern characteristic of the Long cadence. But somehow the upper voices do not assist the effort. Galeazzi does not seem quite up to the task of creating the broad *slancio* ("dash" or "swoop") of his famous contemporaries. Only when, following his principal motive, he reverts to the schemata of his galant training does *il filo* seem to have been spun out with real fluency.

In the 1790s, Italian maestros from the "old school" still had considerable prestige. As late as 1806, Haydn wrote a letter of recommendation for Mozart's son Karl to study with Bonifazio Asioli (1769–1832), a maestro in Milan who, like Galeazzi, would eventually commit his copious musical knowledge to print in a comprehensive textbook.[24] The movement of Italian maestros to Paris, and their prominence in the teaching of music, extended the influence of the galant style for several more generations, though in a propaedeutic role. The full story of that particular nineteenth-century reverberation of galant practice would warrant a separate study. But perhaps one example will suffice. Gustavo Carulli (1801–1876), son of an Italian musician, was born in Paris and there became a well-known teacher of singing. Teaching pieces from his 1838 *Méthode de chant* figured prominently in the famous compendium *Solfège des Solfèges*, a nineteenth-century series of graded studies still in print today.[25] As shown in example 29.11, Carulli, though living in the Paris of Berlioz, Liszt, and Chopin, was fluent in the galant phraseology of the 1780s. Even without their implied basses, the galant schemata should be clearly evident in what Galeazzi would call Carulli's "principal motive" (mm. 1–19) and the start of his "second motive" (mm. 21–24). This "second motive" uses the same choice of modulating Prinner that Galeazzi made for the analogous moment in his *melodia* and that Koch made for his second ritornello. Though relegated to the practice room, galant syntax thus continued to be inculcated in conservatories and private studios.

EX. 29.11   Carulli, solfège (1838), reprinted in Dannhauser, vol. 3, no. 1, Andantino

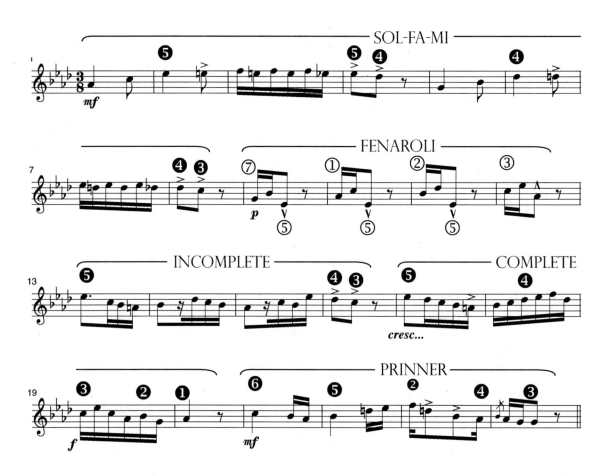

In example 29.12 I have reproduced Galeazzi's entire *melodia* and added a bass to help clarify the various schemata. As mentioned, Galeazzi was, in the 1790s, a conservative composer. The scope of the movement, his "laying out" of schemata, and his melodic style are all more reminiscent of Leduc in the early 1770s than, say, Viotti in the 1790s. Yet I do not mean to diminish the importance of his treatise. Churgin's insightful remarks of 1968 still accurately describe a treatise of great historical significance. By viewing Galeazzi's musical examples in a more detailed, historicized light, I find his treatise more, not less, interesting.

EX. 29.12   Galeazzi's model sonata with a bass added to clarify the schemata

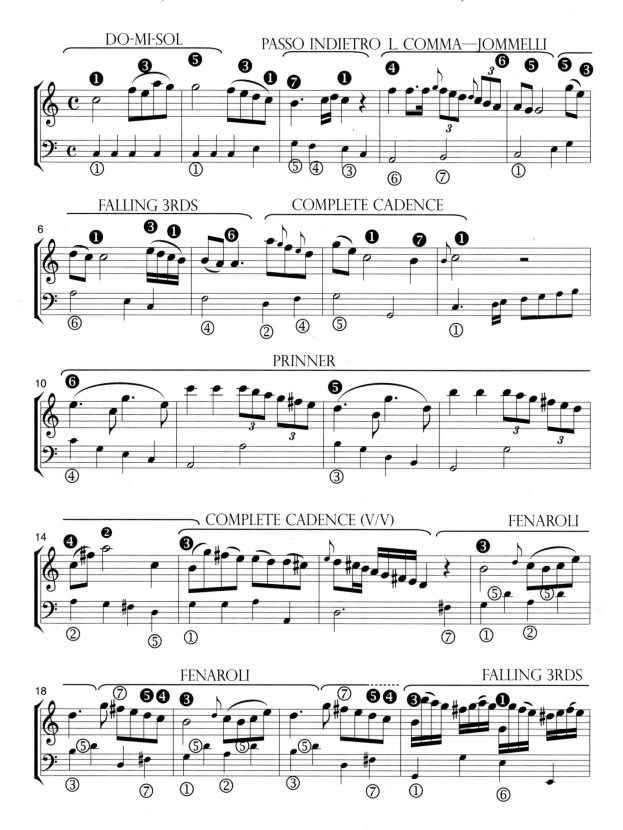

30

SUMMARY AND CADENZA

A EUROPEAN EXPERT ON THE MUSIC OF THE BEATLES, Tuomas Eerola, made a careful study of their experimental style. He compared the distribution over time of Beatles recordings that feature Indian instruments, tape manipulations, psychedelic or nostalgic lyrics, modal scales, changing meters, and so forth with the distribution over time of the Meyer, as reported in my *A Classic Turn of Phrase*.[1] A graph of his comparison is shown below, with the much longer time scale of the Meyer contracted to match the relatively short period of Beatles recordings:

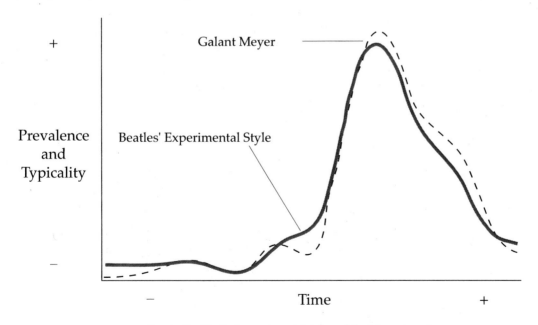

FIGURE 30.1   Eerola, the Beatles' experimental style and the Meyer (1997)

There is little direct connection between the Beatles and galant music. But the very high correlation of these graphs suggests that the hypotheses put forth in A *Classic Turn of Phrase* about the nature of theoretical categories in a music history may have broad applicability, which was the point of Eerola's comparison.

This graph allows a number of inferences to be made about the nature of stylistic categories or schemata. First and foremost, typicality is tied to prevalence. That is, we tend to recognize the most typical exemplars as stemming from the period of a schema's greatest use. Usage of the Meyer peaked in the early 1770s, at the same time that we find especially numerous clear and direct examples of it. Likewise, the Beatles' experimental style peaked in early 1967 at the time of the *Sgt. Pepper* album, which in turn is widely considered the prototype of that style. Second, as a corollary of the first point, there is a marked decline in typicality at the margins of a schema's history. A concept like "the world's first Prinner" would be just as questionable as "the world's last Prinner," because at the margins there may be only a tenuous connection to the schema. Prior knowledge of the schema can make the marginal exemplars subjectively seem to belong, but a different schema might objectively be more appropriate. Third, the resemblance of the graphs to bell-curve–like charts of probabilities is more than accidental. The graph does in fact represent rough probabilistic estimates of the chance of encountering a particular schema in a particular repertory at a particular time in history. A graph of the Monte would peak somewhat earlier than the graph of the Meyer. A graph of the Quiescenza would peak somewhat later. A graph of the Do-Re-Mi or Fonte would stretch across a broader time period. A graph of the Indugio would be focused more tightly on the 1770s and 1780s. All these microhistories, when combined, would form a composite graph of the galant style. Isolated aspects of galant practice appear already in the late seventeenth century, and remnants of it persist well into the nineteenth century, especially where aristocratic society and patronage is involved (Chopin and Tchaikovsky come to mind). Yet this imagined graph of the galant style would show a high probability of the style only within the period of perhaps 1725 to 1785, peaking in the vicinity of 1765.

The central thesis of A *Classic Turn of Phrase*—that one's theory of a musical style or pattern defines or delimits how one views its history, and vice versa—seems to have been borne out in a long history of various misreadings of the galant style. Overly strong music histories, constructed more by analogy with German art-historical fashions than by intrinsically musical resemblances, created an imaginary eighteenth-century moiety in which each composer had to belong to either the Baroque or the Classical clan. The galant world hardly fits into that stark dichotomy, and one sees the resulting discomfort in the endless remarks in surveys and encyclopedias about musicians whose compositions "show characteristics of both Baroque and Classical styles." One might conclude that all but the most one-dimensional eighteenth-century composers were stylistically uncertain of their true identities. These dichotomous histories went hand in hand with overly strong, dichotomous music theories. An early manifestation was the "second theme" and "second key area" becoming the fetish markers of the Classical sonata form as opposed to the reified

Baroque practice of "spinning out" works without form. The later American embrace of the chauvinistically German doctrines of Arnold Schoenberg and Heinrich Schenker resulted in what can be described as theory-driven historiography. That is, some of the publications from professional music theorists seem to reinforce the curious notions (1) that all music before 1700 is not quite "tonal" and thus the sole property of music antiquarians, (2) that all music from Corelli to Mahler should be understood through Schenker's totalizing ideology of a transcendent tonality, and (3) that music after Mahler is the province of set-theory as the patrimony of Schoenberg. Again, the galant style can find no place in this essentialist fantasy of "pretonal, tonal, and post-tonal" music.

What I would like to suggest further is that the galant style is not alone in its discomfort. The grand dichotomies of histories past and the totalizing theoretical ideologies of the early twentieth century have been revelatory for no style at all. The appeal of a Manfred Bukofzer or a Heinrich Schenker can, of course, be quite strong. In a discussion of the generation of architects who followed early twentieth-century giants like Frank Lloyd Wright or Le Corbusier, Rupert Spade wrote in 1971 about the American architect Paul Rudolf, who had been stung by one of Wright's pointed remarks.

> To such a denunciation, uttered as it were over the space of half a century, a man in Rudolph's position could make no adequate riposte. The rigid utterances of the nineteenth-century men—"Form follows Function," "Less is more," "Ornament is crime," "A house is a machine to live in"—cannot be *refuted*, any more than are the remnants of the giant statue of Ozymandias ridiculed by Shelley's famous poem. The writings and works of the great pioneers *do* stand like "vast and trunkless legs of stone"; but to their bombastic utterances men of Rudolph's generation can only reply with complexities, qualifications, amendments, explanations.[2]

In proposing a focus on schemata—microhistories with corresponding microtheories—I hope to make a detour around those "great pioneers," to engage galant music more through its own concepts and less through the discourse of "nineteenth-century men" who were often hostile not only to its artistic premises but also, certainly in Schenker's case, to the ethnicity of the artists who developed it. Had those nineteenth-century men known more about galant music, I suspect that their substantial musical understanding coupled with their aptitude for the craft of composition would eventually have disabused them of some of their more farfetched claims. As Spade might put it, when a Schenker says "Origin is destiny," I can make no adequate riposte.

The world of galant courts was not a realization of some trenchant aphorism or the unfolding of some overarching principle. And the music that both supported and was supported by those courts is similarly not the result of the spirits of tonality or the sonata. The deep roots of the styles of the sixteenth and seventeenth centuries were plainly in view in the eighteenth century. The Romanesca, for example, spanned this whole period. The Clausula Vera had been a meaningful cadence when the Renaissance was still young. Various past traditions were thus part of the galant present. Balancing the force of the past was the strong desire for fashionable novelty. In the course of this book we have seen a full range of works extending from the simplicity of a Somis minuet to the enormous intricacy of a Jommelli duet or a Haydn quartet movement. Schemata like the Indugio or the Quiescenza seem to have risen in tandem with those larger works. The Indugio, for instance, served to hold back an expected big cadence, thereby heightening anticipation. The Quiescenza, by contrast, served to quiet things down *after* a big cadence. Neither function was needed in a small minuet. So in considering the world of those musical courtiers, we should bear in mind that genre mattered, tradition mattered, fashion mattered, their training mattered, and all the elements that Pierre Bourdieu might have described as their musical *habitus* mattered in how they constituted their musical world.

> The *habitus*, a product of history, produces individual and collective practices—more history—in accordance with the schemes generated by history. It ensures the active presence of past experiences, which, deposited in each organism in the form of schemes of perception, thought and action, tend to guarantee the "correctness" of practices and their constancy over time, more reliably than all formal rules and explicit norms. This system of dispositions . . . [is] a present past that tends to perpetuate itself into the future by reactivation in similarly structured practices.[3]

Like each of the galant schemata, the Prinner was saturated in the associations and practices of a living tradition. It was neither essentially a chord progression nor fundamentally a parallel descent of outer voices, though it was correlated with such patterns. As Romantic music theory moved to make harmony the essential element of music, the Prinner, in its two harmonically incompatible forms (the modulating and nonmodulating variants), became more and more invisible, more and more unhearable. This potsherd has lain in the musical rubble of the ancien régime for almost two centuries. Yet any assiduous reader of this book will now begin to recognize Prinners when listening to eighteenth-century music. Prinners were ubiquitous in the galant style because they formed useful ripostes, and the details of their construction operated within modes of harmonic-contrapuntal thought that had been conditioned by ritualized training in figured bass, partimenti, and solfeggi. For someone within this courtly music culture, the Prinner required presentation, not explanation. The child Mozart, for example, learned to present the basic Prinner when he was only five years old (KV1c; see ex. 25.3), and he no doubt wrote hundreds of versions of it over the next thirty years. Each of them was localized in a web of styles, references, compositional techniques, and rhetorical practices.

Mozart is a special case because he often located his utterances at the margins of what was acceptable musical behavior. Thus his work could delight or repel depending on the listener or performer. Dittersdorf, a reliable, centrist composer with great success at court, recalled an imperial minister likening Dittersdorf's music to "a well-furnished, daintily arranged table. The dishes are well served up. One can take a good helping from each, without risk to the digestion."[4] Mozart's late style, by contrast, seems to have been an acquired taste. Dittersdorf and Mozart knew each other well. They even played together, along with Haydn and Wanhal, in a friendly string quartet. By the later 1780s, however, Dittersdorf had begun voicing reservations about Mozart's esoteric, mannered style. In a letter to the publisher Artaria from August of 1788, he offered his recent string quartets for sale and claimed, "I am sure that you will do better with mine than Mozart's (which according to my, as well as the great theorists', judgment are worthy of the highest praise, but which, however, because of their unrelenting extreme artfulness are not everyone's purchase)."[5] Dittersdorf returned to this complaint when, in his autobiography, he recounts a conversation with the Austrian emperor. The emperor had asked him what he thought about Mozart's music, and Dittersdorf replied:

> He is unquestionably one of the greatest original geniuses, and I have never yet met with any composer who had such an amazing wealth of ideas; I could almost wish he were not so lavish in using them. He leaves his hearer out of breath; for hardly has he grasped one beautiful thought, when another of greater fascination dispels the first, and this goes on throughout, so that in the end it is impossible to retain any one of these beautiful melodies.[6]

What Baron von Grimm praised in the seven-year-old Mozart as a "wealth of ravishing ideas, ideas which he nevertheless knows how to place one after the other with taste and without confusion"[7] became, for Dittersdorf, the "amazing wealth of ideas" that the adult Mozart seems to place one on top of the other with resulting confusion and frustration for the listener.

In the summer of 1788, shortly before Dittersdorf wrote to Artaria about the relative merits of his and Mozart's quartets, Mozart was hard at work finishing his famous G-minor symphony. In the Trio of its third movement, he set what could have been a very simple sequence of schemata: (1) Do-Re-Mi, (2) cadence, (3) Prinner, and (4) cadence. The actual movement, though lovely, is anything but simple. Indeed, Leonard Meyer devoted sixty-nine pages of closely argued, heavily footnoted text to the discussion of Mozart's mere forty-two measures of Trio.[8] As shown in example 30.1, its opening gambit (mm. 1–4) is a blend of Do-Re-Mi and Pastorella (note the parallel thirds), which seems appropriate to the movement's general character. A small cadence (mm. 4–6) closes off the first section. Then the oboes begin a modulating Prinner (mm. 7–12). Before they have completed even two measures, a flute begins to play their motive and quickly rises above them. A bassoon then enters below the oboes with the same motive and helps lead the passage to a deceptive cadence (m. 12), followed immediately by the requisite complete cadence (mm. 13–14) and coda-like echoes of that cadence (mm. 14–18). Were we, as listeners, focused intently on hearing the oboes complete their Prinner, we might concur with Dittersdorf that "hardly [have we] grasped one beautiful thought, when another of greater fascination dispels the first."

EX. 30.1   Mozart, Symphony in G Minor (KV550), mvt. 3, Trio, Allegretto, m. 1 (1788)

But would we go as far as Dittersdorf and conclude that "in the end it [was] impossible to retain any one of these beautiful melodies"? Some might object that Dittersdorf's
comments were small-minded sneers motivated by professional jealousy. Yet two years
earlier (1786), when Mozart's *Don Giovanni* vied with Dittersdorf's *The Doctor and the
Apothecary* for the public's attention, Dittersdorf's work was easily the more popular, even
if aimed somewhat below a courtly audience. If we do accept Dittersdorf's reactions, and
accept them as characteristic of courtly society, then we should conclude that modes of
listening have since changed. If the courtiers were listening for the details of familiar schemata, then Mozart's complications could indeed cause confusion. As a patron, the emperor
would have been prudent to inquire about Mozart. Being confused by a musical servant
could put at risk one of the central functions of galant art—the public display of discernment and good taste. When we hear a reviewer of Beethoven's Opus 10 piano sonatas
complain in 1799 that "his abundance of ideas . . . leads Beethoven too often to pile one

thought wildly upon another,"[9] it may be further evidence of the increasing failure of traditional galant strategies of listening.

Almost any eighteenth-century source that discusses the genres of music will note the three main divisions of church, chamber, and theater. Courts categorized their music by venue because each required different musical forces with different talents. Older and pensioned musicians could play in the very large ensembles used for religious festivals and feasts. Elite instrumentalists in their prime vied for favor in aristocratic chambers. Famous singers commanded huge sums to grace the court theater and sing the allegorical praise of its patrons. All three sides of this musical triangle were part of musical life at a wealthy court, and almost every composer was well versed in the requirements of each. Today we may find it difficult to place these parts into a coherent whole. Pianists learn the sonatas of Mozart and Haydn but usually not their masses. Singers learn Mozart operas but often not Haydn quartets and certainly not the quartets of Galuppi. Violinists learn Bach solo sonatas, but not Jommelli arias and never the sacred motets of Durante. When the practices of the one sphere spill over into another, we may interpret the effect not as a reference to the other sphere but as some special artistic initiative. Frequently invoked terms like *Sturm und Drang* ("storm and stress") or "the learned style," for instance, may partly reflect the modern tendency to attribute acts of personal artistic expression to what in many cases were merely musical behaviors typical of the church or theater making an appearance in music for the chamber.

Mozart was especially prone to mix styles. In March of 1784 he wrote a masterful quintet for keyboard, oboe, clarinet, horn, and bassoon (KV452)—a mixture of wind instruments usually associated with outdoor entertainment or other light fare. For its slow movement he crafted an intricate Prinner more commonly found in high church music (see ex. 30.2). The Prinner plays out over a dominant pedal point (⑤). While the upper two voices descend in a chain of 2–3 suspensions, the keyboard player performs arpeggios and repeated notes. The bassoon, in the tenor range, provides the normal bass tones first of a Fonte and then of a Long Comma.

That particular combination of 2–3 suspensions, Prinner melody, the equivalent of the bassoon part, and alternating 6/5 and 5/3 sonorities was previously introduced in chapter 17. An example from the solfeggi of Porpora (ex. 17.1) was suggested as a prototype. Giuseppe Bonno, the imperial chapel master in Vienna, had been sent to Naples for study when Porpora still taught there. Because Bonno was a teacher of Dittersdorf, a possible connection was suggested between Porpora's Neapolitan type of contrapuntal Prinner and a very similar phrase from one of Dittersdorf's string quintets (ex. 17.2). While both these examples share much with the elaborate Prinner in Mozart's quintet (ex. 30.2), Porpora's was completely diatonic, and Dittersdorf's was similarly diatonic save for some fleeting chromatic appoggiaturas in the tracery of the first violin. Neither had the Fonte-like chromatic inflection of Mozart's example. More importantly, neither played out over a dominant pedal point. It is that ⑤ held by the French horn and reinforced each measure by the keyboard player that helps to give Mozart's example its harmonic pungency.

EX. 30.2   Mozart, Quintet (KV452), mvt. 2, Larghetto, m. 108 (1784)

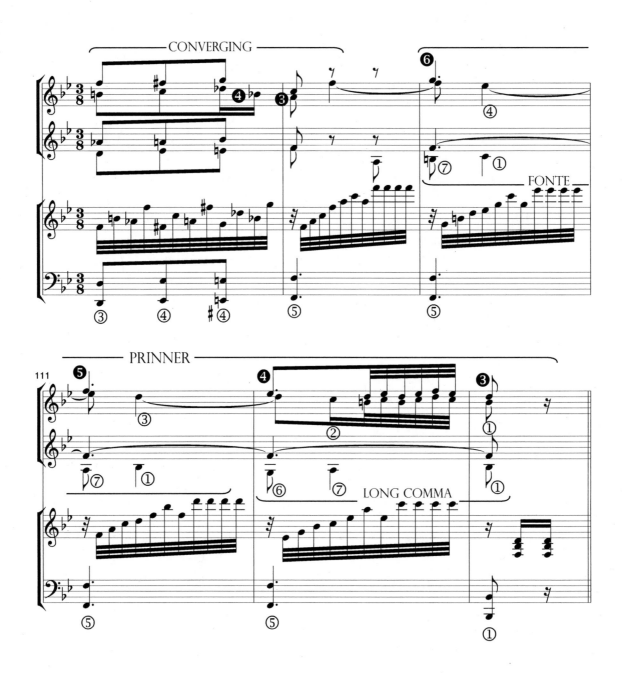

In an earlier keyboard work (KV205b, 1775) Mozart had already equated this type of contrapuntal Prinner with a normal if nonetheless ornate version featuring the *la-to-sol* flourish. The contrapuntal version, with all four voices compressed into little more than an octave, comes first. The more florid version, with the double use of the *la-to-sol* flourish in the style of Aprile (ex. 9.15) or Eckard (ex. 26.1), comes second:

EX. 30.3   Mozart, Sonata (KV205b), mvt. 1, Allegro, m. 33 (1775)

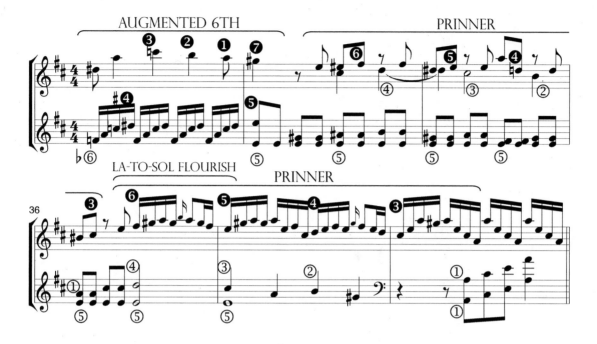

Haydn likewise paired a standard Prinner in A major with a contrapuntal, minor-mode version. Here is just the contrapuntal version from his keyboard concerto in D major, written near the time of Mozart's quintet:

EX. 30.4   Haydn, Concerto in D (Hob. XVIII/11), mvt. 2, Larghetto, m. 53 (ca. 1784)

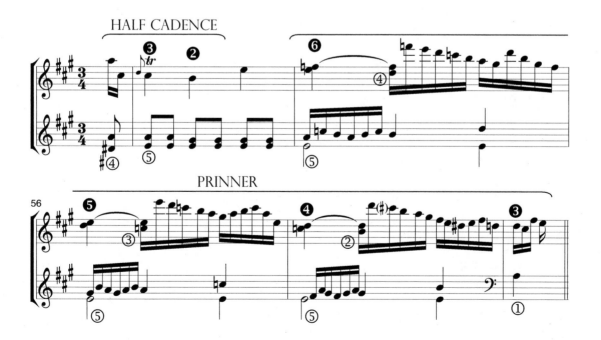

While any number of explanations can be imagined for the similarity of Haydn's and Mozart's contrapuntal Prinners, one of the most probable is that these phrases reflect a tradition within the sphere of church music, a subtype of Prinner made deeply memorable by the closing Amen from the *Stabat Mater* of Giovanni Battista Pergolesi (1710–1736):

EX. 30.5   Pergolesi, *Stabat Mater*, Presto assai, m. 45 (ca. 1736)

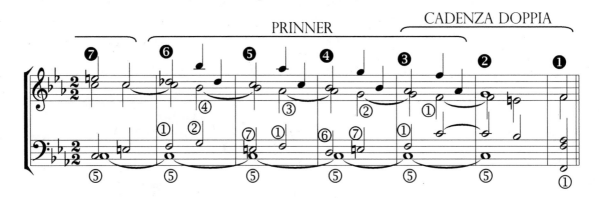

This work, of which the passage shown here is only a small fragment, was enormously popular and influential. Isabelle de Charrière was so fond of it that she had the dying heroine of her novel *Caliste* request it during her last moments. The musicians finished the *Stabat Mater* as Caliste drew her final breath.[10]

"Cadenza Doppia" (It., "double cadence") of course refers to the Neapolitan term for the sacred-style cadence that graced the final measures of a huge number of partimenti (see chap. 11). Pergolesi was a product of the Neapolitan conservatories, and in turn later Neapolitan partimenti replicated patterns found in his *Stabat Mater*. Here is the final passage from a partimento by Paisiello showing a major-mode version of the "Stabat Mater" Prinner (bass and figures, Paisiello; upper voices, mine):[11]

EX. 30.6   Paisiello, *Regole*, p. 34, m. 58 (1782)

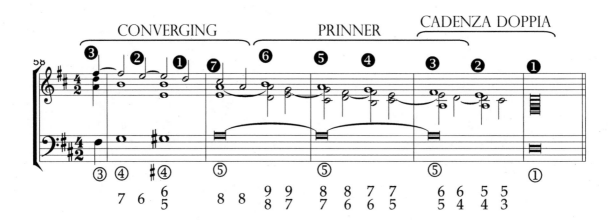

Note that Paisiello's thoroughbass figures do not specify a tenor voice (the bassoon part in Mozart's quintet). Alfred Einstein, in his *Urtext* edition of the Pergolesi *Stabat Mater*, also failed to provide a tenor part for Pergolesi's Prinner because one was not explicit in an early manuscript.[12] Many modern recordings thus have no tenor part. But that tenor part was explicit in Neapolitan performance traditions and in eighteenth-century traditions generally. The tenor part shown in the Pergolesi excerpt above is taken from a Schirmer publication, circa 1900.[13] Though not intended as a scholarly edition, it does convey an authentic nineteenth-century performance tradition based on real galant norms.

The fame of the *Stabat Mater* extended even into Lutheran domains. Late in his life J. S. Bach made an arrangement of it for use in Leipzig:[14]

EX. 30.7   J. S. Bach, arrangement of the *Stabat Mater*, m. 45 (Leipzig, 1745–47)

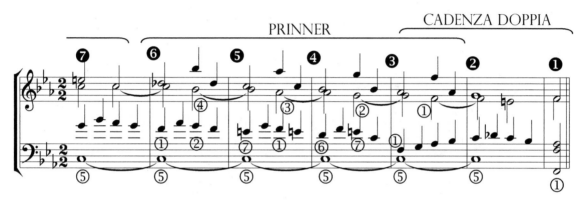

The surviving copy, in the hand of Bach's student and copyist Johann Christoph Altnickel, includes a tenor part played by the viola. For the above Prinner, its core tones fall on the first and third quarter-notes of each bar.

Even Mozart's idol J. C. Bach knew this specialized schema. In an otherwise cheerful Allegro movement in B♭ major, the London Bach inserted a doleful passage in D minor:

EX. 30.8   J. C. Bach, Opus 12, no. 6, mvt. 1, Allegro, m. 71 (Paris, 1773–74)

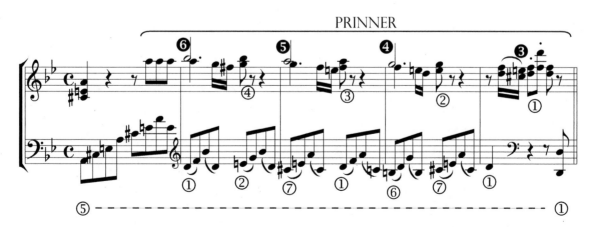

It is the Stabat Mater Prinner shorn of its pedal point, thus making the passage more like the Bonno-Dittersdorf type. Yet, alternatively, one might think of it as having a pedal in the *style brisé*, the manner in which lute players and harpsichordists often gave the illusion of more voices than were actually concurrent. The low A2 in measure 71 could form a memory that only connects to another low tone in that register (D2) at the conclusion of the passage.

As the examples by Mozart, Haydn, and J. S. Bach show, an overt tenor part was clearly incorporated in the received Stabat Mater Prinner, and it was absolutely required in the Bonno-Dittersdorf type. Even Italian models likely predating Pergolesi's work confirm the presence of a separate tenor part, as in an elegant passage from a flute concerto by Leo (note how the deceptive cadence and augmented sixth delay by one measure the Prinner's expected ❹–❸ ending):

EX. 30.9   Leo, Concerto in G Major, mvt. 2, Adagio, m. 58 (ca. 1730s)

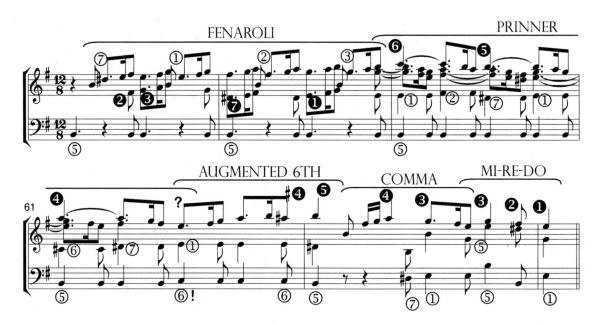

The deeply sedimented tradition of courtly schemata was too complex and multifaceted to be taught directly. Young composers absorbed it indirectly through the rituals of copying scores, imitating famous works or passages, singing and accompanying solfeggi, and realizing partimenti. As one might imagine, important schemata like the Stabat Mater Prinner were included in advanced partimenti. The *lezione* (It., "lesson") by Tritto in example 30.10 is such a work. The realization presented here (bass by Tritto, figures [not shown] probably by a Neapolitan student or copyist, and upper voices by this author) demonstrates how a student would learn to place a Stabat Mater Prinner in both major- and minor-mode contexts (mm. 24–27, 69–72). Saturated in the schemata of the galant style, didactic works by maestros like Tritto faithfully replicated the formulas found in the

earlier partimenti by Durante, Leo, and Tritto's own maestro Cafaro. Students could not
just read this music—they had to rediscover it in the act of performance:

EX. 30.10   Tritto, *Partimenti regole generali* (Naples, ca. 1816)

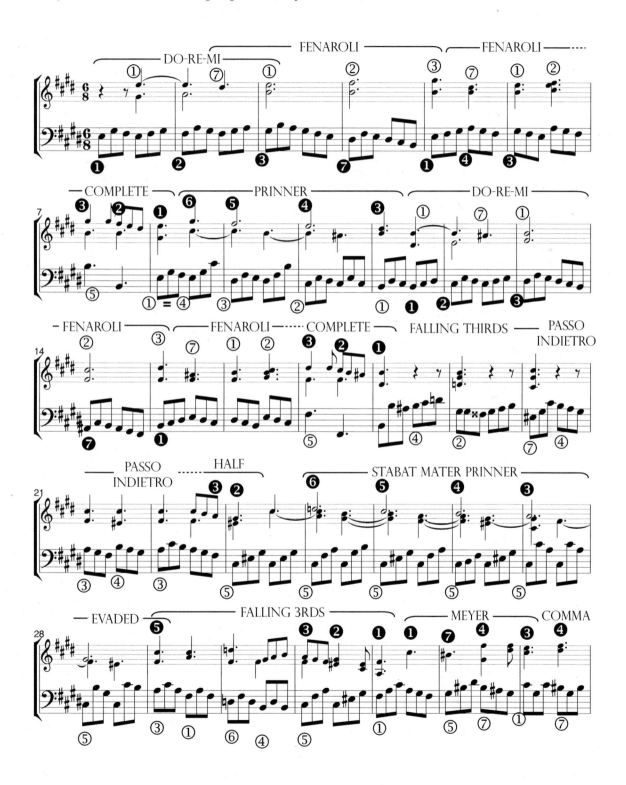

EX. 30.10   (continued)

EX. 30.10   (continued)

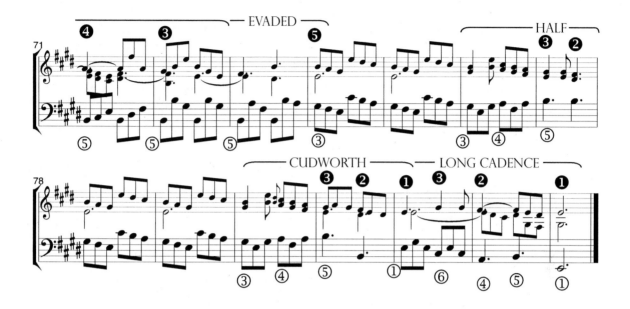

At eighty-four measures long, Tritto's *lezione* is of a moderate size for an advanced partimento. Some extend to over two hundred measures. They constitute the clearest examples
of eighteenth-century instruction in large musical forms. Any student who studied and
internalized a hundred or more partimenti of this scope would have little difficulty in
fashioning an original work of similar size.[15]

Whether one looks at the influence of important exemplars like the *Stabat Mater*, the
training of future chapel masters through the realization of partimenti, the practicing of
solfeggi, the memorization of ornamental figures according to intervallic patterns as out-
lined by Quantz, or the guarding of correct behaviors by maintaining the traditions of
individual schemata like those detailed in the preceding chapters, one sees converging
evidence that the schematization of courtly musical utterances was so pervasive as to constitute a dominant mode of thought. If musicians learned, wrote, and taught this way, did
they not *listen* this way as well? I believe the answer is a qualified "Yes." Moreover, I
believe that in listening this way many of them actually *heard* more. This music was a
richer experience for them because the music and its mode of listening had co-evolved
and co-adapted during the long reign of the ancien régime.

Were this book a concerto, we would now be ready for the cadenza. In the Bolognese
tradition of partimenti, which reflected the teaching of Padre Martini through his disciple

Padre Stanislao Mattei, who in turn taught Rossini and Donizetti, partimenti were often called *cadenze*.[16] Like cadenzas, partimenti were loose frameworks made of schemata suitable for improvisation and musical fantasy. When, as Quantz describes, more than one soloist participated in a cadenza, it needed to be more firmly formulaic, with each new formula introduced by a reliable cue.[17] In the aforementioned quintet for winds and keyboard, Mozart gives the final movement a *cadenza in tempo* for all five performers. That is, the cadenza maintains a beat and meter throughout, and everyone participates. This tour de force (ex. 30.11) begins with one of Quantz's recommended interval progressions,[18] but continues to rise with more voices and more complexity (mm. 109–14) until one can imagine Dittersdorf thinking "hardly [have we] grasped one beautiful thought, when another of greater fascination dispels the first, and this goes on throughout." The peak of complexity (mm. 114–15) is followed by a series of completely regular schemata—two Stabat Mater Prinners with J. S. Bach's active tenor voice in the bassoon part, a large Monte with chromatic bass, and a glorious leaping version of the Romanesca with brilliant figuration in the keyboard part. A circle-of-fifths harmonic progression then connects three bravura statements of the High ❷ Drop and Comma led by oboe, clarinet, and then oboe again. The third such statement is followed by a huge passing-6/4 Indugio, which initiates several delays of the final cadence. That cadence is an elongated, decorated form of the Cadenza Doppia.

Mozart's players would have found all these schemata immediately recognizable. Had more than one of them intended to further ornament their parts, the strongly schematized plan of the *cadenza in tempo* would have allowed them to do so without creating inadvertent clashes with the other players. There was freedom to improvise, but it was constrained by the mutually recognized strictures of these galant schemata.

EX. 30.11   Mozart, Quintet (KV452), mvt. 3, Andante, m. 108 (1784)

EX. 30.11   (continued)

EX. 30.11   (continued)

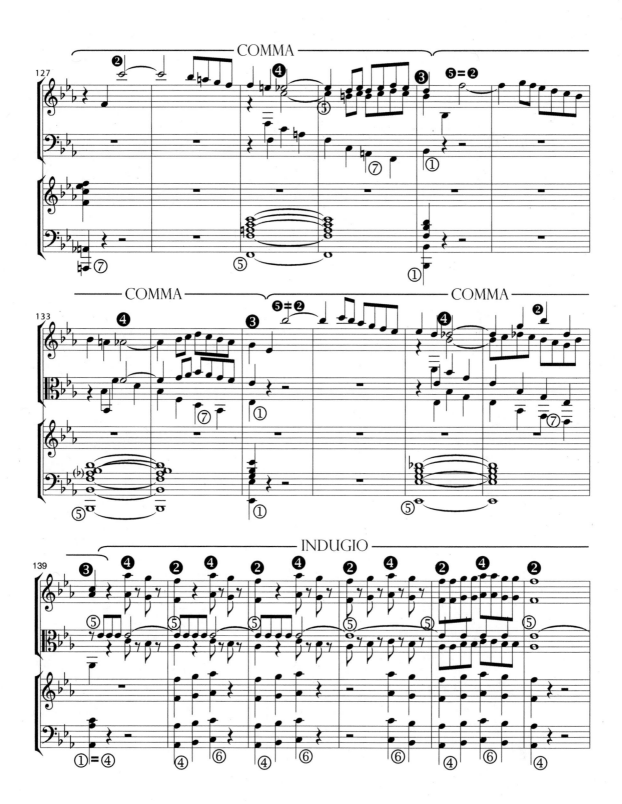

EX. 30.11   (continued)

rondo theme

There is a long list of true statements that one might make about Mozart's cadenza. In terms of an overall harmonic plan, it is clear that the cadenza serves as a gigantic embellishment of the "compound" form of the complete cadence. In terms of a large-scale melodic plan, the general trend is a rapid rise to a peak in measures 113–14 and then a gradual descent to the final trill on ❷, interrupted of course by several intermediate rises and falls. Yet those statements could as easily describe cadenzas by Brahms or Prokofiev. Mozart's cadenza was a very specific presentation of galant schemata—the "compulsory figures"—by a supremely accomplished artist. He knew all the basics, but his invention and flair far surpassed the merely correct. One is reminded of a pronouncement by the haughty Miss Bingley in Jane Austen's *Pride and Prejudice*. Expounding on the subject of being "accomplished," she declares, "A woman must have a thorough knowledge of music, singing, drawing, dancing, and the modern languages, to deserve the word; and besides all this, she must possess a certain something in her air and manner of walking, the tone of her voice, her address and expressions, or the word will be but half deserved."[19] Every detail of courtly behavior mattered, and musical behavior was no less constrained. Long and assiduous training in partimenti and solfeggi could make many musicians accomplished, but Galuppi, Jommelli, Piccinni, Mozart, Haydn, and other real masters of the galant style possessed "a certain something" that transcended mere propriety. They attained the Earl of Chesterfield's ideal of "a superior gracefulness."[20]

In digging down through the many layers of reinterpretation that have built up since the nineteenth century, I hope to have uncovered authentic potsherds of galant music. When we see and hear all the shards pieced together, whether in a masterwork like Mozart's *cadenza in tempo* or in a humble *lezione* by Tritto, I believe we have reconstructed something of that musical world. The schemata in Mozart's cadenza, and indeed in his whole quintet, were the common currency of galant music. These "stock speeches" of the courtly musical language can all be found in the partimenti and solfeggi taught to generations of galant musicians, and the ubiquity of these ritualized presentations helped to mold the responses of the aristocratic audiences. There was potential rigidity in all this schematization, but there could also be art of real depth and significance. Speaking of his own quintet, Mozart wrote to his father that the work "was applauded extraordinarily; I myself consider it the best work I have composed in my life. . . . I only wish you could have heard it."[21] To hear this music more as a Mozart might have heard it, to imagine musical behaviors more consonant with the premises and goals of those who lived at galant courts, and to seek a more realistic account of how galant musical craftsmen fashioned raw tones into finished art has been the aim of this book. The art of eighteenth-century court music extended beyond knowing all the schemata, to be sure. One needed experience in writing fugues, setting liturgical or operatic texts, and constructing an appropriate sequence of schemata for any occasion and musical genre. Yet these were added skills. To "speak" at court, it was first necessary to learn the courtly vocabulary and phraseology, for which the galant musical schemata were central.

APPENDIX A

SCHEMA PROTOTYPES

THE CONVENIENCE OF REPRESENTING MUSIC PROTOTYPES in standard music notation has no doubt made the practice common. Yet standard music notation over-specifies a prototype's constituent features. The Romanesca is a case in point. The schema "Romanesca," that is, a mental representation of a category of galant musical utterances, is likely in no particular key, may or may not have a particular meter, probably includes no particular figurations or articulations, may be quite general as to the spacing of the voices, their timbres, and so on. All that useful indeterminacy would vanish were the schema to be presented as a small chorale in whole notes, probably in the key of C major with a 4/4 meter. To avoid that kind of false specificity, I will represent schema prototypes in a more abstract form. On the following pages you will find prototypes of the schemata presented in the previous chapters. Each schema's individual events are shown as gray lozenges containing a bundle of features. For illustration, imagine an initial event in which the keynote typically occurs in both the melody and the bass:

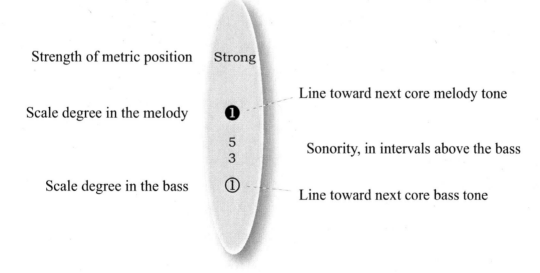

The important musical features—meter, melody, bass, harmony, contour—together shape an event, which in turn can form part of one or more schemata. The above event, for instance, could begin or end several different schemata. Each of the following pages will summarize one of the schemata introduced in previous chapters.

The Romanesca

The Romanesca (see chap. 2) was used primarily as an opening gambit. Its period of greatest currency was the 1720s and 1730s, though it remained an option throughout the century. As the first schema for an Adagio, the galant Romanesca was so common as to be almost a cliché during the first half of the century.

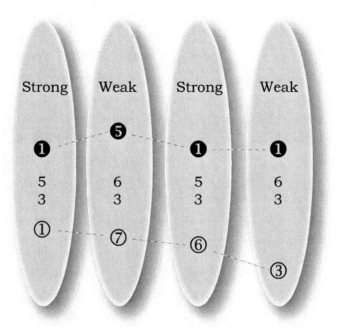

Central Features

- Four equally spaced events, with the first beginning on a metrically strong position, usually a downbeat.
- In the melody, an emphasis on ❶ and ❺ (the particular contour and order are variable).
- In the bass, an initial stepwise descent from ①, with the odd-numbered tones supporting 5/3 sonorities and the even-numbered tones 6/3 sonorities.
- A sequence of four triads with roots (and mode) on ① (major), ⑦ (major), ⑥ (minor), and ③ (major).

Variants

- A leaping type, in which the bass alternately leaps down a fourth and steps up a second, all with 5/3 sonorities (the fourth of which was minor). This was the seventeenth-century norm.
- A stepwise type, in which the bass descends entirely by step, with alternating 5/3 and 6/3 sonorities.

The Prinner

The Prinner (see chap. 3) was often used as the riposte or answer to an opening gambit. Its period of greatest currency was the 1720s to the 1770s, though it remained an option throughout the century. The presence of a Prinner riposte is one of the best indications of a musical style grounded in the Italian galant.

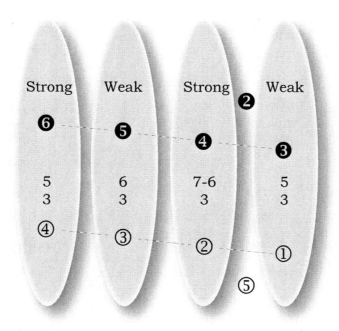

Central Features

- Four events presented either with equal spacing, with an extended third stage, or in matching pairs.
- In the melody, an emphasis on the stepwise descent ❻–❺–❹–❸ (to effect a stronger cadence, a high ❷ is often inserted before the final ❸).
- In the bass, an emphasis on the stepwise descent ④–③–②–① (to effect a stronger cadence, a ⑤ is often inserted before the final ①).
- A sequence of chords in 5/3, 6/3, 6/3, and 5/3 positions. The third stage is often dissonant, while stages one, two, and four are consonant and in the same mode.

Variants

- A type with a canon on ❻–❺–❹–❸ in melody and bass. There is usually a pedal point on ①, with ❹–❸ in the one part sounding against ❻–❺ in the other.
- A precadential type, in which often only the first two stages appear before a standard cadence. See the Passo Indietro, chap. 11.
- A circle-of-fifths type, in which every other core tone in the bass matches the schema.

THE FONTE

The Fonte (see chap. 4) served to digress from, and then return to, a main key. It was used throughout the eighteenth century, being especially common immediately after the double bar in minuets or other short movements. In concertos, arias, and other long works, large Fontes often function as digressive episodes.

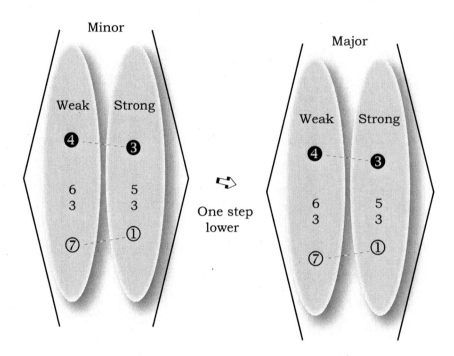

Central Features

- Four events presented as two pairs or dyads. The Fonte's first half is in the minor mode while the second half is in the major mode one step lower.
- In the melody, a short scalewise descent that ends ❹–❸, often ❻–❺–❹–❸. Occasionally the melody arpeggiates the local dominant chord.
- In the bass, ascents from leading tones to local tonics, that is, ⑦–①. Other possible basses involve typical cadential moves like ⑤–① or ②–①.
- Two pairs of sonorities: each pair concludes with a relatively stable 5/3 preceded by a more unstable or dissonant 6/3, 6/5/3, or 7/5/3.

Variants

- A type with the normal melody in the bass and what would be the normal bass in the melody.
- A rare, three-part type with the first two parts in the minor mode and the third in the major mode.

The Do-Re-Mi

The Do-Re-Mi (see chap. 6) was one of the most frequent opening gambits in galant music. It was used in every decade and in every genre. It often had its normal bass part in the upper voice and its "melody" in the bass. The ease with which it could be thus inverted made it a favorite schema for movements in which the bass begins with an imitation of the melody, a procedure especially common early in the eighteenth century.

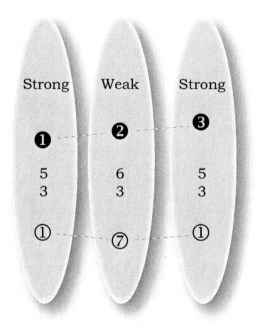

Central Features

- Three events equally spaced, or occasionally presented with an extended first stage. In brisk tempos, each event will likely fall on a downbeat.
- In the melody, an emphasis on the stepwise ascent ❶–❷–❸. Variants may include chromatic passing tones.
- In the bass, an emphasis on ①–⑦–① (sometimes ⑤ substitutes for ⑦)
- A sequence of chords in 5/3, 6/3, and 5/3 positions. Delaying the bass descent from ① to ⑦ creates a dissonance during the second stage.

Variants

- An Adeste Fidelis type with a melody featuring leaps down to and up from ❺.
- A two-part, "Do-Re . . . Re-Mi" type.

THE MONTE

The Monte (see chap. 7) was the preferred schema for an ascending sequence. In the earlier eighteenth century, Montes of three or more sections could effect relatively distant modulations. In the later eighteenth century, Montes usually had only two sections that highlighted the subdominant and dominant keys, often in advance of an important cadence.

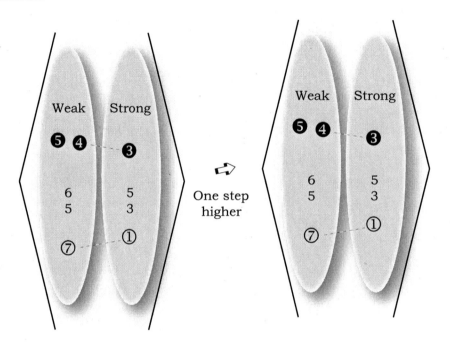

Central Features

- Two or more main sections, with each succeeding section one step higher.
- In the melody, an overall rise, with local descents that complement the ascending leading tones in the bass.
- In the bass, consecutive chromatic ascents from leading tones to local tonics. In the diatonic variant, the bass rises similarly but without the chromatic semitones.
- A sequence of two or more pairs of sonorities where 6/5/3 precedes 5/3. The mode of the stable 5/3 sonority often cannot be predicted.

Variants

- Extensions of the rising IV-to-V sequence to VI or even to VII and I.
- Diatonic types featuring the 6–5–6–5 . . . interval pattern.
- A Principale type with all 5/3 sonorities and a bass that alternately leaps up a fourth, then down a third.
- A Romanesca type with an up-a-fifth, down-a-fourth bass and characteristic 4–3 suspensions.

The Meyer

The Meyer (see chap. 9) was often chosen for important themes. Its period of greatest currency was the 1760s through the 1780s. In earlier, shorter examples, the core melodic tones constitute a major fraction of the perceived melody. In later, longer examples, the two paired events constitute brief moments of punctuation amid a profusion of decorative melodic figures.

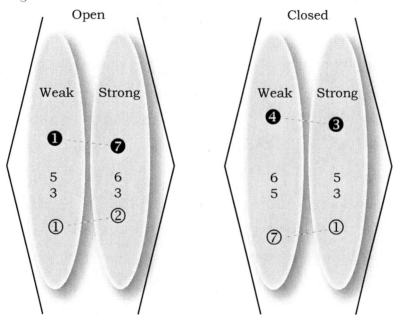

Central Features

- Four events presented in pairs at comparable locations in the meter (e.g., across a bar line, or at mid-bar, with one, two, or four measures between the pairs).
- In the melody, the descending semitone ❶–❼ is answered by a subsequent descent ❹–❸ (in the "typical Italian solfeggio" both dyads are *fa–mi* in major).
- In the bass, the ascending step ①–② is answered by a ⑦–① ascent (or ⑤–①).
- A sequence of four sonorities, usually 5/3, 6/3, 6/5/3, and 5/3. The first and last seem stable while the middle two seem unstable.

Variants

- The ❶–❼ may be higher or lower in pitch than the ❹–❸.
- The related Jupiter schema has a ❶–❷–❹–❸ melody, sharing its opening dyad with the Do-Re-Mi and its closing dyad with the Meyer.
- The related Pastorella schema has a ❸–❷–❹–❸ melody, also sharing its closing dyad with the Meyer.
- The related Aprile schema has a ❶–❼–❷–❶ melody, sharing its opening dyad with the Meyer.

THE QUIESCENZA

The Quiescenza (see chap. 13) marks a short period of quiescence following an important cadence at the end of an important section. As a framing device, it could also appear as an opening gambit (usually not repeated), though this usage was less common. The Quiescenza's period of greatest currency was the 1760s to the 1790s, and it was especially favored in music written for Vienna or Paris.

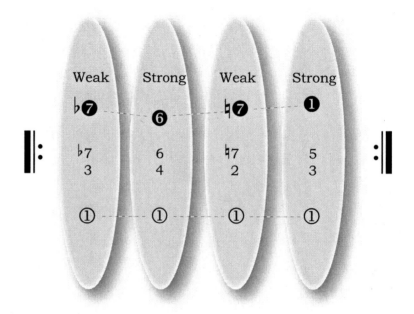

Central Features

- Four events, with the whole schema usually played twice in succession.
- In the melody, the descending semitone ♭**❼**–**❻** is answered by the ascending semitone ♮**❼**–**❶** (in the "typical Italian solfeggio," *fa–mi* is answered by *mi–fa*).
- In the bass, a pedal point on ①, or a figuration that reiterates ①.
- A sequence of four sonorities, usually ♭7/3, 6/4, ♮7/4/2, and 5/3. The first seems unstable in relation to the second, while the third sonority seems highly unstable in relation to the last, tonic sonority.

Variants

- A diatonic type with a rising **❺**–**❻**–**❼**–**❶** melody.
- A rare type that presents two Prinners over a tonic pedal.

The Ponte

The Ponte (see chap. 14) was a "bridge" built on the repetition or extension of the dominant triad or seventh chord. In minuets, this bridge was placed immediately after the
double bar and connected the just-cadenced "second" key with a return to the original
tonic key. More generally, in the latter half of the eighteenth century the Ponte was part of
various delaying tactics employed to heighten expectation prior to an important entry or
return.

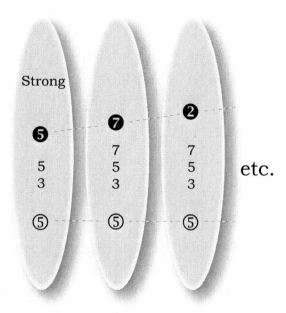

Central Features

- Several events that may be extended until a stable return to the tonic harmony
  offers some degree of closure.
- In the melody, scales and arpeggios focused on the tones of the dominant seventh
  chord: ❺, ❼, ❷, and ❹. The contour is generally rising.
- In the bass, repetitions of ⑤ or even a pedal point on ⑤.
- A sequence of sonorities emphasizing the dominant triad or seventh chord,
  sometimes in alternation with forms of the tonic chord in metrically weaker
  positions.

Variants

- A type with a descending stepwise melody ❺–❹–❸–❷.

THE FENAROLI

The Fenaroli (see chap. 16), usually repeated, was most often introduced following a modulation to the dominant key. In the nineteenth-century sense, it was thus one of the earliest types of "second theme," though it was too processive to meet the Romantic expectations for a "true" theme. A Fenaroli could be initiated on either event one or event two, so a given event could be metrically weak or strong depending on the choice of starting point.

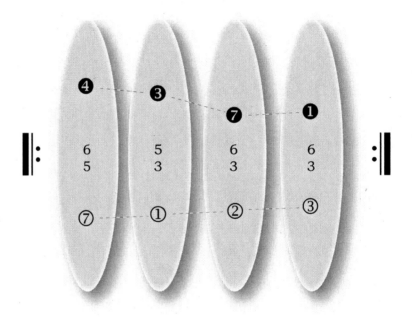

Central Features

- Four events, equally spaced, with the whole schema usually repeated.
- The bass features ⑦–①–②–③, which is *mi–fa–re–mi* in a galant solfeggio.
- The other voice is more variable. Sometimes ❹–❸–❼–❶ is matched against the bass's ⑦–①–②–③. At other times a ❷–❸–❼–❶ melody creates a canon with the bass. An upper or internal pedal point on ⑤ is also common.
- A sequence of four sonorities, usually 6/5/3, 5/3, 6/3, and, 6/3. The ending on a 6/3 sonority contributes to the schema's lack of finality.

Variants

- The full Durante countermelody is ❺–❹–❸–❶–❼–❺–❶–❸, with two tones for each of the four tones ⑦–①–②–③. Either voice may be placed in the bass.
- The ⑦–①–②–③ pattern may be replaced by ⑦–①–④–③, thus emphasizing the semitones in the major mode and enabling a canon with the ❹–❸–❼–❶ countermelody.

The Sol-Fa-Mi

The Sol-Fa-Mi (see chap. 18) was often chosen for important themes. Its period of greatest currency was the 1750s through the 1790s. With its descending melody perceived as perhaps less assertive than, say, a Do-Re-Mi, the Sol-Fa-Mi was most common in movements of slow or moderate tempo, or as a "second theme" in fast movements. It was a favorite schema for Adagios in the minor mode.

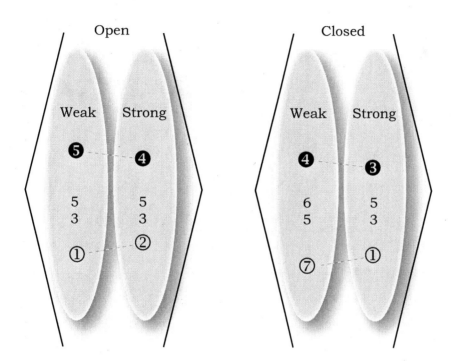

Central Features

- Four events presented in pairs at comparable locations in the meter (e.g., across a bar line, or at mid-bar, with one, two, or four measures between the pairs).
- In the melody, the descending whole step ❺–❹ is answered by a subsequent descent of ❹–❸ (a half step in major, a whole step in minor).
- In the bass, the ascending step ①–② is answered by a ⑦–① ascent (or ⑤–①).
- A sequence of four sonorities, usually 5/3, 5/3, 6/5/3, and 5/3. The second sonority is typically minor or diminished.

Variants

- The second event may have the more major-sounding sonority of 7/5/3 above ⑤, or of 6/3 above ②.

THE INDUGIO

The Indugio (It., "tarrying" or "lingering"; see chap. 20) served as a teasing delay of the approach to a Converging cadence. Uncommon in the first half of the eighteenth century, it quickly became a cliché in the second half. For compositions in the major mode, the Indugio allowed, as does the Fonte, the insertion of a brief passage in the minor mode. Often associated with this "darkening" are "storm and stress" syncopations.

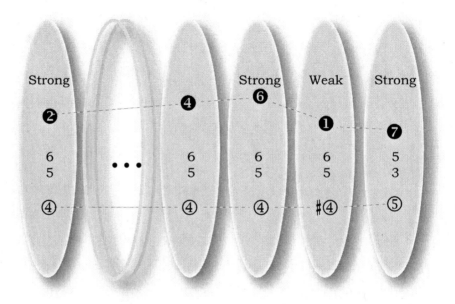

Central Features

- Several events, leading up to a Converging cadence in most instances. The pair of open lozenges above, with the three dots of ellipsis, indicates an open-ended repetition of the opening sonority or figuration.
- The bass features iterations of ④ leading to ⑤, often with an inflection to ♯④ just prior to ⑤.
- The melody usually emphasizes ❷, ❹, and ❻, with frequent approaches to these tones from below by way of chromatic leading tones.
- A prolongation of the 6/5/3 sonority above ④ in the bass, ending with a 5/3 sonority on ⑤ that is optionally the dominant of the main key or the tonic of the new key.

Variants

- A more diatonic type without the bass's ♯④.
- A passing-6/4 type with a more active bass that passes stepwise up and down between ④ and ⑥. When passing through ⑤, a 6/4 sonority helps to maintain iterations on ①, which may act as an internal pedal point.

Appendix B

∾ ∿

PARTIMENTI

CIMAROSA, WEALTHY CHAPEL MASTER TO IMPERIAL COURTS, began his musical career as an indigent boy at the Conservatorio di Santa Maria di Loreto in Naples. There, as mentioned in chapter 2, he studied for a decade under several great maestros. An important component of his studies involved solving progressively more difficult problems in the realization of partimenti, as evidenced by his preserved *zibaldone* ("lessonbook"). A partimento, of course, was an instructional bass, meaning a bass written for a pedagogical purpose. Given a particular partimento to be played at the keyboard with the left hand, a student would work toward its solution and realization by testing various additions of chords or contrapuntal voices with the right hand. Mastery of the lesson was demonstrated when the student could ably perform, with both hands, a series of stylistically appropriate musical behaviors from the beginning to the end of the partimento.

How did young students like Cimarosa in the 1760s develop skills that can challenge even adult musicians today? Part of the answer seems to lie in the students' memorization of a rich repertory of small musical patterns that could be drawn upon for possible matches to the local topography of a given passage in a partimento. In speaking of commedia dell'arte, Pietro Maria Cecchini (1563–ca. 1630) emphasized that "the actor must see to it that his mind controls his memory (which dispenses the treasure of memorized phrases over the vast field of opportunities constantly offered by comedy)."[1] A young musician with a mind trained to control a "treasure of memorized phrases," some of them learned through singing and playing solfeggi, could quickly apply them to the "opportunities" in a partimento. After all, the human mind excels at connecting memories with complex stimuli, for instance when we immediately recognize a known face or voice.

The smallest contexts to be learned were individual tones, intervals, and the combinations of intervals that make up chords. Included in this knowledge was an understanding of basic musical notation, of hexachord syllables labeling specific pitches and local intervallic contexts (*do, re, mi*, etc.), of scale degrees (*prima di tono, secondo di tono*, etc.), and of the shorthand for figured bass ($7 = 7/5/3$, $6/5 = 6/5/3$, etc.). As suggested in chapter 2, these small domains of knowledge were interconnected more strongly then than now. Take for example the notation symbols for sharps and flats. Modern students learn them as instructions to alter a pitch, whereas in Cimarosa's time they still functioned as signs for a change of hexachord syllable and local context. The flat sign occurring as an accidental meant "treat this note as *fa* so that there will be a whole step above it and a half step below it," and the sharp sign meant "treat this tone as *mi* so that there will be a half step above it and a whole step below it." Local context was thus woven into even these rudiments of galant music.

Cadences often came next in the curriculum. Chapter 11 introduced dozens of the cadences known to adult musicians. For young students the world of cadences was reduced to three possibilities—simple (*semplice*), compound (*composta*), and double (*doppia*). The rhythm and contour of the bass determined which cadence to employ. Shown below are these three types of cadences in the particular guise of C major and 4/4 time (ex. B.1). The distinctive feature of how ⑤ moves to ① is marked with a bracket:

EX. B.1   The three partimento cadences for beginners

For the novice, it was efficient first to memorize the models and then to employ the one that best matched the target partimento. In example B.2 I have provided the last few measures of three partimenti by Fenaroli, one of Cimarosa's teachers. Again, brackets highlight the final move from ⑤ to ①:

EX. B.2   The endings of three partimenti by Fenaroli (Naples, ca. 1800)

The best match for ending A is the *cadenza composta*, with the partimento's octave leap from upper to lower ⑤ aligning with the similar leap in the model. Note that even though the meter of A differs from the model, the upper parts of the model can easily be mapped onto the partimento. The best match for ending B is the *cadenza semplice*. And the best match for ending C is the *cadenza doppia*, with its four beats on ⑤ aligning with the model's whole-note ⑤ and the four chords above it. Even for children, the matching would be "child's play." A more advanced student might recognize, for example, that ending B includes two instances of the *cadenza lunga* or "Long cadence" of Sala, with the first one likely to have some form of evasion in the melody. But a beginner, lacking perhaps that broader understanding, could still perform the passage correctly by mapping onto it two instances of the *cadenza semplice*.

The recognition of a best match depends on a holistic evaluation of all the musical features. For instance, in a fast tempo, the bass of example B.3 matches the *cadenza semplice* with the standard ③–④–⑤–① bass. But in a slow tempo none of the three basic cadences would be a good fit. Instead, the passage would match the descending form of the "Rule of the Octave."

EX. B.3   *Presto ⇨ cadenza semplice; Largo ⇨ Rule of the Octave*

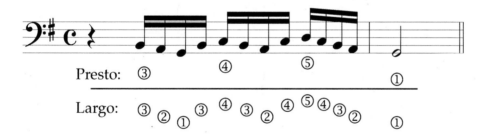

The Rule of the Octave for a young musician, like the Rule of St. Benedict for a monastic novice, was really a collection of rules woven together into a code of conduct. The many component parts of the Rule of the Octave had diverse histories, and Heinichen (1711), as mentioned in chapter 1, treated what he called this "schema" for the major or minor modes as a combination of several two-note contexts. The Rule itself could vary when taught by different maestros in different cities and decades. So to avoid a level of detail better treated in specialist studies,[2] I present below a synchronic, systematized, and slightly idealized exposition of the Rule, conforming in the main to what students in the Neapolitan conservatories would have absorbed from their teachers.

The diagram below (fig. B.1) shows an abstraction of how eighteenth-century musicians may have conceptualized the relative stability or instability of the different scale degrees across an octave in the bass. The dark boxes represent positions deemed stable points of arrival, and the light circles indicate positions felt to be unstable and more mobile. As a first approximation of the Rule of the Octave, we can assign the stable scale degrees 5/3 chords (i.e., play simple triads on ① and ⑤) and the unstable degrees some form of a chord with a 6, perhaps 6/3. This simplified version highlights the great continuity in the traditions of Western European polyphonic music, inasmuch as the association of an "imperfect" sixth with instability and a "perfect" fifth with stability was a central feature of fifteenth-century traditions of improvised *fauxbourdon* singing in cathedrals, a tradition believed to have survived until at least the seventeenth century.

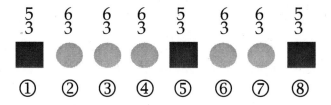

FIGURE B.1   A first approximation of the Rule of the Octave

Like the melodic minor scale, the Rule of the Octave is not quite the same ascending and descending. So for a closer approximation to real practice, let us examine movement up and down separately. Figure B.2 shows the ascending version. Dissonances (the starred clashes between an adjacent "6" and "5") were added to the scale degrees that precede the stable positions. So as one ascends the scale in the bass, maximum instability comes just before a return to stability:

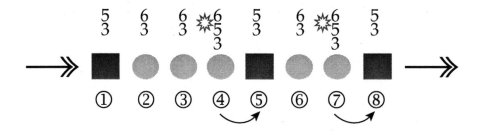

FIGURE B.2   A second approximation—the Rule ascending

The same general principle of maximum instability coming just before the return to stability applies when descending, though the dissonances are now between a "4" and a "3" (see fig. B.3). In the descent from ⑥ to ⑤, the tone corresponding to the "6" above ⑥ is raised a half step to create a leading tone (F♯ in a C-major context) to the stable octave above ⑤, thus giving scale degrees ② and ⑥ the same sonority.

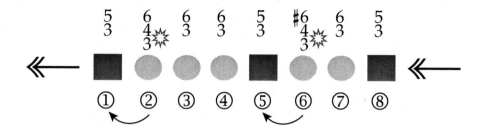

FIGURE B.3   A second approximation—the Rule descending

There is still one more complication. The third scale degree was deemed partly stable, partly mobile. Following the principle of dissonance preceding stability, musicians often added a "4/3" dissonance to a rising ②, and almost always added a "4/2" dissonance to a ④ passing in descent between ⑤ and ③ (see fig. B.4). The Rule of the Octave is thus not a fixed set of chords, but rather a summary of central tendencies in the fluid and highly contingent practices of eighteenth-century musicians.

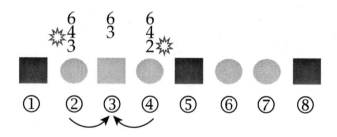

FIGURE B.4   A third approximation—the approach to ③

The Neapolitan maestro Giovanni Furno (1748–1837), in a discussion titled *Regole delle cordi del tono* [The Rules of Scale Steps],[3] detailed further, more particular contingencies relating to departures from scalar movement. Example B.4 on the following page shows one of Furno's partimenti for the rank beginner. As you can see, cadences and scalar passages account for all but the opening gesture. I have marked with asterisks three departures from the normal Rule of the Octave. For the first type (cf. m. 5), Furno recommended a 5/3 chord where ④ has not continued a descent from ⑤. This adjustment matches the Prinner. For the second type (cf. m. 6), he recommended a 5/3 chord where ⑥ does not descend to ⑤. This matches the *cadenza lunga* ("Long cadence"). And for the third type (cf. m. 7), he recommended a 5/3 chord where ⑤ does not ascend to ⑦. This matches the *cadenza finta* ("deceptive cadence"). In his treatise Furno never mentions these larger contexts, though his partimenti suggest that knowledge of them was assumed. I present one of the many possible realizations of this small partimento in example B.5.

EX. B.4   A beginner's partimento by Furno. Cadences (dashed lines) and scalar passages (gray lines) comprise almost the whole exercise

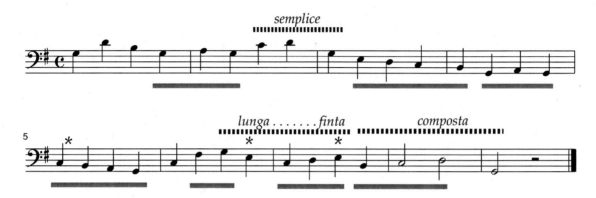

EX. B.5   The author's realization of ex. B.4, using only basic cadences and the Rule of the Octave

Furno's *Metodo Facile breve e chiaro delle prime ed essensiali regole per accompagnare Partimenti senza numeri* [An Easy, Brief, and Clear Method Concerning the Primary and Essential Rules for Accompanying Unfigured Partimenti] (Naples, 1817),[4] from which example B.4 was taken, appeared during a period of reorganization and reevaluation at the conservatories, and his title betrays the growing influence of nineteenth-century "how-to" books. Traditional instruction in partimenti was anything but brief or easy, as Furno had learned from his own maestro Cotumacci. Cadences and the Rule of the Octave alone do not consitute a rich enough vocabulary for galant practice.

Instruction in partimenti also included figured basses, which developed students' skills in sightreading thoroughbass accompaniments, helped beginners learn which harmonies to play, and could supply hints aimed at the realization of stock contrapuntal combinations. A small figured bass (ex. B.6) by the Bolognese maestro Stanislao Mattei (1750–1825), pupil of and successor to Padre Martini (1706–1784), does not appear at first glance to have any clear organization:

EX. B.6 Mattei, *Piccolo basso*, G major, no. 4, m. 1 (Bologna, ca. 1790s)

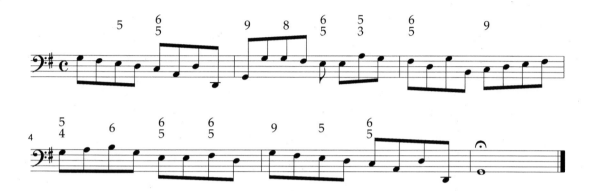

But in playing this exercise a good student might begin to hear patterns emerge whose implications, if recognized, could lead to a strongly contrapuntal, three-voice realization:

EX. B.7 The author's realization of ex. B.6

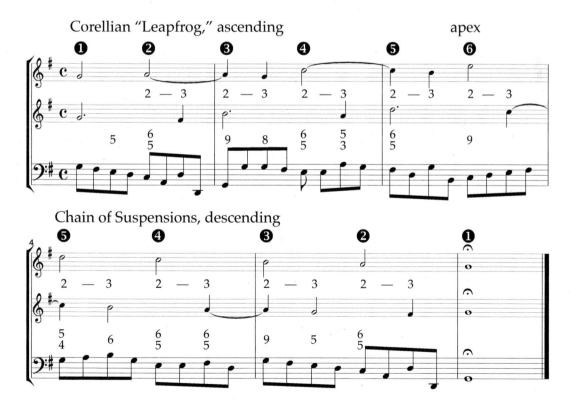

Mattei's whole exercise demonstrates what Cimarosa's lessonbook would have titled
"*Caminare di 2a e 3a*"—"progressing by 2–3 suspensions."

Many such common progressions had long ago crystallized into stock schemata.
Furno, like the older maestro Fedele Fenaroli in his published set of *Regole* [Rules]
(Naples, 1775), described a great number of such progressions as *movimenti* or "special
moves." If the Rule of the Octave described, by analogy to the game of chess, the simple,
straightforward moves of pawns, movimenti described all the sequences of leaps and/or
steps available to a Knight or Queen. Among the schemata presented in the previous
chapters, the leaping-bass Romanesca, the Monte, the Monte Principale, the Monte
Romanesca, and the large circle-of-fifths Prinner all appear in various *regole* as movimenti.
For students, these learned sequences and other phrase-size schemata thus complemented
the default reliance on the Rule of the Octave and helped to add a number of jewels to
their "treasure of memorized phrases."[5]

Movimenti were described by their bass motion within each module of a sequence.
Among the first to be taught was that of a bass that "falls a third and rises a second."[6] The
rule was that the lower tone of the descending third should take a 6/3 or 6/5/3 chord, and
that the following tone (a step higher) should take a 5/3 chord. "And thus," as Fenaroli
said, "one successively alternates the accompaniments [6/5 and 5/3] until the end of the
motion."[7]

Durante wrote the modest partimento shown in example B.8 as an illustration "Of the
Formation of the 5th and 6th," meaning the proper disposition of 6/5/3 chords in the
movimento that opens his exercise. The annotations—a "thick description"[8] of overlapping and nested schemata—are mine. A student like Cimarosa, of course, saw only the
bass and the few figures provided. His task was first to recognize the match between the
opening bass pattern and the "falls-a-third-and-rises-a-second" movimento, and then to set
6/5/3 chords on the lower tones of each descending third. I have labeled Durante's particular instantiation of this movimento "Phrygian" to indicate that the bass tones receiving
5/3 chords descend through the Phrygian tetrachord from E4 to B3. Recognizing that this
opening pattern is a movimento would greatly simplify the student's task, since the Rule
of the Octave offers no help at all and would, in fact, be misleading.[9] Note that Durante
does not provide an explicit solution to the problem posed by the opening movimento
until measures 8–9, where he inserts the figures "6/5."

Durante's partimento, though still more of an exercise than a fully fashioned work of
art, is nevertheless considerably more artful than Furno's (ex. B.4). Whereas Furno scarcely
repeats any of the patterns in his exercise, Durante makes repetition, transposed repetition, and slightly altered repetition a central part of the student's experience, helping
thereby to foster an understanding of the underlying prototypes or schemata. The movimento appears four times in two keys, and the *cadenza semplice* (with the full ③–④–⑤–①
bass) appears six times in five keys. In two places, a one-step-lower repetition of the
Comma-*semplice* combination forms the larger pattern of a Fonte. And the still larger
complex of "Phrygian-to-Do-Re-Mi-to-Fonte" occurs first in E minor and second in

EX. B.8   Illustration no. 34 from Durante's *Regole* (Naples, ca. 1740)

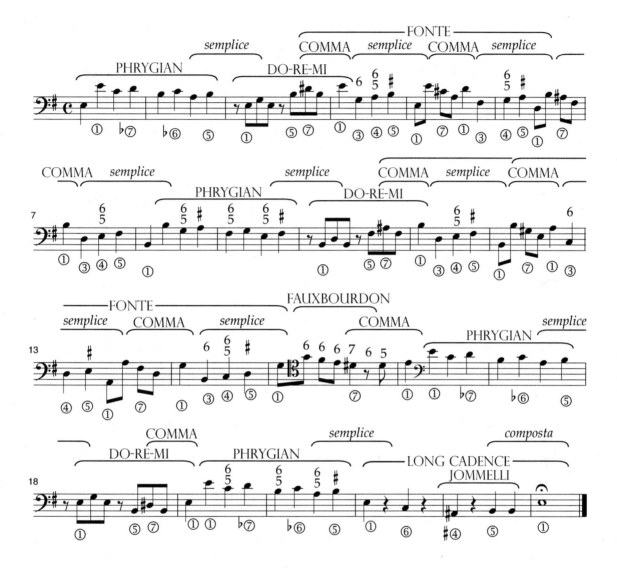

B minor, giving the partimento a common type of exposition. Following the contrast of the fauxbourdon, Durante closes with restatements of the movimento and the Do-Re-Mi in the home key. The Fontes have no place in the final section because there is no longer a need to modulate. I provide one of several possible realizations of Durante's partimento in example B.9. Because the above partimento already provides thorough schematic annotations, only the most important schemata are marked on this example. Note that, in the opening movimento, the sequence is compatible with *caminare di 2a e 3a*. That is, a student who can associate this movimento with a chain of 2–3 suspensions has essentially solved the musical problem posed by the partimento.

EX. B.9   The author's realization of ex. B.8

Furno's small partimento (ex. B.4) was entirely pedagogical. Mattei's march up and down the hexachord in 2–3 suspensions (ex. B.6) was too regular for most real performances in the galant style. Even Durante's larger partimento (ex. B.8) was still constrained to reiterate its point about 6/5 chords. When a student advanced to tackle a full-size, freestanding partimento, he or she faced a significant increase in the music's scope and complexity. Realizing a full-size partimento was—and still is—a significant challenge. A basic level of proficiency can be demonstrated by matching appropriate schemata to the various patterns in the bass. At this basic level the avoidance of error may be uppermost in the student's mind. A second, intermediate level will involve introducing motivic connections between the different phrases and passages. One might describe the student as shifting, by analogy to sport, from defending to attacking, hoping to score artistic points. And an advanced level requires intuiting or deriving opportunities for brief canons and other points of imitation. This is especially true for partimenti written in Durante's era, when imitative counterpoint was pervasive. The student able to perform at this level is demonstrating considerable fluency in the style.

While early nineteenth-century copies of partimenti included overt clues such as *"Imitazione"* or *"Imit."* written where an imitation was expected, the earlier partimenti did not. Presuming that the maestro did not immediately tell the student where to place imitations, the student needed to recognize what today we might call the contrapuntal *affordances*[10] or what an eighteenth-century musician might think of as "opportunities." That is, one needed to learn to recognize the cues and special configurations in the bass that would permit a known contrapuntal treatment. The following remarks relate to the opportunities for counterpoint in example B.10, my realization of one of Durante's full-sized *partimenti numerati*, something of a misnomer since not a single figure (*numero*) appears. The bottom staff, of course, is Durante's original partimento and the top staff is my realization of it. The astute reader may recognize in the opening of this partimento the prototype for Tritto's later partimento shown in chapter 7 (ex. 7.20).

The stepwise bass descent of measures 1–6 affords a presentation of the stepwise Romanesca, which further affords a parallel stepwise descent in the melody. That stepwise descent affords the opportunity to highlight the Prinner by shifting that segment of the descent up one octave. The resulting parallel thirds further afford the opportunity for imitation on a chain of 2–3 suspensions, as demonstrated when the Romanesca returns (mm. 40–45), though choosing that option means abandoning the Prinner. The same types of affordance apply to the descending scales beginning in measure 8. One could set the melody in imitation at either the third or the sixth. Choosing imitation at the sixth realizes an inverted form of the Prinner, which will arrive "on schedule" back on the tonic triad in measure 15. An ascending scale (m. 28) and another descending scale (m. 35) allow for similar treatments. This is also true for the Falling Thirds patterns (mm. 47–50 and 56–59). Perhaps the most characteristic imitation occurs in the passages marked Monte Principale (mm. 50–53, 59–62, and 75–77). Though not immediately apparent, those passages are set in imitation at the fifth, with the accompaniment leading the bass by one quarter-note. The model for this treatment comes from a number of widely copied partimenti and, in particular, Durante's own *Studio* no. 2 (see ex. 7.16).

For the Monte in measures 15–19 the accompaniment works equally well in a diatonic or chromatic guise. With unfigured partimenti, such choices lie with the performer, not the composer. Note also that although the chromatic Monte provides a series of leading tones to local foci on V, VI, and I, no leading tone is provided to VII (no F$\times$4 before G$\sharp$4 in m. 17). Whether through affinity to the Long Comma or merely to avoid a double sharp, that diatonic ending to an extended chromatic Monte was part of galant tradition. The final cadence, measures 80–81, with its doubled note values, invites the *cadenza composta*. Nevertheless I chose to use a slower version of the *cadenza semplice* to allow for one last appearance of the opening motive, the ornamental resolution of a 2–3 suspension.

EX. B.10   The author's realization of Durante's *partimento numerato* no. 14

EX. B.10 (continued)

EX. B.10   (continued)

The passage from the second half of measure 19 to the first half of measure 27 is one of the most difficult to interpret from the bass alone. The eye may be drawn to the whole notes in the even-numbered measures as the likely core elements. But the best match to those four bass tones (E3, D3, C#3, B2) would be a large Prinner in B minor, which would not end properly with the bass's final ascent to C♯ in measure 27. That stepwise ascent happens after each whole note, and if one pays special attention to the notes on the downbeats, the whole passage matches the down-a-third-up-a-second movimento described earlier. Applying that frame, one can then give the whole notes unstable 6/5/3 chords and the downbeat half notes stable 5/3 chords. The overall pattern, thus instantiated, matches the same Phrygian tetrachord found in the opening two measures of the Durante partimento shown earlier in example B.7. The ending chord, C♯ major in measure 27, works very nicely as a half cadence in F♯ minor, the relative minor of the preceding and following A-major contexts.

Readers interested in the still more advanced challenges of Durante's *partimenti diminuiti* ("embellished partimenti") and partimento fugues may wish to consult the author's Internet site, *Monuments of Partimenti*.[11] There one can also find the full texts of the treatises of Furno and Fenaroli in both English and Italian, Durante's *Regole*, hundreds of partimenti, charts of the eighteenth-century maestros of the great conservatories, models for the emulation of galant musical style, and indices of partimento incipits.

The maestros in charge of young students in Naples needed practical, musically worthy teaching material that would slowly but surely transform boys into professional musicians. Lessons learned needed to be retained for life, and the combination of visual, aural, and tactile sensations in partimenti and solfeggi seems to have created especially vivid, well-remembered experiences. The boys gradually built up the rich nonverbal knowledge of how to integrate melody, harmony, counterpoint, characteristic gestures and textures, improvisation, large-scale form, and motivic coherence. And whether or not the correlation is causal, it is nevertheless a historical fact that the heyday of training in partimenti and two-part solfeggi coincided with the period of European dominance by musicians trained at Italian conservatories. The partimento may thus have been a preindustrial but cognitively advanced technology that was especially well adapted to the task of training young musicians for later service at galant courts, theaters, and chapels.

When galant society faltered at the end of the eighteenth century, the study of partimenti slowly transformed from a training of the musical imagination to a training in a canon of fixed exercises. The changes attendant with that transformation parallel the transition from an aural to a literate culture, and the overt marker of that change was the appearance, beginning in the 1820s, of published realizations of Fenaroli's partimenti. That is, the basses designed to train the musical imagination became the left-hand parts of "piano pieces" to be read at the keyboard. Whereas the transition from improvised commedia dell'arte to the literary plays of Pierre de Marivaux (1688–1763), Goldoni, and Charles Simon Favart (1710–1792) changed one art form into another, the change of partimenti into stale exercises essentially extinguished their advantage over humbler exercises in harmony or simple counterpoint. Ossified partimenti continued to be taught as part of a revered tradition. Nadia Boulanger (1887–1979), for instance, was one of the last French teachers in an unbroken partimento tradition, including both her father and her grandfather, that extended back to the first years of the Paris Conservatory in the 1790s.[12] Italian editions of partimenti continued to be published until the 1950s.[13] Yet it was only with Karl Gustav Fellerer's studies in the 1930s at the Santini collection in Münster that a modern appreciation of the original partimento tradition began to emerge. Fellerer's small but insightful *Der Partimentospieler*[14] appeared in Germany shortly after the onset of World War II and was thus largely overlooked in the postwar era. The present volume represents a second stage of rediscovery, one in which many distinguished scholars are currently participating.

NOTES

⚖

CHAPTER 1

1. Philip Dormer Stanhope, *Earl of Chesterfield, Letters to His Son on the Art of Becoming a Man of the World and a Gentleman* (New York: Chesterfield Press, 1917), no. 68, April 19, 1749.

2. Norbert Elias, *The Court Society*, trans. Edmund Jephcott (New York: Pantheon Books, 1983), 8, 55; originally published as *Die höfische Gesellschaft. Untersuchungen zur Soziologie des Königstums und der höfischen Aristokratie, mit einer Einleitung: Soziologie und Geschichtswissenschaft* (Neuwied: Luchterhand, 1969).

3. The absence of "hello" was verified by a computer search of the complete texts. The first versions of *Pride and Prejudice* and *Sense and Sensibility* date from 1795–98. Austen began work on *Emma* in 1814.

4. Baron Friedrich Melchior von Grimm, s.v. "Poème lyrique," in *L'Encyclopédie ou Dictionnaire raisonné des sciences, des arts et des métiers, par une Société de Gens de lettres*, ed. Denis Diderot (Paris, 1751–72), 12:823; translated in Enrico Fubini, *Music and Culture in Eighteenth-Century Europe: A Source Book* (Chicago: University of Chicago Press, 1994), 121. Baron von Grimm is not related to the brothers Grimm, the German philologists and collectors of fairy tales.

5. See http://faculty-web.at.northwestern.edu/music/gjerdingen/galant_book/index.htm. If this URL changes in the future, a search for the keywords "gjerdingen" and "partimenti" should lead to the appropriate site.

6. Baldassare Castiglione, *Il libro del Cortegiano*, ed. Giulio Preti (Turin: Giulio Einaudi, 1965), bk. 1, sec. 26: "usar in ogni cosa una certa sprezzatura, che nasconda l'arte e dimostri ciò che si fa e dice venir fatto senza fatica e quasi senza pensarvi." Unless noted, all translations are mine.

7. In French, one would not describe a gentlewoman as "galante," since the term carried negative connotations. In his paper "Sexism and Language: What Can the Web Teach Us?" (presented at the Congress of the Social Sciences and the Humanities, May 27–28, 1998, University of Ottawa, Ontario, Canada), Fabienne Baider commented, "*Une femme galante* has been and still is a '*courtisane*' whereas *un galant homme* has been since the beginning of the 16th century '*un homme du monde*'; *un homme galant* 'a courteous man.' "

8. Marjorie R. Theobald, "The Sin Of Laura: The Meaning of Culture in the Education of Nineteenth-Century Women," *Journal of the Canadian Historical Association*, n.s. 1 (1990): 257–72.

9. Castiglione, *Il libro del Cortegiano*, bk. 3, sec. 9: "voglio che questa donna abbia notizie di lettere, di musica, di pittura e sappia danzar e festeggiare."

10. " 'Poco A Poco'—Memoires of the Family of Finney, of Fulshaw, (Near Wilmslow) Cheshire, by Samuel Finney of Fulshaw, Esquire.–1787," *The Cheshire and Lancashire Historical Collector*, ed. T. Worthington Barlow, no. 7 (September 1, 1853).

11. Claude Palisca, though tasked with defining "baroque" for *The New Grove Dictionary*, provided a great deal of evidence for the inappropriateness of the term. While "baroque" did have a

pejorative meaning in eighteenth-century French music criticism, its adoption as the name for a style period is a twentieth-century phenomenon rooted in late nineteenth-century German art criticism. See "Baroque," in *The New Grove Dictionary of Music and Musicians*, 2nd ed., ed. Stanley Sadie and John Tyrrell (London: Macmillan, 2001), 2:749–56.

12. Daniel Heartz and Bruce Alan Brown point out many of the ironies of the term "Classical," including Johann Forkel's (1802) use of the term to describe the keyboard music of J. S. Bach, and Mozart's wife's reference to fragments of classical literature in her attempts to market Mozart's incomplete manuscripts. See "Classical," in *The New Grove Dictionary of Music and Musicians*, 2nd ed. (2001), 5:924–29.

13. Leonard G. Ratner, *Classic Music: Expression, Form, and Style* (New York: Schirmer, 1980), xv.

14. Daniel Heartz, *Music in European Capitals: The Galant Style, 1720–1780* (New York: Norton, 2003).

15. For arguments in favor of a narrow use of the term, see Mark A. Radice, "The Nature of the 'Style Galant': Evidence from the Repertoire," *Musical Quarterly* 83 (1999): 607-47.

16. Robert Lewis Marshall, "Bach the Progressive: Observations on His Later Works," *Musical Quarterly* 62 (1976): 313–57.

17. Johann Joseph Fux, *Gradus ad Parnassum* (Vienna, 1725). Also in Fubini, *Music and Culture*, 34.

18. Taken from the skater's Web site, October 20, 2002: http://perso.wanadoo.fr/icegallery/mikkeline-routines.htm.

19. Chesterfield, *Letters*, no. 91, November 24, 1749.

20. See Domenico Pietropaolo, "Improvisation in the Arts," in *Improvisation in the Arts of the Middle Ages and Renaissance*, ed. Timothy J. McGee (Kalamazoo, Mich.: Medieval Institute Publications, 2003), 3.

21. *The Commedia dell'arte in Naples: A Bilingual Edition of the 176 Casamarciano Scenarios*, trans. and ed. Francesco Cotticelli, Anne Goodrich Heck, and Thomas F. Heck, 2 vols. (Lanham, Md.: Scarecrow Press, 2001), 1:67.

22. Niccolò Barbieri, "What is a Buffoon?" trans. from *La supplica* (1634), in *Actors on Acting*, ed. Toby Cole and Helen Chinoy, 2d ed. (New York: Crown, 1954), 53.

23. Carl Ditters von Dittersdorf, *Lebensbeschreibung* (Leipzig, 1801).

24. Francesco Galeazzi, *Elementi teorico-pratici di musica con un saggio sopra l'arte di suonare il violino analizzata, ed a dimostrabili principi ridotta*, vol. 2 (Rome, 1796), 54–55: "non far come taluni, che coll'ajuto di un Zibaldone, o libraccio de rancide lezioni, pretendono dar ad ogni qualunque Scolaro opportune lezioni."

25. Modern editions of the Attwood and Ployer studies are listed under "Mozart" in the index of music sources at the back of this volume.

26. Immanuel Kant, *The Critique of Pure Reason*, trans. J. M. D. Meiklejohn (Chicago: Encyclopedia Britannica, 1952); *Plato's Republic*, trans. I. A. Richards (Cambridge: Cambridge University Press, 1966), bk. 6; Max Weber, *Basic Concepts in Sociology*, trans. H. P. Secher (New York: Citadel Press, 1962), a translation of vol. 1, chap. 1 of Weber's *Wirtschaft und Gesellschaft* (Tübingen: Mohr, 1922); Ludwig Wittgenstein, *Philosophical Investigations*, ed. G. E. M. Anscombe and Rush Rhes (Oxford: Basil Blackwell, 1953), aphorism no. 69; Northrop Frye, *Anatomy of Criticism* (Princeton: Princeton University Press, 1957), 99–105; Michael I. Posner and Steven W. Keele, "On the Genesis of Abstract Ideas," *Journal of Experimental Psychology* 77 (1968): 353–63; Hilary Putnam, "The Meaning of 'Meaning,' " in *Language, Mind, and Knowledge*, ed. Keith Gunderson (Minneapolis: University of Minnesota Press, 1975), 131–93; Eleanor Rosch, *Basic*

Objects in Natural Categories (Berkeley: University of California Language Behavior Research Laboratory, 1975); also Eleanor Rosch and Carolyn B. Mervis, "Family Resemblances: Studies in the Internal Structure of Categories," *Cognitive Psychology* 7 (1975): 573–605.

27. William James, *The Principles of Psychology*, 2 vols. (New York: Holt, 1890), 1:488.

28. Michael I. Posner, "Empirical Studies of Prototypes," in *Noun Classes and Categorization*, ed. Colette Craig (Philadelphia: John Benjamins, 1986), 53–61.

29. Michael A. Erickson and John K. Kruschke, "Rules and Exemplars in Category Learning," *Journal of Experimental Psychology: General* 127 (1998): 107–40.

30. Douglas L. Medin and E. J. Heit, "Categorization," in *Cognitive Sciences*, ed. David E. Rumelhart and Benjamin Martin Bly (San Diego: Academic Press, 1999), 99–143.

31. Carl Dahlhaus, *Studies on the Origin of Harmonic Tonality*, trans. Robert O. Gjerdingen (Princeton: Princeton University Press, 1990); originally published as *Untersuchungen über die Entstehung der harmonischen Tonalität* (Kassel: Bärenreiter, 1967).

32. Jacob Grimm and Wilhelm Grimm, *Kinder- und Haus-Märchen* (Berlin, 1812–15).

33. The standard numbering of these tales identifies their position in the 1812–15 edition.

34. Robert Darnton, *The Great Cat Massacre and Other Episodes in French Cultural History* (New York: Basic Books, 1984), 9–74.; and Stith Thompson, *The Folktale* (New York: Dryden Press, 1946).

35. Erich Fromm, *The Forgotten Language: An Introduction to the Understanding of Dreams* (New York: Rinehart, 1951); and Bruno Bettelheim, *The Uses of Enchantment: The Meaning and Importance of Fairy Tales* (New York: Knopf, 1976).

36. Antti Aarne and Stith Thompson, *The Types of the Folktale*, 2nd rev. ed. (Helsinki: Academia Scientiarum Fennica, 1961).

37. Antti Aarne, *Verzeichnis der Märchentypen* (Helsinki: Suomalainen Tiedeakalemian Toimituksia, 1910).

38. Jean M. Mandler, *Stories, Scripts, and Scenes: Aspects of Schema Theory* (Hillsdale, N.J.: Lawrence Erlbaum Associates, 1984).

39. Robert O. Gjerdingen, *A Classic Turn of Phrase: Music and the Psychology of Convention* (Philadelphia: University of Pennsylvania Press, 1988).

40. Edward E. Lowinsky, *Secret Chromatic Art in the Netherlands Motet* (New York: Columbia University Press, 1946).

41. Johann David Heinichen, *Neu erfundene und gründliche Anweisung . . . zu vollkommener Erlernung des General-Basses* (Hamburg, 1711), 201–4.

42. Thomas Christensen, "The *Règle de l'Octave* in Thorough-Bass Theory and Practice," *Acta Musicologica* 63 (1991): 91–117.

43. Baron von Grimm, "Poème lyrique"; translated in Fubini, *Music and Culture*, 122.

44. Aldous Huxley, *Brave New World* (London: Chatto and Windus, 1932). The title is taken from *The Tempest*, act 5, scene 1, speech of Miranda.

45. Herbert Butterfield, *The Whig Interpretation of History* (London: G. Bell and Sons, 1931).

46. Michel Foucault, *The Archaeology of Knowledge*, trans. A. M. Sheridan Smith (London: Tavistock, 1972); originally published as *L'archéologie du savoir* (Paris: Gallimard, 1969).

47. Henry Adams, *The Education of Henry Adams: An Autobiography* (Boston and New York: Houghton Mifflin, 1918), 5.

48. Adams, *Autobiography*, 284.

49. Adams, *Autobiography*, 72.

50. Adams, *Autobiography*, 80–81.

51. Michel Foucault, *The Order of Things: An Archaeology of the Human Sciences* (New York: Pantheon, 1970), xvii; originally published as *Les mots et les choses: Une archéologie des sciences humaines* (Paris: Gallimard, 1966). With regard to musical form, a similar point was made in Scott Balthazar, "Intellectual History and Concepts of the Concerto: Some Parallels from 1750 to 1850," *Journal of the American Musicological Society* 36 (1983): 39–72.

52. André Gide, *Morceaux choisis* (Paris: Nouvelle Revue Français, 1921), 93: "L'oeuvre d'art classique ne sera forte et belle qu'en raison de son romantisme dompté."

53. Henry Glassie, *Passing the Time in Ballymenone: Culture and History of an Ulster Community* (Philadelphia: University of Pennsylvania Press, 1982), 621.

54. Leopold von Ranke (1795–1886) was in many respects the first modern historian. He distrusted the grand narrative and relied on primary sources, which could reveal the past "as it really was" ("wie es eigentlich gewesen ist"). See the preface to his *Geschichten der romanischen und germanischen Völker von 1494 bis 1535* (Leipzig: G. Reimer, 1824).

55. Nicholas Kenyon, ed., *Authenticity and Early Music* (Oxford: Oxford University Press, 1988); and Richard Taruskin, *Text and Act: Essays on Music and Performance* (New York: Oxford University Press, 1995).

56. Hermann Phleps, *Die Farbige Architektur bei den Römern und im Mittelalter* (Berlin: Ernst Wasmuth, 1930).

57. It is worth noting, however, that by the standards of mass-market cinema, ancient temples have recently become more colorful. Compare, for instance, the 1963 film *Cleopatra* with the 2005 television series *Rome*.

58. Arnold Dolmetsch, *The Interpretation of the Music of the XVIIth and XVIIIth Centuries Revealed by Contemporary Evidence* (London: Novello, 1915).

59. James Boswell, Esq., *The life of Samuel Johnson, LL. D. : comprehending an account of his studies and numerous works, in chronological order; : A series of his epistolary correspondence and conversations with many eminent persons; : and various original pieces of his composition, never before published. : The whole exhibiting a view of literature and literary men in Great-Britain, for near half a century, during which he flourished. : In two volumes* (London: Henry Baldwin, 1791), entry for April 8, 1773.

60. Paul Antoine Nolivos de Saint-Cyr, *Tableau du siécle* (Geneva, 1759), 132: "La Ville est, dit-on, le singe de la Cour."

61. Samuel Johnson, *Dictionary of the English Language* (London, 1755), title page.

CHAPTER 2

1. Giovanni Maria Bononcini, *Musico prattico che brevemente dimostra il modo di giungere alla perfetta cognizione di tutte quelle cose, che concorrono alla composizione de i canti, e di ciò ch'all'arte del contrapunto si ricerca, opus 8* (Bologna, 1673), preface: "viva voce di ben fondato Maestro."

2. Giacomo Tritto, *Scuola di contrappunto, ossia Teorica Musicale* (Milan: Ferd. Artaria, [1816]), 21, no. 8.

3. Stanislao Mattei, *Piccolo basso: In tutti li toni per introduzione alli bassi numerati ó siano partimenti* (MS Od.2.18, I-Nc, Naples), fol. 12r, "Sol terza maggiore no. 1."

4. Giovanni Paisiello, *Regole per bene accompagnare il partimento* (St. Petersburg, 1782), 30. In Italy, to my knowledge, no collections of partimenti were published in the eighteenth century.

Only in the early nineteenth century do prints of partimenti become common. The special circumstances of Italian music in Russia, and the very high status of the patroness (the future tzarina), may have made Paisiello's print possible.

5. Some of the earliest mentions of the Romanesca are found in Spanish sources, though its development is an Italian phenomenon. It shares many features with other early musical formulas like the *passamezzo antico*. See Elena Ferrari Barassi, "A proposito di alcuni bassi ostinati del periodo rinascimentale e barocco," in "Memorie e contributi alla musica dal medioevo all'età moderna offerti a Federico Ghisi nel settantesimo compleanno (1901–1971)," *Quadrivium* 12 (1971): 347–64; but see also Georg A. Predota, "Towards a Reconsideration of the Romanesca: Francesca Caccini's *Primo libro delle musiche* and Contemporary Monodic Settings in the First Quarter of the Seventeenth Century," *Recercare* 5 (1993): 87–113.

6. Carl Dahlhaus, *Studies on the Origin of Harmonic Tonality*, trans. Robert O. Gjerdingen (Princeton: Princeton University Press, 1990), 97.

7. *Partimenti di Domenico Cimarosa per violino* [sic], MS Gamma.L.9.26, Estense Library, Modena.

8. Heinrich Schenker, *Neue musikalische Theorien und Phantasien, i: Harmonielehre* (Stuttgart, 1906; Eng. trans., 1954/R); ii/1: *Kontrapunkt: Cantus firmus und zweistimmiger Satz* (Vienna, 1910; Eng. trans., 1987); ii/2: *Kontrapunkt: drei- und mehrstimmiger Satz, Übergänge zum freien Satz* (Vienna, 1922; Eng. trans., 1987); iii: *Der freie Satz* (Vienna, 1935; rev. ed., 1956, by Oswald Jonas; Eng. trans., 1979).

9. Monsieur de Saint Lambert, *Nouveau traité de l'accompagnement du clavecin, de l'orgue et des autres instruments* (Paris, 1707); trans. and ed. by John S. Powell under the title *A New Treatise on Accompaniment with the Harpsichord, the Organ, and with Other Insruments* (Bloomington: Indiana University Press, 1991), 45.

10. Guido of Arezzo, *Micrologus* (ca. 1026); trans. in *Hucbald, Guido, and John on Music: Three Medieval Treatises*, ed. Claude V. Palisca (New Haven, Conn.: Yale University Press, 1978).

11. Giuseppe Tartini, *De' principi dell'armonia musicale contenuta nel diatonico genere* (Padua, 1767); trans. in Enrico Fubini, *Music and Culture in Eighteenth-Century Europe: A Source Book* (Chicago: University of Chicago Press, 1994), 145.

12. Leopold Mozart, *Versuch einer gründlichen Violinschule* (Augsburg, 1756).

13. Jean-Philippe Rameau, *Traité de l'harmonie reduite à ses principes naturels* (Paris, 1722); trans. by Philip Gossett under the title *Treatise on Harmony* (New York: Dover, 1971).

14. Fausto Fritelli, *Il modo di solfeggiere all'uso Francese* (Sienna, 1744).

15. Joseph Riepel, *Anfangsgründe zur musicalischen Setzkunst: Nicht zwar nach alt-mathematischer Einbildungs-Art der Zirkel-Harmonisten sondern durchgehends mit sichtbaren Exempeln abgefasset, ii: Grundregeln zur Tonordnung insgemein* (Frankfurt and Leipzig, 1755), 10–15. Johann Friedrich Daube, *General-Bass in drey Accorden, gegründet in den Regeln der alt- und neuen Autoren* (Leipzig, 1756); trans. in Barbara Kees Wallace, "A Translation and Commentary on *General-Bass in drey Accorden* by Johann Friedrich Daube" (Ph.D. diss., North Texas State University, 1983).

16. Johann Jacob Prinner, *Musicalischer Schlissl* (1677); autograph manuscript, ML 95 P 79, Library of Congress, Washington, D.C.

17. Bononcini, *Musico prattico*, 35: "In vece della sillaba Ut i moderni si servono di questa Do, per essere piu risuonante."

18. Francesco Durante, *Partimenti numerati e diminuiti e fughe del maestro Francesco Durante* (n.d.; MS 24.2.4, I-Nc, Naples), fol. 8r.

19. *Sieben kleine Kirchenkompositionen für 1–5 Solostimmen und Generalbass* (Lottstetten/ Waldshut: Edition Kunzelmann, ca. 1986).

CHAPTER 3

1. Isabelle de Charrière, *Une liaison dangereuse: Correspondance avec Constant d'Hermenches, 1760–1776*, ed. Isabelle Vissière and Jean-Louis Vissière (Paris: Éditions de la Différence, 1991), from her letter of July 21–22, 1764, "La nuit entre samedi et dimanche."

2. Johann Jacob Prinner, *Musicalischer Schlissl* (1677); autograph manuscript, ML 95 P 79, Library of Congress, Washington, D.C., microfilm fol. 58.

3. This piece was likely composed much earlier, though the date of the print shows its currency during Wodiczka's study in Italy. See Eleanor Selfridge-Field, *The Music of Benedetto and Alessandro Marcello: A Thematic Catalogue with Commentary on the Composers, Repertory, and Sources* (New York: Oxford University Press, 1990).

4. Reinhard Strohm, ed., *The Eighteenth-Century Diaspora of Italian Music and Musicians* (Turnhout, Belgium: Brepols, 2001).

5. Saverio Valente, *Partimenti* (MS Noseda Q.13.17, I-Mc, Milan), 9. In this manuscript, the natural sign was placed under "8" rather than to the right of "6." The other similar examples on the same page show the proper placement of the accidental.

6. Valente, *Partimenti*, 14: "per uscire alla quinta del tono in terza maggiore."

7. *Oeuvres complètes / Isabelle de Charrière (Belle de Zuylen)*, ed. Jean-Daniel Candaux et al. (Amsterdam: G. A. van Oorshot, 1979–84), vol. 10.

8. Hugo Riemann, *Verloren gegangene Selbstverständlichkeiten in der Musik des 15.–16. Jahrhunderts* (Langensalza, 1907).

9. Niccolò Zingarelli, *Partimenti del Signor Maestro Don Nicolò Zingarelli* (Milan: Ricordi, post 1838), 31.

10. Zingarelli, *Partimenti*, 36.

11. Zingarelli, *Partimenti*, 1.

CHAPTER 4

1. Riepel's magnum opus—*Anfangsgründe zur musicalischen Setzkunst: Nicht zwar nach alt-mathematischer Einbildungs-Art der Zirkel-Harmonisten sondern durchgehends mit sichtbaren Exempeln abgefasset*—was written over a long period, with the earlier parts published in a series of "chapters," which were in fact each significant treatises focusing on different aspects of galant musical art. I will cite Riepel's works by chapter and page number. A reprint edition of the chapters, including new typesettings of Riepel's unpublished treatises, is now available: *Anfangsgründe zur musicalischen Setzkunst: Sämtliche Schriften zur Musiktheorie*, ed. Thomas Emmerig, 2 vols. (Vienna: Böhlau, 1996).

2. Riepel, *Anfangsgründe*, chap. 2, p. 44.

3. Riepel, *Anfangsgründe*, chap. 2, p. 46.

4. Giacomo Tritto, *Scuola di contrappunto, ossia Teorica Musicale* (Milan: Ferd. Artaria, [1816]), 25, no. 3, m. 52, originally in G major.

5. Riepel, *Anfangsgründe*, chap. 4, p. 2.

6. Riepel, *Anfangsgründe*, chap. 2, p. 44.

7. Riepel, *Anfangsgründe*, chap. 2, p. 124.

8. Riepel, *Anfangsgründe*, chap. 2, p. 103.

9. Riepel, *Anfangsgründe*, chap. 2, p. 103.

10. Wolfgang Budday, *Grundlagen musikalischer Formen der Wiener Klassik* (Kassel: Bärenreiter, 1983). The list of Fontes can be found in his appendix, pp. 225–26.

11. Riepel, *Anfangsgründe*, chap. 2, p. 102.

12. Pierre Rameau, *The Dancing-Master: or, The Art of Dancing Explained*, trans. J. Essex (London: J. Essex and J. Brotherton, 1728).

13. Guy de Maupassant, *Stories*, trans. Albert C. McMaster, A. E. Henderson, and Louise C. G. Quesada (New York: Thompson-Barlow, 1922), "Minuet," first published in French as "Menuet" (1882): "Le menuet, Monsieur, c'est la reine des danses, et la danse des Reines, entendez-vous? Depuis qu'il n'y a plus de Rois, il n'y a plus de menuet."

CHAPTER 5

1. Joseph Reipel, *Anfangsgründe zur musicalischen Setzkunst: Sämtliche Schriften zur Musiktheorie*, ed. Thomas Emmerig, 2 vols. (Vienna: Böhlau, 1996), chap. 1, p. 1.

2. The notebooks of Attwood and Ployer, who studied with Mozart, bear this out. See "Mozart" in the index of music sources at the back of this volume; see also Robert Lach, *W. A. Mozart als Theoretiker* (Vienna: Kaiserliche Akademie der Wissenschaften in Wien, Philosophisch-historische Klasse 61/1, 1918).

3. Riepel, *Anfangsgründe*, chap. 1, p. 2.

4. Please see http://faculty-web.at.northwestern.edu/music/gjerdingen/galant_book/index.htm. Should this address change in the future, a search for the keywords "gjerdingen" and "partimenti" should lead to the appropriate site. Enrico Gatti's performance can be heard on *La scuola piemontese nel XVIII secolo* ([Italy]: Symphonia, 1992), SY 92S13, recorded January, 1992 at the Chiesa di S. Chiara, Bra, Italy.

5. Giovanni Battista Somis, *Sonate da camera* [opus 1] (Paris: J. Roger, 1717): "a quell' Augusto Nome, che acclamato in tutte li Corti"; "in queste mie Cifere presento a tutto il Mondo un Ritratto Simbolico delle Sue gloriose qualitá"; "in queste mie Note alte, e basse, e in questi tuoni acuti, e gravi dalla loro contrarietá, e opposizione ridotte con arte ad armonic, e consonanza riscontrerá ogn' una Somma Maesta congiunta ad una Somma doldezza, un contegno affabile, una gravitá lieta, e Serena, insomma un concerto d'altura e dimestichezza, di moderazione e di splendore, d'autoritá e condiscendenza."

CHAPTER 6

1. I have named this schema after the core tones of its melody. Prof. Elwood Derr taught this pattern, by this name, to his students of fugue at the University of Michigan in the 1980s, and no doubt others have made the same connection.

2. Albert Bates Lord, *The Singer of Tales* (Cambridge: Harvard University Press, 1960), 54.

3. Neal Zaslaw, "Leclair, Jean-Marie," in *The New Grove Dictionary of Music and Musicians*, 2nd ed., ed. Stanley Sadie and John Tyrrell (London: Macmillan, 2001), 14:445–48.

4. Leonard B. Meyer, *Style and Music: Theory, History, and Ideology* (Philadelphia: University of Pennsylvania Press, 1989), 4.

5. Niccolò Zingarelli, *Partimenti del Signor Maestro Don Nicolò Zingarelli* (Milan: Ricordi, post 1838), 3.

6. François-Joseph Fétis, *Traité complet de la théorie et de la pratique de l'harmonie* (Paris: Maurice Schlesinger, 1844), 104–12.

7. Students who take melodic dictation sometimes confuse *do-re-mi* with *do-mi-sol*, giving some support to the notion that the mistake is one of "alphabet" (triadic in place of diatonic). See Diana Deutsch and J. Feroe, "The Internal Representation of Pitch Sequences in Tonal Music," *Psychological Review* 88 (1981): 503–22.

8. From the verse of "Do-Re-Mi" sung by the character Maria in *The Sound of Music* (New York, 1959).

CHAPTER 7

1. Joseph Reipel, *Anfangsgründe zur musicalischen Setzkunst: Sämtliche Schriften zur Musiktheorie*, ed. Thomas Emmerig, 2 vols. (Vienna: Böhlau, 1996), chap. 3, p. 1.

2. Niccolò Zingarelli, *Partimenti del Signor Maestro Don Nicolò Zingarelli* (Milan: Ricordi, post 1838), 7. The example has been transposed up a whole step for comparison with example 7.1.

3. Riepel, *Anfangsgründe*, chap. 1, p. 18.

4. Riepel, *Anfangsgründe*, chap. 4, p. 22: "Er findet sich aber betrogen."

5. Riepel, *Anfangsgründe*, chap. 4, p. 22.

6. Riepel, *Anfangsgründe*, chap. 4, pp. 28–29: "nicht gar vertilgt werden."

7. Scarlatti would likely have known Pierre Rameau, the dancing master mentioned in chapter 4 (no relation to the French composer). But whereas the patroness of Rameau was Elisabetta Farnese, Scarlatti was allied to her successor as queen, Maria Barbara.

8. Darrell M. Berg, "The Keyboard Sonatas of C. P. E. Bach: An Expression of the Mannerist Principle" (Ph.D. diss., State University of New York at Buffalo, 1975).

9. Riepel, *Anfangsgründe*, chap. 2, pp. 25–31.

10. Giovanni Furno, *Metodo facile, breve e chiaro delle prime ed essenziali regole per accompagnare i partimenti senza numeri* (Naples, ca. 1810), 12: "When the partimento rises a 5th and falls a 4th, one accompanies it with a 4th, a 5th, and an 8ve, and the said 4th is prepared by the 8ve and resolves to a minor 3rd above the same note."

11. Johann Joachim Quantz, *Versuch einer Anweisung die Flöte traversiere zu spielen* (Berlin, 1752), 106; trans. by Edward R. Reilly under the title *On Playing the Flute*, 2nd ed. (London: Faber and Faber, 1985), 190.

12. Giacomo Tritto, *Scuola di contrappunto* (Milan: Ferd. Artaria, [1816]), 26, no. 2.

13. Riepel, *Anfangsgründe*, chap. 4, pp. 32–33: "so alt."

14. Riepel, *Anfangsgründe*, chap. 2, p. 45.

15. Riepel, *Anfangsgründe*, chap. 2, p. 45: "zwei gleiche Absätz hinter einander nicht gut lauten."

CHAPTER 8

1. Judith Leah Schwartz, "Phrase Morphology in the Early Classic Symphony (c. 1720–c. 1765)" (Ph.D. diss., New York University, 1973).

2. Joseph Reipel, *Anfangsgründe zur musicalischen Setzkunst: Sämtliche Schriften zur Musiktheorie*, ed. Thomas Emmerig, 2 vols. (Vienna: Böhlau, 1996), chap. 4, p. 29.

3. Riepel, *Anfangsgründe*, chap. 4, p. 29.

CHAPTER 9

1. The practice continues today; for example, a violinist might describe herself as a student of Galamian, or a guitarist as a student of Ghiglia (who was a student Segovia, and so forth).

2. Giacomo Tritto, *Scuola di contrappunto* (Milan: Ferd. Artaria, [1816]), 21, no. 13; see also p. 20, no. 5.

3. Robert O. Gjerdingen, *A Classic Turn of Phrase: Music and the Psychology of Convention* (Philadelphia: University of Pennsylvania Press, 1988).

4. Leonard B. Meyer and Burton S. Rosner, "Melodic Processes and the Perception of Music," in *The Psychology of Music*, ed. Diana Deutsch (New York: Academic Press, 1982), 317–41. In subsequent publications Meyer replaced the term "archetype" with "schema."

5. Leonard B. Meyer, *The Spheres of Music: A Gathering of Essays* (Chicago: University of Chicago Press, 2000), 189–225; a reprint of "Exploiting Limits: Creation, Archetypes, and Style Change," *Daedalus* 109 (1980): 177–205.

6. Stefan Eckert, "Ars Combinatoria, Dialoque Structure, and Musical Practice in Joseph Riepel's *Anfanggründe zur musicalischen Setzkunst*" (Ph.D. diss., SUNY at Stony Brook, 2000); see pp. 82–100.

7. Michel Foucault, *The Order of Things: An Archaeology of the Human Sciences* (New York: Pantheon, 1970), 203; originally published as *Les mots et les choses: Une archéologie des sciences humaines* (Paris: Gallimard, 1966).

8. Leonard G. Ratner, "Ars Combinatoria: Chance and Choice in Eighteenth-Century Music," in *Studies in Eighteenth-Century Music: A Tribute to Karl Geiringer on His Seventieth Birthday*, ed. H. C. Robbins Landon and Roger E. Chapman (New York: Allen and Unwin, 1970), 343–63.

9. A. Peter Brown, "Eighteenth-Century Traditions and Mozart's 'Jupiter' Symphony K. 551," *Journal of Musicology* 20 (Berkeley: University of California Press, 2003): 157–95. Brown details the historiography of the Jupiter motto.

10. Jean-Marie Morel, *Théorie des jardins* (Paris, 1776), 37; cited in Jill H. Casid, "Queer(y)ing Georgic: Utility, Pleasure, and Marie-Antoinette's Ornamented Farm," *Eighteenth-Century Studies* 30 (1997): 304–18.

11. Johann Joachim Winkelmann, *Gedanken über die Nachahmung der Griechischen Werke in der Mahlerey und Bildhauer-Kunst* (1755).

12. Leonard G. Ratner, *Classic Music: Expression, Form, and Style* (New York: Schirmer, 1980); see also his "Topical Content in Mozart's Keyboard Sonatas," *Early Music* 19 (1991): 615–19.

13. Meyer, *Spheres of Music*, 197 n. 16.

14. Meyer, *Spheres of Music*, 55–125; a reprint of "Grammatical Simplicity and Relational Richness: The Trio of Mozart's G-Minor Symphony," *Critical Inquiry* 2 (1976): 693–761.

CHAPTER 10

1. Writing variations had great importance for Haydn. See Elaine Sisman, *Haydn and the Classical Variation* (Cambridge: Harvard University Press, 1993).

2. In a major key, adjacent triads with the higher one minor and the lower one major can be found on ②–① and ⑥–⑤. In a minor scale, there are no such pairs due to the peculiar pattern caused by lowering the third and sixth degrees while raising the seventh.

3. Riepel, *Anfangsgründe*, chap. 2, pp. 25–31.

CHAPTER 11

1. S.v. "Clausula," in *A Latin Dictionary*, ed. Charlton T. Lewis and Charles Short (Oxford: Clarendon, 1879).

2. Johann Walther, *Praecepta der musicalischen Composition* (1708; MS, D-WRtl); ed. Peter Benary (Leipzig: Breitkopf & Härtel, 1955), ms. p. 296. The manuscript is dedicated to Walther's pupil, Prince Johann Ernst.

3. Andreas Werckmeister, *Harmonologia Music* (Frankfurt, 1702), p. 48, sec. 86 (reprint, New York: Hildesheim, 1970).

4. Walther, *Praecepta*, ms. p. 298.

5. For a similar approach applied to a related though somewhat earlier repertory, see Heinrich Deppert, *Kadenz und Klausel in der Musik von J. S. Bach* (Tutzing: Hans Schneider, 1993).

6. Domenico Pietropaolo, "Improvisation in the Arts," in *Improvisation in the Arts of the Middle Ages and Renaissance*, ed. Timothy J. McGee (Kalamazoo, Mich.: Medieval Institute Publications, 2003), 4.

7. Charles Cudworth, "Cadence galante: The Story of a Cliché," *The Monthly Musical Record* 79 (1949): 176–78.

8. Francis Bacon, *The Advancement of Learning* (1605), bk. 2, sec. 5, par. 3.

9. Alexandre E. Choron, *Principes de composition des écoles d'Italie* (Paris, 1808), vol. 1, bk. 1, pt. 2, no. 44, p. 12.

10. Choron, *Principes*, no. 73, p. 24.

11. Choron, *Principes*, no. 40, p. 11.

12. Janet M. Levy, "Texture as a Sign in Classic and Early Romantic Music," *Journal of the American Musicological Society* 35 (1982): 482–531.

13. Vincenzo Manfredini, *Regole armoniche, o sieno Precetti ragionati* (Venice, 1775; 2nd ed., enlarged, 1797), 41.

14. Alexander Malcolm, *A Treatise of Musick, Speculative, Practical, and Historical* (Edinburgh, 1721), 269.

15. Francesco Galeazzi, *Elementi teorico-pratici di musica con un saggio sopra l'arte di suonare il violino analizzata, ed a dimostrabili principi ridotta*, vol. 2 (Rome, 1796), 261.

16. Johann Friedrich Daube, *General-Bass in drey Accorden, gegründet in den Regeln der alt- und neuen Autoren* (Leipzig, 1756), chap. 6, p. 13.

17. Daube, *General-Bass*, chap. 6, p. 13.

18. Johann Joachim Quantz, *Versuch einer Anweisung die Flöte traversiere zu spielen* (Berlin, 1752), 127–28; trans. by Edward R. Reilly under the title *On Playing the Flute* (London: Faber and Faber, 1966), 150.

19. Quantz, *Versuch*, 127; *On Playing the Flute*, 150.

20. Quantz, *Versuch*, 127–28; *On Playing the Flute*, 150.

21. The term *clausula vera* appears frequently in nineteenth- and early twentieth-century manuals for students of counterpoint, but infrequently in historical sources. W. S. Rockstro (1823–1895)

wrote the article "Cadence" for the second edition of the original Grove dictionary. His emphatic statement that "the most important Close employed in polyphonic music, is the Clausula vera, or true Cadence, terminating on the final of the mode" may have elevated the term to general use. See *Grove's Dictionary of Music and Musicians*, ed. J. A. Fuller Maitland (London, 1908–10), 1:435–35.

22. The Cadenza Doppia has also been called a "consonant fourth" cadence. This refers to the second beat, where the (dissonant) fourth between bass and middle voice appears to be the (consonant) preparation for the dissonance on the third beat. Since the main counterpoint occurs between the upper two voices, the focus on that particular interval with the bass somewhat misses the mark. Nevertheless, in pedantic approaches to counterpoint the legitimization of this configuration vis-à-vis the bass was a necessary expedient.

23. "Cadence longue" is attributed to Sala in Alexandre E. Choron, *Principes de composition des écoles d'Italie* (Paris, 1808), 2:1.

24. Giovanni Paisiello, *Regole per bene accompagnare il partimento* (St. Petersburg, 1782).

25. Daube, *General-Bass*, chap. 5, p. 5.

26. Saverio Valente, *Partimenti* (MS Noseda Q.13.17, I-Mc, Milan), 9.

27. Manfredini adopted both the three-chord model of Daube and a version of Rameau's fundamental bass.

28. Choron gives several versions of this cadence, all true to the "Italian school," in his *Principes* 1:70.

29. James W. Carey, *Communication as Culture: Essays on Media and Society* (Boston: Unwin Hyman, 1988), 13ff.

30. "Harmony Simplified" was the English title of Riemann's harmony textbook aimed at a general audience. See Hugo Riemann, *Vereinfachte Harmonielehre oder die Lehre von den tonalen Funktionen der Akkorde* (London and New York, 1893; Eng. trans., 1896); see also Francis L. York, *Harmony Simplified* (Boston: Oliver Ditson, ca. 1900).

31. Choron, *Principes*, no. 115, p. 55.

CHAPTER 13

1. Niccolò Zingarelli, *Partimenti del Maestro Nicolò Zingarelli*, vol. 2 (MS Noseda I.140.II, I-Mc, Milan), 1–2: "Il pedale si forma dall' accordo del basso fondamentale."

2. Zingarelli, *Partimenti del Maestro*, 2: "Si puo dar partimenti la settima minore come si andasse nella natura della quarta del tuono."

3. Paul Bryan, *Johann Wanhal, Viennese Symphonist: His Life, His Symphonies, and His Musical Environment* (Stuyvesant, N.Y.: Pendragon, 1997).

4. In spite of the key signature, the local key preceding the excerpt is C major. The partimento is reprinted in Camillo de Nardis, *Partimenti dei maestri C. Cotumacci, F. Durante, . . .* (Milan: Ricordi, ca. 1900–1910), bk. 3, no. 11.

CHAPTER 14

1. Joseph Reipel, *Anfangsgründe zur musicalischen Setzkunst: Sämtliche Schriften zur Musiktheorie*, ed. Thomas Emmerig, 2 vols. (Vienna: Böhlau, 1996), chap. 2, p. 44; "Monte, **Berg**

zum hinaufsteigen. Fonte, **Brunn** zum hinabsteigen. Ponte, **Brücke** zum hinübergehen (the bold type is Riepel's).

2. Riepel, *Anfangsgründe*, chap. 1, p. 79: "Musik ist ein unerschöpliches Meer."

3. Riepel, *Anfangsgründe*, chap. 2, p. 46: "Ich will das Ponte auch ein wenig herum wenden."

4. Riepel, *Anfangsgründe*, chap. 2, p. 46.

5. Riepel, *Anfangsgründe*, chap. 2, p. 47: "Auch gut."

6. Riepel, *Anfangsgründe*, chap. 2, p. 47: "Lang nicht so gut wie das vorige."

7. Riepel, *Anfangsgründe*, chap. 2, p. 48: "Sofern es das Gehör leidet, oder erfordert."

8. Riepel, *Anfangsgründe*, chap. 2, p. 48.

9. Riepel, *Anfangsgründe*, chap. 2, p. 49: "Ungeachtet es weder zu Monte, noch zu Fonte und Ponte gehört."

10. Riepel, *Anfangsgründe*, chap. 2, p. 123: "Aus der Tonart C entlehnet."

11. Riepel, *Anfangsgründe*, chap. 4 passim.

12. Isabelle de Charrière, *Une Liaison dangereuse: Correspondance avec Constant d'Hermenches, 1760–1776*, ed. Isabelle Vissière and Jean-Louis Vissière (Paris: Éditions de la Différence, 1991), from her letter of July 9–10, 1764: "Ce que j'aime surtout ce sont les beaux trios ou quartetti dans le gout de Campioni et de Pugnani."

13. Though Prinners occur in several of Riepel's treatises, he never refers to smaller ones by any special term. He terms large ones, those with a circle-of-fifths harmonic pattern and a chain of suspended sevenths, "seventh progressions" (*Septimegänge*; chap. 4, pp. 1–3), a term he reserves for large Prinners even though many other types of "seventh progressions" can be found in the galant style.

14. William Drabkin defines "Schusterfleck" and its Italian equivalent, "Rosalia," as "a pejorative name, taken from an old Italian popular song *Rosalia, mia cara*, for the identical repetition of a melody a step higher, often involving transposition." See "Rosalia," in *The New Grove Dictionary of Music and Musicians*, 2nd ed., ed. Stanley Sadie and John Tyrrell (London: Macmillan, 2001), 21:681–82. Thomas Christensen has noted that H. F. M. Langlé (1741–1807), writing in his *Traité de la basse sous le chant, precede de toutes les regles de la composition* (Paris: Maderman, 1799), mentions the *rosalie* as characteristic of Italian music (p. 214). Unlike the IV–V tonal movement of the Monte, the Rosalia is characterized by a I–II, major-to-minor movement in the opening, parallel phrases of a theme.

CHAPTER 15

1. Percy A. Scholes, ed., *Charles Burney: An Eighteenth-Century Musical Tour in France and Italy* (Oxford: Oxford University Press, 1959), 134, report of Thursday, August 16, 1770.

2. Baldassarre Galuppi, *Concerti a quattro a due violini, viola e basso obbligati* (Milan: Stradivarius, 1993), STR 33316, recorded on May 18, May 24–25, and June 6, 1993, at the Chiesa di S. Maria del Popolo, Vigevano, Italy by the Quartetto Aglàia.

CHAPTER 16

1. For an excellent introduction to the facts and fables of these lineages, see Jesse Rosenberg, "The Experimental Music of Pietro Raimondi" (Ph.D. diss., New York University, 1995), 171–225.

2. See Rosa Cafiero, "La didattica del partimento a Napoli fra Settecento e Ottocento: Note sulla fortuna delle Regole di Carlo Cotumacci," in *Gli affetti convenienti all'idee: Studi sulla musica vocale italiana, Archivio del teatro e dello spettacolo,* no. 3 (Naples: Edizioni Scientifiche Italiane, 1993); Giorgio Sanguinetti, "Un secolo di teoria della musica in Italia: Bibliografica critica 1850–1950," *Fonti musicali italiane* (1997): 155–248.

3. Gaetano Cesari and Alessandro Luzio, eds., *I copialettere di Giuseppe Verdi* (Milan, 1913); rev. Eng. trans., abridged, as *Letters of Giuseppe Verdi,* ed. Charles Osborne (New York: Holt, Rinehart and Winston, 1971), 242, 320.

4. An introduction to the Rule can be found in appendix B. For a historical treatment, see Thomas Christensen, "The *Règle de l'Octave* in Thorough-Bass Theory and Practice," *Acta Musicologica* 63 (1991): 91–117.

5. See Roger Kamien, "Style Change in the Mid-18th-Century Keyboard Sonata," *Journal of the American Musicological Society* 19 (1966): 37–58; and Kamien, "The Opening Sonata-Allegro Movements in a Randomly Selected Sample of Solo Keyboard Sonatas Published in the Years 1742–1744 (Inclusive)," 2 vols. (Ph.D. diss., Princeton University, 1964).

6. Joel Lester, *The Rhythms of Tonal Music* (Carbondale: Southern Illinois University Press, 1986), 229ff.

7. Giovanni Paisiello, *Regole per bene accompagnare il partimento* (St. Petersburg, 1782), 36.

8. Carlo Antonio de Rosa, Marchese de Villarosa, *Memorie dei compositori di musica del regno di Napoli* (Naples: Stamperia Reale, 1840), 72.

9. Jonathan Swift, *The Adventures of Capt. Gulliver in a Voyage to the Islands of Lilliput and Brobdingnag* (Darlington: John Sadler, 1773), 19.

10. Riepel, *Anfangsgründe,* chap. 3, p. 40: "Von einigen berühmten Meistern."

11. Daines Barrington, "Account of a Very Remarkable Musician [W. A. Mozart]. In a Letter from the Honourable Daines Barrington, F.R.S. to Mathew Maty, M.D. Sec. R.S.," *Philosophical Transactions of the Royal Society* 60 (1770): 54–64.

12. The prevalence of Fenarolis in Mozart's string quartets was pointed out to me by the Toronto music theorist Mikki Leung.

13. Franz Liszt, *Frederic Chopin,* trans. Edward N. Waters (New York: Free Press of Glencoe, 1963), 34; the original edition was published in Paris in 1852.

CHAPTER 17

1. Titles like Choron's *Principes de composition des écoles d'Italie* (Paris, 1808) and his earlier *Principes d'accompagnement des écoles d'Italie* (Paris, 1804) helped to make "the Italian school" a common term.

2. See Norton E. Dudeque, "Music Theory and Analysis in the Writings of Arnold Schoenberg (1874–1951)" (Ph.D. diss., University of Reading, 2002), sec. 4.3.1.

3. See, for example, George Robert Hill, "The Concert Symphonies of Florian Leopold Gassmann" (Ph.D. diss., New York University, 1975).

CHAPTER 18

1. Cited in the notes to the recording *Galuppi: Motets / Confitebor / Arripe alpestri ad vallem*, performed by Gérard Lesne, Véronique Gens, Peter Harvey, and Il Seminario musicale (Virgin Veritas 45030).

2. The comedy *The Ladykillers*, dir. Alexander Mackendrick (Ealing Studios, 1955), starring Alec Guinness, Herbert Lom, and a young Peter Sellers.

3, William Drabkin, "Rosalia," in *The New Grove Dictionary of Music and Musicians*, 2nd ed., ed. Stanley Sadie and John Tyrrell (London: Macmillan, 2001), 21:681–82.

4. Joseph Reipel, *Anfangsgründe zur musicalischen Setzkunst: Sämtliche Schriften zur Musiktheorie*, ed. Thomas Emmerig, 2 vols. (Vienna: Böhlau, 1996), chap. 4, p. 29: "Sieht aus, wie ein alltägliches Fonte."

5. Riepel, *Anfangsgründe*, chap. 4, p. 29: "Zieren ihn einige Componisten auf deise Art."

CHAPTER 19

1. *The Letters of Mozart and His Family*, trans. Emily Anderson (London: Macmillan, 1938), 2:889. In his letter of August 13, 1778, Leopold writes, "Das *Kleine* ist *Groß*, wenn es natürlich—flüssend und leicht geschrieben und gründlich gesetzt ist. Es so zu machen ist schwerer als all die den meisten unverständliche Künstlichen Harmonischen progressionen, und schwer auszuführende Melodyen. hat sich Bach dadurch heruntergesetzt? — keines wegs! Der gute Satz, und die Ordnung, il filo—dieses unterscheidet den Meister vom Stümper auch in Kleinigkeiten." The complete German text of this letter can be found in *Mozart, Briefe und Aufzeichnungen* (Bärenreiter, 1962).

2. Albert B. Lord, *The Singer of Tales* (Cambridge: Harvard University Press, 1960), 130–31.

CHAPTER 20

1. Joseph Reipel, *Anfangsgründe zur musicalischen Setzkunst: Sämtliche Schriften zur Musiktheorie*, ed. Thomas Emmerig, 2 vols. (Vienna: Böhlau, 1996).

2. Johann Joachim Quantz, *Versuch einer Anweisung die Flöte traversiere zu spielen* (Berlin, 1752); Carl Phillip Emanuel Bach, *Versuch über die wahre Art das Clavier zu spielen*, 2 vols. (Berlin, 1753, 1762), Eng. trans., ed. W. J. Mitchell, as *Essay on the True Art of Playing Keyboard Instruments* (New York, 1949); Leopold Mozart, *Versuch einer gründlichen Violinschule* (Augsburg, 1756).

3. Friedrich Daube, *General-Bass in drey Accorden, gegründet in den Regeln der alt- und neuen Autoren* (Leipzig, 1756).

4. Giacomo Tritto, *Partimenti regole generali: Per conoscere qual numerica dar si deve a vari movimenti del basso* (Milan: Ferd. Artaria, [1816]), 7, lezzione 3.

5. Norbert Elias, *Mozart: Portrait of a Genius*, ed. Michael Schröter, trans. Edmund Jephcott (Berkeley: University of California Press, 1993), 10ff. The book is a posthumous collection.

6. Program notes presented by BBC3, London, 2003 (http://www.bbc.co.uk/radio3/classical/pizarro/sonata18.shtml).

7. Grace (Dalrymple) Elliot, *Journal of My Life During the French Revolution* (London: R. Bentley, 1859), 17–18.

CHAPTER 22

1. Joseph Reipel, *Anfangsgründe zur musicalischen Setzkunst: Sämtliche Schriften zur Musiktheorie*, ed. Thomas Emmerig, 2 vols. (Vienna: Böhlau, 1996), chap. 1, p. 1.

CHAPTER 24

1. Saverio Mattei, *Memorie per servire alla vita del Metastasio ed elogio di N. Jommelli* (1785; reprint, Bologna: A. Forni, 1987), 75.

CHAPTER 25

1. Friedrich Melchior, Baron von Grimm, *Correspondance littéraire, philosophique, et critique, adressée à un souverain d'Allemagne, depuis 1753 jusqu'en 1769* (Paris, 1813), 528–29, letter of December 1, 1763.

CHAPTER 26

1. See, for instance, Leonard G. Ratner, "Harmonic Aspects of Classic Form," *Journal of the American Musicological Society* 2 (1949): 159–68.

CHAPTER 27

1. Galuppi is quoted in Percy A. Scholes, ed., *Charles Burney: An Eighteenth-Century Musical Tour in France and Italy* (Oxford: Oxford University Press, 1959), 134, report of Thursday, August 16, 1770.

2. *The Letters of Mozart and His Family*, trans. Emily Anderson (London: Macmillan, 1938), 2:889, letter L.323, August 13, 1778.

3. *The Letters of Mozart*, ed. Anderson, 2:889.

4. Reinhard Strohm, ed., *The Eighteenth-Century Diaspora of Italian Music and Musicians* (Turnhout, Belgium: Brepols, 2001).

5. Francesco Durante, as related by Francesco Florimo in his *La scuola musicale di Napoli*, 3 vols. (Naples: Morano, 1881–83), 2:180–81: "Miei cari, fate così, perchè così va fatto. Dev'essere così, perché il vero ed il bello è uno, e non m'inganno. Io non so dirvi le ragioni che mi dimandate; ma siate pur certi che i maestri che verranno dopo di me le traverranno, e dei precetti che ora vi do, essi faranno tanti assiomi che diverranno regole infallibili." See Jesse Rosenberg, "The Experimental Music of Pietro Raimondi" (Ph.D. diss., New York University, 1995), 202–3.

6. Giovanni Furno, as related by Francesco Florimo, *La scuola musicale di Napoli* 2:292: "Fate così e come io vi dico, perchè così m'insegnò di fare il mio maestro Cotumacci."

7. Howard Brofsky, *New Grove*, s.v. Stanislao Mattei.

8. Paul F. Berliner, *Thinking in Jazz: The Infinite Art of Improvisation* (Chicago: University of Chicago Press, 1994), 205.

9. Berliner, *Thinking in Jazz*, 227.

10. Domenico Pietropaolo, "Improvisation as a Stochastic Composition Process," in *The Science of Buffoonery: Theory and History of the Commedia dell'Arte*, ed. D. Pietropaolo (Toronto: Dovehouse Editions, 1989), 167–76.

11. The sampled repertory included the featured movements of chapters 5, 8, 10, 12, 15, 17, 19, 21–24, 26, and 28–29. Because the version of Haydn's quartet movement given in this chapter differs from his published version, it was not included in the statistics.

12. See, for example, Leonard B. Meyer, *Style and Music: Theory, History, and Ideology* (Philadelphia: University of Pennsylvania Press, 1989); Eugene Narmour, *The Analysis and Cognition of Basic Melodic Structures: The Implication-Realization Model* (Chicago: University of Chicago Press, 1990); and Robert O. Gjerdingen, *A Classic Turn Of Phrase: Music and the Psychology of Convention* (Philadelphia: University of Pennsylvania Press, 1988).

13. Carl Dahlhaus, "Some Models of Unity in Musical Form," *Journal of Music Theory* 19 (1975): 2–30, esp. 14.

14. Albert B. Lord, *The Singer of Tales* (Cambridge: Harvard University Press, 1960), 130–31.

15. Friedrich Melchior, Baron von Grimm, *Correspondance littéraire, philosophique, et critique, adressée à un souverain d'Allemagne, depuis 1753 jusqu'en 1769* (Paris, 1813), 528–29, letter of December 1, 1763.

16. Both Meyer and Narmour discuss unrealized implications at length. See, for example, Eugene Narmour, *Beyond Schenkerism: The Need for Alternatives in Music Analysis* (Chicago: University of Chicago Press, 1977).

17. Johann Joachim Quantz, *Versuch einer Anweisung die Flöte traversiere zu spielen* (Berlin, 1752); trans. by Edward R. Reilly under the title *On Playing the Flute* (London: Faber and Faber, 1966), chap. 18, par. 46.

18. This partimento fugue is printed in Karl Gustav Fellerer, *Der Partimento-spieler: Ubungen im Generalbass-spiel und in gebundener Improvisation* (Leipzig: Breitkopf & Härtel, 1940), 19.

19. See the index of music sources, s.v. "Mozart," *Skizzen.*

20. *Streichquartette, "Opus 20" und "Opus 33,"* ed. Georg Feder and Sonja Gerlach, in *Joseph Haydn: Werke*, ed. J. Haydn-Institut, Cologne, ser. 12, vol. 3 (Munich: G. Henle, 1958–), 191.

21. Because of the inclusion of the sketched Monte, my measure numbers will differ from those of Haydn's finished work.

22. Leonard B. Meyer, "Grammatical Simplicity and Relational Richness: The Trio of Mozart's G-Minor Symphony," *Critical Inquiry* 2 (1976): 693–761.

CHAPTER 28

1. A letter from Krause to the poet Johann Wilhelm Ludwig Gleim, December 20, 1747, cited in James Harry Mallard, "A Translation of Christian Gottfried Krause's *Von der musikalischen Poesie.* . . ." (Ph.D. diss., University of Texas at Austin, 1978), 205: "Bach ist ein Milton. . . . Man muß mit seinen Melodien vorher recht bekannt werden, ehe sie gefallen."

2. In the case of the libretto for the opera *Montezuma*, for instance, Frederick was the "author," although a court poet assisted behind the scenes. Quantz or other professional musicians may have served in similar roles for Frederick's compositions. See Heinz Klüppelholz, "Die Eroberung

Mexikos aus preussischer Sicht: Zum Libretto der Oper Montezuma von Friedrich dem Grossen," in *Oper als text: Romanistische Beiträge zur Libretto-Forschung*, ed. Albert Gier (Heidelberg: Winter, 1986), 65–94.

3. Johann Joachim Quantz, *Versuch einer Anweisung die Flöte traversiere zu spielen* (Berlin, 1752), 106; trans. by Edward R. Reilly under the title *On Playing the Flute*, 2nd ed. (London: Faber and Faber, 1985), 190.

4. Quantz, *Versuch*, chap. 13, par. 4.

5. Quantz, *Versuch*, table 12, fig. 8.

6. Quantz, *Versuch*, table 9, fig. 3.

7. Quantz, *Versuch*, chap. 13, par. 6, from the Reilly translation.

CHAPTER 29

1. Bathia Churgin, "Francesco Galeazzi's Description (1796) of Sonata Form," *Journal of the American Musicological Society* 21 (1968): 181–99; rev. trans. in *Source Readings in Music History*, ed. Wye Jamison Allanbrook, rev. ed. (New York: Norton, 1998), 5:85–92.

2. Francesco Galeazzi, *Elementi teorico-pratici di musica con un saggio sopra l'arte di suonare il violino analizzata, ed a dimostrabili principi ridotta*, vol. 1 (Rome, 1791), vol. 2 (Rome, 1796).

3. Carl Dahlhaus, "Some Models of Unity in Musical Form," *Journal of Music Theory* 19 (1975): 2–30.

4. Galeazzi, *Elementi* 2:253: "nell' esatta condotta di un intero pezzo di Musica."

5. Galeazzi, *Elementi* 2:253: "nel tirare le Melodie."

6. *The Letters of Mozart and His Family*, trans. Emily Anderson (London: Macmillan, 1938), 2:889, letter L.323, August 13, 1778: "dieses unterscheidet den Meister vom Steumper."

7. Heinrich Christoph Koch, *Versuch einer Anleitung zur Composition*, vol. 3 (Leipzig, 1793), 2ff.: "Von der Verbindung der melodischen Theile, oder von dem Baue der Perioden."

8. Koch, *Versuch* 3:218, sec. 70: "die Parenthese, oder die Einschaltung." The musical examples are his Figures 5 and 6, pp. 221–22.

9. Koch, *Versuch*, vol. 2 (1787), 431.

10. Koch, *Versuch* 3:209: "Man kann aber auch vermittlest der Versetzung eines Gliedes in eine andere Tonart moduliren."

11. Koch was born and worked in Rudolstadt, a small Protestant court at some distance from the great centers of the galant style. His bass D4 in measure 4 of example 29.5, while respecting the Prinner's harmony, was not quite comme il faut. An F#4 would have been the more galant choice.

12. Koch, *Versuch* 3:365.

13. Koch, *Versuch* 3:229.

14. Koch, *Versuch* 3:426.

15. Galeazzi, *Elementi* 2:256; the melody appears in his Table 7, Ex. 1.

16. Galeazzi, *Elementi* 2:256.

17. Jane Austen, *Pride and Prejudice, a Novel* (London: T. Egerton, 1813).

18. Herbert Simon, "The Organization of Complex Systems," in *Hierarchy Theory: The Challenge of Complex Systems*, ed. Howard H. Pattee (New York: George Braziller, 1973), 1–28.

19. James Edward Austen-Leigh, *Memoir of Jane Austen by Her Nephew James Edward Austen-Leigh*, intro. R. W. Chapman (Oxford: Clarendon, 1926), reprint of 2nd ed. (1871), letter sent from Chawton, Thursday, February 4, 1813.

20. Galeazzi, *Elementi* 2:253.

21. Galeazzi, *Elementi* 2:258: "Un pensiero affatto nuovo, ed estraneo . . . per maggior sorpresa."

22. Adolf Bernhard Marx, *Die Lehre von der musikalischen Komposition, praktisch-theoretisch*, 4 vols. (Leipzig: Breitkopf & Härtel, 1837–47), vol. 3 (1845), quoted in Heinrich Schenker, *Die Tonwille* (Vienna: Universal, 1921–24), Eng. trans. ed. W. Drabkin, 2 vols. (New York: Oxford University Press, 2004), 1:66.

23. Schenker, *Die Tonwille*, Eng. trans., 1:66.

24. Bonifazio Asioli, *Principj elementari di musica* (Milan, 1809), and *Trattato d'armonia e d'accompagnamento* (Milan, 1813). The recommendation from Haydn is mentioned under "Asioli" in *The New Grove Dictionary of Music and Musicians*, 2nd ed., ed. Stanley Sadie and John Tyrrell (London: Macmillan, 2001), 2:112–13.

25. Adolphe Danhauser, *Solfège des solfèges* (New York: Schirmer, 1891); Henry Lemoine, Gustavo Carulli, Adolphe Danhauser, Albert Lavignac, and Léon Lemoine, *Solfège des solfèges* (Paris: H. Lemoine, 1910).

CHAPTER 30

1. Tuomas Eerola, "The Rise and Fall of the Experimental Style of the Beatles: The Life Span of Stylistic Periods in Music" (M.A. thesis, University of Jyväskylä, 1997), 67.

2. Rupert Spade, *Paul Rudolph* (New York: Simon and Schuster, 1971), 9–10.

3. Pierre Bourdieu, *The Logic of Practice*, trans. Richard Nice (Stanford: Stanford University Press, 1990), 54; originally published as *Le Sens pratique* (Paris: Éditions de Minuit, 1980).

4. Karl Ditters von Dittersdorf, *The Autobiography of Karl von Dittersdorf*, trans. A. D. Coleridge (London: R. Bentley, 1896), 249–50; originally published as *Lebenbeschreibung* (Leipzig, 1801).

5. Carl Ditters von Dittersdorf, letter to Artaria, August 18, 1788, I.N. 69578, Stadt-und-Landesbibliothek, Vienna, trans. Leo. F. Balk.

6. Dittersdorf, *Autobiography*, 251–52.

7. Baron Friedrich Melchior von Grimm, *Correspondance littéraire, philosophique, et critique, adressée à un souverain d'Allemagne, depuis 1753 jusqu'en 1769* (Paris, 1813), 528, letter of December 1, 1763: "une foule d'idées ravissantes qui'l sait encore faire succéder les unes aux autres avec goût et sans confusion."

8. Robin Wallace, *Beethoven's Critics: Aesthetic Dilemmas and Resolutions During the Composer's Lifetime* (Cambridge: Cambridge University Press, 1986), 8.

9. Leonard B. Meyer, *The Spheres of Music: A Gathering of Essays* (Chicago: University of Chicago Press, 2000), 55–125; a reprint of "Grammatical Simplicity and Relational Richness: The Trio of Mozart's G-Minor Symphony," *Critical Inquiry* 2 (1976): 693–761.

10. Isabelle de Charrière, *Caliste ou Lettres écrites de Lausanne* (Paris: J. Labitte, 1845), 204–5.

11. Giovanni Paisiello, *Regole per bene accompagnare il partimento* (St. Petersburg, 1782), 34.

12. Giovanni Battista Pergolesi, *Stabat Mater: For Soprano, Alto and String Orchestra, Edited from the Autograph MS in the Library of the Monastery Montecassino by Alfred Einstein* (London: Eulenburg, n.d.: Einstein's preface, 1927). In Einstein's edition the pedal point is marked "tasto solo."

13. Giovanni Battista Pergolesi, *Stabat Mater: For Two-Part Chorus of Women's Voices with Piano Accompaniment* (New York: G. Schirmer, n.d.).

14. Johann Sebastian Bach, arrangement of Pergolesi's *Stabat mater* (Psalm 51, "Tilge, Höchster, meine Sünden"), BWV 1083, ca. 1745–47.

15. Giacomo Tritto, *Partimenti regole generali: Per conoscere qual numerica dar si deve a vari movimenti del basso* (Milan: Ferd. Artaria, [1816]), 9, lezzione 6. The tenor voice of the Stabat Mater Prinner is overtly specified in the printed figures.

16. Stanislao Mattei, *Piccolo basso: In tutti li toni per introduzione alli bassi numerati ó siano partimenti* (MS Od.2.18, I-Nc, Naples), fol. 12r.

17. Johann Joachim Quantz, *Versuch einer Anweisung die Flöte traversiere zu spielen* (Berlin, 1752), chap. 15, sec. 19.

18. Quantz, *Versuch*, Table 20, Fig. 11.

19. Jane Austen, *Pride and Prejudice, a Novel* (London: T. Egerton, 1813), chap. 8.

20. Philip Dormer Stanhope, Earl of Chesterfield, *Letters to His Son on the Art of Becoming a Man of the World and a Gentleman* (New York: Chesterfield Press, 1917), no. 68, April 19, 1749.

21. Mozart to Leopold, April 10, 1784: "und dann ein Quintett, welches ausserordentlichen beyfall erhalten; — ich selbst halte es für das beste was ich noch in meinem leben geschrieben habe. — es besteht aus *1 oboe, 1 Clarinetto, 1 Corno, 1 fagotto*, und das *Piano forte*; — Ich wollte wünschen sie hätten es hören können!"

APPENDIX B

1. Pietro [or Pier] Maria Cecchini, *Frutti delle moderne comedie et avisi a chi le recita* (Padova, 1628), trans. and excerpted in *Actors on Acting*, ed. Toby Cole and Helen Chinoy, 2d ed. (New York: Crown, 1954), 50–52.

2. Thomas Christensen, "The *Règle de l'Octave* in Thorough-Bass Theory and Practice," *Acta Musicologica* 63 (1991): 91–117; Rosa Cafiero, "La didattica del partimento a Napoli fra Settecento e Ottocento: Note sulla fortuna delle Regole di Carlo Cotumacci," in *Gli affetti convenienti all'idee: Studi sulla musica vocale italiana*, Archivio del teatro e dello spettacolo, no. 3 (Naples: Edizioni Scientifiche Italiane, 1993).

3. Giovanni Furno, *Metodo facile, breve e chiaro delle prime ed essenziali regole per accompagnare i partimenti senza numeri* (Naples, ca. 1810), 2.

4. Furno, *Metodo*, 7.

5. Chapter 2, "Fundamental Progressions of Harmony," in William Caplin's *Classical Form: A Theory of Formal Functions for the Instrumental Music of Haydn, Mozart, and Beethoven* (Oxford: Oxford University Press, 1998), gives a modern listing of patterns related to Neapolitan movimenti; for important early German and French adaptations of Italian listings of movimenti, see J. G. Albrechtsberg's *Kurzgefasste Methode den Generalbass zu erlernen* (Vienna, ca. 1791) and Charles-Simon Catel's *Traité d'harmonie* (Paris, 1802).

6. Fedele Fenaroli, *Regole musicali per i principianti di cembalo* (Naples, 1775), 44–48.

7. Fenaroli, *Regole*, 45: "e così successivamente si alterneranno gli accompagnamenti fino alla terminazione del movimento."

8. Clifford Geertz, "Thick Description: Toward an Interpretive Theory of Culture," in *The Interpretation of Cultures: Selected Essays* (New York: Basic Books, 1973), 3–30.

9. The Rule of the Octave can be applied to the lowered sixth and seventh scale degrees (C♮ and D♮ in the key of E minor) when they directly *descend*, as in the melodic minor scale. In example B.8, however, the bass *ascends* to those degrees.

10. See Donald A. Norman, "Affordances, Conventions and Design," *Interactions* 6 (1999): 38–43.

11. The URL is <http://faculty-web.at.northwestern.edu/music/gjerdingen/partimenti/index.htm>. It may also be found by searching for "gjerdingen" and "partimenti" jointly.

12. Boulanger's students often studied from the harmony book of Théodore Dubois (*Traité d'harmonie théorique et pratique* [Paris, 1921]), which contains a small collection of basses titled "partimenti." She preserved a composition of her student, Walter Piston, titled *Fugue pour quatuor à cordes sur un sujet de Fenaroli*, MS Mus 245 (ca. 1924–26), Houghton Library, Harvard University.

13. See Camillo de Nardis, *Partimenti dei maestri C. Cotumacci, F. Durante, . . .* (Milan: Ricordi, ca. 1900–1910); Jacopo Napoli, *Bassi della scuola napoletana, con esempi realizzati* (Milan: Ricordi, 1959).

14. Karl Gustav Fellerer, *Der Partimento-Spieler: Übungen im Generalbass-Spiel und in Gebundener Improvisation* (Leipzig: Breitkopf & Härtel, 1940). Fellerer wrote an introduction to partimenti and then provided a selection of partimenti from the Santini collection in Münster. See also his earlier "Le Partimento et l'organiste au XVIIIe siècle," *Musica Sacra* 41 (1934): 251–54.

Index of Music Sources

All composers whose works appear as musical examples are listed alphabetically. For each composer, citations are provided for widely available modern editions (if such exist), manuscripts, or recordings, and cross-references are given to the individual examples. The captions of the examples provide opus number, movement, tempo, measure number and, if they can be determined, place of composition and date of publication or first performance.

L'ABBÉ LE FILS (1727–1803)

 Mid Eighteenth-Century Masters: Continuo Sonatas for Violin, ed. Jane Adas (New York: Garland, 1991). Exx. 3.17; 13.7

APRILE, GIUSEPPE (1732–1813)

 Solfeggi / Per voce di Soprano / Con accompagnamento di Basso / Del Signore Giuseppe Aprile / In Napoli Strada Toledo No. 177 Sotto le Reali Finanze (MS Solfeggio.4, olim Od.1.15, Naples Conservatory Library, Naples). Exx. 3.16; 9.15

BACH, CARL PHILIPP EMANUEL (1714–1788)

 Carl Philipp Emanuel Bach, 1714–1788: The Collected Works for Solo Keyboard, ed. Darrell Berg (New York: Garland, 1985). Exx. 7.13–14.

 Versuch über die wahre Art das Clavier zu spielen, vol. 2 (Berlin, 1762). Ex. 13.5

BACH, JOHANN CHRISTIAN (1735–1782)

 Keyboard Music, ed. Stephen Roe, vol. 42 (1989) of *The Collected Works of Johann Christian Bach, 1735–1782*, ed. Ernest Warburton (New York: Garland, 1984–99). Exx. 2.23; 11.11, 20, 38; 19.1–3; 30.8

BACH, JOHANN SEBASTIAN (1685–1750)

 Inventionen und Sinfonien, ed. Georg von Dadelsen, ser. 5, vol. 3 (1970) of *J. S. Bach: Neue Ausgabe sämtlicher Werke (Neue Bach-Ausgabe)*, ed. Johann-Sebastian-Bach-Institut, Göttingen, and Bach-Archiv, Leipzig (Kassel: Bärenreiter, 1954–). Ex. 13.3

 Varia: Kantaten, Quodlibet, Einzelsätze, Bearbeitungen, ed. Andreas Glöckner, ser. 1, vol. 41 (2000) of *J. S. Bach: Neue Ausgabe*. Ex. 30.7

 Werke für Flöte, ed. Hans-Peter Schmitz, ser. 6, vol. 4 (1954) of *J. S. Bach: Neue Ausgabe*. Ex. 16.3

BARBELLA, EMANUELE (1718–1777)

 Late Eighteenth-Century Masters: Continuo Sonatas for Violin, ed. Jane Adas (New York: Garland, 1991). Ex. 11.27

BEETHOVEN, LUDWIG VAN (1770–1827)

 Sonaten für Klavier und Violine, ed. Walther Lampe and Kurt Schäffer, ser. 5, vol. 1 (1975) of *Neue Ausgabe sämtlicher Werke*, ed. Joseph Schmidt-Görg et al. (Munich: G. Henle, 1961). Ex. 13.23

 Klaviersonaten, ed. Hans Schmidt, ser. 7, vols. 2–3 (1976) of *Neue Ausgabe*. Exx. 16.17; 20.13

BOCCHERINI, LUIGI (1743–1805)

 Sei quintetti per 2 violini, viola, 2 violoncelli, op. 11, vol. 2 (1970) of *Le opere complete di Luigi Boccherini*, ed. Pina Carmirelli (Rome: Istituto italiano per la storia della musica, 1970–85). Exx. 11.10; 18.5

DURANTE, FRANCESCO (1684–1755)

Sei sonate per cembalo divisi in studii e divertimenti, ed. Pinuccia Carrer (Rome: Stravaganza, 1986), reprint of 1747–49 Naples edition. Exx. 7.15–17; 11.44; 16.1–2, 5

Der Partimento-Spieler: Ubungen im Generalbass-Spiel und in gebundener Improvisation, ed. Karl Gustav Fellerer (Leipzig: Breitkopf & Härtel, 1940). Ex. 27.3

Regole di partimenti numerati e diminuiti del maestro Francesco Durante (MS 34.2.3, Naples Conservatory Library, Naples, n.d.). Ex. 2.20; B.8–10.

EBERLIN, JOHANN ERNST (1702–1762)

See Mozart, *Skizzen*. Exx. 27.4–5

ECKARD, JOHANN GOTTFRIED (1735–1809)

Complete Keyboard Works, Miklos Spanyi, clavier, Hungaraton Classic HCD 32313-14. Exx. 25.19; 26.1

FENAROLI, FEDELE (1730–1818)

Regole musicali per i principianti di cembalo (Bologna: A. Forni, 1975), reprint of 1774 Naples edition. Exx. 7.11–12; 11.45

Partimenti ossia basso numerato (Bologna: A. Forni, 1978), reprint of 1863 Florence edition (of copies possibly dating from the 1790s). Exx. 16.4, 6; B.2

FERRÈRE, AUGUSTE JOSEPH FREDERICK (fl. 1782)

Recueil des ballets (MS Rés. 68, Bibliothèque-Musée de l'Opéra, Paris, ca. 1782). Ex. 4.10

FURNO, GIOVANNI (1748–1837)

Metodo facile, breve e chiaro delle prime ed essenziali regole per accompagnare i partimenti senza numeri (Naples, ca. 1810). Exx. B.4–5

GALEAZZI, FRANCESCO (1758–1819)

Elementi teorico-pratici di musica con un saggio sopra l'arte di suonare il violino analizzata, ed a dimostrabili principi ridotta, vol. 2 (Rome, 1796). Exx. 11.30; 29.9–10, 12

GALLO, DOMENICO (fl. 1750s)

Sonate a tre per 2 violini e basso continuo, vol. 5 (1940) of G. B. Pergolesi: *Opera omnia*, ed. Francesco Caffarelli (Rome: Gli Amici della Musica da Camera, 1939–42). Ex. 3.9

GALUPPI, BALDASSARE (1706–1785)

Concerti a quattro : a due violini, viola e basso obbligati, Quartetto Aglàia, Stradivarius STR 33316 (Milan). Recorded on May 18, 24–25 and June 6, 1993, at the Chiesa di S. Maria del Popolo, Vigevano, Italy. Exx. 11.14, 43; 15.1

Galuppi: Motets / Confitebor / Arripe alpestri ad vallem, Gérard Lesne, voice, Virgin Veritas 45030 (London). Ex. 18.1–2

La diavolessa, intro. Howard Mayer Brown (New York: Garland, 1978). Ex. 23.1

Sonate italiane del sec: XVIII, per cembalo o pianoforte novamente date in luce, ed. Domenico De Paoli (London: Chester, 1939). Ex. 26.5

GASPARINI, FRANCESCO (1661–1727)

Il Bajazet, intro. Howard Mayer Brown (New York: Garland, 1978). Ex. 4.4

GAVINIÉS, PIERRE (1728–1800)

Mid Eighteenth-Century Masters: Continuo Sonatas for Violin, ed. Jane Adas (New York: Garland, 1991). Exx. 11.6; 13.8; 18.13; 20.3, 7

Late Eighteenth-Century Masters: Continuo Sonatas for Violin, ed. Jane Adas (New York: Garland, 1991). Ex. 13.9

GENERAL INDEX